Third Edition

The Flexible Writer

A BASIC GUIDE

Susanna Rich

Kean College of New Jersey

For Ally —
Because you Matter!
Love,
Susanna Rich
16 September 16

ALLYN AND BACON

Boston   London   Toronto   Sydney   Tokyo   Singapore

Vice President, Humanities: Joseph Opiela
Editorial Assistant: Kate Tolini
Marketing Manager: Lisa Kimball
Production Administrator: Rowena Dores
Editorial-Production Service: Lauren Green Shafer
Text Designer: Pat Torelli
Cover Administrator: Linda Dickinson
Composition Buyer: Linda Cox
Manufacturing Buyer: Suzanne Lareau

Library of Congress Cataloging-in-Publication Data
Rich, Susanna.
    The flexible writer : a basic guide / Susanna Rich.—3rd ed.
      p.   cm.
    Includes index.
    ISBN 0-205-26599-5
    1. English language—Rhetoric. 2. English language—Grammar.
  3. Report writing. I. Title.
  PE1408.R558 1997
  808'.042—dc21   97-16434
                                       CIP

Credits
Pages 22–23: From Daniel Goleman, "Hope Emerges as Key to Success in Life," *The New York Times,* December 24, 1991. Copyright © 1991 by The New York Times Co. Reprinted by permission.

Credits continued on page 502, which constitutes an extension of the copyright page.

Printed in the United States of America
10 9 8 7 6 5 4 3   00 99

Contents

Chapter 12   Writing to Learn I: Becoming a Responsible Thinker   304

To Instructors

> The point is that students must be
> at the center of their own learning.
> —*John Mayher, Nancy Lester, Gordon Pradl*

When I first started to teach developmental writing, I found myself order-ing three texts for my classes: a rhetoric, a reader, and a handbook. I soon found it hard to justify three texts for a course focused on writing. Serving as coordinator of a developmental writing program with a constantly changing population of instructors, I found it even more difficult to pre-order texts for other instructors that would suit a broad range of teaching styles in a multicultural community. We needed a more flexible textbook that incorporated the benefits of rhetorics, readers, and handbooks and focused directly on meaning and purpose, person and process. We needed a textbook that would help students of different ages and cultural back-grounds write for different purposes: personal, interpersonal, academic, and professional. I wrote *The Flexible Writer* to address these needs. Here are its features:

Flexibility.   *The Flexible Writer* can be used as a rhetoric, a reader, and a handbook. The book is organized to serve students and instructors with different styles and approaches to basic writing. You can use chap-ters in sequence or as the need for them arises in your course. Also, the text has ample materials for programs that offer a sequence of develop-mental writing courses that would lead from personal to interpersonal and academic writing.

A Dynamic Model of the Writing Process.   There are no shortcuts or mechanical formulas for real writing. *The Flexible Writer* offers a dynamic recursive model of the writing process that reflects the practical experiences of writers. This model focuses on purpose and audience and includes the processes of consulting and revising. Separate chapters offer detailed discussions and Explorations of seven identified phases of the writing process.

Emphasis on Writing.   Learning to write, like any worthwhile activity, takes time, patience, commitment, and practice, practice, practice. Writing leads to more writing. Therefore, *The Flexible Writer* offers numerous opportunities for writing.

Focus on Purpose and Audience.   Writing is a process of finding and making meaning in particular contexts—for different purposes and audiences. Part III of *The Flexible Writer* helps students appreciate these dynamics and offers opportunities to write for different purposes, from the most personal ("Writing to Remember") to the most public ("Writing for Power"). "Writing to Bridge Cultures" invites students to explore experiences of ethnicity, gender, age, race, and religion. Two chapters on "Writing to Learn" are devoted specifically to strategies of academic writing.

Numerous Student Models.   New writers are much encouraged and inspired by learning about each other's processes and experiences in writing. Therefore, *The Flexible Writer* offers numerous models of student writing not only as polished products, but through multiple drafts.

Student-Centered Explorations.   Students write more and better when they write about what interests them. Therefore, *The Flexible Writer* offers students a broad range of Explorations through which to pursue their own interests. By understanding and developing their own points of view, students can appreciate and develop strategies to negotiate other points of view.

Emphasis on Community and Collaboration.   Writing, like other language activities, is more easily learned in the company of others. *The Flexible Writer* offers a balanced range of Explorations (marked *Together* and *Solo*) to help you and your students create a writing community. Students become conscious of and confident about the linguistic insights they already have and therefore better appreciate and incorporate the insights of others.

Connections Between Reading and Writing.   Practicing writers know how to read. Therefore, *The Flexible Writer* guides students to read with an emphasis on how the writing process is reflected in the product. The third edition of *The Flexible Writer* includes not only numerous student examples but also a rich source of over forty published works by a broad range of our finest professional writers. These all serve as prompts for further writing. Each chapter provides a strong component of focused questions to pose while reading—such as "Reading for Purpose and Audience" or "Reading to Bridge Cultures"—that can be applied in other classes and contexts.

Multicultural Perspective.   Writing is a process of learning how to communicate with audiences of cultural backgrounds that vary in ethnicity, gender, age, race, religion, experience, and interests. *The Flexible Writer* provides insights and opportunities to explore the dynamics of how language works in different cultural contexts.

Preparation for Academic Writing.   *The Flexible Writer* provides students with the basic conceptual skills they need for writing to learn. Two chapters focus specifically on reading and responding to academic texts across the curriculum.

In addition, *The Flexible Writer* offers technological guidance on the use of computers for writing and academic assessment tools such as evaluation checklists and methods for constructing a portfolio.

Critical Thinking Strategies.   As student Bruce Inge stated it, "Writing is a learning process." Thinking shapes writing; writing shapes thinking. Critical thinking strategies and Explorations are provided throughout *The Flexible Writer.*

Flexible Handbook Focused on Meaning.   Leo Tolstoy said, "To the teacher the simplest and most general appears as easiest, whereas for a pupil only the complex and living appears easy." Part IV of *The Flexible Writer* is a handbook that shows students how grammar and punctuation function to create the complex of meanings in effective writing. Stylistic issues are approached not as a system of merely learning and applying general rules but as a process of developing sensitivity to purpose and audience in multicultural communities. The Explorations in this section, under the heading "Developing Style," are designed to help students to learn and directly apply grammar and punctuation strategies to their own writing.

A Solid Base in Theory and Research.   *The Flexible Writer* is based on my eighteen years of experience as a writer in a wide range of genres, including essays, articles, a novel (and a dissertation about writing it), humor, business memos, translations, and reams of poetry. It is based, as well, on eighteen years of guiding a broad spectrum of students and instructors in composition, creative writing, critical thinking, and research on the teaching of college writing. The approaches and methods that are formulated in *The Flexible Writer* reflect the most carefully developed current research on the writing process.

How to Use This Book

The purpose of *The Flexible Writer* is to support you and your students in creating a community of writers that suits your styles and needs. The Explorations are a special feature of this book. Sometimes an Exploration suggests a series of steps to be taken together or solo, or alternating between the two. The purpose of the Explorations is to help students write and talk about writing. Students don't have to take every step or answer every question. Many breakthroughs occur when student writers follow ideas that occur to them independently during the process. The purpose of the suggested class discussions is to practice talking about writing, not to settle on "correct" answers.

Finally, even as you are working together as a class on one portion of this book, you can refer students to other portions you feel they need. In some classes, you and your students can decide together which chapters to turn to next and which Explorations to do. Sidebars, shaded gray for easy identification, summarize and highlight important writing strategies. Encourage your students to photocopy select sidebars to keep at close reference as they develop their skills. For additional support, the *Instructor's Manual* that accompanies *The Flexible Writer* offers suggestions for how to sequence and combine chapters for different purposes, styles, and needs.

The enthusiasm, successes, and breakthroughs of students and instructors who have worked with *The Flexible Writer* are recorded and reflected throughout the book. I hope you will write to me about your experiences with *The Flexible Writer*, as well.

A Word on the Third Edition

Readers of the previous editions will notice the following new features developed in response to the needs of classes using the text:

- Over forty new published readings by professional writers
- A strong component of strategies for reading for specific purposes
- Portfolio assessment instruments
- Strategies for writing with a computer
- Refocusing of the Grammar and Punctuation chapters to emphasize *Developing Style*
- Reorganization of sidebars for at-a-glance reference.

Acknowledgments

Writing *The Flexible Writer* taught me much about the dynamics of the writing process in general and my own in particular. The single most important lesson I learned was just how central understanding *purpose and audience* is to the making of meaning, even if the only purpose is to express and the only audience oneself. I learned just how inextricable *consulting* is to the writing process, whether it's as simple as consulting a dictionary for spelling or as complex as consulting teachers about different thinking styles.

I could not have written a textbook flexible enough to fulfill the purposes and serve the broad audience I set out to reach if it weren't for the many people I consulted during the process—some as distant as the memory of my sixth-grade English teacher, some as immediate as the remarks of a current student. The guidance I offer in this book is my current best synthesis of the guidance and support I received from consulting with others in decades of becoming a writer myself. A comprehensive list of them would fill a city phone book. I mention here only those who have been most obviously focal to the creation of this book.

First, I would like to thank my students at Kean College of New Jersey, Montclair State University, the University of North Carolina at Chapel Hill, New York University, and Sussex County Community College, who inspired me to create the materials that comprise this book. They were models for me in their willingness to write, write, and revise, and to work with and for each other. Their insights, creativity, energy, and successes dispelled any of the fears I had when I first started to teach developmental writing.

I am grateful to my past and current teachers who continue to be a source of inspiration for me. They include Paul Ziff, Carl Schmidt, Mitchell A. Leaska, John Mayher, Gordon Pradl, Lil Brannon, Dixie Goswami, Nancy Sommers, Mimi Schwartz, Neil Postman, Joan Aleshire, John Skoyles, Sharon Olds, and Robert Wrigley. In addition, there are those teachers who have mentored me only through their writings: Mina P. Shaughnessy, Peter Elbow, Mike Rose, Janet Emig, Ann E. Berthoff, James Moffett, Kenneth Bruffee, and Grace M. Fernald. I thank these teachers for inspiring what is worthy in this book.

Many of my colleagues at Kean College worked with these materials in process and provided invaluable insights, ideas, student feedback, and encouragement. They have taught me much by their example about effective teaching and collaboration. I am especially grateful to Dorothy Goldberg, Ruth Hamann, Sid Krueger, Jay Mahoney, and Bernie Weinstein. My special thanks to Carole Shaffer-Koros and Bob Cirasa, past and present Chairs of the English Department at Kean; to Dean Ed Weil, and Mark Lender; and to Kean College of New Jersey for providing the context, time, resources, and encouragement I needed to write this book.

In addition, the generous, detailed comments of many other writing instructors helped transform *The Flexible Writer* into its present form. My thanks to Jeanne Costello, Fullerton College; Sandra Lloyd, Tomball College; Mary Sauer, Indiana University–Purdue University, Indianapolis; and Geraldine J. Winter, Kent State University, for their helpful comments on the present edition. I would also like to thank the following instructors whose comments helped shape the earlier editions of this text: Peter Adams, Essex Community College; Peter Carino, Indiana State University; Duncan Carter, Portland State University; Theresa Enos, University of Arizona; Timothy J. Evans, Richard Bland College; Pamela Gay, SUNY–Binghamton; Eric Hibbison, J. Sargeant Reynolds Community College; C. Jeriel Howard, Northeastern Illinois University; Frances Kurilich, Santa Monica College; Cecilia Macheski, La Guardia Community College; Eileen Master, Rowan College of New Jersey; Martin McCoski, University of Akron; E. Jennifer Monaghan, Brooklyn College; Randall Popken, Tarleton State University; Arthur B. Powell, Rutgers University; Sylvia Robb, Tomball College; Rick Shannon, Community College of Allegheny County; Judith Stanford, Rivier College; Kathryn Waltz-Freel, Indiana Vocational Technical College; and Fran Zaniello, Northern Kentucky University.

I wish to thank Kate Tolini, Rowena Dores, and Ellen Mann at Allyn & Bacon for the energy and creativity they devoted to helping *The Flexible Writer* reach its audience and fulfill its purpose. My thanks also to Lauren Green Shafer and Kathryn Graehl for their patience, thoroughness, and perseverance in bringing *The Flexible Writer* through production.

There are three persons without whom this book could not have been written, and to whom I am most grateful. Joe Opiela is a writer's ideal editor. His devotion to producing quality English textbooks, his patience, flexibility, expertise, accessibility, and diplomacy allowed me to develop what is best in *The Flexible Writer*. Priscilla Donenfeld is a textbook writer's ideal research assistant. Her devotion, patience, flexibility, teaching, research, and writing were crucial to the realization of this text. Most of all, I would like to thank Morton D. Rich for being a writer's ideal husband and friend. He was my first methods teacher twenty-six years ago and still dazzles me with the depth and creativity of his teaching. His devotion and patience, ideas and expertise, flexibility and support allowed me, through this process, to discover what is best in me as a teacher, writer, and person.

Susanna Lippoczy Rich
Kean College of New Jersey

To Students

Part of becoming a writer is the desire to have
everything mean something.

—*Louise Erdrich*

If you are like most student writers, you may be worried about writing. Perhaps you have been discouraged by previous experiences. You may feel as other students have felt at the beginning of a developmental writing course: deprived, scared about what others will say, out of place, and panicky.

Know that you are not alone. Most writers, even professionals, have these feelings. The difference between them and you is that they have learned strategies for making the writing process satisfying, no matter how they feel at first. These writers know that writing is not a matter of following rigid rules, that writing is a process that takes time, practice, patience, and commitment. *The Flexible Writer*—based on my years of writing and working with writers like you—offers you the strategies of practicing writers so that you too can enjoy the following:

- The confidence that comes from recognizing that you already know more about writing than you thought you did
- The productive habits of practicing writers
- The chance to practice writing without fear of mistakes
- The freedom to choose topics that concern and interest you
- The opportunity to write for different purposes and audiences
- The ability to use a variety of writing strategies
- The skills of reading as a writer
- The skills of a responsible thinker
- The opportunity to learn through writing

- The means to bridge cultural, intellectual, and other gaps between you and others
- The opportunity to work collaboratively with your peers

Features of This Book

In order to help you gain the benefits of writing, this book has these features:

- Numerous opportunities to practice writing
- A strong focus on the writing process
- Student models and reflections on writing
- Professional models of writing to inspire you
- Opportunities to write alone (solo) and together
- Opportunities to revise your writing
- Sidebars and quotes you can use as reminders
- Strategies for developing style in grammar and punctuation

How This Book Is Organized

The Flexible Writer is divided into four parts:

Part I offers you practical suggestions for arranging your time, space, and habits for writing. This part introduces you to the experiences of other writers and offers you strategies for success.

Part II offers you a dynamic model of the phases of the writing process, which starts with needs and ends with results. The phases in between are these: identifying purpose and audience, collecting and drafting, focusing, organizing, drafting, consulting, and revising. A separate chapter is devoted to each of these phases. With your instructor, you can decide whether to work through these chapters one after another or to refer to them as needed while you work with chapters in Part III.

Part III offers you opportunities to write for different purposes: to remember, to bridge cultures, to learn, and to assert power.

Part IV is a handbook that helps you to appreciate how your grammar and punctuation affect meaning. Explorations in *Developing Style* will offer you dynamic ways to adjust your writing for different purposes and audiences. Here, too, you can decide whether to work through both chapters or to refer to portions as you need them. The Table of Contents and the Index will help you to find what you need.

How to Use This Book

The purpose of *The Flexible Writer* is to provide you with the support you need to become a writer with your own style. Even as you are working together with your instructor and fellow students, turn to other portions of this book that you need. Have the courage and independence to take what this book has to offer, whether or not you are assigned to work with a particular section. Review portions that you need to review, even after the class has stopped working on those portions.

The Explorations are a special feature of this book. They are marked *Together, Solo*, or a combination of *Together* and *Solo. Together* Explorations are designed for class and small group work. *Solo* Explorations are designed for individual work. Sometimes an Exploration suggests a series of steps to be taken together or solo or alternating between the two. In doing Explorations, remember that the most important purpose of them is to help you to start and keep writing. If an Exploration inspires an idea that is not explicitly suggested in the Exploration, follow your inspiration. As long as you are writing, don't feel as if you have to take every step or answer every question. Remember, as well, that the point of class discussions is to develop ideas about writing, not to settle on "correct" answers.

Notice, also, that throughout *The Flexible Writer* there are sidebars that are shaded gray for easy reference. These sidebars offer you quick summaries of important points. You might want to photocopy those which you need to learn and post them by your desk or in the cover of your notebook. Use them often.

I enjoyed writing *The Flexible Writer* and hope you will enjoy it, as well. Send me some of your writing and tell me of your experiences with the book.

Susanna Lippoczy Rich
Kean College of New Jersey

Chapter *1*

Becoming a Writer

This chapter offers opportunities to

—Explore **myths** and **fears** about writing

—**Freewrite**

—Make a **commitment** to writing

—Create the **time, space,** and **habits** for becoming a writer

—Discover the dynamics of **language and beliefs**

> Everybody is talented and original and
> has something important to say.
> —*Brenda Ueland,*
> *Writer, Teacher*

> The feeling that the work is magnificent, and the
> feeling that it is abominable, are both mosquitoes
> to be repelled, ignored, or killed, but not indulged.
> —*Annie Dillard,*
> *Naturalist, Essayist*

Why Write?

A father needs to reassure his son, so he tacks a note onto the refrigerator saying, "Back by noon." A student rewrites her notes to prepare for an exam. Two heads of state want to end a war, so they write and sign an agreement. People write for many reasons: to express feelings, to remember, to develop their senses, to learn, to solve problems, to ask for help or to offer it, to have fun, to complain, to argue, to mourn. In short, people write to live. One student writer says, "I write because I like that 'Wow' feeling I get when I find out I know more than I thought I knew." Another student writer, who is very career oriented, says she writes in order to create high expectations in a prospective employer. "Then I have something to live up to," she says. I'm writing this book because I love to write and want more people to enjoy the benefits of writing, too.

Free Yourself to Write

Writing can be very flexible and useful. So it's a wonder that more of us don't write more often. Some people suffer from "writer's block," an inability to write because of fears, false beliefs, and unproductive habits. This section offers some insights and explorations to help you to free yourself from writer's block and become a flexible writer.

Myths About Writing

The word *myths* applies to stories of heroes and heroines, fantastic dragons and unicorns, quests for magical powers, and perfect solutions to human problems. Such myths can tell the history of a people, reflect their emotional and spiritual needs, and offer hope and moral guidance. For example, the movie *Star Wars* is a cinematic myth for the twentieth century. In it, Luke Skywalker uses technology to call on "the Force," a creative, spiritual energy that enables him to encounter and survive a destructive force represented by Darth Vader. Princess Leia is no "damsel in distress" who must wait for someone to save her. She is active and powerful, and she collaborates *with* the hero. One of the lessons of this myth is that technology must be used for positive purposes. It reminds us of the values of courage and friendship, and it discourages mere hunger for power. It is a myth that embodies the newfound power women have embraced in the past century.

But the word *myth* also applies to superstitions and false beliefs that can rob people of their powers to grow and create. A long-distance swim-

mer, Melanie, once told this story of how a myth limited her ability to
swim:

> For twenty years I couldn't swim the crawl because I believed you
> *had* to blow the air out into the water before you come up for air. But the
> bubbles flew back into my face, disorienting me. I kept swallowing water
> and gasping for air. I gave up swimming.
>
> One day while I was wistfully watching people doing laps, I asked
> the lifeguard if there was any other way to manage my breathing. "Sure,"
> she said, "Just blow out the air when you come up. You can take your
> next breath right after." I tried it and a whole new world opened up for
> me. Before long I was swimming a half mile regularly with strong, even
> strokes. I'm training now for a long-distance race. Recently, I experi-
> mented with blowing the air out with my face in the water. Because I
> have greater confidence as a swimmer now, I'm not disturbed by the bub-
> bles anymore. I can even swim faster: the bubbles just trail behind me.

Unquestioned beliefs and rigid rules can stop you from writing just as
Melanie's rigid belief about breathing stopped her from swimming. Here
are some myths about writing that may be stopping you from immersing
yourself in the process.

Myth 1: Writers are born, not made.

If you believe writers are born, not made, you may feel like giving up
even before you start. But the ability to write is learned, not given to you.
If you can speak a language, you are already 80 percent there. After all,
you have been learning, helping, arguing, and so on since you first started
to talk. Just like ballet dancers, concert pianists, football players, and
master carpenters, writers train for years, decades, and lifetimes to perfect their writing. Perhaps you may be only a weekend jogger and not a
winner of marathon races, but to be a runner you have to run. You may
not want to be a professional writer, but if you are to enjoy the benefits of
writing, you have to work and play like a writer.

Myth 2: There is one right way to write.

If you believe there is one right way to write, you may feel so tense and
discouraged by your early exploratory attempts that you give up too soon.
But minds are not mass-produced pages to be shaped and filled in the same
way. You have to develop your own mind so that it will be uniquely your
own and not just a copy of those around you. Writing is one of the most
effective tools you have for knowing and developing your mind. To seek a
right way is just to follow someone else's way. Find your own. The *A* paper

usually takes risks and sounds unique. It would be comforting if there were *one* right way, but ultimately that would be stifling.

Myth 3: You have to get it right the first time.

The most destructive belief that beginning writers may have about writing is that if you don't get it right the first time, you can never get it right. But in reality, what you read on a published page is rarely, if ever, a first draft. Novelist Ernest Hemingway revised his book *The Old Man and the Sea* more than two hundred times. Marcy Syms, chief operating officer of Syms Stores, says that in her office people are constantly checking with each other on how to phrase and rephrase thoughts in letters and in memos. A teacher's first draft may need more work than a student's. The difference between a piece of writing that works and one that doesn't may be the number of times it's been rewritten.

Myth 4: You have to get it right all the time.

You wouldn't devote the same amount of attention to choosing every outfit you wear—every minute of every day—or you would never get out of your closet and on with your life. Yet, some new writers waste so much energy perfecting one response to an exam question that they fail because they don't move on to the others. They worry so much about their first sentence in a first draft of a paper that they lose ideas that would have emerged had they kept writing.

If you believe that everything you write has to be perfect, you will miss the pleasure of the new ideas and subjects that develop with a more flexible approach to writing. Especially for a new writer, it's important to explore many new directions. Informal writing such as freewrites (defined on pages 13–16), diary entries, informal letters to your instructor, and early drafts of your papers may include tangents, changes of subject, and errors. Polished writing such as job résumés and term papers deserve more attention, more drafts, and more time.

Myth 5: Only better is good enough.

This myth is a variation on Myth 4. Some new writers feel that unless later drafts are better than earlier ones, they will never succeed. Discouraged, they may give up, saying, "I just don't have what it takes." But this is not true. Writing does not develop in a straight, upward-sloping line, any more than health regimens or achievements in sports do. Often people find that they get worse before they get better: fevers, rashes, and other "detox" symptoms are sometimes necessary for regaining health. Successful workouts are often followed by aches, setbacks, and frustration.

The more you commit yourself to excellence, the more likely it is that your work will get worse before it gets better. Your standards will rise, and sometimes you'll stumble. Frustration is a badge of commitment, not an invitation to failure.

Myth 6: Product is more important than process.

In a finished piece of writing, what you see is not how the writer got there but what he or she got to. When you buy a worthwhile garment, you rarely, if ever, will see the patterns, loose threads, chalk marks, pins, scissors, and leftover scraps of material needed to make it. It takes many, many people to get that garment to your store.

When you read a book, you don't see the twenty attempts to start, the crumpled drafts, the worn-out dictionary and library card. The really effective beginning is often written last—after the writer has thought things through in the process of writing. If there is a thesis sentence (a sentence that states the main point the author wants to get across), it is often discovered and reshaped as the writer writes. The arrangement of paragraphs, the purpose, and the author's sense of the audience will often change in the process of writing. The Foreword of this book was written and rewritten as ideas unfolded and developed in the process. It was finished last.

Being too worried about grades is partly a result of focusing too much on the end product and not on the activities of the writing process. Being impatient with yourself and what you write is also an indication that you are putting too much emphasis on the product. Engage fully in the *process* of writing. The more you do, the better your final product will be.

Myth 7: Writing is just recorded speech.

If you believe writing is just recorded speech, then you may be confused by the demands teachers make on you in writing classes. Here are some ways in which writing and speaking differ:

- Writing is *permanent,* whereas speech (unless it is recorded) is gone as soon as it is spoken.

- Writing is *solitary.* When you speak, your face, body, and voice help express what you mean. But when you write, the words you choose and the way you arrange them have to communicate some of what your face, body, and voice would if you were speaking instead of writing.

- Writing can be *riskier* than speaking. When you write, you are never sure who will pick up your writing. You can't be there to reinterpret or soften what you say. That's why you have to make even more careful decisions about what you decide to leave in finished papers. Others can hold you to something in writing much more than they can hold you to your spoken word.

- Writing can be *safer.* When you speak, words can tumble out before you realize what you are saying and what effect it can have.

Once you have said something, it's hard to take it back. One of the benefits of writing is that you can adjust what you write before it reaches your intended audience. So, for example, it's helpful to write some letters you never send: you express your feelings without having to cope with the consequences of having done so. Having formulated your ideas, the next time you speak with the person you will be able to express yourself more clearly and with more control.

- Writing is *solid.* When you put your thoughts on paper, they become as real as clay. While you are writing, you can change and learn from your words because you can see and manipulate them. You can't hold silent thoughts or spoken words in the same way.

- Writing is *independent* of speech. Writing doesn't just record speech, although early drafts may approximate it. How you punctuate does not always follow the rhythms of speech. How you hear a word in English is not always how you spell it. How you communicate on the page may be very different from how you communicate in person.

Myth 8: No pain, no gain.

In the past you may have become convinced that writing is painful, and so now, naturally, you avoid it. But although writing is work, so is playing football, creating a special meal, building an engine, or breeding cats. Meaningful work—a labor of love—is what people seek. It is human nature to do so.

A closed fist can only punch and pound. A relaxed hand is flexible enough to create a world. Writing doesn't have to hurt. Writing is a process of experimenting with ideas and words until you find the ones that work. Researchers have noticed that the students who do best in writing are the ones who know how to design their schedules, choose their topics, work with others, and challenge themselves in ways that enable them to *enjoy* writing. As you develop as a writer, notice your strengths and use them. If you are bored, challenge yourself. If you are frustrated, relax. Try another strategy or topic for a while.

On the other hand, don't fall into the pleasure trap: just because something is easy or you like it doesn't mean that it's as good as it can be. Writing is satisfying work, but it is *work.* And sometimes work is hard. The better you are as a writer, the more aware you are of problems, and the higher your standards will be. Listen to what others suggest about your writing, and grow. Listen to your own best instincts. Writing develops over time.

Myth 9: You have to go it alone.

Many of the benefits of writing stem from its being a solitary activity: you have time to think things through, opportunities to change your mind, space to be your own person on your own terms. But although part of writing is done alone, more often than not, writing happens as a result of anticipating an audience and consulting with others. Just read the Acknowledgments at the beginning of this book and you will see that hundreds of people were involved in its creation. You, as an anticipated reader, are crucial to my process. Biographies of great authors are filled with stories of how poets, novelists, playwrights, humorists, and essayists worked with and for each other. Business, legal, medical, and scientific professionals are constantly collaborating with each other in the preparation of documents.

Myth 10: Only the teacher knows.

Some students and teachers believe that it is the writing teacher's job to tell the student exactly what to write and how to write it, and then to correct the student's grammar and punctuation. These students become discouraged because they don't feel in charge of their own minds and development. They don't write what they really want or need to say because they don't want to be criticized for it. They don't take risks. Teachers become frustrated, as well, if they feel they are doing the work students need to learn to do for themselves.

The teaching of writing has gone through many changes in the past decades. Teachers realize more fully that writing is an expression of a whole human being. Students have many insights into language that the teacher may not have. In addition, students know things that their writing teachers may not but would like to learn. The teacher's role is seen to be more like that of a coach. Teachers can't write it for you, but they can help you to find your way. Teachers and students find the new ways of learning to write more meaningful and exciting. The purpose of this book is to help you discover your strengths.

*E*xplorations _____

1. *Together or Solo.* Discuss which of the ten myths about writing you have believed. How have these myths affected you as a writer? Offer a specific incident as an example of a myth in action.

2. *Together.* Discuss how the following myths formulated by student writer Sandra Spillman would affect you as a writer:

   a. Each sentence when writing a paper must be perfect. If it is not, I may not go on to the next.

   b. When finished with writing the paper, I must not need corrections and, therefore, do not need to make changes.

   c. My vocabulary must sound intelligent—the more complex, the better.

d. Each piece of work must be finished at the end of each session. I may never hand in an incomplete work.

e. I must keep to my regular format and not try anything different in case it may be wrong.

f. I must not write about anything that may not interest every single reader of my work.

g. My work must sound as though an English major wrote it.

3. *Together or Solo.* List some rules about writing that you learned or adopted during your years in elementary and high school. How have each of these rules benefited or hindered your development as a writer?

4. *Solo.* Choose one of the following topics, and write about how you developed beliefs about writing from your experience:

   • Your earliest experience with writing

   • Your worst experience with writing

   • Your best experience with writing

5. **a.** *Solo.* Write a letter introducing yourself to your classmates. Decide how you want them to see you, whether it be entertaining, serious, outgoing, shy, or assertive. Tell them what is most important about you. Relate how you feel about writing, what you hope to gain from the class, and how you can contribute to the class.

   b. *Together.* In small groups, read these letters to each other. Ask questions that arise. Note similarities and differences between group members.

   c. *Solo.* Rewrite your letter, including aspects of yourself that occurred to you during the small group conversation.

   d. *Together.* Form small groups with other students to read and discuss your rewritten letters.

Fears About Writing

If you fear writing, you may become so paralyzed that you won't write. Naming fears is a first step to facing them. Here are some insights that other students have had into why they fear or avoid writing:

Fear of Success.   Sometimes success can be even worse than failure. It can put pressure on you, as it did on Jane. She wrote this:

> I avoid doing well in school because whenever I do well my parents and teachers expect too much out of me. I can't take the pressure. So I go sour on school and do as little as I can. I tell myself I can't do it, so I don't.

The problem was that Jane exchanged one set of pressures for another. Instead of having to cope with pressures to succeed, she had to cope with the pressures of not having the skills she needed to land a satisfying job.

Fear of Failure. If you have had difficulty with grammar in the past, you might write sentences that are too simple to express your ideas. If you have difficulty with spelling, you might avoid writing interesting words that you don't know how to spell. If an instructor gave you a low grade because you disagreed with a popular political statement, you might avoid taking a stand in your work. But writing to avoid failure—writing "safe"—diminishes you and your skills.

Fear of failure breeds failure. What makes gold medals at the Olympic Games, landings on the moon, flourishing vegetable gardens, and best-selling books is the ability to fall down and get right up again. A professional basketball player will have made more mistakes than an amateur. A successful student or writer is someone who is willing to work through mistakes until a piece of writing fulfills its purpose.

The best way to develop confidence in writing is to write, write, write. Here's what student Sharon DiNicola discovered:

> I couldn't wait to finish revising to tell you how I am improving. You were right. I was very negative about my last paper and felt too discouraged to do anything about it. Well, this time around, I sat down and said I was going to have a positive attitude toward this revision. I told myself, "I know what I'm doing. I *can* do this."
>
> I expanded a few paragraphs and used more effective words to make my point clearer. I am learning to write and go back and fix certain areas. Every time I revise, I feel more and more proud of myself.

Fear of Losing Friends. Sam's friends made fun of him when he showed interest in classes. They called him a "nerd," so Sam hid his books, stopped asking questions in classes, and refused invitations from teachers to join debates and the school newspaper staff. He was afraid of losing his friends if he did well. They were afraid of the same thing. The trouble was, he became bored and irritable because he was starving his mind. His friendships suffered.

Fear of Exposure. You may feel embarrassed or shy about revealing who you are to people you don't know. This is what Kerrie Losche wrote:

> My shyness supposedly keeps me safe from any kind of embarrassment and stops me from taking risks. I've been shy my whole life, stopping myself from doing little things like oral reports, raising my hand in

class to give an answer, introducing myself to a class, and especially writing well-developed essays. I always told myself I would sound dumb and I really believed it.

The problem for Kerrie was that the more she retreated, the less she learned and the more she needed to hide her lack of knowing.

Fear of Change.   Another student felt torn about learning to speak and write in English. José Campis was born in Puerto Rico and loved the beautiful landscapes, people, and way of life he knew as a youngster. He wanted to do well when his family moved to New Jersey, but somehow, adopting standard academic English felt as if he were betraying his Puerto Rican heritage. Many of us closely identify with the language of our family and community. Adopting a different language or way of communicating may threaten our sense of belonging. José felt more and more torn and lost.

Misery Likes Company.   Sometimes you can adopt another person's fears. Ed realized that succeeding in a world of words threatened his relationship with his father, who had not had the same educational opportunities. In writing the following, Ed was able to appreciate why he held back from greater involvement in his school work:

> I really get interested in some things about science and nature. This sometimes hurts me when I talk to my father. If he is doing something and I tell him an easier way to do it, he sort of shuns me. He mainly does this if there are other people around. I think he does it because he resents his son being able to tell him something that he doesn't know. This makes him look dumb in front of people. He still loves me, but I don't think he can accept my knowledge about certain things he doesn't know. I usually don't let this bother me, but sometimes if I know something more about what my dad is doing, I just keep quiet. I also don't put much effort into school anymore.

Ed decided that his failing school would just make his father feel worse. Ed hoped that by doing well in school he would eventually make his father proud of him.

Commitment

Commitment is the cure for myths and fears. Commitment is taking charge of your life. You stop waiting for others to push you or "do it for you." You decide to make things happen in your life, for yourself. If you don't, you will probably settle for superficial novelty and pleasure that soon wear off. Falling in love is novelty and pleasure; marriage is a commitment to work through hard times so as to enjoy a lasting and meaningful relationship.

Writing is a commitment. If you write only when it's easy or safe, you will enjoy such superficial pleasures as "getting it over with." But success comes from working through as many rough drafts as is necessary to realize the potential of your writing projects. Resisting writing tasks because they might be inconvenient is self-defeating. A successful writer is willing to write something more challenging and meaningful than a merely error-free, easy essay. A successful writer takes on challenging topics, recognizes problems, and then revises a piece of writing until it fulfills a satisfying purpose.

When fears arise about writing, when you find yourself resisting a writing task, take a deep breath and *do it anyway*. The more you write, the more you assert that you *are* a writer. Get organized; make a commitment to yourself as a writer. Here are two lists that contrast the actions of a committed and an uncommitted writer:

Committed writer	**Uncommitted writer**
Buys both the more complete hardcover dictionary for home and a portable paperback for commuting.	Reluctantly buys the cheapest dictionary and loses it—buys a new CD with the money saved.
Attends all writing classes and makes special arrangements to be on time.	Gets to classes only when the weather is suitable and no work is due.
Asks the instructor for appointments. Arranges for a tutor when necessary. Asks questions often in class.	Complains to others that the instructor doesn't explain things. Doesn't talk to the instructor directly.
Types and proofreads all papers.	Writes papers on the bus on the way to class. Drops them into a puddle.
Makes contact with several other students in class to study together and review class notes and assignments.	Makes excuses for not knowing assignments.

Committed writer	Uncommitted writer
Uses school work as a way to cope with personal and family difficulties by studying family and social relationships, researching diseases, and so on. Develops a firmer hold on life by adopting teachers for suppport.	Frequently uses personal and family difficulties as excuses for not attending class and doing assignments.
Treats "mistakes" as necessary for growth. Welcomes adjustments and critiques offered by teachers and others.	Uses "mistakes" as excuses for giving up too soon.
Organizes time and space to support writing.	Procrastinates.
Goes to the college writing center.	Goes to the game room.

*E*xplorations

1. *Solo.* Write about a time when you overcame a fear to succeed at something important to you. Choose one or more of these questions to inspire you:

   - What did you fear?
   - What myths did you believe?
   - How did you avoid confronting your fear?
   - What finally caused you to confront your fear?
   - What did you do?
   - What happened?
   - What did you learn?

2. *Solo.* Write about a particular time when you failed at something, such as writing, a sport, a relationship, or a project. Respond to one or more of these questions to inspire you:

   - What happened?
   - Who was involved?
   - What changed?
   - What did you fear?
   - What myths did you believe?

- If you had to do it over again, what would you do?

3. *Solo.* Write about someone you know or have heard of (this could be you, as well) who overcame a fear or handicap in order to succeed. Discuss in detail the person's problems and how he or she overcame them. What did you learn from writing about this person that you can further apply to your own life?

4. *Solo.* Poet Diane Wakoski said, "We become the words we speak." Language can shape your life through self-fulfilling prophecies and social prejudices. For example, if a teacher expects a student to be intelligent, then she or he will treat the student with more respect. That respect can help the student develop the confidence needed to work and thereby succeed. On the other hand, making snap judgments about a person because of how she or he seems can lead to misunderstandings, at the very least. Write about some experience you have had with social prejudice, whether because of your age, sex, race, religion, physical traits, past record, or cultural background. The prejudice may be positive or negative. What were the beliefs that shaped this experience? What were some of the words others applied to you? What did you learn about how language changes the way we perceive and behave?

5. **a.** *Solo and Together.* Add to the lists of actions of committed and uncommitted writers. Draw on your experience. Be honest.

   b. *Solo.* Write a letter to your instructor, making a commitment to actively participate in your writing class. Record any problems that you anticipate and how you plan to solve them. Ask for specific kinds of support. From time to time during the semester, revise and add to this letter.

Freewriting

The best way to learn *how* to write is to write: learn by doing. *Freewriting* is a special strategy that will help you write past myths and fears. When you freewrite, you get words onto the page or computer screen as fast as possible. You are like a runner leaping over the hurdles of worries and indecision, speeding past the blocks of confusion and resistance. Freewriting helps you relax so your ideas can flow. As one student writer, Satonya Gardner, put it, "Freewriting helps you break down walls." Frank Kisselman, another student, said, "Sometimes when I freewrite, my mind wanders. Sometimes what emerges is more worth writing than what I started out with."*

---

*The concept of freewriting was formalized by Peter Elbow in *Writing Without Teachers* (New York: Oxford, 1973).

How to Freewrite

1. *Focus.* Choose a topic (for example, a word, idea, image, or quote) and record it at the top of a sheet of paper or a clear computer screen.

2. *Time.* Commit yourself to writing for a specific number of minutes. (Start with sessions of five or ten minutes.) If you need to write longer, go ahead.

3. *Speed.* Write as quickly as you can without physically hurting yourself. Speed helps you run through blocks and distractions.

4. *Flow.* Keep your pen or keyboard active. If you feel stalled, repeat the same word or expression until you find something else to write.

5. *Freedom.* Don't reread or correct while you are freewriting. If you can't think of a word, draw a line to fill in later. Spell words any way that lets you move on. Follow novelist John Steinbeck's advice:

> Write freely and rapidly as possible and throw the whole thing on paper. Never correct or rewrite until the whole thing is down. Rewriting in process is usually found to be an excuse for not going on. It also interferes with flow and rhythm which can only come from a kind of unconscious association with the material.

The elements of freewriting are focus, time, speed, and freedom. Read the basic procedure detailed in the sidebar on how to freewrite.

To keep going as you freewrite, you may want to record your reflections on the writing process as you proceed. Be honest! You may have to start by writing, "I don't know where to start." Remember that focus is the first element of freewriting, even if it means to focus on your not being able to focus. You'll be surprised how this can loosen you up. When you freewrite another time, you may want to choose a favorite sentence, image, or word from a previous freewrite.

Strange, silly, or forbidden thoughts and words may come to your mind as you freewrite. *Write them down.* No one has to see a freewrite that you don't want to show. At times, a mind is like a clogged faucet—jammed with words held back for fear of someone's disapproval, especially your own. Once you get the "sludge" out—the old rusts and "musts"—you get a clear flow. The idea you needed may be just behind one you don't want. And you never know—on second thought, one of those silly or forbidden thoughts may turn out to be exactly the one you were looking for.

Virginia Woolf is one of the most admired writers in English literature. Notice how flexibly she uses freewriting to focus herself in "A Sketch of the Past":

> Two days ago—Sunday 16th April 1939 to be precise—Nessa said that if I did not start writing my memoirs I should soon be too old. I should be eighty-five, and should have forgotten—witness the unhappy case of Lady Strachey. As it happens that I am sick of writing Roger's life, perhaps I will spend two or three mornings making a sketch. There are several difficulties. In the first place, the enormous number of things I can remember; in the second, the number of different ways in which memoirs can be written. As a great memoir reader, I know many different ways. But if I begin to go through them and to analyse them and their merits and faults, the mornings—I cannot take more than two or three at most—will be gone. So without stopping to choose my way, in the sure and certain knowledge that it will find itself—or if not it will not matter—I begin: the first memory.
>
> This was of red and purple flowers on a black ground—my mother's dress; and she was sitting either in a train or in an omnibus, and I was on her lap.

*R*eflections

1. Which parts of Virginia Woolf's freewriting sound as if she's talking to herself? Point to particular words, phrases, and sentences.
2. Which parts may need further explanation?
3. Which parts are most interesting to you? Why?
4. How did freewriting help Woolf clear her mind and find ideas on which to write?

When to Freewrite

Freewriting can help you with any writing task. Here are some purposes it can help you satisfy:

- To express a strong feeling
- To generate ideas
- To discover and choose details

- To get warmed up for an essay exam—freewrite your answer on a separate sheet of paper before writing on the exam paper
- To start writing when you are tired
- To rehearse a conversation
- To test different beginnings for a writing project
- To entertain different solutions to a problem
- To pass time

Exploration

Together and Solo.

1. Choose a thing (such as snow, roses, milk, or beer) or a person (such as a talk show host) that the whole class knows. Individually, do a timed ten-minute freewrite about the subject you chose together.

2. Read aloud to each other what you wrote, and compare the different directions people took from the same starting point.

3. Name any fears or concerns about writing that occurred as you wrote.

4. Choose your favorite sentences, phrases, or ideas from your freewrites. You might want to record them on a board. Discuss what you like and why. Do another freewrite starting with a sentence, phrase, or idea from your own or someone else's freewrite. Read portions of these freewrites to each other and discuss what you learned.

The Practice of Writing

The following practical ideas will help you manage your time, tools, space, and habits so that you can put into practice your commitment to being a writer.

Writing Time

To manage your time, you need goals, regularity, flexibility, and planning. With your instructor, set a *goal* for the number of papers and pages you are to submit on schedule. Then strive to be *regular* in your writing habits, the way most practicing writers are. So, for example, just like a runner deciding to run a mile every day at 6:30 P.M., you may decide to practice writing every day for fifteen minutes at 6:30 P.M. Then do it wherever you are. Let your friends think you are strange when you go off to another room during a party. They will admire you, too. And it might be fun to go

OCTOBER 1997	SUN	MON	TUES	WED	THU	FRI	SAT
				1	2	3	4
	5	6	7	8 PAPER ASSIGNED LIST TOPICS	9	10 CONSULT MR. JAUGS ON FOCUS	11
	12	13 LIBRARY— COLLECT INFO.	14	15 ORGANIZE— DRAFT LEAD	16	17	18 DRAFT PAPER
	19 CONSULT BRUCE ON PAPER	20 COLLECT MISSING INFO.	21	22 REVISE TYPE	23 PROOF WITH MARY	24 PAPER DUE	25
	26	27	28	29	30	31	

FIGURE 1.1   A Writing Time Plan

off and gossip with yourself about them in writing. Use made-up names in case others find what you wrote.

Be *flexible* in how you plan, so your schedule will work *for* you. For example, because campus parking is difficult, several students decided to drive to school by 7:45 A.M. so that they could park where they wanted to, without wasting time. During the hours before class, they found places in the library or in an empty auditorium, studio, classroom, or lounge to study or work. Three other students, with small children, arranged for one babysitter to care for all of their children one afternoon a week. The students used those afternoons to meet at the library to work on their papers together.

Plan your writing time. Start early and make and beat your *own* deadlines. Break down your writing projects into manageable parts. The next chapter maps out the different phases of the writing process. Once you become familiar with it, you will be able to decide which phase of the writing process you want to do next *before* you stop a particular writing session. Then you will feel more confident because you will know where to start. Figure 1.1 shows how one student planned his time to write a long paper. He wrote his writing time plan in pencil and made frequent adjustments as he went along.

Procrastination.   *Procrastination* means "to put off until tomorrow." There are two kinds of procrastination: creative and self-deceiving. *Creative procrastination* is taking time off from a particular phase of a task *already started* to reorganize, re-energize, and give ideas and events time to evolve. It can also be staying at your workplace and doing either nothing or your work. The first seven minutes of a task are usually the hardest, and 50 percent of the task is getting yourself settled. One student, working on a long paper, would sit for an hour at her desk without producing more than a paragraph. But sitting there reaffirmed her commitment. After a while, she had few dry spells. It was more interesting to work on her writing than to sit there doing nothing.

The point of *self-deceiving procrastination*, the second type, is to avoid giving enough time to a task. Self-deceiving procrastination shows up in two ways: putting off the task constantly, or trying to "get it over with" too soon. Either way, the person puts off real development for another day. The self-deceiving procrastinator tends to claim, "I work best under pressure." If you put work off, this is what can happen:

1. You tend to make more errors because you're working too fast.
2. You may run out of time, because it's hard to judge exactly how long a project will take.
3. You are cheating yourself because you don't give yourself the opportunity to develop your skills.
4. If you realize that you could have done the task if you had started earlier, you will probably lose confidence and self-esteem. Loss of confidence is an invitation to give up too soon.

Writing Tools

Instruments.   Mechanics have their wrenches; writers have their pens. Your tools are there to serve you the way a scalpel serves a surgeon. As a student writer in the 1990s, your challenge is to experiment with different writing instruments. You will need a typewriter or computer for college and work-related writing so that you can produce presentable materials. In addition, studies have shown that, for many writers, a typewriter or computer enhances not only the speed with which they compose but also the process of developing ideas. (This works even if you are only a two-finger typist, as fiction writer John Cheever was.)

Tape Recorder.   If you are a talker but freeze when facing a page, make the most of your gifts by talking your early drafts into a tape recorder. Then you can play back and write down your ideas. In addition, if you are a commuter, you may find that ideas come to you while you are riding. Tape them for later.

Supplies. If you were a lawyer, you wouldn't tell the judge you couldn't complete your case because your printer's ink cartridge ran out the night before. *Being a student is your profession.* Part of a profession is to keep plenty of supplies (such as paper, back-up cartridges, pens, and notecards) so that you can complete your work properly. Next time you run out of paper, be ready to go to class and tell your instructor, "I ran out of paper." Watch the person's face change, ready for the excuse. Then say, "But I had an extra package, and here's the freshly printed copy." Then you can both laugh.

Writing Space

Incense, flowers, high ceilings, organ music, and a pulpit invite a congregation to worship. Loud, rhythmic music and strobe lights inspire people to dance. To write, you need to find or create the right conditions. When you establish that a place is a writing place, just going there will help you to get started or at least to practice creative procrastination.

William Oatman, a student, wrote about how he created his writing space:

> First of all, when I write, I have to bring myself into my own world. I'll put Marvin Gaye's "What's Going On" on the tape recorder to block out noise that will bring my mind back into reality. When I write, I have to be physically alone: anyone around me seems to be a threat. It's like they're looking over my shoulder trying to correct or give me advice. Even if the person doesn't know me, I feel uncomfortable.

Robin Livelli, another student, reported some of the discomfort she had while writing:

> My body becomes very tense because most of the time when I write I am not using a table; I use my lap. Therefore, I have to make a hard enough surface to write on. My head is always swaying from side to side. Don't ask me why. I think that maybe by moving my head around, I feel it will shake the information out. My hand always cramps because I hold my pen or pencil too tight. In grammar school, I was taught that if the teacher could not pull the pen or pencil out of your hand easily then you were holding it incorrectly. But I still hang on too tight.

Her classmate Raul Sanchez gave her some ideas about how to cope:

> When I write I sit in a chair in an upright position with both my feet on the floor so that there's a consistent blood flow. This helps me to relax my body. Once I relax the writing gets better. Once in a while I get up to stretch, walk around, or even do some sit-ups. I also have to have a good lamp and a desk with a big surface.

Writing Habits

To establish the habits of a writer, take the following advice adapted from William James's essay "Habit: Its Importance for Psychology":*

1. Launch yourself into writing with energy.
2. Make no exceptions to your routine until the new habit is established in your life.
3. Start today.
4. Write every day (even if only for ten minutes).

Writing is its own reward. But *do* reward yourself for your new habits with a treat: a new something, a game of basketball, a hot bath, or a walk in the park. Keep a record of how much you write on any given day, what research you did, and what you learned so you can monitor and be proud of your progress.†

*E*xplorations _____

1. **a.** *Solo.* One writer writes on an ironing board; another prefers writing in bed. Describe what happens in your mind, body, and emotions when you write: How do you create your environment to enhance your work? What changes could you make in your environment or in your habits to help you better harness your writing energies?

   b. *Together.* Read your essays to each other and swap and develop strategies.

2. **a.** *Solo.* List problems that you anticipate in creating or acquiring the time, tools, space, and habits that are conductive to becoming a writer.

---

*William James, "Habit: Its Importance for Psychology," in *The Writings of William James*, ed. John J. McDermott (Chicago: University of Chicago Press, 1977), pp. 11–19.
†Turn to Chapter 4 for further suggestions on writers' tools and habits.

   b. *Together.* In small groups, share these concerns and then devise strategies that will help you turn problems into opportunities. If possible, find ways in which you can work to support each other, such as forming study groups or car pools, sharing supplies and tools, or swapping services (for example, typing a paper for an oil change).

3. *Solo.* Keep a record of your writing activities. Each time you perform some writing task, mark it down in a particular place such as the inside cover of your notebook. This will help you to monitor your work. If you haven't worked, it can remind you to do so. If you have progressed, it can enhance your self-esteem and inspire you to do more.

4. *Together.* Using insights you developed through reading and working with this chapter, write a group letter of advice to student writers.

WRITERS WRITING

Read and discuss the essays that follow, using these reflection questions and suggestions to guide you.

*R*eflections _____

1. *Together or Solo.* Choose your favorite essay. Discuss the following:
   - Why you like it more than the others
   - What similar experiences you have had in your life
   - Which words, phrases, or sentences are most powerful
   - What purpose you think it served the writer
   - What questions you would ask the writer

2. *Solo.* Write a letter to the writer in response to her or his essay.

3. *Solo.* Write about an experience you remembered while reading one of the essays.

From *Hope Emerges as Key to Success in Life*

Daniel Goleman

Daniel Goleman, Ph.D., covers the behavioral sciences for The New York Times *and has authored numerous books in this area.*

Psychologists are finding that hope plays a surprisingly potent role in giving people a measurable advantage in realms as diverse as academic achievement, bearing up in onerous jobs and coping with tragic illness. And, by contrast, the loss of hope is turning out to be a stronger sign that a person may commit suicide than other factors long thought to be more likely risks.

"Hope has proven a powerful predictor of outcome in every study we've done so far," said Dr. Charles R. Snyder, a psychologist at the University of Kansas who has devised a scale to assess how much hope a person has.

For example, in research with 3,920 college students, Dr. Snyder and his colleagues found that the level of hope among freshmen at the beginning of their first semester was a more accurate predictor of their college grades than were their S.A.T. scores or their grade point averages in high school, the two measures most commonly used to predict college performance. The study was reported in part in the November issue of The Journal of Personality and Social Psychology.

"Students with high hope set themselves higher goals and know how to work to attain them," Dr. Snyder said. "When you compare students of equivalent intellectual aptitude and past academic achievements, what sets them apart is hope."

People who score high on the hope scale are understandably better able to bear up in dire circumstances, other researchers are finding. In a study of 57 people with paralysis from spinal cord injury, those who reported more hope, compared with those having little hope, had less depression, greater mobility (despite similar levels of injury), more social contacts and more sexual intimacy.

"Those with high hope were more adaptive in all realms, regardless of how long they had been injured, whether just a month or 40 years," said Dr. Timothy Elliott, a psychologist at Virginia Commonwealth University in Richmond, who reported the study in the October issue of The Journal of Personality and Social Psychology....

Traits Among the Hopeful

Dr. Snyder found that people with high levels of hope share several attributes:

- Unlike people who are low in hope, they turn to friends for advice on how to achieve their goals.

- They tell themselves they can succeed at what they need to do.

- Even in a tight spot, they tell themselves things will get better as time goes on.

- They are flexible enough to find different ways to get to their goals.

- If hope for one goal fades, they aim for another. "Those low in hope tend to become fixated on one goal, and persist even when they find themselves blocked," Dr. Snyder said. "They just stay at it and get frustrated."

- They show an ability to break a formidable task into specific, achievable chunks. "People low in hope see only the large goal, and not the small steps to it along the way," Dr. Snyder said.

From *What It Is I Think I'm Doing Anyhow*

Toni Cade Bambara

*Dancer, actress, and prolific writer, Bambara was a
founding member of the Southern Collective of African-
American Writers.*

Writing is one of the ways I participate in struggle—one of the ways I
help to keep vibrant and resilient that vision that has kept the Family
going on. Through writing I attempt to celebrate the tradition of resistance, attempt to tap Black potential, and try to join the chorus of voices
that argues that exploitation and misery are neither inevitable nor necessary. Writing is one of the ways I participate in the transformation—one
of the ways I practice the commitment to explore bodies of knowledge for
the usable wisdoms they yield. In writing, I hope to encourage the fusion
of those disciplines whose split (material science versus metaphysics versus aesthetics versus politics versus...) predisposes us to accept fragmented truths and distortions as the whole. Writing is one of the ways I
do my work in the world.

From *A Way of Writing*

William Stafford

*Poet, essayist, and revered teacher, Stafford has been
the inspiration for many generations of writers.*

A writer is not so much someone who has something to say as he is
someone who has found a process that will bring about new things he
would not have thought of if he had not started to say them. That is, he
does not draw on a reservoir; instead, he engages in an activity that brings
to him a whole succession of unforeseen stories, poems, essays, plays,
laws, philosophies, religions, or—but wait!

Back in school, from the first when I began to try to write things, I felt
this richness. One thing would lead to another; the world would give and
give. Now, after twenty years or so of trying, I live by that certain richness, an idea hard to pin, difficult to say, and perhaps offensive to some.
For there are strange implications in it.

One implication is the importance of just plain receptivity. When I
write, I like to have an interval before me when I am not likely to be
interrupted. For me, this means usually the early morning, before others
are awake. I get pen and paper, take a glance out of the window (often it

is dark out there), and wait. It is like fishing. But I do not wait very long, for there is always a nibble—and this is where receptivity comes in. To get started I will accept anything that occurs to me. Something always occurs, of course, to any of us. We can't keep from thinking. Maybe I have to settle for an immediate impression: it's cold, or hot, or dark, or bright, or in between! Or—well, the possibilities are endless. If I put down something, that thing will help the next thing come, and I'm off. If I let the process go on, things will occur to me that were not at all in my mind when I started. These things, odd or trivial as they may be, are somehow connected. And if I let them string out, surprising things will happen.

If I let them string out.... Along with initial receptivity, then, there is another readiness: I must be willing to fail. If I am to keep on writing, I cannot bother to insist on high standards. I must get into action and not let anything stop me, or even slow me much. By "standards" I do not mean "correctness"—spelling, punctuation, and so on. These details become mechanical for anyone who writes for a while. I am thinking about such matters as social significance, positive values, consistency, etc. I resolutely disregard these. Something better, greater, is happening! I am following a process that leads so wildly and originally into new territory that no judgment can at the moment be made about values, significance, and so on. I am making something new, something that has not been judged before. Later others—and maybe I myself—will make judgments. Now, I am headlong to discover. Any distraction may harm the creating.

So, receptive, careless of failure, I spin out things on the page. And a wonderful freedom comes. If something occurs to me, it is all right to accept it. It has one justification: it occurs to me. No one else can guide me. I must follow my own weak, wandering, diffident impulses.

A strange bonus happens. At times, without my insisting on it, my writings become coherent; the successive elements that occur to me are clearly related. They lead by themselves to new connections. Sometimes the language, even the syllables that happen along, may start a new trend. Sometimes the materials alert me to something waiting in my mind, ready for sustained attention. At such times, I allow myself to be eloquent, or intentional, or for great swoops (Treacherous! Not to be trusted!) reasonable. But I do not insist on any of that; for I know that back of my activity there will be the coherence of my self, and that indulgence of my impulses will bring recurrent patterns and meanings again.

This attitude toward the process of writing creatively suggests a problem for me, in terms of what others say. They talk about "skills" in writing. Without denying that I do have experience, wide reading, automatic orthodoxies and maneuvers of various kinds, I still must insist that I am often baffled about what "skill" has to do with the precious little area of confusion when I do not know what I am going to say and then I find out what I am going to say. That precious interval I am unable to bridge by skill. What can I witness about it? It remains mysterious, just as all of us must feel puzzled about how we are so inventive as to be able to talk along through complexities with our friends, not needing to plan what we are going to say, but never stalled for long in our confident forward progress. Skill? If so, it is the skill we all have, something we must have learned before the age of three or four.

A writer is one who has become accustomed to trusting that grace, or luck, or—skill.

Owning My Words

Student Annie E. Lee

It felt like someone was constantly whispering in my ears, "You don't know how to articulate your words. Your grammar is horrible. How can people understand you?" These fears were always there, causing me to fear speaking before a group.

I guess it began when I came to New Jersey from the south. Southern people have a deep accent and some have a tendency to talk fast—I was one of them.

Some people criticized me for my southern accent. I had this one friend in particular, Karen Jones, who thought she was more intelligent than others. Whenever I talked, she listened very closely to see how I pronounced words. She told me that I added endings to words such as "mucha" instead of "much" and "hurted" instead of "hurt." Or, I might leave endings off words such as "start" when it was appropriate, instead of saying "started." Sometimes we could be talking and she would say to me, "I don't know what you are trying to say: spell it out for me." She even told me once that I don't put my words in the right places. She always was trying to correct me and always in the presence of other people. This made me feel stupid and insecure and caused me not to want to talk to people. Or, I would choose certain words that I thought people would understand. I started to lose confidence in myself and it hindered me for a long time. I came to the point where I didn't want to talk with her because I was so afraid that I would say the wrong thing. She was the only person I had this problem with.

Just this past Sunday, I had dinner at my house with some friends and invited Karen over. I was sharing my experience of baking my first cake with my friends. The first cake I baked fell because I put too much baking powder in it. I was baking this cake for a birthday, so I had to call my mother and get the right ingredients. Where I put three teaspoons of baking powder, I should have put ¼ teaspoon. I told my friends that my mother said to use confectioners' sugar instead of granulated sugar. Well, not only did Karen have a better solution, but she also tried to correct me again. With her head up high and a tone in her voice that said, "You don't know what you are talking about," she said, "If you don't have confection*ary* sugar, you can always sift granulated sugar and it will be just as good." Her statement made me feel stupid and embarrassed because she emphasized "confection*ary*" as a way to not-so-subtly correct my saying "confection*ers'*." My attention was not directed to my guests any more. I was sitting there thinking that I misused "confectioners'." My fears started to work on me, saying, "You can't, you didn't, you shouldn't..." So, to put my mind to rest, I looked at the name on the box of sugar I used and also consulted *The American Heritage Dictionary,* and I saw that the correct expression *was* "confection*ers'* sugar." It made me feel much more in control, and Karen doesn't seem so intimidating to me anymore.

---

*C*hapter Review

1. *Solo.* Define yourself as a writer, using the ideas, readings, discussions, and strategies you explored in this chapter. You may want to ask these questions of yourself for inspiration:

   - Where have I been as a writer? Why?
   - Where am I as a writer now? Why?
   - What are my specific challenges as a writer?
   - Where do I want to be as a writer? How am I going to get there?

2. *Together.*

   a. In a small group of three or four, write a letter to your instructor saying what you hope to gain from your writing class. Mention your fears. Ask your instructor to clarify her or his expectations of you as a writer. Make a commitment as a class to helping everyone develop as a writer. Suggest any ideas that you believe will help make this a satisfying venture for all of you.

   b. Read your small group letters to the whole class. Notice what they had in common and how they were different. How does your instructor react? What did you learn from this group review?

Chapter *2*

The Writing Process

This chapter offers opportunities to

—Identify **seven phases of the writing process**

—Distinguish **formal** from **informal** writing

—Discover your **style of composing**

—Learn what an **essay** is

> You write by sitting down and writing.
> —*Bernard Malamud, Novelist*

> You are like a mechanic trying to design something, sitting at a table with…little bits and pieces scattered about, sorting them out with a forefinger, pushing one to the side, ousting another altogether, bringing the first one back, finding it doesn't match with something that you've meanwhile chosen; deciding, perhaps, that it's so good that you must consider abandoning all the rest and starting over again with this as the main component.
> —*Christianna Brand, Mystery writer*

> You have to try something harder to do better.
> —*Laura Silwones, Athlete, Massage therapist*

Writing for Meaning

Writing is a process that leads from a need to a product and, ideally, a result that is meant to satisfy the need. What a piece of writing *means* to you is determined by the combined effect of your need, purpose, audience, and results. If you write only to have an instructor read and grade what you write, the writing itself may not mean much to you. If you write because you are horrified at drug dealers in your neighborhood (you have a need to protect yourself) and want to convince the government (your audience) to provide more police protection (your purpose is to persuade), the writing itself will be very meaningful. If, as a result of writing, the situation actually changes as you want it to, you will be experiencing the full power of written language.

The more important the need, purpose, and results of writing are to you, the more meaningful your writing will be. The less important the need, purpose, and results of writing, the less it will mean.

Needs + Purpose + Audience + Results = Meaning

Often, you can't control needs or the results of writing. These are relatively *passive* phases of the writing process. But you *can* decide whether and how to react to needs and results. Your options are the seven *active* phases of the writing process: identifying purpose and audience, drafting, collecting, focusing, organizing, consulting, and revising. By working through these active phases, you will discover how needs can lead writers to satisfying results.

This chapter offers an overview of the seven phases of the writing process. This model emphasizes the importance of writing for meaning and for an audience that includes, at the very least, not only your instructor but your peers. You may decide to work through the chapters that are devoted to different phases of the writing process first. Or you may decide to explore writing for different purposes in Part III of *The Flexible Writer*—to remember, to bridge cultures, to learn, to gain power—and return as the need arises to explore the phases of the writing process in Part II.

Phases of the Writing Process

How you write (the process you go through) is not *what* you finally produce (the product or result). The rehearsal (the process) is not the play (the

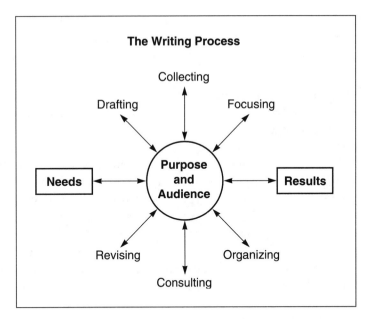

FIGURE 2.1   The Writing Process

product or result)—the production line is not the car. Much work goes into the process of producing a Madonna for her audience: long daily workouts with a personal trainer; hours of nail, hair, and skin work by beauty experts; lessons with dance, voice, and acting coaches; experiments with wardrobe consultants, composers, musicians, technicians, and many more. Her music videos are a product of much trial and error, outtakes, and surprises in the process. You see only the results, not the many hours of preparation and mistakes. So too with writing—what is published is the result of consulting with peers and experts, trial and error, outtakes, and surprises in the process.

The writing process can be divided into nine phases, as shown in Figure 2.1. You enter the process because of some need. The center of the writing process is identifying your purpose (what you hope to accomplish for yourself and others through writing) and identifying your audience (who you want to reach with your writing). The writing process culminates in some result, which in turn may create another need to write.

As you can see, this model of the writing process is not a straight line leading from a need to a result. According to this model, there is no set order in which to move through the phases of the writing process. Also, the way you move between phases will change for different writing tasks. Notice that the arrows pointing to the phases go both ways. This is to illustrate that any phase can be repeated as needed. As you move into one phase of the writing process, ideas for other phases of the writing process will probably arise. Look at the summary of these phases in Figure 2.1.

Needs.   The writing process begins with a need. This need may be as simple as a need to design a schedule or as complex as a need to express anger over a political issue. Educator Claire Weinstein distinguishes two kinds of needs for learning: *performance* and *mastery.* If you do your assignments just to get a grade and pass a course, then you are only creating a performance. You will expend your energy figuring out what the instructor wants and will fulfill only the requirements you perceive. You make your instructor a dictator and thus give over your power. If you do your assignments to master a body of information or a set of skills, then your interest is mastery. You will perceive the instructor as a guide, not a dictator. Assignments will be a stimulus for exploration and discovery. You will take initiative and assume responsibility for your own development.

What Weinstein says about learning applies to writing in most situations. For example, you might write a memo in order to perform for your boss, just so he will notice you for the next promotion. Or you might write the same memo to develop your ideas about marketing a new product. The irony is that the person who works for mastery is the person who is most likely to perform well. The person who works only to perform may become stuck in a mere power struggle. *This bears repeating: focus on mastery and the performance will take care of itself.*

The least inspiring motivation for writing may be to merely fulfill a course requirement. But you can turn almost any assignment into something satisfying if you can discover some way to address more basic needs such as curiosity, a need for adventure, a need to assert your individuality, a need for precision, a need to be included in a community, or a need to express yourself. A given piece of writing may fulfill a single need or a complex of needs. To understand this phase of the writing process, ask yourself such questions as these:

- How do I feel about this topic?
- Which aspect of this topic is important to me?
- What human interest do I find in this?
- What basic need could writing this satisfy for me?
- What does writing this *mean* to me?
- Am I writing for performance or mastery?

Identifying Purpose and Audience. When you enter the active phases of the writing process, you make a commitment to fulfill your need. This commitment to action transforms your need into a purpose. Since writing is communicating, as soon as you enter the writing process you are also anticipating who your audience (or receiver) will be, even if it's just yourself as reader.

Your purpose and audience will determine what and how you write. For example, if you write a letter to your senator (your audience) to win a vote against a nuclear plant in your city (your purpose), you would not want to attack her personal campaign strategies. This could alienate her and undermine your purpose. However, you could write an additional letter to the editor of your local newspaper stressing your concerns and thus make the senator more willing to please her constituents.

The purposes and audiences for writing are as varied and numerous as there are life situations. Any given piece of writing may have more than one purpose and audience, although some may be more important to you. To engage in this phase of the writing process, ask yourself these questions:

- Why am I writing this?
- Is my reason personal, intellectual, economic, physical, or social?
- Who is my audience?
- What does my audience know?
- What does my audience want?
- How can I capture and keep my audience's attention?
- How can I best fulfill my purpose?

Drafting. To experiment with and learn from writing, you put words on the page. Drafting is this process of actually creating the written document. You may use many different methods of drafting: audiotaping, writing longhand, typing, cutting and pasting, or word processing. To manage your documents so that you can monitor and ensure your progress, you create a filing system. To engage in this phase of the writing process, ask yourself this question:

- What tools in which environment would best support my writing process?

Collecting. To discover, develop, and create ideas that will serve your purpose and reach your audience, you need to collect memories, sensations, experiences, and ideas. You will read, talk, watch films, and listen to the radio. You may visit a museum, try hang gliding, or cook seaweed so that you can better understand your subject. Chapter 1 invited you to experiment with *freewriting,* a basic tool for collecting and creating ideas. Additional collecting strategies are introduced in Chapter 4: *listing, brainstorming, clustering, interviewing,* and *writing journals.* To engage in this phase of the writing process, ask yourself these questions:

- What information, experiences, and ideas do I need in order to accomplish my purpose?
- How can I most effectively collect what I need?

Focusing.   To divide your writing task into manageable bits, and to hold your own attention as well as that of your audience, you focus your writing. By focusing, you create *unity* in your work—including all and only those ideas that are relevant and necessary to fulfill your purpose.

1.   *Strategies.* Six focusing strategies are explored in Chapter 5: choosing, specifying, illustrating, questioning, quoting, and stating. To engage in this phase of the writing process, ask yourself these questions:

- What's relevant to my purpose?
- What choices do I need to make?
- How can I be more specific?
- Which examples could enliven my writing?
- What exactly am I writing about?
- What questions do I need to answer to be clearer?
- How can I state my purpose and point of view?

2.   *Sense appeal.* To enliven your writing and engage your audience, you focus on sensory images of sight, hearing, smell, taste, and touch as well as bodily sensations of motion, pleasure, and pain. Chapter 6 offers you strategies for giving your work sense appeal. You will learn how to describe, how to distinguish showing from telling, how to balance objective and subjective approaches to writing, and how to use comparisons to enliven your work. To engage in this phase of the writing process, ask yourself these questions:

- Have I used sensory images?
- Have I ignored any senses that might be relevant?
- How can I prime my senses with objects, photographs, or audio- and videotapes?

- What firsthand experience could prime my senses?
- Do I illustrate important claims?
- What do the images mean to me?

Organizing.   To guide yourself and your reader, you organize your work so it holds together. A well-organized piece of writing will thereby have *coherence.* You pay special attention to titles, leads (beginnings), the body of your work, transitions, and endings. Chapter 7 offers you strategies for managing these elements of your writing and also for developing, shaping, and outlining your work. To engage in this phase of the writing process, ask yourself these questions:

- How can I shape this writing so that it will engage me in the process of developing ideas?
- How can I organize this writing so that it holds my audience's attention, from an effective beginning through a body of ideas to a memorable last impression?

Consulting.   To grow as a writer, a thinker, and a person, you consult with others who can help you develop. These people may include peers, teachers, writing center staff, librarians, family, friends, and others. To develop your own writing intuitions, you, in turn, respond to the writings of others. Helping them, you help yourself. We learn best what we teach. To engage in this phase of the writing process, ask yourself these questions:

- Who can respond to my work?
- What do I want others to help me do in my writing?
- How can I best help other writers?

Revising.   To develop your early drafts, you look for opportunities to improve and build on them: this is the process of revising. In revising, you reconsider your purpose and audience and decide which phases of the writing process you need to repeat. The best way to learn how to adjust your writing for your purpose and audience is to consult with others. To engage yourself in this phase of the writing process, ask yourself these questions:

- How can I revise this writing to most effectively do what I want it to do?
- What am I learning from revising?

Results.   A stopping point in a particular writing process is publication. This may be as limited as reading a paper aloud in class or sending in a résumé to a prospective employer. It may be as broad as having a book published. Other results may occur, including return mail, a grade, a job offer or rejection, money, a new love, or ideas for more writing. A most disappointing result may be no reaction or result at all. You may follow up any result by choosing to address a different need, a different purpose, a different audience, or a different way of presenting your ideas.

Publication of some sort—either in print or in a public speech or reading—is often the desired result of writing. In school, publication may be as limited as handing in a paper to your instructor or as wide as having your work published in a newspaper, magazine, or book. The results may be as limited as a grade or as far-reaching as finding an instructor who becomes actively engaged in helping you with your academic career.

Because publication is so motivating in the real world of writing, you may want to set a goal of producing a class newsletter or magazine. You may want to arrange for an evening of reading your work for family, friends, and members of the campus and community. Sometimes you can pair up with another section of a course and present your work to each other. Working toward such goals offers opportunities for community and accomplishment. To respond to this phase of the writing process, ask yourself these questions:

- Am I satisfied with this result?
- With whom can I further share my writing?
- How can we, as a community, publish together?
- Do I need to write more or differently?

*E*xplorations _____

1. *Solo.* The purpose of this exploration is to help you further understand process. Identify some specific activity—serious or humorous—at which you consider yourself to be an expert. Here are some examples:

Throwing a fastball	Messing up relationships
Eating pizza	Making peanut butter sandwiches
Arranging flowers	Mowing a lawn
Losing things	Growing snap peas
Rebuilding a carburetor	Upsetting others
Throwing parties	Breeding dogs

Describe how you go from need to result in your chosen activity. You may want to use different phases of the writing process as a guide. So, for example, you *need*/crave an apple pie; the *purpose* for it may be to celebrate a raise; the *audience* can be your friends; the *collecting* activities may include picking apples; and so on. For each phase of your activity, offer special instructions. *How* do you select apples? *How* do you make the crust flaky?

2. *Together.* Read what you wrote in Exploration 1. Discuss your different processes. If two people wrote about a similar activity, compare their processes. Discuss what lessons you can draw for your writing process from what you know about process in other activities.

3. *Solo.* Describe how you wrote your last piece of writing. Identify which phases of the writing process you used and which you didn't. Would you have written the paper differently if you had used the model of the writing process described in this chapter? If so, how? If not, why not?

4. *Together.* Set a goal for publishing your work this semester either by creating a class book or by giving a public reading to family, friends, and members of the campus and the community.

Formal and Informal Writing

Different writing tasks emphasize different phases of the writing process. If you are writing a diary entry, you are less likely to move into the consulting and revising phases of the writing process than if you were writing a business proposal. Similarly, if you are writing a first draft of a paper, you may be less concerned about organizing your thoughts than you are in just collecting and drafting what comes to mind.

In considering how to approach the phases of the writing process, it is helpful to distinguish *informal* and *formal* writing tasks. One definition of the word *formal* is "shaped." Informal writing does not have to be shaped as carefully as formal writing does. Informal writing focuses more on the drafting and collecting phases of the writing process. The more formal a piece of writing is, and the more important its audience, the more fully you must enter every phase of the writing process. Notice how some characteristics of formal and informal writing compare:

Formal	Informal
Clean printout	Illegible handwritten draft
Focused	Exploratory
Concise	Searching

Formal	Informal
Researched	Incomplete
Organized	Digressive (with tangents)
Passed consultation	Unreviewed
Revised	Uncorrected

Here are some parallel examples of formal and informal writing:

Formal	Informal
Polished paper	Freewrite
Business proposal	Short memo
Letter to a senator	Letter to a good friend
Exam essay	Class notes
Produced play	Party charade

Figure 2.2 shows how your purpose and familiarity with your audience affect the level of formality of your writing.

The Essay

An essay is a composition focused on a single topic, supported by examples and illustrations. One purpose of writing an essay is to explore ideas. In fact, the verb form of the word *essay* means "to try" or "to make an attempt." Another purpose of writing an essay is to present your personal point of view on a topic. Often, the essay is an attempt to convince your audience to see the world as you do. The essay is a fundamental form of writing that helps you develop as a student and a professional.

The model of the writing process in *The Flexible Writer* is tailored to help you write essays. Focusing helps you to commit yourself to a single topic. It helps you to illustrate your topic so you can, in turn, focus your audience's attention on what you have to say. Collecting invites you to explore and test different ideas and sensations. Organizing allows you to develop a structure that will support your focus. Consulting and revising offer you opportunities to test and learn more about your purpose, your audience, and your topic.

Styles of Composing

You may discover that you have special abilities in particular phases of the writing process or that you prefer some phases of the writing process

Less

Audience:	Self, friends, some family and peers	Audience:	Co-workers, some authorities
Purpose:	Personal	Purpose:	Practical, social, business
Examples:	Journal Personal letter Shopping list	Examples:	Interoffice memo Some reports Quiz

Line of Formality

Less ———————————————————————————————— **More**

Audience:	General audience	Audience:	Authorities, critics
Purpose:	Varies	Purpose:	Argument, demonstration, negotiation
Examples:	Anecdote Family history How-to article	Examples:	Term paper Résumé Proposal Editorial article Professional journal article

Line of Familiarity

More

FIGURE 2.2   Formality in Writing

over others. You may discover that you are a natural researcher and prefer collecting information to revising. You may be an editor and enjoy revising more than drafting. You may be a doer who likes to dive right into drafting. You may be social and enjoy the consulting phase over organizing. This section offers you some insights into tastes in and styles of composing.

The Planner's Style

As you practice writing, you may discover that you have a current favorite way of moving from one phase of the writing process to another. For example, you may prefer a particular straight-line style because you tend to be a *planner:* collect information, choose a topic, organize an outline, write a focused statement, draft your paper, proofread, submit. A planner tends to know ahead of time how a writing project will look when it is finished. The benefit of the planner's style is the security of knowing what to do next. This style works well for papers in which you report simple information.

The drawback of the planner's straight-line style is that it may restrict the writer. One of the benefits of writing is that you learn and create new ideas during the process. Often in the writing process new insights arise in one phase that will require you to refocus, reorganize, or redraft if you are to include them. If you adhere too strictly to your original plans and ideas, you lose the benefit of writing your way to better ideas. Also, different writing tasks call for different approaches. What may work for you in writing academic papers may not necessarily serve you in writing business letters or project proposals. Longer, more creative writing projects take more time, readjustment, and flexibility than short writing pieces that are meant only to transfer simple information.

The Explorer's Style

The person who takes an *explorer's* approach to the writing process moves back and forth between different phases as needed and is comfortable with revising as many times as is necessary. For example, an explorer may draft several attempts first, find a focus, collect information, draft again, consult with others, organize, revise, refocus, collect more information, redraft, publish. The benefit of the explorer's style is freedom and the discovery of new ideas.

The drawback of the explorer's style is that it may initially confuse or frustrate you. Planning can help you steady your mind when you focus and organize your thoughts. Having a clear plan can offer you the structure you need to develop confidence in yourself as a thinker and social being. If you entertain too many ideas at once, you may confuse yourself and become bored. Shorter tasks such as essay exam questions do not require the same kind of exploration as longer, more creative papers, proposals, and projects do.

Experiment with both the planner's and the explorer's styles. Ask yourself which writing tasks call for which approach, and when. Although you may favor one style over the other (and some writing tasks require more of one and less of the other), you will find yourself both planning and exploring in most tasks. Here, as in any aspect of the writing process, be flexible.

New Versus Practicing Writers

New Writers

Being a new writer can be very exciting. It is a time for discovering abilities you already have but didn't recognize in yourself. It is a time for exploration, adventure, and discovery—it is a time for developing friendships with other writers. Each time you start a kind of writing with which you are unfamiliar, you have an opportunity to recapture this excitement. If you are fully engaged with the process, you can take on the attitude of a new writer each time you write.

But some new writers—afraid of criticism—get stuck in a familiar phase of the writing process. Often this is the revising or consulting phase. Even before they start putting words on the page, these new writers *revise* in their heads. They believe statements such as "That won't work," "I can't write that," "They won't understand." It's almost as if they were trying to avoid the disapproval of a harsh authority figure. So they give up before they have to and depend almost entirely—without discussion or negotiation—on teachers or tutors to perform the other phases of writing *for* them, including assigning topics (identifying purpose and audience, and focusing), offering ideas to include (collecting), telling them how to organize their work, and correcting their grammar and punctuation (a part of revising). These writers may rush through their assignments and thus lower their satisfaction in writing. The purpose of this textbook is to help you to gradually make these choices for yourself.

Then there are new writers who go to the other extreme and won't take any advice at all. They tend to believe statements such as "My writing is just fine. What's good is just a matter of my taste against yours." They are suffering from denial. Shutting themselves off from others' reactions, these blocked writers can slow their growth or even stunt it.

The problem for both the underconfident and the overconfident new writer is fear of not getting it *right* the first time. If you fear not being able to write *right,* you let others perform phases of the writing process for you or you make believe you don't need any help.

Ignore your fears. Focus on experimenting with the different phases of the writing process for yourself. If you get stuck in one phase, skip to another. You may find your answer there. Keep moving. Become a *practicing* writer.

Practicing Writers

Flexibility is the hallmark of practicing writers. They move more easily from one writing phase to another and back, as needed. For example, when practicing writers get too involved collecting information (to the point of being jammed with more research than will ever be needed to write a certain paper), they may return to the center of the writing process and ask, "What is my purpose in writing this paper?" They may move to revising an introduction (noticing that it is more likely to engage an audience) and then move right to drafting. Practicing writers acknowledge that they may need more practice in a particular phase of writing and then get it. Acknowledging that different writing tasks may call for different approaches to the writing process, practicing writers don't get stuck with any particular sequence in which to perform the phases.

Practicing writers are *aware* of their audience, so they consult with others to read drafts. Practicing writers are willing to *revise* as many times as needed to fulfill their purposes and reach readers. Because they consult with others and experiment with different versions of what they write, practicing writers know how to talk about writing and become more and more *aware* of their own writing processes.

Becoming a Flexible Writer

The difference between a new and a practicing writer is that the practicing writer has probably made more mistakes in writing than the new writer has—just as a tennis pro has hit more balls out of bounds in a career than an amateur has. There are days and days of frustrating rehearsal, miles of rejected film, and sometimes millions of dollars worth of false starts, bloopers, and outtakes behind the smooth surface of a finished movie. There can be years of work and piles of rejected words behind a well-written book. Have the courage to be imperfect. The more you practice one kind of writing, the more perspective and flexibility you'll have for other kinds of writing. A practicing writer gets through possible blocks by being willing to experiment, explore, and try as many ways as needed to create the desired results. The practicing writer makes enough time for writing, so that new ideas can emerge and the process can be enjoyed. The more you practice as a writer, the more automatically you can move from one phase of the writing process to another.

One student, Edem Ikurekong, summarizes the benefits of learning to be flexible during the writing process: "Not trying to be too perfect while I'm in the writing process enables me to be a man of my own and be able to say what I want to say and not what I'm expected to say. If I was trying to be too perfect, I'd be searching for somebody else's *right way* to write." The good news is that you can become a practicing writer very quickly, just by committing time, energy, and attention to the process. Each time you write notes, experiment with an idea on paper, consult with someone, turn to a book (such as this one) to guide you, collect information, or even just shop for the proper supplies, you are acting as a practicing writer, a flexible writer.

Chapter Review

1. *Solo and Together.* Answer "yes" or "no" on the lines of the following questionnaire to determine whether you currently prefer a planner's or an explorer's style of composing. Check the Answer Key below, and then discuss your results.

   a. _____ Do you write an outline before starting to write?

   b. _____ Do you need to know exactly how to write something?

   c. _____ Once you start, do you need to finish writing quickly and be done with it?

   d. _____ Do you revise when you get new ideas as you write?

   e. _____ Do you look forward to learning as you write?

   f. _____ Do you prefer thinking things through before writing?

   g. _____ Do you write down your ideas first and revise later?

   h. _____ Do you like to revise?

   i. _____ Do you prefer reading to writing?

   j. _____ Do you believe that there is a right sequence of steps to take in the writing process?

2. *Solo.* Determine which phase of the writing process has given you the most difficulty in the past. Read the chapter that is devoted to that phase. Freewrite a letter to your instructor, quoting your three favorite statements from that chapter. In your letter, make a commitment to becoming an expert on that phase. Adopt that chapter; refer to it often; help others with that phase of the writing process.

3. *Solo.* For your next essay—and whenever possible—write a self-review by responding to these questions:

   a. Why did I write this?

   b. Who is my audience?

Answer Key:

The planner tends to answer "yes" to a, b, c, f, i, j. The explorer tends to answer "yes" to d, e, g, h.

c. How did I maintain focus?

d. How did I organize?

e. How did I collect information?

f. What did I learn from consulting others?

g. What efforts did I make to revise?

h. What problems did I have in the process?

i. What did I learn about my writing process and skills?

j. What more could I do to enliven this work for myself and for my readers?

Chapter 3

Purpose and Audience

This chapter offers opportunities to

—Identify **purpose** and **audience** in the writing process

—Find **meaning** and **purpose** in writing

—Learn how to **engage readers**

—Distinguish four purposes of education: **information, skills, interpretation,** and **experimentation**

—Explore the dynamics of **denotation** and **connotation**

Why write? To live, of course.
—*Gunter Kunert,*
Author of over sixty books

Ancient Egyptians believed that the mere action of writing could provide protection against calamity.
—*Joseph Campbell, Mythologist*

Purposes for Writing

The writing process is usually motivated by some combination of real-life needs: personal, emotional, intellectual, physical, social, or economic. If you choose to satisfy your need through the act of writing, you transform your need into a purpose. Some purposes are more inspiring than others.

If you write merely to avoid disapproval—to get an assignment "over with"—the reward of writing may be as removed from your real-life needs as a grade on a dusty transcript. It is far more meaningful to write in order to explore feelings, questions, ideas, topics, and interactions that concern you fully and directly. How engaged you are shows in the writing. If you're bored with your writing, your reader will be too. Even if you are writing only for someone else's approval, paying attention to the phases of the writing process will help you discover some way to transform each writing task into something that satisfies you more fully and directly— something that meets *your* approval. Your work itself will thereby improve, and so will your grades. But then the grade won't have to be the point any more.

Kinds of Purposes

Writing can serve three kinds of needs or purposes: (1) *self-expressive*— the need to be heard; (2) *interpersonal*—the need to get something done with others; and (3) *aesthetic*—the need for order, beauty, pleasure, and creativity.* A given piece of writing may serve some or all of these purposes, depending on the writer's purpose and audience. Practicing writers know how to gauge the kind of writing (or combination of kinds of writing) that is appropriate in a given situation. These writers don't try to write a mostly self-expressive piece when an interpersonal one is in order, nor do they treat something aesthetically when they mean only to be self-expressive.

Self-expressive Writing.   Self-expressive writing helps you to formulate your experiences in words so that you can "get them out of your system." The main purpose of self-expressive writing is to fulfill the need to be heard. Self-expressive writing allows you to vent your anger as well as to express love, to remember your childhood as well as to dream of your future. Sometimes the purpose of this kind of writing is fulfilled just in

---

*These distinctions are an adaptation of James Britton's, "Notes on a Working Hypothesis about Writing," in *Prospect and Retrospect: Selected Essays of James Britton*, ed. Gordon M. Pradl (Montclair, N.J.: Boynton/Cook, 1982).

> ### *When to Explore Purpose and Audience*
>
> 1. You are beginning a writing project.
> 2. You are worried about readers' reactions.
> 3. Readers don't respond as you had hoped they would.
> 4. You are bored or frustrated.
> 5. You don't know what to do next.

the act of writing. Self-expressive writing often takes the form of first-draft diary entries, letters, autobiographies, poems, and songs. Here is a self-expressive paragraph written by student Samantha Renner:

```
     I am terrified of the idea of war. All I can think of are
those films of houses gutted by bombs, children lying half-
naked and dead in the streets, and blood everywhere. Some-
times at night, I wake up to the sirens from the fire station
down the block, and I panic: What if they are not signaling
for a fire? What if, somehow, there are planes coming to bomb
our town? This must be just a little of what people must feel
who are actually in a war zone. It's terrible.
```

In this example, Samantha is expressing her feelings about war. The self-expressive purpose of the piece is fulfilled by writing, itself.

Interpersonal Writing. Interpersonal writing is social. The main purpose of interpersonal writing is to help you connect, break, or negotiate lines of communication between different aspects of yourself and others. These others are called your *audience,* a word that literally means "those who listen." Your anticipated audience may be as far away as a reader in another country whom you may never meet, or your audience may be as close as yourself. Your anticipated audience may be as specific as your instructor or as general as all college students. More than one audience may exist for a given piece of writing. Your task is to decide which audiences you mainly want to reach.

In interpersonal writing, you try to get someone else to recognize you, to do something for or with you, to agree with you, or to change in some way. The *essay,* a written interpretation of experiences and information, is a very important form of interpersonal writing in the academic world, in journalism, and in business and the professions. In the essay, you show what you know and contribute your perspectives to the community. Interpersonal writing may take other forms such as letters, proposals, reports, business and legal memos, recipes, instructions, exams, legal documents, and editorials. The following paragraph is an example of interpersonal writing that contrasts with the self-expressive writing in Samantha's paragraph about war. In this second paragraph, Samantha is trying to persuade the audience of her position:

> Before a country declares war on another country I believe that several things should take place:
>
> 1. There should be an open debate on television between those who are for the war and those who are against it. The debators should include the parents of draftable people, military personnel, lawmakers, and conscientious objectors.
> 2. There should be films of wars played on television showing people who have been hurt or killed.
> 3. There should be a vote taken by the general population.
> 4. There should be an active campaign to ensure that at least 50 percent of the population votes.
> 5. The people of the country on whom we are planning to declare war should be allowed to speak to the people of this country. In short, we should spend at least as much time, money, and thought in deciding on whether to declare war as we do on a presidential campaign.

Aesthetic Writing.   The main purpose of aesthetic writing is the challenge and pleasure of learning how to use language in interesting ways. When you focus on your writing style for its own sake, you are writing for an aesthetic purpose: to create beautiful language. Even a harsh situation can be aesthetically described if the language is precise and effective. Writing about your feelings about war may start out to be a self-expressive act, but if you then revise it into a polished poem, play, story, or creative essay, you are writing for an aesthetic purpose. Samantha transformed her paragraph into a poem. She shaped her work using techniques that display the beauty and power of language: clear images, meaningful line breaks, musical sounds, appropriate rhythms, and comparisons. Using these strategies, she engages her readers' attention so that she can more effectively relate her message on a difficult subject:

```
              When Will We Awaken?

The sirens shriek,
3:30 in the morning, again.
Somewhere nearby there is a fire.
This one will be cooled by water.
The children will be carried
By people in wet rubber coats.
What of the shrieking in another place
Where no one can carry the children
Away from bombs bursting in air
Giving proof through the night
That a flag may wave?
```

Combinations. Good writing often satisfies different needs or purposes at the same time. For example, it is hard to separate the aesthetic from the self-expressive and from the interpersonal in some writing. A poem that is written to satisfy an aesthetic need may also satisfy a self-expressive purpose, as Samantha's poem does. This same poem may serve to convince others to avoid war. Paying attention to how words are put together—writing something in an aesthetic way—often helps you to better satisfy your self-expressive and interpersonal needs. Furthermore, self-expressive writing can form the basis for interpersonal writing, and, in turn, interpersonal writing can lead to more self-expression, as it did for Samantha.

In your own writing, balance self-expressive, interpersonal, and aesthetic purposes. The following Explorations help you to identify different purposes for which you may write or have written.

*E*xplorations _____

1. **a.** *Together.* List different kinds of writing you've done, from shopping lists to essay exams, telephone messages to formal proposals.

    b. *Solo.* Choose two pieces of writing you've done: a particularly meaningful piece and one that you found less satisfying. For each piece, consider the following:

- The purpose for writing
- Who the audience was or would be
- The difficulties you may have had in writing
- How you managed problems with writing
- Who supported you in the writing
- The satisfactions you had from the writing
- The results of the writing

c. *Together.* As a whole class or in small groups, discuss what you learned from this exploration.

2. *Together.*

a. There are some down-to-earth reasons people need to write. These include personal, emotional, intellectual, economic, and social purposes such as the following:

- To release stress
- To make others like them
- To be heard when no one seems to listen
- To earn a good grade

Add to this list, being as honest and straightforward as you can be.

b. Group the reasons on your list into the following categories, according to the main need they satisfy for you: self-expressive, interpersonal, aesthetic.

c. Discuss which reasons for writing are the most satisfying to you. Which reasons cause you the most tension? Which of these are more directly related to writing? Which of these are indirectly related to writing?

3. a. *Together.* Add to this list of professions:

Mechanic	Real estate broker
Homemaker	Psychiatrist

b. *Solo and Together.* Interview a person from a profession or business with which you aren't familiar but that interests you. Ask the person to show you samples of the kinds of writing done in the normal course of her or his duties. Use these questions to guide your discussion of individual pieces of writing:

- Why did you write this?
- Who were your anticipated readers?

- What problems did you have in writing this?
- How did you solve your writing problems?
- Whom did you consult?
- What advice helped you the most?
- What satisfactions did you have from writing this?
- What results did this piece bring?
- Would you do it differently next time? If so, how?

c. *Together.* Bring the materials and ideas you collect to class and discuss what you learned.

Identifying Your Purpose

Purpose and audience are closely connected in the writing process. What you want to accomplish—your purpose—will determine your choice of audience. The audience you're writing to or for determines—to a great extent—what purposes you can fulfill.

The range of things you can do with language is as broad as life itself. For example, expressing, proposing, promising, betting, and naming can be done entirely with words and don't necessarily anticipate reactions from others. Just stating "I promise" is a promise. Just stating "I bet" is a bet.* Other actions—such as persuading, negotiating, arguing, and stopping—anticipate reactions from others and may require a more complex statement. You have to learn about your audience's interests, access to information, and expectations. You have to anticipate your audience's responses to shape your own.

By writing, you *connect* with, *separate* from, or *negotiate* with others. For example, to marry, apologize, compliment, or inform is to attempt to connect with others. To argue against, ridicule, intimidate, or blame may serve to create separation. To discuss, plan, or persuade is to negotiate.

The following Explorations will help you to discover some of the purposes that language can serve and to see how it allows you to connect, separate, or negotiate.

---

*From J. L. Austin, *How to Do Things with Words* (New York: Oxford University Press, 1962).

Explorations _____

This Exploration provides the language you need to discuss the purposes of your own papers.

1. *Together.*

    a. Generate a list of thirty-five verbs that refer to verbal communication. You may wish to use dictionaries and thesauruses. Start with these words:

discuss	scold
argue	flatter
persuade	ask
entertain	insult

        Let the words above lead to other words that lead to other words. Strive for variety and quantity.

    b. Group these language activities according to whether they help you *connect* with, *separate* from, or *negotiate* with others.

    Letters often focus on well-defined purposes. The following Explorations offer you focused opportunities to explore how awareness of purpose and audience shapes writing.

2. *Together and Solo.* Referring to the verbs listed in Exploration 1a, name the purposes of different sentences in the following letters. For example, Cornelius Vanderbilt starts by *accusing the reader of cheating him.* What does he do next?

    a.

    Dear Sir:

    You have undertaken to cheat me. I will not sue you because the law takes too long. I will ruin you.

    Sincerely,

    Cornelius Vanderbilt

    b.

    Dear Miss,

    After three years of schooling at Barbiana I took, in June, my exams for the intermediate diploma as a private-school candidate. The composition topic was: "The Railroad Cars Speak."

    At Barbiana I had learned that the rules of good writing are: Have something important to say, something useful to everyone or at least to many. Know for whom you are writing. Gather all useful materials. Find a logical pattern with which to develop the theme.

Eliminate useless words. Eliminate every word not used in the spoken language. Never set time limits.

That is the way my schoolmates and I are writing this letter. That is the way my pupils will write, I hope, when I am a teacher.

But, facing that composition topic, what use could I make of the humble and sound rules of the art of writing in all ages? If I wanted to be honest I should have left the page blank, or else criticized the theme and whoever had thought it up.

But I was fourteen years old and I came from the mountains ... I tried to write the way you want us to. I can easily believe I was not a success.

c.

Dear Mrs. Allen,

Don't you hate to hear the ring of the alarm clock early in the morning? I do. I suspect my reason is that I dislike to be reminded of an obligation.

I guess that's common with everybody. We all have a feeling of irritation when reminded of something we might overlook or forget. So, I want you to know that I don't like to remind you of the account of $435.40 that was due a few days ago. But, like the alarm clock, I must speak my piece.

If you've already placed your check in the mail, please ignore this note and consider it bookkeeping on our part.

And, thank you!

Sincerely yours,

P.S. I'm sure we'll both continue to dislike—but recognize the necessity of—pesky reminder devices. Right?

3. *Together or Solo.*

   a. Suppose you have just accidentally damaged a car you borrowed from a family member or friend. Imagine the accident in as much detail as you can. Write letters to each of the following: the owner of the car, the officer who is going to file the accident report, and someone who would be on your side.

   b. Read these letters aloud to each other. Using words you discovered in Exploration 1a, decide on the following for each letter:

   - The purposes of the letter
   - The most important purpose
   - Why the letter is or is not likely to accomplish your purpose
   - Whether the letter attempts to connect, separate, or negotiate
   - How you could change the letter so that it would be more likely to achieve its purpose

4. a. *Solo.* Write a letter that you *don't* intend to send. Your audience should be someone with whom you have an important relationship, such as a family member, a friend, a lover, a boss, a co-worker, or an instructor. Your subject should be something that concerns you deeply. Your purpose in this letter is to express your feelings and position.

b. *Solo.* Write another letter to the same person and on the same subject, this time with the intention of sending it. As you write and modify what you write, decide on your purpose and the result you want.

c. *Solo or Together.* Compare your sets of letters. What changes have you made in the letters you intend to send? What did you include, exclude, emphasize, or de-emphasize? Which letters are more likely to succeed, and why?

5. a. *Together and Solo.* Choose a controversial public figure who is currently in the news and write her or him a letter with a specific purpose in mind. As you write, adjust your approach. Discuss your purpose as it develops in the writing.

b. *Solo.* Choose a person you admire (either alive or dead) to whom you would like to say something. This person can be either a private or a public figure. Write a letter to this person, noting your purpose.

c. *Together.* Discuss the letters you wrote to persons you admired, paying special attention to purpose and audience.

Purposes in Education

To focus your studies in a particular academic course, become conscious of the major purpose or emphasis of the course. Four major emphases of courses are (1) information, (2) skills, (3) interpretation, and (4) experimentation.

Information.   When the focus is on *information,* you concentrate on what people in a particular academic discipline consider to be important and relevant facts. When information is emphasized, you tend to concern yourself with others' statements and points of view: You memorize more and question less. You take more short-answer exams. There certainly are benefits and satisfactions in knowing a lot of information. Otherwise, games like Jeopardy and Trivial Pursuit—based on information—wouldn't be as popular as they are. It *is* satisfying to score 100 percent on a multiple-choice test. But more important, knowing what others know in an academic community helps you become a part of that community. Fundamentally, knowledge *is* power.

Remember, however, that just because people believe something is a fact doesn't mean that it is or that it shouldn't be questioned. For example, at one time some scientists erroneously believed that women were intellectually inferior to males. "Facts" sometimes are no more than statements that are commonly believed by a group of people. Maintain the position of a responsible thinker. Have the courage to question "facts." If you disagree with the information you are offered, the more you know about it, the better you can question it and convince others of your point of view: *you* become a maker of knowledge.

Skills. When the focus in a course is on *skills,* you will engage in a variety of activities that go beyond collecting and memorizing what others consider to be important information. The focus of this book is on skills. Approaching this book as if it were focused on information would be inappropriate. You could memorize this whole book and be able to score 100 percent on a multiple-choice test about it. But, if you didn't write and consult with others about writing, you wouldn't acquire the skills this book can help you develop.

Interpretation. When the focus in a course is on *interpretation,* you combine a command of information and general skills with the ability to respond as an individual. Morals and art, for example, are considered to be more matters of "point of view" than matters of "fact." Each discipline and subdiscipline provides you with skills for responding to subject matter in an individual way. For example, in an art course, you are taught how to interpret the mood or statement that a painting suggests through the use of colors, shapes, shadows, and organization. In a poetry course, you are taught to interpret the feelings or insights a poem suggests through the use of sound, rhythm, and sensory images. Be careful to notice if, in a particular course, someone claims that a certain interpretation is "the right one." That person may have confused a matter of fact with a matter of interpretation. One interpretation may be clearer or may account for more parts of a painting or a poem than another, but that doesn't mean that that is the *only* good interpretation.

Experimentation. When *experimentation* is the focus in a course, you concentrate on questioning, experimenting, and exploring. You are encouraged to *discover* information more through trial and error than through collecting and memorizing. Whereas an information-based course offers the security of easy ways of learning and testing, an experimentation-based course offers you the excitement and satisfaction of creating and inventing new ideas and skills.

There is no easy way to assign these emphases by disciplines because much depends on your instructor's style of thinking and teaching and your style of thinking and learning. But courses such as basic chemistry may emphasize information and structured experimentation more than interpretation. Your writing course is more likely to emphasize skills, interpretation, and experimentation over information. Whenever you move from one class or situation to another, and whenever there is a shift in what you are required to do in a class, identify the main emphasis of your work.

*E*xplorations

1. *Together.* Bring college catalogs to class. List a number of interesting courses representing the full range of disciplines. Using catalog descriptions as aids, state in your own words the purpose or emphasis of each course and the academic discipline of which it is a part.

2. *Together.* List the courses that members in the class are currently taking or have recently taken. For each course, arrange the following in terms of their importance to each class: information, skills, interpretation, experimentation.

3. *Together.* List the different kinds of tests, papers, and reports you are required to do in the courses you are currently taking or have recently taken. Which assignments stress information? Skills? Interpretation? Experimentation? Which assignments require you to have a command of more than one of these?

Audiences for Writing

Kinds of Audiences

Writing has three kinds of audiences: (1) general, (2) focused, and (3) specific. If you are writing for a *general audience,* you must consider that it may include people of different sexes, ages, and ethnic origins, with a variety of tastes, interests, and political and religious beliefs. Large newspapers and national magazines are likely to be written for a broad general audience. Writing for general audiences is difficult because so many different factors must be considered, including the following:

- How much information can you assume that everyone knows?
- On what kinds of information would most people agree?

- What are the most popular interests of your audience?
- How many people would stop reading the publication if you included certain topics and information?

As a student writer, develop your skills by writing for *focused audiences,* such as children from eight to ten years old, photographers, stamp collectors, homemakers, or college students. The amounts and kinds of information that would interest such a focused audience are easier to gauge. Magazines, small newspapers, and books on topics of more limited interest are usually written for special audiences.

Finally, a *specific audience* will include only one person or at most a few people. This audience may be just yourself, your instructor, a group of co-workers, your boss, a business associate, or a friend. Journals, letters, and memos are often written for specific audiences.

Identifying Your Audiences

How much information you offer in a piece of writing is determined by the main audience you target for your writing. If, for example, you were trying to decide whether to pursue your college degree now, you could write about it to clarify the pros and cons, decide what to do, and ultimately ease the discomfort of being split by indecision. Because you know yourself and the details of your situation, you would be less likely to include information that would be necessary if you intended your writing to be read by someone else. The following journal entry, written by student Manny Ricardo when he was in high school, may be meaningful to him, but it leaves out information that an audience beyond him and his family would need to know:

> Dad has his reasons for wanting me to wait a year before entering college and when I'm talking to him I agree. But when I walk away I don't feel right. There are so many things I need to learn and I want to get started right away. I wish Mom would talk to him because she agrees with me.

However, if you were writing a letter introducing yourself to a prospective college admissions officer, you would be wise to research the college, its offerings, and its admissions requirements. In writing the letter you would be creating lines of communication between what you believe the college wants and what you know and want. You would have to convince the people in the admissions office to accept you by telling them relevant information about yourself. In a letter he drafted for his application to college, Manny included information that he would not have needed to include in a quick journal entry:

> Ever since I was eight years old, scuba diving in a lagoon near my family's cottage, I have been fascinated by the ecological balance between different forms of marine life. I am applying to Ocean State College to make my dream of becoming a marine biologist and educator come true because you have one of the most reputable departments in the field. As my résumé shows, I have spent many summers serving as a Marine Life Counselor training children. I hope that you will consider me as a candidate.
>
> My only concern at this point is financial. My father recently sustained a permanent injury and the funds that were saved for my education are now being used for living and medical expenses. I believe that if I can win a scholarship, including room and board, I can start my education, ease the financial burdens of my family, and more quickly find a job in the field so that I can support them in turn.

Because this letter was written to people who didn't know Manny, he was careful to include information that would support the purpose of his application: to gain admission to Ocean State College with a full scholarship. As he broadened his audience, Manny included more information. His original letter would appeal to the special audience of admissions personnel. With some changes, he wrote a paper that could appeal to an audience of college students:

> Ever since I was eight years old, scuba diving in a lagoon near my family's cottage, I have been fascinated by the ecological balance between different forms of marine life. It has been important to me that I be able to devote my time and energy to this interest. Very early on I looked for jobs that were related in some way to the ocean. I spent many summers serving as a Marine Life Counselor training children. During the winter I worked at a scuba diving store that serviced people who vacationed in the Bahamas and Virgin Islands. Every time I had to write a paper in school I asked my teacher if there was some way I could pitch it toward some topic on marine life.

Who your prospective audience is determines—to a great extent—what and how much you write. You might write a friend to express your anger about the job market, but only under extraordinary circumstances would you include this information on your college application. Also, you would not write the same words on an exam as you would write to someone who has demolished your new car—unless your purpose was to shock the professor and fail the exam. In general, don't assume that what you notice is exactly what your reader will notice. Be as clear and thorough as is appropriate to your task.

The following Explorations will help you sharpen your awareness of audience—the person or persons who may read what you write.

*E*xplorations _____

1. *Together or Solo.* Read through the following excerpts and determine the likely audience for each. Is the audience general, focused, or specific? Who is not likely to read a particular excerpt? Why? Consider such factors as these:

age	education	nationality
sex	economic status	family role
occupation	politics	residence
health	religious leanings	hobbies
experience	environment	life style

   a. When you get your new camera, read the instruction booklet that comes with it before you try to use it. The battery and film go in only one way, and you want to do it right so your first roll of film is good.

   b. Among the new films, Kodak's Ektar 25 offers the finest definition, resulting in high acutance at all apertures. Ektar shot at small apertures with a tripod-mounted camera will enable you to make grainless 16 × 20's of a portion of a 35-mm negative.

   c. The camera you are holding is an ideal travel companion. Compact, easy to hold and set, weatherproof, and comfortable for eyeglass wearers, this camera will faithfully record all those places you have dreamed of visiting.

   d. You can now make a fashion statement with the camera you sport. Formerly colors were limited to chrome or black, but several new models are available in a creamy off-white that blends well with any outfit you choose for day or evening.

   e. Here's the camera I promised to send. I've already loaded it with high-speed film because you told me you want to take some indoor pictures of your team without using the flash. You said the flash really annoys the players when they're playing. When you turn the camera on, you'll need to turn the flash off. It has a red button with an arrow on it. Just point and shoot. Make a few baskets for me.

2. **a.** *Solo.* Write three sets of directions for a specific everyday activity you know well, such as baking chocolate brownies, changing a tire, braiding hair, or cleaning a window. Vary the audience and therefore the directions and information you include. The first audience can be a peer who has never done the activity; the second, a child; and the third, an expert in the activity.

    b. *Together.* Read these directions to each other and notice what changes as the audience changes. How does the amount and kind of information vary with the audience?

3. *Together or Solo.* Describe a particular place on campus to these three audiences: a person from the time of the American Revolution, a person from another planet, and a contemporary interior decorator. Notice how the information changes as you adjust to what you believe will interest your audience and what your audience already knows. Notice how much you need to learn to better understand your audience and topic.

4. *Together.* In small groups or as a class, read some essays you are writing for a class, or consider memos and other documents you are writing for other purposes. Identify the audience or audiences that would be interested in this writing. Does the writer show an awareness of audience? Which words, phrases, or sentences show this awareness? What is the writer's purpose? Will that purpose be satisfied as a result of this paper? Why or why not?

Audience Appeal

To be effective, your writing needs *audience appeal*. Otherwise, readers won't engage with your work long enough for you to fulfill your purpose. Think of what appeals to *you* as a reader: a clear focus, sensory details, striking examples, a memorable story, a surprising new fact, a neatly organized argument, humor, helpful suggestions, a well-paced mystery. This book will help you to use appropriate writing strategies that will appeal to your readers. But, to have audience appeal doesn't necessarily mean to please—it means to engage and interest. In order to appeal to your audience, *take care of your readers.* Even if you disagree with your readers or want to express hostility, consider how you can best help them to get your point.

Whether your audience finds your work appealing depends on the attitude you convey. If you are fearful or dishonest, your audience will not find your work as appealing as if you are confident and honest. Using the suggestions in the Reflections below, compare the difference in attitude, and therefore appeal, that student Ziggy Jamieson brought to two drafts he wrote about writing:

First draft

I will try to do my best in this class. In the past I didn't understand the assignment. Now I will read the book and do the assignment. I will hand it in on time. I will be a good writer. I will pass this course. The teacher knows what is best and I will do that.

Second draft

I never liked to write. I never felt that my teachers listened to what I was writing about. Sometimes I felt that they didn't even read what I wrote. So why should I care? I was good at art though. In that class, I could try different things. Always my teacher seemed to like me and what I did. So I worked even harder. I'm afraid I just can't feel that way about writing. I don't know if I could get a teacher to make me feel good enough so I will want to try.

*R*eflections

1. Which draft do you prefer? Why?
2. Who is Ziggy's anticipated audience?
3. What are Ziggy's feelings and attitudes toward the audience in the first draft? In the second draft?
4. Point to specific words, phrases, and sentences that show Ziggy's feelings and attitudes.
5. What is Ziggy's purpose in the first draft? In the second draft?
6. What changed between the first and second drafts?
7. What's the difference in audience appeal between the two drafts?
8. What do you think helped Ziggy to change?
9. Does Ziggy take care of his reader in the first draft? In the second draft? How or how not?
10. What are the likely responses and results to the first draft? To the second draft?

Whenever you get stuck in a particular phase of the writing process, remind yourself of your purpose and audience. Write an informal "pretend" letter to your audience to help you puzzle out your attitude and whether or not it will appeal to your audience. Another purpose of this letter is to discover how to take care of your reader. Here are some questions to ask yourself and your intended audience while writing your letter:

- What is my purpose?
- What are my feelings and attitudes toward you as my audience?
- As my audience, what are your feelings and attitudes on this subject?
- What do you already know?
- What do you need to know?
- Would this writing appeal to you?
- What more do I need to know or convey about this topic so as to best fulfill my purpose with you as my audience?

*E*xplorations

1. *Together.* Generate a list of words that refer to writers' attitudes toward audiences. You may want to use dictionaries and thesauruses. Here are some words to help you get started:

fearful	self-enhancing
friendly	hostile
unsure	playful
bored	worried

2. *Together.* Using words generated in Exploration 1, compare the following introductory paragraphs of two student papers on Megan's Law. What attitudes does each convey? Which paper has more audience appeal? Why? Do class members disagree on which has more appeal? If so, why? How would you change these essays?

Student A

The topic of Megan's Law has become controversial. Meaning everyone has their beliefs and views on the situation. Some people are for it, meaning that they believe that all sex offenders should be reported to the community. Some people feel that everyone deserves a second chance. I feel the issue is controversial.

Student B

I will be student teaching next fall. As part of Megan's Law, I have to prove that I am not a sex offender going into the schools. I will have to pay $50, get fingerprinted at a police station, fill out an annoying report, and pay for it to be notarized all as part of a background check. In other words, I have to prove that I am innocent of sex crimes. This contradicts one of our basic civil rights--to be presumed innocent until proved guilty.

3. **a.** *Solo.* Bring an essay in process to class. Using specific words such as those listed in Exploration 1, write a brief statement of your purpose, your feelings, and your attitudes toward the anticipated audience of the essay.

   b. *Together.* In small groups or as a class, read each of the essays aloud.

   - Determine its intended audience.

   - Name and discuss the feelings and attitudes the writer seems to have toward the anticipated audience.

   - Point to specific words, phrases, and sentences that convey these feelings and attitudes.

   - Decide whether the essay has audience appeal.

   - Anticipate what purpose this essay might serve with its intended audience.

   c. *Together and Solo.* For each essay, compare the writer's statement of feelings and attitudes with those ascribed by the group discussion. If there are differences, develop ways to revise the essay to best fulfill its intended purpose. If a better purpose arose in the discussion, suggest ways to satisfy this new purpose.

4. *Solo.* Write a "pretend" letter to the anticipated audience of a particular letter, memo, or essay you are writing. Using insights you develop in the letter, adjust your attitude toward your audience and revise your work accordingly. What did you learn about yourself and writing from doing this exploration?

Denotations and Connotations

If you want your writing to reach a broader audience than yourself or those who know and already agree with you, and if you want to satisfy your purposes, you need to anticipate your audience's reactions to your tone and your point of view. In writing, just as in speaking, *tone* is the feelings and attitudes that come through in *how* you use words. Your attitude is the point of view about persons, places, objects, ideas, and events that your choice of words communicates. The following sections of this chapter invite you to explore how tone and attitude are created in writing.

In writing, your attitude toward your topic is shown by your choice of words. For example, a person named Harriet Sloan can be referred to— among many other ways—by these expressions:

Dr. Sloan	Dearie
Mrs. Sloan	Mommy
Ms. Sloan	Harriet
Reverend	Honey
That witch	Lady
Miss Know-It-All	The doctor

All these expressions can be used to refer to the same person, so they all have the same denotation. A *denotation* is the meaning that most people would agree a word has. A denotation is the meaning that the dictionary will offer. But each of the expressions used for Harriet Sloan also suggests different attitudes and feelings toward her. These terms have different meanings or connotations. A *connotation* is the attitude or feeling that a word or expression conveys.

Unless used humorously or sarcastically, "Dr. Sloan" shows an attitude of respect, for it recognizes Harriet Sloan as a member of an educated culture. The expression is likely to be used in a professional setting. "Mrs. Sloan" focuses on Harriet Sloan's marital status and can suggest a culture in which women are subordinate to their husbands. However, if Harriet Sloan was born closer to the beginning of the century, when marital status was a matter of more prestige, she might consider "Mrs. Sloan" to be respectful. "Ms. Sloan" is meant to be more neutral and signals a culture in which the issue of the equality of the sexes is recognized. Furthermore, the term a person uses says as much about his or her cultural leanings as it does about Harriet Sloan. If a person insists on calling her "Mrs. Sloan" in a professional setting where "Dr. Sloan" would be more appropriate, that person may be expressing disrespect.

What is true of names is true of most words. In a given situation, a word can convey a positive, negative, or neutral tone. Some words are more strongly positive or more strongly negative. To say someone is a "bulldozer" conveys a strong negative tone. To say the person is "aggressive" is a weaker negative comment. To say someone is "assertive" can be a strong compliment. But to refer to someone as an "entrepreneur" conveys a much stronger positive tone.

When you write, decide how strong you want your tone to be. Using the right words will help you emphasize or de-emphasize those points that will enable you to fulfill your purpose with a given audience. To deepen your understanding of denotation and connotation, turn to pages 112–116 in Chapter 5, which will help you distinguish strong from weak statements.

Do one or more of the following Explorations to sharpen your sense of how your choice of words conveys different connotations and attitudes toward your audience.

Explorations ————————————————

1. *Together.* Discuss the terms that can be used to refer to Harriet Sloan, considering the following questions:
   - In which situations are they respectful?
   - In which situations are they disrespectful?
   - What attitudes, feelings, or cultural leanings would a person have in using each of these terms? What circumstances could change the connotations?

2. **a.** *Together.* List some words used to exclude or diminish people who don't belong to your social group.

   b. *Solo.* Write about a time when you were made uncomfortable by others who used diminishing terms about you. Contrast this with examples of how diminishing words can be used playfully or affectionately within a group.

   c. *Solo.* Write about how you use diminishing language to separate yourself from people who are different from you.

3. **a.** *Together.* In small groups, choose one of the following words. Recall or find as many words as you can with the same *denotation.* (You may want to use dictionaries and thesauruses.) Be sure to include terms that occur to you from your own experience.

mentally ill	persuade
thrifty	humorous
intoxicated	lie
request	play
slim	different

   b. In each group, put the words in order, beginning with the word with the strongest *negative connotation* and ending with the word with the strongest *positive connotation*. Decide which word you think is most neutral and why.

   c. Present the findings of each group to the class. Add further words and insights as a class.

4. *Solo or Together.* The practice essay "A Lot of Got" is filled with forms of the verb *to get.* *Get* tends to be a weak word. Underline every occurrence of it in the essay. Then replace forms of *get* with stronger verbs. Add to, delete from, and reorganize the essay to make it more engaging and interesting. Write another paragraph or two to finish the story. Avoid forms of *get, do,* and *have.* Use strong verbs instead.

A Lot of Got

I got up this morning and realized I had gotten a headache. I got myself over to the medicine cabinet and got out the aspirin. I got it down with some water that my sister got for me. I got better.

I got myself outside to get the newspaper where it had gotten lost under the bushes. I got my breakfast. After getting through that and the newspaper, I got dressed. It was getting late, so I got outside and got the bus to get to work. No sooner had I gotten my seat than I realized I had forgotten my briefcase. I got really mad. How do I get myself into these situations? I had gotten an interview with the CEO of my company and now I was going to get there without all the charts I had gotten ready the night before (which is probably why I got a headache).

5. *Together and Solo.*
   a. Choose some papers that you are currently writing for either your writing class or other purposes. Underline ten strong words in each. Discuss the connotations of these words and how they would affect a reader in a given situation.
   b. Underline ten weak words in each paper. Using dictionaries and thesauruses, find stronger words that will better serve the purpose of each paper.

Purpose and Audience in the Writing Process

Focusing

Meaningful writing responds to real-life needs. Sometimes you may recognize the need before you start writing. Often you may discover it as you move through different phases of the writing process.

The same is true for identifying your purpose and audience. Sometimes you discover your purpose and audience as you write. For example, you may start writing a letter thanking your aunt for the weekend you spent at her shore house. As you write, you may notice that you keep thinking of how your two cousins were arguing about who would paint the house this summer. You may find you want to readjust your purpose in writing the letter and offer to help paint the house. So your purpose will expand from merely *thanking* your aunt to *offering to help* her.

Your audience may shift as well. Suppose you start writing about some painful incident in your family. At first, you may be writing just for yourself—to assert how you feel. Then you may realize you want to adopt your cousin as your audience. As you write, you may decide to write a paper as an appeal for sympathy from a more neutral audience.

A given piece of writing may serve many purposes and address a variety of audiences. But, at some point in the writing process, you need to choose what your *main* purpose and audience will be. Devote your energies to this. Chapters 5 and 6 offer you specific strategies for focusing so that you will earn the trust and interest of your audience.

Collecting

Even if your audience is very focused or specific, do not assume that your audience knows what you know or is interested in what interests you. Even if your audience knows what you know, refreshing your audience's

---

Strategies for Managing Purpose and Audience

- *Identify the main need or purpose* a particular piece of writing is meant to satisfy. Ask yourself, "Why am I writing this? Am I writing it mainly for a self-expressive, interpersonal, or aesthetic purpose?"

- *Identify the relevant characteristics of your anticipated audience.* Ask yourself, "Which audience am I trying to reach? What is my anticipated audience like?"

- *Adjust the amount of information* you give to your audience. Ask yourself, "What information does my audience already know? What information do I need to offer or emphasize?"

- *Be aware of connotations.* Ask yourself, "What attitude do these word choices convey to my reader? Are my words appropriately strong?"

- *Write a letter* to your anticipated audience. Ask your audience, "What is your perspective? How can I connect with, separate from, or negotiate with you?"

memory is usually a good idea. It helps you to clarify your position and engage your reader. Collect the kinds of information and examples that will engage your readers and enliven your writing. Chapter 4 offers you basic strategies you can use to collect the kinds of information that will best capture your audience.

Organizing

Shape your writing with the purpose of guiding your readers. Offer them a clear sense of the direction you are taking. Help your readers remember what you want remembered. How you begin a letter or essay is crucial for establishing both your relationship with your audience and the purpose for which you are writing. How you develop the body of your writing determines whether or not you will maintain your audience's attention. How you end a piece of writing determines whether or not you leave a

Reading for Purpose and Audience

As you answer the following questions about your readings, point to particular words, phrases, and sentences to support your claims. Consult your dictionary for further insights into both familiar and unfamiliar words.

1. Is the purpose of this piece self-expressive, interpersonal, aesthetic, or a combination of these?
2. Is the purpose of this piece to connect with, separate from, or negotiate with others?
3. How might the writer state the need or purpose that motivated this piece?
4. If this is an academic piece, is the emphasis on information, skills, interpretation, or experimentation?
5. Who is the anticipated audience for this piece?
6. Is the anticipated audience general, focused, or specific?
7. On a scale of 1 to 10, where 10 is best, how would you rate the audience appeal of this piece? Why?
8. What is the writer's point of view?
9. What are the strongest words? What are their connotations?
10. Do you anticipate the writer will satisfy what seems to be the purpose of the piece with its intended audience? Explain.

lasting impression that serves your purpose. Chapter 7 helps you to develop and strengthen your organizing skills.

Consulting

The ideal way to identify your purpose and audience and accomplish what you want with your writing is to consult with other readers. Voice your concerns to them. Listen to their responses and watch their reactions. Adjust your writing with the insights you gain from them. Chapter 8 offers you strategies for successfully consulting with others.

Revising

Once you have spoken something, it's hard to take it back. One of the benefits of writing is that you can adjust it before it reaches your audience. In some cases, you can negotiate with the anticipated audience. For example, some instructors will allow you to revise before you hand in work for a final grade, and bosses may support you in revising proposals before they are formally submitted. If that opportunity is not offered, request it. The request itself shows respect and commitment and will help you to accomplish your purposes with your audience. Chapter 9 offers you strategies for effectively revising your work.

*C*hapter Review _____

1. *Solo.* Copy three statements from this chapter that you want to remember for yourself. For each statement, write a sentence saying why or for what purpose you chose it.

2. *Together.* Using the sidebar on reading for purpose and audience, discuss the readings at the end of Chapter 12. Notice the different points of view that the writers take on the topic of AIDS.

3. *Together.* Using the sidebar on reading for purpose and audience, discuss your own papers in process.

Chapter 4

Collecting and Drafting

This chapter offers opportunities to

—*Collect* interesting subjects for writing

—Create a *journal*

—Practice *listing, brainstorming,* and *clustering*

—*Interview* people

—Experiment with different modes of drafting: *audiotaping, writing longhand, typing, photocopying,* and *word processing*

—Create a *portfolio*

> Science is built with facts, as a house is with stones. But a collection of facts is no more a science than a heap of stones is a house.
>
> —*Jules-Henri Poincaré,*
> *Mathematician, Physicist*

The Dynamics of Collecting

Supermarket carts overflowing on a Friday evening, long lines of cars queuing up at gas stations during a fuel crisis, stacks of family photographs, stadiums filled with fans—for survival and for happiness, people collect.

Learning is a process of collecting and a powerful human need. We collect and transmit much learning by way of letters, the telephone, television, movies, computer networks, newspapers, magazines, and books. Writing is our most effective tool for collecting and remembering what we want to pass on to others.

What you collect for your writing will be determined by your purpose and your intended audience. The four main sources from which you can collect information, observations, and ideas—moving from the more direct to the more indirect—are (1) *yourself* (what you remember and experience); (2) *the world* (what you observe directly of the physical world, including people); (3) *other people* (what they say and show you); and (4) *documents* (what you can learn from visual, audio, and written reports of the experiences and interpretations of others).

Here is a list of sources from which to collect what you need for your writing:

Memory	Interviews
Direct observation	Surveys
Conversations	Photographs
Lectures	Video- or audiotapes
Experiences	Written documents

Different writing tasks may require different methods of collecting. For example, notice how you would proceed in college courses. In chemistry, you would probably collect observations by experimenting directly with chemicals in the laboratory; in early childhood education, you would be likely to observe and interact with young children directly; and in art, you would develop skills by handling different materials. In other courses, the favored method of collecting could be reading. Of course, which methods of collecting information are emphasized in a course will depend on your instructor's objectives and how you interpret them. When you write papers, reports, and answers to exams, use the collecting method that best suits the purpose of the course.

Chapter 1 introduced you to freewriting—a basic way of collecting what you already know. The main tools and strategies presented in this chapter are the journal, listing and brainstorming, clustering, and interviewing.

How you collect your information and ideas will be determined not only by your purpose, your audience, and the availability of sources but also by your particular style. If you are a planner, you may prefer writing a *focused* journal and listing. If you are an explorer, you may prefer freewriting and brainstorming. Artists, especially, and people who like physical activity enjoy clustering. If you are a talker, interviewing may be for you. If you are shy, reading may feel more secure.

> ### *Collecting Guide*
>
> Ask yourself these six questions whenever you begin to collect information and ideas:
>
> 1. What do I already know?
> 2. What do I already have that I can use?
> 3. What do I need to find?
> 4. What can I directly observe or do to find what I need?
> 5. Whom can I ask directly?
> 6. What can I read?

How you collect your information and ideas will also be determined by your writing tools and methods, which may include audiotaping, writing longhand, typing, photocopying information, and word processing. (See pages 18–21 in Chapter 1 for further discussion of writers' tools.) How you organize and store what you collect may also affect your success in collecting. For example, if you use a loose-leaf binder, you can rearrange your materials. A portfolio (featured on pages 90–94) allows you to showcase and to monitor your progress as a writer.

As you experiment with different methods of collecting, notice which work best for you and in which circumstances. Strive to be flexible.

*E*xplorations

1. *Together.* On the board, list things people tend to collect, such as stamps, newspaper clippings, Star Trek souvenirs, or photographs. Think of unusual collections. What do you learn?

2. *Solo.* Choose something you or someone close to you collects. Write an essay about the collection. What is collected? How is it collected? What does the collection mean? How does the collecting and the collection affect you, the collector, or other people?

Collecting and the Writing Process

Purpose and Audience

Just as you need bricks, wood, metal, and other materials to build a house (or people, telephones, printing presses, and the mail to run a political campaign), so too you need subjects, ideas, experiences, and information to develop your writing. But even if you collect all the information in the world, if you don't have a purpose, you will just end up with clutter. Throughout this book you will be offered specific strategies for collecting what you need in order to write for particular purposes and audiences. This chapter offers you some *basic* ways to streamline your collecting of subjects, information, and ideas so that you can reach the audiences you want to reach and satisfy the purposes for which you are writing. Tailor your collecting activities to best suit your style and achieve your purposes.

To monitor your purpose and audience while collecting, ask yourself these questions:

- Why am I writing this?
- What does my audience need to know?

Collecting and Focusing

Collecting and focusing are complementary phases of the writing process. Just as the heart has to expand and contract to control the flow of blood, in the writing process, you need to both collect—expand—and focus—contract. Sometimes while you collect information, observations, ideas, and memories, your focus will emerge in the process. You may find yourself moving back and forth between scanning for or collecting your thoughts and focusing on or choosing certain ones. Once you focus, choose only relevant details: those that will help you most effectively fulfill your purpose. Remember that a starting focus makes your collecting easier and more productive. Notice that throughout this chapter all the collecting activities focus on a word, phrase, statement, or question.

To keep yourself focused while collecting, ask yourself these questions:

- Which details are most relevant?
- How can I enliven my work with examples?

Collecting and Organizing

Collecting and organizing are also complementary activities. To avoid overwhelming or confusing yourself or your readers, ask yourself these questions:

- Which ideas and what information belong together?
- What is the most effective order in which to arrange them?

Signals to Collect

- You have a focus.
- You feel as if you have nothing to say.
- You are not interested in an assigned topic or in what you already have to say.
- Your readers need more details or examples.
- A new focus emerges.

Develop a working plan for how to organize what you choose to include. Be careful, however, not to slow down the collecting by organizing your material into a rigid plan too soon. During the writing process you will move in and out of the collecting and organizing phases.

Collecting, Consulting, and Revising

The collecting phase does not stop with your first draft. You will find, as you reread your work and consult with others, that you may be missing some important materials that would help you better fulfill your purpose with a larger audience. Return to the collecting phase as needed. Ask others for support in finding the sources you may need.

Journals

> Anyone who doesn't write doesn't know how wonderful it is.... I am grateful...for this gift, this possibility of developing myself and of writing, of expressing all that is in me.
>
> —*Anne Frank*

In this book, the word *journal* is used instead of *diary*. Both words come from words that mean "day" in Latin. But the word *diary* most often applies to personal daybooks, whereas *journal* can apply to many more kinds of daybooks, including not only the personal daybook but daybooks with special purposes. A journal is a home base for collecting what interests you and concerns you, what happens *to* you and *because* of you. The more focused your journal is, the easier it will be for you to continue to write one. Here are some focused journals you can keep.

Personal Journals

During World War II, Anne Frank and her family had to hide in an attic from the Nazis. Keeping a diary helped Anne to understand and find meaning and dignity during a time of terrible oppression and hardships. Her diary was, in many ways, her best friend, and she started her entries with "Dear Kitty." Of course, the person she was writing to was a part of herself—her perfect listener. In writing a diary she created and re-created herself. Her diary satisfied a need to express herself, but it also created a record of her experiences for others.

Many students have found writing personal journals for the purpose of self-expression very satisfying. Sean keeps a personal journal to release pent-up tensions and concerns. Victor is able to steady himself during family conflicts by keeping a journal to show his counselor. Jane writes Bible quotations in her journal and writes about how they apply to her life.

A personal journal—unless it is focused—can become merely a listing of events or a jumble of complaints. From time to time, choose a focus for your personal journal such as one of the following:

Wedding	Leaving home
Children	Religious concerns
Managing the budget	Grandpa
Surviving school	Health

Process Journals

A lawyer keeps a record of the proceedings of a murder trial; a scientist records observations and theories about a series of drug experiments for AIDS; a pastry chef records changes and variations in a new chocolate mousse recipe—all these people are keeping *process* journals. A process journal is a notebook in which you follow your progress, experiments, and failed attempts in a particular endeavor.

Writer's Journals

Practicing writers often keep their journals nearby so they can talk to themselves about what they are writing, what they would like to accomplish with it, how they feel, what they need or plan to do, and which phase of the writing process needs more attention. At times, practicing writers begin and end writing sessions by writing in their journals. You might find it very helpful, as you write, to reflect on your processes in a writer's journal.

Learning Journals

In any intensive learning situation, such as school, travel, or projects, a journal is a tool to help you focus, plan, and direct your energies and to collect and test ideas. Writing helps you learn. One of the most basic ways to use a learning journal is to record a particular question, statement, or event that interests or puzzles you. Then freewrite about it to discover what you already know, name what you need to learn, make connections between different courses and learning situations, and engage more fully in the learning process. You can devote a separate journal to each course or keep a larger journal for them all. Starting a learning journal is simple if you remember to begin your freewrites with a focus. Student James Anglin learned a great deal about himself and the world by keeping a focused journal while reading Alice Walker's *The Color Purple*. Student José A. López keeps a journal to help him monitor his learning process in his mathematics courses. Here are some other possible focuses for your learning journal:

Readings	Chemistry problems
A current event	Medical facts
Legal issues	Your first year in college

Training Journals

Athletes, especially, find a journal very helpful in their training and development. For example, runners record how far and fast they run each day, what physical changes they felt, how the route affected their workout, and what other exercises they performed. They plan their training in the journal and entertain different solutions to physical obstacles and limitations. Runners also write about their psychological blocks and breakthroughs during the running process. A journal is also a place for a runner to record experiences of races won and awards earned. If you are training for sports, dance, singing, acting, pottery, painting—or any other activity—start and maintain a training journal. Here are some possible focuses:

Dieting	Drawing
Weight lifting	Playing an instrument
Singing	Landscaping

Other Focused Journals

Throughout history, politicians, explorers, scientists, adventurers, parents, and artists (among others) have kept journals for particular purposes. Some people like to keep focused journals dedicated to one interest. In *The Golden Notebook,* novelist Doris Lessing writes about a character who keeps five different journals responding to five different aspects of her life. Here are some more ideas for focused journals:

Travel journal	Solving-a-problem journal
Journal of a campaign	Business transactions
Journal of an illness	Family events

Reflections

1. *Together.* Read the journal entries below. Choose your favorite one. Write about it, discussing the following:

   - Why you like the entry more than the others
   - What similar experiences you have had in your life
   - Which words, phrases, or sentences you especially like
   - What purpose you think the entry served for the writer
   - What audience or audiences are anticipated by the writer, if any
   - What you learn about writing a journal

2. *Together or Solo.* Write a letter to the writer in response to a journal entry below.

3. *Solo.* Write entries in your journal that are inspired by the ones you read here.

Journal Entries

a. Here's my journal entry on finishing one of the drafts of Chapter 2, "The Writing Process." If you like, you might want, as a class, to compare a paragraph from that chapter with how I write in my journal. Discuss, too, how my journal might have been different if I had written it only for myself. What might I have excluded or included?

6/5/96 12:30 P.M.

I have just finished redrafting the chapter "The Writing Process"—two hours of intense work. Time to break. I think I'll go back to Chapter 1 and make sure I haven't repeated myself. I do talk about confidence and fears in both chapters and don't want to belabor the point. I'm feeling the usual excitement and fear when I finish one phase of this project and go on to the next. (I notice that, since I decided to include this entry in the book, I'm more conscious of what I believe would be helpful to my readers. It's amazing how writing changes when you expect someone will read it.)

In any case, I need to recheck my working outline to see what I want/need to do next or else I'll be too agitated to enjoy lunch. Originally, the plan was to include "focusing" in this chapter but I still believe it needs its own. Since the original plan, I combined the chapters "Why Write" and "Audience and Purpose" to form Chapter 2 and decided to use "The Writing Process" as a chapter title because most writing teachers could relate to it. I hope Joe will like the outline I've developed, since we revised the earlier one together.

Of course here I am still writing away after I decided it was time for a break. See you later.

12:40

b. This is a short series of excerpts from writer Joan Didion's essay "On Keeping a Notebook."

> *How it felt to me:* that is getting closer to the truth about a notebook. I sometimes delude myself about why I keep a notebook, imagine that some thrifty virtue derives from preserving everything observed. See enough and write it down, I tell myself, and then some morning when the world seems drained of wonder, some day when I am only going through the motions of doing what I am supposed to do, which is write—on that bankrupt morning I will simply open my notebook and there it will all be, a forgotten account with accumulated interest, paid passage back to the world out there:
>
>   . . .
>
> I imagine, in other words, that the notebook is about other people. But of course it is not…. *Remember what it was to be me:* that is always the point.
>
>   . . .
>
> Our notebooks give us away, for however dutifully we record what we see around us, the common denominator of all we see is always, transparently, shamelessly, the implacable "I."

c. This is what student Altovise Smith wrote:

> Well as I was reading my *Learning to Learn* textbook, a question came to mind. The question was how could I generate questions about my interest in criminal justice. So I thought of things such as how should a lawyer prepare for a case, how should a lawyer make a person seem like he or she is innocent when really guilty, and how in the world of law and justice I could come to conclusions about those issues.

I figured studying might help me for the knowledge part but I won't actually know how to do it unless I set my mind on actual court cases so I would be prepared for my first court appearance. But it would never stop there. You still have so much to learn. You have to know about kinds of people you are defending. The personalities you studied about might not be the personalities you are working with. So being a lawyer you have to try very hard to enforce your honesty and good judgment. I know it's hard because you always get people who are guilty and they know that you have to prove that they are innocent because you were hired to protect them.

d. Student John Gaines reflected on his literature class in his learning journal:

This is my first English Literature class today and it seems it is going to be very interesting. We discussed the poem "The Chimney Sweep" by William Blake. There was an enormous amount of input by us students. We discussed the different meanings that the poem created for us. I interpreted the poem as someone standing from afar watching what became of this boy as these things happened to him. I did not relate it as others did. Some related it to Martin Luther King and Cinderella. I did not relate it to anyone else because I don't make an attempt to relate poems to something outside of them. I make an attempt to take what was written for itself. I occasionally have a problem understanding things. I don't make a connection to try to relate it to something so I can understand it. My teacher has taught me to take what I have in front of me, whether familiar or not, and try to apply it to something that I do know and do understand.

e. This is what runner Beth Avery wrote in her training journal:

Another tough day. Cold, wet, sinuses kicked in halfway through the run. Decided to walk the rest of the five miles. Coach says it's the distance not the speed, for now. Dad says why do it? Thought a lot about the meet as I walked. I've trained too hard and long not to give this my best shot. Will experiment with not eating any dairy, meat, or sugar. Seems that some people say that will help my sinuses. Will use the steamer before the run, too. Take my time to prepare: steam, stretch, walk, run, cool down.

Keeping a Journal

Choose a journal book that pleases you. You can keep your journal in a spiral-bound notebook, in a blank artist's pad, or in an accountant's ledger. You can handwrite or type your journal, or you can keep the pages in a ring binder. You can use a word processor and keep your entries on file.

Be creative. Your journal is *your* record. If you like to draw, you might want to draw in yours.

Plan a regular time for writing in your journal and, in the beginning, especially, stick to the schedule to develop the habit of it. Record the date, day of the week, and time you are writing. Bring this journal book to class to do your in-class writing Explorations. This journal can be a resource of ideas and topics from which you can choose to develop longer papers. (If at any time you feel inspired to write something off the topic, do so. It's *your* journal.)

*E*xplorations _____

1. *Solo.* Choose one of the following kinds of journals. Commit yourself to writing it for a week. Find or create a journal book or use a new computer disk. Write in this journal at a particular time each day.

    a. *A personal journal* in which you record the highlight and low point of each day. Or, you might want to focus on a particular concern for the week, such as a relationship. A journal of just your dreams might be interesting as well.

    b. *A process journal* in which you record experiences with a particular project you are doing. Record what you did, what you learned, and what you want to do next.

    c. *A writing journal* in which you record your concerns with writing. Before or after each writing session (and class), freewrite for ten minutes on what you did, what you learned, and what you want to do next.

    d. *A learning journal* in which you record experiences with a course of learning. For each assignment (and class), choose a particular statement or question and freewrite for ten minutes on what it means to you and what more you need to learn.

    e. *A training journal* in which you record your experiences with training in some performance activity such as a sport, dancing, singing, an art, or a craft.

    f. *A current events journal* in which you record your reactions to news items. For example, clip an article, attach it to your journal, and freewrite. If possible, follow that issue for a week.

2. *Solo.*

    a. Write a journal with another focus for a week. At the end of the week, write about the benefits and challenges of having written this kind of journal.

    b. Commit yourself to keeping a journal for another month or for the whole semester.

    c. Once a month, reread your journal, noticing what changes and what stays the same. Recommit yourself to writing for another month.

3. *Together.* Read portions of your journals to each other in small groups. Discuss the benefits of having written focused journals. Write letters to each other in response to certain entries.

Listing and Brainstorming

Listing

Whenever you are presented with a writing or thinking task, one of the most basic ways you can respond is by listing words, phrases, or sentences. Write and underline a short descriptive title. Write your list underneath it. For example, when student Anita Morrow was presented with the assignment to write about the effects of television, she listed the following possible topics:

<u>Television</u>

Window to the world	Commercials
Relax	Cable
Learn anything	Multicultural
Fast-growing industry	World events
Twenty-four hours a day	Soap operas
Children's	

As you will see on page 99, Anita used this list to start a paper.

Brainstorming

When you brainstorm, you say or write whatever comes to mind, without stopping to wonder whether you're right or whether the ideas are relevant or make sense. Listing remains focused on a chosen topic. Brainstorming is more like freewriting in that it can take any direction you want. It allows you to clear your mind, create a flow of ideas, and discover new connections. This strategy is best done without much reflection. *Allow your brainstorming to be as long as you like. Cover an entire board space or page. Or decide to brainstorm for a certain time.* Your brainstorming may take the form of a list, or you can write over a page (or board) at random. Notice the different directions some students took while brainstorming on the topic of drugs:

<u>Drugs</u>

Prison	AIDS
Crack	Homeboys
Neighborhood	Pushers
Needles	High
Stealing	Trouble

This brainstorming showed the kinds of things that concerned the people involved. If anyone had stopped to question the connections, other ideas might not have emerged. By not stopping and by allowing themselves freedom to let one idea lead to another, the students were able to collect enough ideas so they could identify topics they wanted to write about. Brainstorming works just as effectively if you do it by yourself. Try using a computer to speed the flow of your ideas.

Once you have listed or brainstormed, you will be able to see some of your options in writing. Choose the item or idea that is most interesting or relevant to your purpose. Start developing your written response: write your chosen item at the top of your page or screen, and freewrite for a particular length of time. From there you will find yourself either listing, brainstorming, or freewriting some more, or maybe you will be ready to move on to another phase of the writing process. Perhaps you will return to collecting more information by interviewing someone or reading. Anita used her list to start a paper that eventually developed into a piece on soap operas. The story of Anita's process and paper is featured on pages 99–126 in Chapter 5.

Joe Brainard—painter, illustrator, and writer—wrote three books of lists in which each sentence begins with the words "I remember" and recalls a past event. Read the following items excerpted from *I Remember* and respond by doing Exploration 1 or 2 below.

I Remember

I remember shoulder pads and cinnamon toothpicks.

I remember baby shoes hanging from car rear-view mirrors.

I remember cold cream on my mother's face.

I remember not understanding why women in dresses didn't freeze their legs off in the winter time.

I remember little boxes of cereals that opened up in back so you could eat it right out of the box. I remember sometimes they leaked.

I remember every other Saturday having to get a haircut, and how the barber was always clicking his scissors even when he wasn't cutting anything.

*E*xplorations _____

1. *Together and/or Solo.* Using Brainard's list as a model, write a list of at least twenty-five memories of a particular time in your life. Start each sentence with the words *I remember.* Then go back and choose the ten best memories. Reorganize them so that they would be most interesting to other readers.

2. *Solo.* Choose a course you are taking or an important activity you are involved in. To review or practice your knowledge of it, write a list of twenty-five items focused on it. Start each item with the words *I remember.*

3. *Together and/or Solo.* Create a list under one of the following headings, or brainstorm on it:

    Things at which I'm an expert

    Things that happen once in a lifetime

    Animals

    Outsiders

    Things to do to get through college

    Medicine

    Things to do to survive your job

    Problems that need to be solved in the United States

    Challenges for the elderly

4. *Solo and Together.* Choose an interesting item or group of items from the lists you created in Explorations 1, 2, and 3. Do a timed ten-minute freewrite on it. Read the freewrite to your classmates and note the different directions people took using the same list. Write an essay focusing on an idea you develop from the lists and freewrites.

Clustering

Although writing occurs in straight lines on the page, the thinking that goes into it is much more complex than a straight line. As you may have noticed from brainstorming, a word or phrase can point you in many

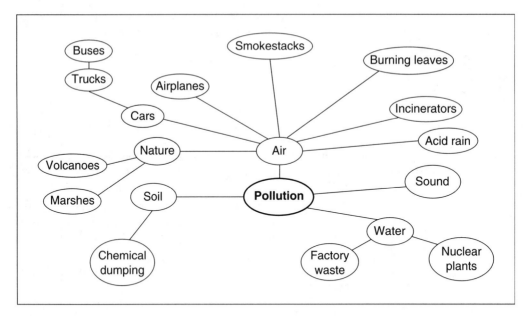

FIGURE 4.1   Clustering

different directions. *Clustering* is a method of collecting your thoughts that reflects this complex shape of thinking.* Artists and people who enjoy physical activities such as sports and dancing especially enjoy clustering because it treats ideas as if they were moving around in space.

Clustering is different from brainstorming in that it shows how one idea is linked to another. Clustering is like brainstorming in that it is freer than focused listing: you can take any direction you want when you cluster.

In Figure 4.1, notice how student Melanie Patel created a cluster to help her design an experiment for her earth science class. She circled the word *pollution* and let it lead to other words that she also circled. She drew lines to show which ideas were connected to others. When she found a word or cluster of ideas that interested her, she created new clusters from them.

Melanie found clustering useful because it helped her to identify some topics that interested her. Some of her written explorations of these topics are featured in Chapters 13 and 14. The process fulfilled many pur-

---

*Clustering was formulated by Gabrielle Lusser Rico in *Writing the Natural Way: Using Right-Brain Techniques to Release Your Expressive Powers* (Los Angeles: J. P. Tarcher, 1983).

poses for Melanie. It helped her develop ideas for lesson plans for the third grade science class she was scheduled to student teach. In addition, it helped her focus on issues she wanted to present at her town meeting about the effects of an incinerator.

Follow clustering just as you would listing and brainstorming. Choose a particular segment of connected thoughts that most interests you. Start developing an essay by freewriting. This freewrite may lead you to another phase of the writing process, or it may inspire some more collecting activities.

*E*xploration

Together.

   a. Brainstorm a list of words that are important to you for some reason. This list may include words that refer to people, events, emotions, objects, or places. Or you might want to consider the courses you are taking and list important terms from them, such as *impressionist painting* (art), *depression* (psychology), *energy sources* (ecology), or *carcinogens* (biochemistry).

   b. Choose a word that interests you. Write your topic down and circle it. Now create clusters around the word. Write, circle, and link ideas as they come to you, anywhere on your page or on the board.

   c. Notice if any particular string of words becomes long and/or very interesting. Do a freewrite, focusing on an idea or cluster of ideas you create in this process.

   d. Read your freewrites to each other.

   e. Brainstorm a list of words that you would use to describe your experience of clustering, and discuss why you would use these words.

Interviewing

When you *interview,* you hold a conversation—much as television talk show hosts do—to learn more from and about another person. Prepare for interviews by formulating some questions. During the interview, take notes or record the interview itself, depending on the situation.

There are many different purposes and audiences for interviews. For example, in a job interview your prospective employer meets with you to tell you about the requirements of the job and to assess whether you meet those requirements. In other interviews you can learn about a famous

Interviewing

1. ***Choose*** the most appropriate and available person to interview. Because they are such valuable resources, focus on older people when you can.

2. ***Tape*** the interview, if at all possible, so that you don't distract yourself or your subject by having to take notes. But as a matter of courtesy, ask for permission *before* the interview. Honor your subject's wishes. If permission to tape is denied, take notes and ask the person to repeat statements if necessary.

3. ***List questions*** you want to ask. Don't ask for information that you could and should have gotten elsewhere. For example, if you are interviewing an author, find that author's books ahead of time. Don't ask what he or she has already published: you should know. Focus on those questions that are most important to you. But know that questions that arise during the interview may be the best ones to ask.

4. ***Use the question star*** (Figure 5.4, page 120) to stimulate questions during the interview.

5. ***Be patient and compassionate.*** Let your subjects tell their own stories. Know that silence during the interview may help them to remember. Let them take tangents. Don't stop them just so you can ask another question.

6. ***Observe*** the person you are interviewing. Notice her or his actions, voice, and facial and hand expressions, and be aware of the environment.

7. ***Acknowledge*** the person you interview in three ways. First, thank the person in a letter. Say what you learned and what it means to you. Second, acknowledge the person in your writing when you include ideas learned during the interview. Use a format such as one of these:

   - In an interview with (*name*), I learned _____.
   - In a conversation we had on (*date*), (*name*) said, "_____." (Note the quotation marks.)
   - I am indebted to (*name*) for telling me that _____.

   Third, if you plan to publish what you write, allow the person to read and adjust what you attribute to him or her.

8. ***Conduct follow-up interviews*** to consider questions that arose while you wrote.

person, your family, how to perform certain tasks, where to find information, and so on. Follow the suggestions in the sidebar on interviewing.

*E*xplorations

1. *Together.*
   a. Brainstorm a list of people you would like to interview, and discuss why you would like to interview them.
   b. In small groups, create a list of questions that you would like to pose to a famous person. Which questions do you think would lead to the most interesting answers? Which questions would be too broad? Which questions would lead only to one-word answers?
   c. Using the sidebar on interviewing, conduct a mock interview. Let one person or a group of people assume the role of the famous interviewee. If you can, focus on a particular ability or experience. Notice which questions just can't be answered by anyone other than the actual person for whom the questions were designed.

2. *Together or Solo.*
   a. List the talk shows that are aired in your vicinity either on television or radio. Include not only big network and syndicated shows but also shows that feature interviews with lesser-known people. Watch or listen to one of these shows (if possible, together), and record the questions asked by both the host and participants. Which questions lead to the most interesting answers? How does the host keep the conversation moving? Notice which questions aren't fully answered.
   b. Watch or listen to a second talk show whose topic or host is very different from the topic or host in the first show. Discuss the differences you notice between these two programs, focusing on the questions asked and the strategies used by the hosts.
   c. Watch a live or videotaped debate between political candidates. Which questions lead to the most interesting answers? Which questions do the candidates dodge, and how?

3. *Solo.* Choose a person in your family or circle of friends who you know has experienced some important historical event, such as a political march, involvement in a war, political imprisonment, meeting an important person, the events surrounding an assassination, or the creation of an institution or church. Focusing on this event, brainstorm a list of questions that will lead the person into telling you stories about the event. Using the sidebar on interviewing, interview the person and write an essay about what you learned.

Drafting

To experiment with and learn from writing, you record words on audio-tape, paper, or a computer screen. This process is called *drafting.* To write effectively, you must know your writing tools and whether they support or frustrate your purposes in writing a particular piece.

Author Richard Selzer claims, "Writing in longhand has a special kind of magic in it for me." Author Donald Murray suggests, "Switch your writing tools...they are a writer's toys, and effective, easy writing is the product of play." Most of you are aware of what it is like to write long-hand. Some of you might have typed copies of your handwritten work. Some of you may compose directly on the typewriter or computer key-board. Audiotaping and writing with others is yet another way to bridge spoken and written English.

Read the following Explorations to discover alternatives to the ways you are used to writing. After the Explorations you will be guided briefly to a discussion of word processing.

*Explorations*_____

1. *Together.*

    a. To explore some of the benefits of speaking instead of directly writing your ideas, pair up with someone in your class and talk to her or him about a topic listed below. As you talk, your partner will write down what you say.

        • A current news item that disturbs you

        • A problem you are trying to solve for yourself

        • Something that has changed in your life

    b. Listen as your partner reads back what you spoke. Together, choose what should remain in the written version of your ideas, what should be removed, what should be further expanded.

2. *Solo or Together.* Do Exploration 1 with a tape recorder as your part-ner. Then do Exploration 1b either solo or with someone else.

Computer Word Processing

Word processors offer all the benefits of typing and none of the drawbacks of having to retype, use correction fluid, erase, and cut and paste drafts.

The flickering light of the computer screen relaxes you the way a television can. Good writing is a result of multiple revisions, and revising on a word processor is fast, clean, and easy. Because you can revise so easily, you are freed from thinking about typing and you can spend your time thinking about ideas. Brainstorming is especially effective on a computer. Since one idea usually leads to another, the speed of the word processor encourages you to write more. When you are free to experiment, you can develop your creativity. Your computer may offer features such as a spelling checker, a grammar checker, a dictionary, a thesaurus, an encyclopedia, graphics, desktop publishing, access to distant libraries, and electronic conferencing. Word processors also offer invaluable assistance to people who must work with special physical challenges such as blindness, muscular impairments, and paralysis of various kinds.

Computers not only network us with other writers in the writing lab, but offer us access to almost anyone on the globe. Being computer literate is becoming more and more crucial not only in finding a job but in a successful career.

You need to learn only a few basic skills to start working with any word processor. Check with your instructor, or read the computer manual for your particular system. The following Explorations will help if you have never used a word processor.

*E*xplorations

1. *Solo.* Using a word processing program, enter the following paragraph exactly as it is written, including mistakes. Learn and practice word processing commands in your system by revising the paragraph.

   > When you write with Emily a pencil, there not much--other than losing your point, run out of lead or eraser--that can go wrong. Jacob lost his way on the beach. Complexity increases chances your of breakdown. You can pluck back a jammed arm in a typewriter. But when the chips are down, how can you cope with something that you can't even see? Typewriters get jammed, run out of ribbon, wear down in the gears. Once you get into computers you're really finished. Computers are not apples. Some people are afraid of computers.

2. *Solo.*

   a. After you have done Exploration 1, write a short essay describing your experience with using the computer. Include benefits, problems, and questions. As you write your first draft, don't concern yourself with errors. If you can't think of a word or idea, just leave room for it. You can go back to fill in later.

b. Revise your essay on the computer and print out the results.

c. Use the computer for your next writing task at school, at work, or in your personal life.

Creating Portfolios

Novelist Thomas Mann once wrote, "Order and simplification are the first steps toward the mastery of a subject—the actual enemy is the unknown." There's nothing as complicated as scavenging for lost notes, drafts, or papers the night before a test or deadline. Even if you have the papers, if you can't link pieces of information together when you need to, you will be facing that enemy—what Mann calls "the unknown"—just the same. Getting organized will save you time. More importantly, keeping organized can help you to see what you know, to ask questions about what you don't know, and to monitor your progress.

In business, professions, science, and the arts, people create portfolios—portable cases with representative examples of their work. A photographer might fill it with photographs; an investment banker, with an itemized list of securities and other commercial papers. They show their portfolios to others as passports to jobs and awards.

In the past, your writing—your passport to a higher grade or better job—may have been judged by your responses to exams and tests. Now, however, writing programs all over the country have started to assess student writing in portfolios. Whether or not you are required to, create your own writing portfolio. Organizing one will be invaluable to your present success as a student and will initiate a practice that will support you in future endeavors.

The simplest writing portfolio is a folder that contains your best or most recent drafts of your papers. By keeping these all in one place, you can appreciate how much work you have done, and how much more you need to do. However, for a writing course, it is helpful to include all your work, carefully organized. Here are some suggestions for starting and maintaining a portfolio. You can use these suggestions for portfolios in all your courses and in your business or personal projects as well:

* Choose portfolio folders that give you room to grow.
* Keep a portfolio for each course or project.
* Put your name, address, and phone number(s) on each portfolio in case you misplace it.

- Place your best or most recent work where you can access it immediately.
- Attach earlier drafts of papers behind your newest ones.
- File your portfolios in a convenient place.

To benefit most from your portfolio, you will need some way to monitor your progress. Two qualities of a responsible learner are the ability to adopt or formulate standards and the ability to adjust or correct oneself (see Chapter 12). Each course or project introduces its own demands. Here are some strategies for adopting and applying standards to your work:

- At the beginning of a project or course, ask for or adopt a list of standards by which to monitor your work.
- Attach this list to one of the portfolio covers.
- List the contents of your portfolio on the front or inside cover.
- Write a letter to your instructor, your boss, the project head, or yourself, in which you detail your experience of your tasks, what you hope to accomplish, and the skills you need to develop. Refer specifically to your list of standards. You don't have to send this letter, but if you do, keep a copy for yourself. (See Chapters 8 and 9.)
- Make dates with yourself to write letters of self-assessment. Write the dates on your calendar, and keep to this schedule.
- Write your letters of self-assessment, referring specifically to your list of standards. If the standards have shifted, make note of that.
- Write a self-assessment at the end of the course or project, detailing what you did, how you grew, and what more you hope to accomplish in setting and meeting standards for yourself.

A portfolio reflects the purpose and audience of your work. If your portfolio will be used to assess your work in a course, you and your instructor will negotiate what to include. The Portfolio Contents Checklist and Progress Review Checklist can help you assess your work in your writing course. Both checklists refer to portions of *The Flexible Writer*.

*E*xplorations

1. *Solo.* Create a portfolio of the work you have done in your writing course, using the Portfolio Contents and Progress Review checklists offered in this chapter. Make changes on the checklist to reflect the needs and concerns of your class.

2. *Solo.* Create a portfolio for your work on a different personal, business, or school project. Develop an appropriate checklist for evaluating the portfolio's contents. Make changes on your checklist as needed.

Portfolio Contents Checklist

In this folder, collect the following pieces of writing. Each letter and paper must include at least one revision. All final drafts must be typed. *Number* your drafts and clip them *under* the final versions.

Date completed

1. _____ A letter from the beginning of the course, in which you relate your experience of writing and state what specific skills you want to develop. Use the Explorations in Chapter 1 and the criteria listed in the Progress Review Checklist.

2. _____ A personal or expressive piece in response to a topic from Chapter 10 or 11 (at least 2–3 typed pages).

3. _____ A persuasive piece in response to an Exploration from Chapter 12, 13, or 14 (at least 2–3 typed pages).

4. _____ A letter from the middle of the term, in which you review your work in the course and project what you still want to accomplish. Use the criteria listed in the Progress Review Checklist. Cite specific examples from your papers. (This letter may be revised.)

5. _____ A major work that is longer and more completely revised than those in categories 2 and 3 (at least 5–7 typed pages). This may be a series of papers on one subject or one longer paper. The focus of a paper written for category 2 or 3 may serve as a basis for this work.

6. _____ A letter of self-evaluation at the end of the course, in which you specifically state what you have learned so far and what aspects of process, usage, or punctuation you need to work on. Use the criteria listed in the Progress Review Checklist. Cite specific examples from your papers.

*C*hapter Review _____

1. *Solo.*

   a. Create a sidebar, listing the collecting strategies mentioned in this chapter. Write and underline "Collecting Strategies" to get started. Include freewriting from Chapter 1.

   b. Write one of the collecting strategies in the middle of a piece of paper and circle it. Create a cluster around this term, incorporating what you learned about the strategy from this chapter, and how you used it yourself.

Progress Review Checklist

This checklist identifies phases of the writing process and lists grammar and punctuation skills. The three columns following each item refer to different times during the course: (1) the beginning, (2) the middle, and (3) the end. Place check marks by skills you still need to develop.

Process	1	2	3	*Punctuation*	1	2	3
Sense of purpose	___	___	___	Apostrophe	___	___	___
Audience awareness	___	___	___	Comma	___	___	___
				Semicolon	___	___	___
Drafting	___	___	___	Colon	___	___	___
Focusing (choices, examples)	___	___	___	Period	___	___	___
				Question mark	___	___	___
Collecting (depth, range)	___	___	___	Quotation marks	___	___	___
Organizing (structure, transitions)	___	___	___	Hyphen	___	___	___
				Dash	___	___	___
Consulting	___	___	___	Parentheses	___	___	___
Revising	___	___	___	Paragraphing	___	___	___

Grammar and Style

	1	2	3		1	2	3
Fragments	___	___	___	Subject-verb agreement	___	___	___
Run-ons	___	___	___	Pronoun agreement	___	___	___
Comma splices	___	___	___	Pronoun shifts	___	___	___
Sentence lengths	___	___	___	Spelling	___	___	___
Modifiers	___	___	___	Word choice	___	___	___
Verb tenses	___	___	___	Other ___	___	___	___
Verb tense shifts	___	___	___	___	___	___	___

    c. Choose a segment of your cluster from Review Question 1b and freewrite for ten minutes, describing the strategy to a new writing student.

2. *Together.* Read and discuss with each other your results from Review Question 1c. What would you have added to or deleted from each description to help the new writing student?

Chapter 5

Focusing I

Strategies

This chapter offers opportunities to
- —Explore the dynamics of **focusing**
- —Create **unity** in your writing
- —Write for **purpose** and **relevance**
- —Distinguish **repetition** from **redundance**
- —Learn how to **choose, specify, illustrate, question,** and **quote**
- —Practice writing **thesis statements**

Keep to one thing and concentrate.
—*Virginia Woolf, Novelist, Essayist*

The hardest work is making up
your mind to one thing.
—*Ruth Stout, Master gardener*

You can't eat everything you see.
—*Bessie Delaney, 101-year-old retired dentist*

The Dynamics of Focusing

You can dribble a basketball all over the court for days, but sinking it into the small center of the basket is what makes the game. A lawyer can divide her attention among five cases, but she is more likely to win in court if she devotes her energies to one case at a time. People create and achieve in sports, in medicine, in law, in academics—in most human endeavors—by focusing their energies.

Writing focuses the mind. Part of the mind's survival instinct is to be constantly scanning for pleasures, dangers, and novelties. When the mind doesn't have a focus outside itself, it starts scanning itself—rehashing yesterday, rehearsing tomorrow. If nothing holds the mind's attention, this scanning can turn into either a scattered, bored state or a spinning, confused one. Without a focus for your writing, you can become bored, confused, and discouraged. Your mind goes into a blur, like an unfocused photograph. You won't know what you're looking at, and after a while you will be too frustrated to care. In this chapter, you will have opportunities to learn how to focus and thereby to engage yourself and your audience.

When a piece of writing is focused, it is said to have *unity*. The word *unity* comes from the Latin word *unus*, which means "one." Unity in writing means that all the parts of a piece fit together to form a whole, a oneness. The writing has a clear purpose and point. There are sufficient examples and evidence to support the main purpose or point of the writing. Everything is *relevant:* nothing distracts from the main purpose of the work. When a point is repeated, it is to good effect. That is, it doesn't belabor an idea (the way this sentence is starting to do): it isn't *redundant*.

Your mind is focused by writing and reading pieces that have unity. Reading such works focuses your mind by clearly showing you something about yourself, the world, the author, or how to use words. Often, pieces that focus your mind are written in such a way that you feel you are learning something new and interesting. Learning to focus in the writing process offers you even more benefits than reading because you are fundamentally learning how to focus and refocus yourself.

Most readers aren't *mind* readers. Even if you know someone well, you can't be certain that what you notice is what he or she will notice. Look at Figure 5.1 on the following page. What do you see? Some people see a profile of young woman with a ribbon around her neck; some people see an old woman with a large chin and a slightly opened mouth. Try to see both for yourself.

Do the following Exploration to discover how this dynamic of shifting focus works with language.

FIGURE 5.1 *Focusing*

*E*xploration

1. *Solo.* Quickly read the following sentences:
   a. Cilantro is a spicy herb to include in avocado dip.
   b. Babies should not suck pacifiers, which can cause tooth deformation.
   c. It's important to use a moisturizer to counter the effects of heat curling.
   d. Major league baseball today is much more politically run than it was in the time of Willie Mays.
   e. Studies show that vitamin B6 may be effective in reducing the growth of tumors.
   f. Windup watches have been entirely replaced in stores by battery-driven quartz timepieces.
   g. Without a proper recovery program, an addict may go from one addiction right into another.
   h. To protect your iris garden, cut rot off the roots, separate the plants, and replant them with ample space for new shoots.
   i. Floppy disks should never be exposed to magnets or cigarette smoke.

j. Use premium gasoline every fourth tankful to keep fuel injectors clean.

Without looking back at the list, write down what you remember of the sentences you just read. What you remember is an indication of what interests you, what you know the most about, or perhaps what you experienced most recently, just as whether you see a young woman or an old woman in Figure 5.1 is determined by the perspective you take. Your choices reflect your point of view.

2. *Together.* Compare what focused (or captured) your attention in doing Exploration 1 with what others remember. Discuss what you think accounts for the differences and the similarities. For example, you might remember that cilantro is good for avocado dip because you are a gourmet cook.

When you write, you need to focus your readers' attention in the same way that certain sentences focused yours. You cannot assume that what you notice is what your reader will notice. If you could be certain, then there would be no reason for language or communication. We would just all know the same thing. You can't even assume that what you notice today is what you will notice tomorrow. It's possible that sometime in the next day or so, you will remember one of the sentences listed above (that you can't recall right now) because some experience will remind you of it.

Focusing and the Writing Process

Rita Williams, a student writer, said, "I find the focus by wandering." Just as there are many ways to sink a basketball and many places where the ball can land, there are many ways to focus and many things on which to focus.

Every writing project begins with some *working* focus followed by some early scanning for ideas. Early freewrites and drafts are exploratory. Sometimes you're lucky and find a clear direction right away. This usually happens with topics that you know well and have lived with for a while. Often you will focus and refocus as you revise and redraft. There's always some point you can clarify. Sometimes you will find a new, more exciting focus and start all over again. It's worth it: focusing steadies your mind and creates a clear message.

Focusing and Purpose

Often, the *need* to write helps you to focus on your purpose and audience. For example, you may need to pass a course in communication sciences for your major. But that is a superficial purpose; a deeper need is for you to understand how the mass media affect you and your community. Or, as another example, you may be haunted by the Vietnam War and need to come to terms with it. When you make a commitment to satisfy such needs through writing, you find your purpose.

Relevance

Throughout this chapter, you will be invited to practice focusing strategies: choosing, specifying, quoting, illustrating, questioning, and stating. The most satisfying focus for a piece of writing will be a focus that *means* something, that is *interesting,* or that serves some *purpose:* in short, something that is *relevant* to you or your subject. The more meaningful the purpose on which you focus, the more you will have to say.

The concept of relevance is crucial to focusing, in another way. Often new writers are reluctant to offer details, quotes, and illustrating examples because they are afraid of adding monotonous and irrelevant points. But to focus is not merely to collect details at random: it is to choose details, quotes, and examples that are *directly relevant* to the purpose of your paper.

For example, Anita Morrow was working on an assignment for a mass communications course in which she was assigned to explore the effects of television. She made a list (see page 81) and freewrote from it.

First draft

```
    Television the window to the world. A place where you can
relax and learn anything about the world. A fast-growing
industry that employs many people. A member of the family
that can be on twenty-four hours a day. Even the poorest
household in America has a television. Children learn their
ABC's. Commercials open a window onto the economics of Amer-
ica. Cable offers all of us an opportunity to express our
cultural backgrounds. Even world events can be in your own
living room. You can watch everything with the flick of a
remote. Nothing is beyond your reach. For example, soap
operas make us a part of a larger family. Television brings
us together. It is definitely the window to the world.
```

Responding to this draft, Anita's peers were not sure what aspect of television she was interested in. They pointed out that she bounced from one topic to another and back. When she wrote her first draft, Anita had not discovered her focus or her purpose. In this chapter, we will consider focusing strategies that Anita used (or could have used) to become more fully engaged with her project.

Repetition and Redundance

Dr. Martin Luther King Jr. inspired a nation and the whole world with his speeches. One of the strategies he used for fulfilling his purposes was *repetition*. For example, we all remember the words "I have a dream." Each time those words resounded in his speech, they gained power and momentum and helped to make him an immortal figure in our history.

Repetition is the very essence of advertising: hear it often enough, and you might buy just to shut the pressure off. Repetition is the heart of humor and the delight of children. Repetition is a basic tool of learning. For example, *The Flexible Writer* offers you reminders, sidebars, and restatements of important points. Even this paragraph employs repetition to make its point. But repetition, if repetitious, can bore and distract.

Looking back at Anita's first draft, notice that three of her thirteen sentences begin with *A* and two begin with *Even.* Beginning so many sentences with the same word can be repetitious. A reader will naturally feel dulled by it.

A writer may also repeat the same idea with different wording. Unnecessary repetition is called *redundance.* For example, the following two sentences say the same thing without adding any new information or insight:

Serious traffic accidents are caused by drunken drivers.
Drunken drivers cause serious traffic accidents.

Notice how Anita restated the same points in each of these sentence pairs:

Television the window to the world.
It is definitely the window to the world.

You can watch everything with the flick of a remote.
Nothing is beyond your reach.

Such repetition is natural in spoken language. But in writing, without further details, such repetition is redundant. Redundance is like superimposing images on a photograph slightly out of register with each other: even if they are the same image, they blur. Blur is the opposite of focus.

Focusing and Collecting

Even as you identify your purpose and audience, you begin to *collect* information, ideas, experiences: you list the effects of the Vietnam War named in an encyclopedia; you recall experiences and consequences of an injury; you reread letters that someone sent you.

Focusing and collecting are complementary processes. As you collect information, you focus on what interests you and is relevant to your purpose. When you focus, you create a center much like a magnet, which helps you to collect more relevant information. Especially in the early stages of writing a particular piece, there are several strategies you can use to focus and to collect relevant information, ideas, and insights: (1) make choices, (2) identify patterns and repetition, and (3) look for surprise, power, and interest. These strategies are especially helpful if a particular piece of writing requires the planner's style of composing.

1. *Make choices.* Some writers subscribe to "the myth of plenty," the belief that the more things you try to write about in one paper, the more you will have to say. In fact—although it seems inside out—the more you try to write about at once, the less you have to say. Too much chocolate makes you too sick to eat; too much oxygen leads to hyperventilation, so you can't breathe; and you might like lobster, cheesecake, pizza, and spicy sausage—but would you ever put them into a casserole together? As architect Ludwig Mies van der Rohe wrote, "Less is more." The more you try to write about at once, the less you'll have to say. The less you try to write about at once, the more room you will have to develop and expand upon your chosen focus.

The basic way to create unity in your writing is to limit the amount you try to write about in any given piece of writing. *The process of focusing means to choose one person, place, time, event, idea, or thing to write about at a time.* For example, you would choose which one effect of the Vietnam War you can write about to fulfill your assignment, which single experience is most directly relevant to your injury, or which specific letter best captures the experiences of a relationship. If you include other effects and experiences, they must be directly relevant to your chosen subject. You may want to use a slogan to remind you, such as "Choose one" or "One thing at a time." Remember the image of the magnet.

2. *Identify patterns and repetition.* Suppose you list the experiences you remember from working through an injury and notice that some of them are very positive and some very negative. You can focus your paper by dividing it into positive and negative experiences. You could write first about the positive and then about the negative. Or suppose you were writing about a series of crimes in your neighborhood, and you noticed that certain seemingly innocent persons seem to be involved in many of the cases. Focus on those persons. You may formulate some crucial insights.

> To focus, look for surprise, power, and interest.

3. *Look for surprise, power, and interest.* Remember, what focuses *your* mind and holds *your* interest when you read might focus your readers' minds as well. Choose to write about the most appealing, unusual, or dramatic thing that will help you focus and capture your audience's attention. If you're bored, your audience will be too. To engage your audience, engage yourself.

Focusing and Organizing

Organizing helps you maintain your own and your readers' focus on what you are writing. Even if you have focused on the most dramatic and interesting ideas, if you don't organize and pace your presentation, you can confuse and thereby lose your reader. In organizing, you pay attention to how you (1) start a piece of writing, (2) develop it for coherence, and (3) end it in a memorable way. The beginning, or lead, of any piece of writing is a crucial place to focus yourself and capture the attention of your audience. The body should develop from the lead and expand upon and support claims with relevant examples connected in clear ways. The end should reinforce the lead and leave a unified impression on your audience. Organizing helps you to maintain focus in your writing.

Focusing, Consulting, and Revising

The writing process is especially conducive to focusing your mind. Therefore, don't expect yourself to find a clear, powerful focus at the very start of a writing project. The model of the writing process in *The Flexible Writer* developed *as* I explored and developed the first draft of the first edi-

---

Signals to Focus

- Too many topics at once
- Too many general terms and ideas
- Treating the reader as a mind reader
- Not enough specific details or examples
- Too many questions unanswered
- Redundance
- Irrelevant details

tion. Even as I revised *The Flexible Writer* for the second and third editions, I learned and developed new perspectives on the model. Therefore, I decided to revise Chapter 2, which summarizes the writing process, *last*— so that the chapter would reflect all I learned during the revision process.

To revise this textbook, I consulted with instructors and students, asking them what was helpful and what was not. Using their responses, I was able to expand, delete, and reorganize material in *The Flexible Writer* so that it would better serve its purposes: to help *you* to become a flexible writer.

Consult with your instructors, tutors, co-workers, family members, and peers to help you develop your focus not only at the start of a project but also during the revising phase. Consult this chapter and the next, which offer you a variety of specific strategies for focusing.

Strategies

Choosing

In the novel *Herzog,* Saul Bellow's title character tells himself, "Choose one." Choosing is the most fundamental focusing strategy that you need to employ over and over in the writing process.

Students are surprised at how much more they have to write when they limit the number of topics they try to cover. They find that when they limit their choices, writing is more satisfying and enjoyable. They are eager to revise.

With the help of her peers, Anita numbered the topics she attempted to cover in her first draft.

First draft

```
  1      Television the window to the world. A place where you
  2    can relax and learn anything about the world. A fast-growing
  3    industry that employs many people. A member of the family
  4    that can be on twenty-four hours a day. Even the poorest
  5    household in America has a television. Children learn their
 6,7   ABC's. Commercials open a window onto the economics of Amer-
  8    ica. Cable offers all of us an opportunity to express our
       cultural backgrounds. Even world events can be in your own
  8    living room. You can watch everything with the flick of a
  8    remote. Nothing is beyond your reach. For example, soap
  9    operas make us a part of a larger family. Television brings
 10,1  us together. It is definitely the window to the world.
```

How to Choose

1. *Number* the topics, ideas, time periods, people, or experiences you try to cover in a particular piece of writing. Use the same number for closely related topics that belong together.
2. *Choose* the topic, idea, time period, person, or experience that is most relevant to you.
3. *Remember:* Less is more.
4. *Save* your early drafts until you are satisfied with your paper. Keep a "great things said by me" file. You will feel more secure about letting go of irrelevant or distracting work if you know you can retrieve it.

She had touched on too many topics: economics, education, advertising, cable television, world news, and soap operas. Anita decided that she was most interested in writing about soap operas. Making a choice, Anita felt both energized, because she is an avid soap opera buff, and worried, because she was afraid she wouldn't have enough to write. As we move through this chapter, you will see how focusing helped Anita create an effective paper.

Choosing is a liberating and energizing process. For example, in the second edition of *The Flexible Writer*, five student papers were used to illustrate the focusing strategies in this chapter. Revising for the third edition, I decided to choose one student paper, instead, so that you could focus on the strategies themselves and not so much on the different topics. In the process, the strategies became clearer to me as well.

*E*xplorations _____

1. *Together.*
   a. Read the following student journal entry, and number the topics on which the writer touches.

   May 14, 1996

   The library was closed. Jessica went in for her tests. Lost the file on frozen orange juice futures. Can't stand the trucks on I-80 anymore. Movie theater went adult. I'm feeling exhausted.

   b. In small groups, choose one of the events on which the writer touches, and write an expanded fictional account of it.

2. *Solo.* Write a journal entry listing significant events of the past week (either personal or public). Choose one event, and write about it in more depth.

3. *Solo.* Choose a paper on which you are working, and number the topics or ideas you try to cover. Are there any you could eliminate so as to focus on the more important portion(s) of your paper? If so, write a revised version, focusing on what's most important, interesting, or engaging.

Specifying

Another version of the myth of plenty is the belief that the more generally you write, the more room you allow for readers to interpret as they need. Language allows you to refer to many objects, persons, activities, experiences, and events at once. This is very efficient. You wouldn't want to have to reinvent the word *chair* every time you wanted to refer to a chair. If you were to tell me you sat in a chair yesterday, and if I know what *chair* means, I would understand, in general, what you meant. But I wouldn't know *exactly*. I would be left to interpret for myself. Maybe it wouldn't be important that you sat in a chair yesterday. But suppose you sat in an *electric* chair yesterday—that would change everything. If you told that to me, my attention would be instantly focused. I would probably want to know why, how you got there, how it felt. It would *mean* a lot more to say you sat in an electric chair. Our interaction would be stronger and more satisfying.

The more a word can apply to, the less it says. Words such as *love, hope, special,* and *good* are only a few words that leave you scanning for something to *hold* your attention. The ultimate general word is *thing.* It applies to everything and nothing. It doesn't say anything much to anyone. If you assigned numbers to words to reflect how many situations they applied to, there would be no number for *thing* because there are an infinite number of things. *Love* could get a number because it is used to refer to fewer situations, but the number would be very high. *Fuzzy* applies to fewer persons, situations, and things than *love,* so *fuzzy* would get a lower number. *Fuzzy* says a lot more than *love. Audre,* a proper name, would apply to fewer persons than the word *person,* which would apply to anyone. *Audre Lorde* applies to still fewer persons, places, or situations and therefore means more. The more you specify exactly what you mean, the more engaging your work will be.

Another way Anita might have arrived at her new focus would have been to create a tree diagram before starting her first draft. Since tree

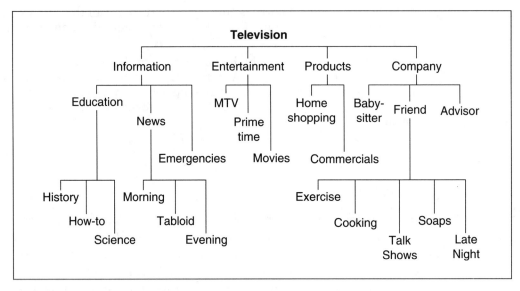

FIGURE 5.2   Anita's First Tree Diagram

diagrams were new to her, Anita decided to backtrack and create one from the word *television*, as shown in Figure 5.2.

Think of the bottom of the diagram as the tips of the tree branches where the apples are. This is where you can harvest your ideas. Trying to cover a broad topic is like trying to eat the trunk of the tree. Once again, you *choose* which item you want to further explore. You can continue to make tree diagrams to further specify. Anita decided to create one with the word *soaps* (referring to soap operas). Her new diagram is shown in Figure 5.3.

The farther you branch from the top in any tree diagram, the more there is to specify about your subject. Notice how the word *addiction* generated nine branches for Anita right away. Often when you arrive at a focus, ideas flow quickly. At this point Anita decided to redraft her paper. Here are the first three paragraphs she generated after doing her second tree diagram:

Second draft

Soap operas allow us to enter the lives of other people. We can learn ways to cope with different human problems by tuning in daily. Watching soap operas helps us escape from

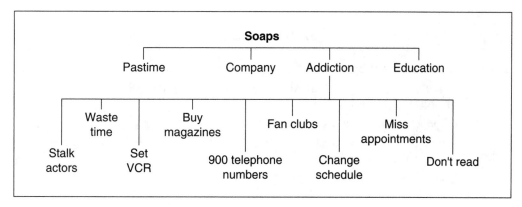

FIGURE 5.3 **Anita's Second Tree Diagram**

our own problems. Soaps give us company. They become daily friends.

Many people are addicted to tuning in at the same time every day. This is true of all soap operas, whether they are daytime soap operas, or one-hour weekly nighttime soap operas. This can be frustrating if you can't get to a television or are at work and can't take a break. Sometimes the VCR doesn't record or your program is preempted by news or a special report.

People do all sorts of things to get their "fix." They change their schedules, cancel appointments, forget to read, and may procrastinate doing other important things such as paying attention to children, completing assignments, or even taking a shower.

*R*eflection _____

Together or Solo. Compare Anita's first and second drafts, using the following suggestions and questions:

a. Compare the lengths of the two drafts.

b. For this item only, don't check the drafts. Record what you remember from each draft. Why are these ideas or phrases memorable?

c. What does Anita save from the first draft, and why? What does she leave out, and why?

How to Specify

1. ***Identify*** an important word in your topic or paper.
2. ***Create*** a tree diagram similar to the one in Figure 5.2. Focus on an interesting portion.
3. ***Choose*** a more specific word, expression, or topic.
4. ***Avoid*** using "thing" words such as *something, anything, everything,* and *nothing.*
5. ***Use proper names*** for people, places, and things.

---

    d. Notice the specific details Anita uses in her second draft.

    e. How does Anita's purpose and sense of audience improve in her second draft? Point to specifics that engaged you.

Explorations

These Explorations help you to discover how specifying enlivens communication.

  1. *Together.* Notice how the items in the following portions of tree diagrams become more meaningful and interesting as they become more specific:

    a. vehicle
　　　　　\
　　　　　　car
　　　　　　　\
　　　　　　　　sports car
　　　　　　　　　\
　　　　　　　　　　1997 red Corvette
　　　　　　　　　　　\
　　　　　　　　　　　　my 1997 red Corvette that stalled on Route 80 during a snowstorm when…

    b. home
　　　　　\
　　　　　　house
　　　　　　　\

        stone house

      \

          175-year-old brownstone

         \

             175-year-old brownstone that Abraham Lincoln visited when…

c. love

    \

      mother love

     \

       Sam's mother's love

      \

        Sam's mother bringing him apple cobbler

       \

         Sam's mother bringing apple cobbler when he's suffering over writing a paper about love

d. abortion

    \

      abortion for rape victims

     \

       my cousin's story

In what ways do the more general items differ from the more specific?

2. **a.** *Together.* Create tree diagrams to discover meaningful specifics, starting with one of the following general topics:

Courage	Environment
Responsibility	Furniture
Biology	People
Conversations	Current events
Freedom	Violence

  b. *Solo.* Harvest a specific from a tree diagram. Put it at the top of a new page, and create a further refined tree diagram. Then freewrite an essay using specifics as your foundation.

3. *Together or Solo.* Review pages 63–66, which show you how to distinguish strong and therefore more specific words from weaker, more general ones.

Stating: The Thesis

Just as questions invite answers, some statements invite further questions, explanation, examples, quotes, and discussion. These statements are called *thesis statements* or *key statements.* They unlock and open your mind as well as your reader's. Key statements assert your main purpose or point in your letters, freewrites, and essays.

In the writing process, good thesis statements can focus your mind, trigger your memory, and guide you to collect whatever you need to support your claim. In considering your audience, the purpose of writing a thesis statement is to stimulate interest in your idea, focus the reader's attention, and inspire confidence in your grasp of the subject. Thesis statements are especially geared for academic and professional papers and examinations.

In the past, writing courses may have required that you write a thesis statement to focus *all* your essays. But writing a thesis statement is only one way to focus a piece of writing. Many effective pieces of writing do not depend on a single thesis statement. As author and mathematician John Allen Paulos wrote,

> I find it oppressive when a piece of writing has a single thesis that is stated early and is then continuously and predictably amplified and repeated. It reminds me of being cornered at a party by someone with interminably boring stories to tell who refuses to omit any detail or to deviate one jot from his sequential presentation.

Whether you use thesis statements in your writing will be determined by your purpose, your audience, and your thinking style. If you are a planner, you are more likely to favor writing thesis statements early in the process. A good thesis statement allows you to plan ahead. If you are an explorer, you are more likely to favor other strategies for focusing. Freewriting and choosing, illustrating, and questioning are more conducive to exploring. You will develop key statements in the process.

Whether you think of yourself as a planner or an explorer, learn how to use thesis statements. If you do, you will be able to write them when you need to. You might find yourself using a thesis statement in an early draft of a paper, only to discard it altogether in later drafts. You might find yourself writing early drafts without a thesis statement, only to begin your later drafts with thesis statements you developed in the process. A thesis statement is the roof under which the building must be built. You might have started your final draft with a thesis statement. But you might have written it later in the process, as you "built" the essay itself. Be flexible. (For a discussion of where to place thesis statements in your essays and how to further develop essays in response to them, turn to pages 179–194 and 318–319.)

Good Thesis Statements

A good thesis statement does this for you:

- Gets you started and keeps you going
- Helps you remember what you know
- Helps you discover that you know more than you thought you knew
- Helps you use and create new knowledge
- Reduces writing anxiety
- Inspires, in your reader, confidence in your knowledge and abilities
- Helps you focus your collecting activities
- Helps you organize your work

Consider these examples of thesis statements:

- Poverty doesn't allow the children of the Williamsburg section of Brooklyn the luxury of summer fun.
- Sulfur is one of the ten or more chemical elements believed to be essential to the growth of plants.
- Lying found its worst expression during Desert Storm.

These thesis statements embody the main or key idea the authors want to relate. They are good thesis statements because they meet some or all of the following standards:

- They are focused.
- They lead to focused questions.
- They lead to other statements.

The first statement meets the three standards. It is focused on a particular group of children and doesn't attempt to account for all the children in New York City. It invites focused questions, such as "What is summer fun in the city?" "How does poverty affect children in Williamsburg?" and "What happens to the children of Williamsburg in other seasons?" And the thesis statement can lead to a long discussion about conditions in Williamsburg, poverty, and children's lives.

Strong and Weak Statements

To stimulate your own mind and earn the attention of your readers, you need to adopt or formulate strong statements that invite further elaboration and thought. To say "Soap operas are popular" may not stimulate you to write or your readers to read on. Currently, most people believe the statement as a matter of course. It is neither interesting nor likely to generate much writing. Let's consider the statement with which Anita started her second draft: "Soap operas allow us to enter the lives of other people." This is still a weak statement. One way to test a statement is to replace a key term or expression with another word. If you can't create a meaningful statement, then the sentence is too general. Replacing "Soap operas" with "Automobiles" makes the statement as uninformative as the original.

A much stronger statement, because it may run against popular beliefs and commercial pressures, would be "Soap operas are addictive." This statement, although more specific, adds nothing new to our knowledge and is therefore weak. When Anita discussed her statement with her peers, many of them told her she should use some of the ideas she discovered in doing her second tree diagram (see Figure 5.3). This was Anita's next draft of her thesis statement: "Soap operas, just like alcohol or tobacco, turn us into addicts." As Anita was typing this statement, she had another breakthrough. This was her next draft of her thesis statement: "Soap operas ruin people's lives as much as alcohol or drug addiction." Notice that she incorporated the word *ruin*, a much stronger verb than *turn*.

Strong statements do the following:

- Respond to some important human need
- Make you think
- Lead to good questions
- Give you an "aha" feeling
- Make you say, "That's a strong statement."
- Question common beliefs
- Take a stand
- Assume a new point of view
- Stimulate strong reactions
- Form the basis for further research and discovery
- Aren't instantly popular
- May meet with resistance from others
- Have the potential for creating breakthroughs

- Require strong supporting evidence
- Lead you to work together with others who are ready for a breakthrough.

Sometimes you don't want to commit yourself to an extreme statement because you don't feel confident about being able to collect and offer enough evidence to support it. You can weaken Anita's statement by using such words as *can be, could be,* or *may be* instead of *is, are,* or *will:* "Soap operas can ruin people's lives as much as alcohol or drug addiction." You can further weaken a statement by revising it with conditions such as *some people believe, it is possible,* or *there are a few.*

Sometimes you want to commit yourself to an extreme or controversial position to prove a point. For example, in "A Modest Proposal," Jonathan Swift proposed that infants should be used as food. He proposed this outrageous solution to starvation in London to emphasize how people were negligent in solving the crisis. This is a challenging strategy that often leads to effective satire.

Unless you are prepared to take up the challenge of writing satire, be careful of trying to support extreme statements. Some statements, such as "Milk is the only food that can sustain life," "Women shouldn't be allowed in the workplace," or "'Soap operas are a CIA plot to control the vote," are strong but irresponsible. These statements lead not to the betterment of life for all people and our environment but to possible destruction and sustained misery. Because strong statements invite further discussion and proof, and because (as you will see in Chapter 14, "Writing for Power") almost any position can be made convincing to unthinking people, irresponsible statements—assumed and acted upon by people in power—are dangerous. The standard that a responsible thinker will always endeavor to meet when making a strong statement is this:

The statement must be made in the spirit of preserving or bettering human relations and the environment.

Notice how Anita's paper becomes more focused and powerful as she revises with her new thesis statement:

Third draft

    Soap operas can ruin people's lives as much as alcohol or
    drug addiction. An addiction, according to twelve-step pro-
    grams, is anything that takes over your life and stops you
    from living your life.

How to Write Thesis Statements

1. *Read* your assignment.
2. *Write* a statement that takes a stand.
3. *Adjust* the strength of your statement to satisfy your purpose and reach your audience.
4. *Revise* your thesis statement as you write your paper.

Many people are addicted to tuning in at the same time everyday or every week. This is true of all soap operas no matter if they are daytime soap operas or one hour weekly nighttime soap operas. This can be very frustrating if you can't get to a television or are at work and can't take a break. Sometimes the VCR doesn't record or your program is interrupted by a special report. Sometimes a soap opera will be canceled for weeks because of a special event like a court case, war reports, or a sports event.

People who are addicted to Soap operas, do many things to make it possible to get their daily fix. For example, they program their VCRs, change their schedules, and miss appointments. As other examples of soap opera addiction, they buy soap opera magazines, spend money on telephone updates, and join fan clubs. Some people even become so addicted, that they stalk soap opera actors.

There are other ways that this addiction hurts people. For instance, watching soap operas can waste so much time that a person does not take care of parenting their children by taking a child to a baseball game. Watching soap operas can also dull your mind so much that you can't concentrate on your school work or your job, As another example, instead of watching a soap opera every day for an hour, you could be reading a book or going out for some fresh air and exercise.

*R*eflections _____

1. *Together or Solo.* Compare Anita's first and third drafts, with special attention to the focusing strategies she used to move from one to the other. Use the following suggestions and questions as a guide:

   a. Compare the lengths of the two drafts. How do you account for the difference?

   b. Without looking back to check, record what you remember of the first draft. Then record what you remember from the third draft. Which draft is more memorable, and why?

2. *Together or Solo.* Compare Anita's second and third drafts, and answer the following questions:

   a. What changes were made between the two drafts?

   b. What makes Anita's third draft more effective?

   c. What suggestions can you offer for revising the third draft?

Explorations

1. *Together and Solo.* Write or discuss your reactions to the statements "Milk is dangerous to your health" and "Women should not be allowed in the workplace." Ask as many questions as you can in response to these statements. Discuss what you learn from this process.

2. *Together.*

   a. Rank the following statements on a scale of 1 (for weakest) to 5 (for strongest) according to the strength of the statements for you.

   • Electroshock therapy is cruel and unusual punishment for people who are already in great mental anguish.

   • Toxic waste dumps exist in the United States.

   • The diet of the average U.S. teenager is about as healthy as skydiving without a parachute.

   • Communities can reestablish a sense of unity by organizing social events together.

   • Drugs are a problem in the world today.

   b. For practice, revise the weaker statements into stronger statements and the stronger into weaker. Whenever possible, do so by adding or crossing out a few words.

   c. Discuss which statements from Explorations 2a and 2b would be most effective in stimulating further research and discussion.

3. *Together and Solo.* Collect statements from the editorial page of a college or city newspaper. Discuss whether the statements are strong, weak, responsible, or irresponsible, and why.

4. *Together and Solo.* Choose a strong statement from something you have read or heard that you only half-believe. Write an essay in response to it, with the purpose of convincing yourself and your audience of the claim. Notice how one statement leads to another and what you learn as you proceed.

5. *Solo.* Revise a paper, with special attention to the strength and relevance of your statements.

Illustrating

Could you imagine reading a Dr. Seuss book without drawings, or a *National Geographic* article on tropical fish without underwater photographs? Of course not. Such drawings and photographs help readers to more fully enjoy and understand what they are reading.

This past century has brought us a carnival of visual and audio media to delight and educate us all. Business professionals often support their presentations with graphics. Music videos are helping to solve social problems such as bringing runaway children home. Medical diagnoses can be made via satellite telecasts. Video games and of course television and the movies have made us all dependent on visual media.

As a writer, you participate in a long tradition of transforming and re-creating the world through words so that others will be able to see it *as you do.* The old saying goes, "A picture paints a thousand words." But just a few words illustrating your points can enliven not only your readers' experience but your own, as writer. Strive to illustrate your ideas in words as visual media illustrate in pictures.

An effective way to focus your work is to offer examples—*illustrations*—of exactly what you mean. In the first paragraph of this section, I could have just written this sentence:

> Illustrations help to enliven books and magazines.

Instead, I stopped to think of some examples that are relevant to my point and that you might recognize as well. So, I chose to write this:

> Could you imagine reading a Dr. Seuss book without drawings, or a *National Geographic* article on tropical fish without underwater photographs?

There is a difference between offering specifics and illustrating. Although in her third draft Anita offers examples of how soap opera addicts behave—buying magazines, joining fan clubs, missing appointments, and so on—she is still not illustrating her point of view. To illustrate means to choose one particular example of your subject and then offer a detailed enough description of it. (Chapter 6 provides you with further strategies for effectively illustrating your work.) Read and reflect on the specific illustration Anita wrote to add to and transform her paper: the story of one soap opera addict, her Uncle Leon.

Fourth draft

At 12:30 every afternoon my Uncle Leon sinks into his old brown leather recliner to start watching his soap operas. He begins with <u>The Young and the Restless</u>, goes to <u>Bold and Beautiful</u>, then <u>As the World Turns</u> and <u>General Hospital</u>. He even comes back at 5:00 to watch <u>Beverly Hills 90210</u>, even though he is eighty years old and that's a program for high school kids.

As a gift for his wife, my Aunt Helen, Uncle Leon bought one of those plates with people from <u>The Young and the Restless</u> painted on it. Aunt Helen hated it because he never pays any attention to her anymore since he is always either watching or talking about all the things that happen on the soap operas. When she tried to get him to go to a marriage counselor about it, he said he couldn't go because he didn't want to miss an upcoming wedding on <u>General Hospital</u>. So my Aunt Helen told me that she said to him, "What's the matter with you? Are you giving the bride away? Or are you having a secret affair with the groom?" (My Aunt Helen still has a sense of humor and is very open to different lifestyles.)

All kidding aside, things really got serious with my Uncle Leon which I will get back to later. For now, I want to ask the question: how do the soap operas make us addicted?

*R*eflections _____

1. Would Anita's illustration engage her audience? If so, how?
2. Will Anita's illustration help her to further clarify and satisfy her purpose in writing her paper? If so, how?
3. Which portions of Anita's illustration are most powerful, and why?
4. How might Anita make her illustration stronger or more relevant?

How to Illustrate

1. **Ask** yourself, "What illustration would enliven this writing?"
2. **Use expressions** such as *for example, for instance, such as,* and *as in* to launch yourself into illustrating.
3. **Rewrite** your draft to reduce unnecessary repetition of words or expressions.
4. **Illustrate** your writing with examples without using suggestion 2.
5. **Focus** on one major illustration or story whenever possible.

---

*E*xplorations _____

1. *Together or Solo.* Read the following sentences. Illustrate the claim made in each. If you are so inspired, write a short essay further illustrating the claim with relevant examples and stories.

   a. The United States has waged many wars.

   b. Many music videos address social problems in a responsible way.

   c. Car manufacturers are creating safety features that are saving lives.

   d. Exercise can be dangerous to your health.

   e. Modern civilization is ruining the planet.

2. *Solo or Together.*

   a. Read the following student paragraph. Mark portions that could have been enlivened by illustrations.

   > Our governor is the best thing that's happened to the state. Before she got in, we had all sorts of social problems that nobody paid attention to. Now we're getting action. Some people are saying mean things about her. All I know is that my problems are not being overlooked anymore. Maybe she's had to change things around to make things happen. But it's worth it. I'm going to help her get reelected in any way I can.

   b. Revise and expand the student paragraph in Exploration 2a into an essay. Use your imagination, and illustrate the claims with relevant examples and stories.

3. *Together and Solo.* Bring essays in process to class. Read them in small groups. Mark portions that could have been enlivened by illustrations. Revise your work to include more examples. If possible, choose one example or story to tell in detail.

Questioning

So far in this chapter, you have had opportunities to explore four focusing strategies: choosing, specifying, stating, and illustrating. All these strategies help you to achieve these objectives:

- Relate *exactly* what you want to relate.
- Create a flow of words.
- Take care of your reader.
- Learn while you write.
- Enjoy writing.

Questioning helps you to practice these four strategies more fully.

Anita's classmates helped her by asking her questions in response to her illustration. Questions were asked as they naturally occurred to the students on hearing the paper read aloud. To boost the process, students referred to the question star (Figure 5.4), which arranges the eight *wh* question words.* It helps to go back to the question star, pick a word, and see if a question forms in your mind.

Here are some of the questions students asked Anita:

- When did your Uncle Leon begin watching soap operas?
- Why did he begin watching soap operas?
- How does Aunt Helen treat him?
- Where do they live?
- How do you feel about your Uncle Leon?
- What do you think soap operas do to get people hooked?

Anita found these questions very helpful. In fact, the last question, "What do you think soap operas do to get people hooked?," inspired her and gave her a direction in which to take her next draft.

---

*All the *wh* words were originally spelled with an initial *hw.* Only *hwuo (how)* was not re-spelled with an initial *wh.* Because *how* comes from the same family of words as the other *wh* words, *how* is included here as an honorary *wh* word.

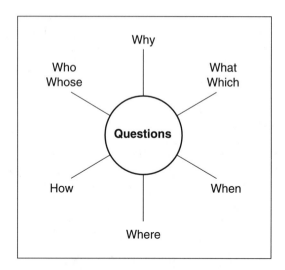

F I G U R E   5 . 4   ***The Question Star***

Anticipate questions that would arise for your readers. Even if your reader is familiar with your topic or illustration, you can't assume that what she or he sees is what you see. Focus your reader's attention on *exactly* what you mean.

*E*xplorations

1. *Solo and Together.* Choose papers that you are working on right now. In turn, read each of them aloud in small groups. Using the question star (Figure 5.4), ask questions of the writers to help them clarify their points with examples and details. Revise your papers by answering these questions and others you anticipate may arise.

2. *Solo and Together.* For an in-depth discussion of questions, turn to pages 311–318. Do the Explorations that follow.

Quoting

As human beings, we live in a constant environment of language, both spoken and written. To offer examples of what others say, either in conversation or through written material, is a most basic and powerful focusing strategy. You draw on the power of others' thoughts to inspire and expand your own. In your academic and professional activities, you will

How to Question

1. *Identify* claims that readers could question.
2. *Ask* questions, using each point of the question star (Figure 5.4).
3. *Consult* with other readers.
4. *Choose* questions to answer.
5. *Answer* important questions, including any questions that occur to you as you revise. Push yourself to answer *exactly* what, which, who, whose, when, where, how, and why.

be referring to written material. The research skills you need to develop in order to do so are not the focus of this textbook. However, you already know certain basic quoting strategies. For example, turn back to page 117 to notice how much Anita introduced into her illustration of Uncle Leon by quoting Aunt Helen's response to his soap opera addiction. Read the sidebar on how to quote, and whenever quotations are relevant, use them to enliven your writing.

How to Quote

1. *Assume* your reader won't know *exactly* which portion of what you heard or read is important to you, even if your reader said or wrote it.
2. *Choose* the relevant excerpt of what you heard or read, and write it down. (An *excerpt* is a chosen portion of what was said or written.)
3. *Quote* your chosen excerpt by putting quotation marks before and after the exact words you are mentioning. (Review the use of quotation marks on pages 483–488 in Chapter 16.)
4. *Indent and single-space* quotes that are longer than four lines of printed material.
5. *Acknowledge* the person and the work you are quoting. Use such expressions as these: *according to (person or title), (person) wrote, (person) said, in (title) (person) wrote.*
6. *Explain* exactly what the quote means to you and how it is relevant to your purpose. When appropriate, requote smaller portions of the work.

*Explorations*_____

1. **a.** *Solo.* Read the following letter that retired public librarian Marvin H. Scilken wrote to *The New York Times.* Write a letter in response to him, saying exactly

   - To which letter you are responding
   - Where the letter first appeared
   - Which of his points were meaningful to you, and why.

   Be sure to quote and requote words, phrases, and sentences as you refer to them. Whenever you use his exact words, place them in quotation marks.

   To the Editor:

   As a retired public librarian I would like to comment on your Sept. 9 article that shows that many Americans cannot read.

   People do what gives them pleasure and avoid doing what gives them pain. Regular library users told me that just after learning to read they read hundreds of pleasure-giving books. This intensive period of reading for pleasure honed their reading skills and enabled them to read with ease for the rest of their lives.

   I believe children who don't experience this early coupling of reading with pleasure rarely become facile readers as adults. Learning to read, like learning foreign languages, is best done early in one's life.

   Schools usually cannot "teach" reading for pleasure because, in their desire to measure a student's progress, they couple reading with the "pain" of tests and book reports. This coupling of reading and "pain" turns many people into aliterates. They can read but don't like to. People who don't read apparently lose some of their ability to read. This may account for some of the shocking literacy figures.

   The public library plays a major, but unrecognized, role in the creation and nurturing of America's good readers. Fortunately, public libraries are very inexpensive, perhaps America's greatest education bargain. New Jersey, for instance, spends about $1,000 per capita (about $7,000 per student) for public schooling while it spends a minuscule $26 a year per capita on public libraries.

   If we are to have a more literate population, the public should see to it that their public libraries are open when children and adults can get to them and that libraries have a sufficient supply of books that kids and adults want to read when they want to read them.

Because libraries are so inexpensive this "keep reading alive" program is within the means of most communities.

Mayor David Dinkins, when he came to office, gutted the libraries. Apparently seeing that this made him unpopular with many voters, he recently gave the libraries money to open six days a week, but he "forgot" to give them more money for books.

It is easier to watch TV than to read. If we want to be a reading country, we have to make desired books and other reading matter easily available.

—Marvin H. Scilken
New York, Sept. 16, 1993

b. *Together.* Read your response letters to each other in small groups or as a class. What point was each letter trying to make? Decide whether the letter used quotes effectively. Were all the quotes relevant? What relevant information, if any, was left out? How would you revise the letter?

2. a. *Solo.* Choose something you have read recently that was important to you, such as a passage from the Bible or the Koran, a newspaper item, a personal letter, a poem, or a book. To clarify what it means to you, and to convince others of its relevance, write an essay in response to your chosen passage. State what it means to you. Assume your readers will not be familiar with your chosen

---

Reading for Focus

Ask these questions to test a piece of writing:

1. Could almost anyone have written this? (This is a measure of how general it is.)
2. Does the writer try to cover too many subjects?
3. Does the writer use strong, specific words and expressions?
4. Can I replace an important word or expression with any other and say as much or more?
5. Does the writer illustrate the claims?
6. Are all the details relevant to a main purpose?
7. Is any of this redundant?
8. Is any of this false or unclear?
9. Are any important questions left unanswered?
10. Are there any thesis statements? Are the statements appropriately strong?

passage or source. Quote and requote words, phrases, and sentences to keep your discussion focused for yourself and for your readers. State the person and the source you are quoting.

b. *Together.* Bring your chosen passage to class along with your essay in response. In small groups, read your essays to each other. Then show each other your passages. Discuss whether you have used relevant quotes. Did you quote sufficiently? If not, what more could you have quoted or requoted to make your essay clearer to readers who won't be reading your chosen passage as you did?

Chapter Review

1. *Together.* Throughout this chapter, you have seen how learning to focus enabled Anita Morrow to write a meaningful paper. Using the sidebar titled Reading for Focus and Meaning, compare Anita's first and fifth drafts of her paper. What further suggestions would you offer her to improve on her fifth draft?

Fifth draft

Brainwashed: Soap Operas and Addiction

At 12:30 every afternoon my Uncle Leon sinks into his old brown leather recliner to start watching his soap operas. He begins with The Young and the Restless, goes to Bold and Beautiful, then As the World Turns and General Hospital. He even comes back at 5:00 to watch Beverly Hills 90210, even though he is eighty years old and that's a program for high school kids.

As a gift for his wife, my Aunt Helen, Uncle Leon bought one of those plates with people from The Young and the Restless painted on it. Aunt Helen hated it because he never pays any attention to her anymore since he is always either watching or talking about all the things that happen on the soap operas. Aunt Helen refuses to watch soap operas with him because she doesn't want to support his habit.

When she tried to get him to go to a marriage counselor about it, he said he couldn't go because he didn't want to miss an upcoming wedding on General Hospital. So my Aunt Helen told me that she said to him, "What's the matter with you? Are you giving the bride away? Or are you having a secret affair with the groom?" (My Aunt Helen still has a sense of humor and is very open to different life-styles.)

All kidding aside, things really got serious with my Uncle Leon, which led me to this question: How do soap operas make us addicted?

First I'm going to define addiction because soap operas can ruin people's lives as much as alcohol or drug addiction. An addiction, according to twelve-step programs, is anything that takes over your life and stops you from living your life.

Many people are addicted to tuning in at the same time every day or every week. This is true of all soap operas, whether they are daytime soap operas or one-hour weekly nighttime soap operas. Some people can get frustrated if they can't get to a television or are at work and can't take a break. Sometimes their VCR doesn't record or their program is interrupted by a special report. Sometimes a soap opera will be canceled for weeks because of a special event like a court case, war reports, or a sports event.

Another point about soap opera people is that they do many things to make it possible to get their daily "fix." For example, they program their VCRs, change their schedules, and miss appointments. As other examples of soap opera addiction, they buy soap opera magazines, spend money on telephone updates, and pay money to join fan clubs. some people even become so addicted that they bother soap opera actors as if they were the real people they acted on television.

There are other ways this addiction hurts people. For instance, watching soap operas can waste so much time that a person does not take care of parenting their children by taking a child to a baseball game. Watching soap operas can also dull your mind so much that you can't concentrate on your school work or your job. Instead of watching a soap opera every day for an hour, you could be reading a book or going out for some fresh air and exercise.

There are many ways soap operas keep us hooked. First, they have a lot of sex and violence, which are cheap ways to get people's attention. Next, they always leave you in suspense before a commercial so that you want to wait to find out what happens. They also do this at the end of the hour and especially on Friday because they know how to play hard to get over the weekend. Everybody knows how playing hard to get in a relationship makes you want the other person more.

Soap operas also take you out of your own life into other people's problems. When somebody doesn't know how to cope with life problems, that person might turn to alcohol or drugs to stop the pain for a while. So, because we are not in the lives of the people on soap operas, it is easier to watch them than to watch our own lives. On soap operas everybody is either all good or all bad. That's an easy way to look at life. In real life, people are not usually so simple to figure out.

Going back to Uncle Leon, he started to watch soap operas when he went into the hospital to have triple-bypass heart surgery. No one knew if he was going to live. He was very overweight because he weighed 325 pounds and was 5 feet, 7 inches tall. So after intensive care they put him into a room to monitor his progress and diet and to start him on exercise. So what he did was walk from his room, where there was a television, down to the dayroom, where there was another television.

So, you can see that instead of facing his problem with his heart and his weight and doing exercise, Uncle Leon buried himself in television soap operas.

There is a bright side to this story because Aunt Helen made Uncle Leon go back to the hospital, where they have a twelve-step program and no television in the room. Uncle Leon has decided to give it a try not to watch soap operas for a month but to let himself read <u>Soap Opera Digest</u> instead. The doctor thinks that this is a good move, especially because when the weather is nice Uncle Leon reads outside. Aunt Helen also makes Uncle Leon walk to the store to buy his magazines.

Professor Neil Postman wrote a book titled <u>Amusing Ourselves to Death</u>. That is what my Uncle Leon almost did. Are you hooked too?

2. *Together.* Read the following student essay. Notice your own reactions. Are you interested? Are you bored? Are you being forced to make up examples yourself to enrich your experience of the essay? Discuss the essay, using the questions in the sidebar on reading for focus and meaning. Notice what happens, for example, if you replace

drug with *exercise* or *diet.* Using the strategies developed in this chapter, offer suggestions for how the writer could have focused. What risks may the author have to take?

                    Drug Abuse Today

   In recent years drug abuse has been increasing at a rapid rate in the United States and throughout the world. The practice occurs mostly among young people who are looking for new sensations or who think that drugs will increase their mental functioning or their ability to understand themselves.

   Some young people begin to take drugs while they are still in elementary school, particularly if their friends have persuaded them to do so. During high school and early in college, more and more people take drugs. By the middle of their college years, most members of this group realize that the practice is dangerous. Most young people who try drugs soon stop, but some find that they cannot, even if they want to. Even among preteenagers, alcohol is now a problem. It seems that the earlier the use, the more likely a young person is to become an alcoholic.

   Sometimes people use a doctor's prescription for a drug unwisely. A person takes too much of the drug or fails to check with the doctor about stopping its use. But very often one person introduces another to drug abuse. The newcomer, in turn, introduces others to drugs. In this way, more and more people, unaware of the dangers of drugs, begin to take them. This is the situation today.

3. **a.** *Together.* Consult with each other about essays you are now writing. Focus on focusing. Refer to specific strategies offered in this chapter.

   b. *Solo.* Revise a paper according to questions and suggestions that emerged in your discussions.

Chapter 6

Focusing II

Sense Appeal

This chapter offers opportunities to

—Give your writing *sense appeal*

—*Describe* persons, places, things, and events

—Distinguish *showing* from *telling*

—Balance *objective* and *subjective* writing

—Use *comparisons* to enliven your writing

Caress the details.

—*Vladimir Nabokov, Novelist*

…touch and taste and hear and see the world, and shrink…from all that is of the brain only, from all that is not a fountain jetting from the entire hopes, memories, and sensations of the body.

—*William Butler Yeats, Poet*

Writing is a mind-taxing process. Using sensory detail makes it more enjoyable.

—*Jen Levine, Student*

The Dynamics of Sense Appeal

Life depends on the ability to perceive everyday sensations such as the color of a traffic light, the texture of rain, the smell of breakfast cooking. Without the senses of sight, touch, hearing, motion, taste, and smell, you would be locked in emptiness. You would not be able to develop your mind or have common sense, good sense, or a sense of humor. In every human endeavor—from noticing the skin texture of a sick person to observing the flight patterns of aircraft, from listening for prowlers in a danger zone to appreciating how light shifts on a landscape you are photographing—the quicker and sharper your senses, the more fully you can live. At times, you may shut off your senses if your environment is unpleasant. At other times, even pleasant stimulation such as music, television, junk food—or the more dangerous experiences of fast driving, alcohol, and drugs—can numb you. You find yourself reaching for more stimulation and so get even more numbed. The antidote is to calm down and start focusing your attention on small sense details that surround you every day.

The greatest achievements in art, science, business, education, sports, and human relations require sharp senses. One of the most powerful ways to develop your senses is to learn how to focus them in the writing process. As you enliven your writing with you-are-there images, you increase its *sense appeal*. The more sense appeal your writing has, the more likely you are to enjoy writing and engage your readers' interest. Your work becomes, in short, *sensational*.

*E*xplorations _____

1. *Solo and Together. Without referring to the real thing,* draw one of the following to test your awareness and memory:
   - The front of a dollar bill
   - A familiar cartoon character
   - A modern pay phone
   - A particular campus building
   - The hallway outside the classroom
   - The lines in your palm (don't look)

   Compare your drawings with the real thing. How accurate were you?

2. *Solo.* If you have had, or currently have, a disability involving a sense or body part, write about your experiences. Relate experiences before, during, and after the disability occurred. You may also write about another person's way of coping with a disability.

3. *Solo.* If you wear glasses or a hearing aid or experience your senses of smell, taste, touch, or motion reduced from time to time, write a description of the difference between having your senses fully functioning and having them impaired.

4. *Solo or Together.* Imagine you had to live forever in the same place and could arrange every detail in that environment. Write a description of this place. What would you be sure to include? Which senses would be most stimulated by the environment you create?

Collecting: Your Six Senses

The five senses you've heard about since grammar school are *sight, hearing, smell, taste,* and *touch.* These senses are focused mostly in your head and fingertips. But you live in more than your head and fingertips. When you ride on a roller coaster, dance, fall, or feel muscle pain, you are experiencing what it means to live in a body. Therefore, *body sensations* have been added to this discussion as the sixth sense.

Here is a list of the kinds of phenomena related to each sense, with specific examples:

Sight: color, shape, size, light/dark, perspective, movement
   Specific Examples: neon pink T-shirt, flickering glints from a heart-shaped diamond, a green river snaking through a valley

Touch: texture, itching, heat/cold
   Specific Examples: prickling wool slacks on a hot day, juiciness of a ripe peach, warm sand trickling through your fingers

Taste: single and combined tastes of sweet, sour, salty, spicy, bitter (taste is closely related to smell)
   Specific Examples: tang of lemonade, sweetness of watermelon, metallic taste from smelling silver polish

Smell: aromas, odors
   Specific Examples: whiff of baby powder, smoky-sweet aroma of barbecue, pungent stench of a frightened skunk

Body Sensations: motion, movements, balance, pressure, pain, tension, pleasure, weight
   Specific Examples: sensations of riding in a roller coaster, release of tension from a massaged muscle, heft of a basket of

apples, stabbing toothache, throb from bass speakers felt through the body

Hearing: pitch, tone, loudness, frequency, rhythm, sound imitations
  Specific Examples: shrill of a lifeguard's whistle, scraping and sloshing sounds of autumn leaves being raked, basso of a Mack truck's horn, hum of bees, quaver of a complaining voice

Read and reflect on this passage from James Dickey's adventure novel *Deliverance,* about four men on a canoe trip down the ravaging white waters of a Georgia rapids. First read this passage about a walk on the riverbank. Then use the Reflections below to guide you in appreciating Dickey's strategies for offering sense appeal.

There was still no light in the sky but moonlight. I turned away from the river where the land shelved back to some boulders and low trees, and felt around. Among the trees, which held the light from me, I could tell nothing except by touch. I put out a foot because I could reach farther that way. Something solid was there. I took a step toward it and was enveloped at once in branches and the stiff pine-hairs. I set the bow down and climbed into the lower limbs, which were very thick and close together, and went up until the tree swayed.

There was a little visibility through the needles, a little flickering light off the river, which the tree set twice as far off as it had been when I looked at it from the grasses at the edge of the cliff. I finally figured out that the part of the river I could see was where it came out of the turn from the last of the rapids below Lewis and Bobby, and calmed and smoothed out, losing its own thready silver for the broad-lying moonlight.

I went back down and got the bow and began to do what I could about setting up a blind in the tree. I had never shot anything—or at anything—from a tree before, not even a target, though I remembered someone's telling me to aim a little lower than seemed right. I thought about this while I worked.

Moving as though I was instructing myself—where does this hand go? Here? No, it would be better over here, or a little lower down—I cleared away the small-needled twigs between myself and the platform of sand. It was not hard to do; I just kept taking things away from between the river-light and my face until there were not any. When I was back against the bole of the tree, I was looking down a short, shaggy tunnel of needles; I would shoot right down that; it even seemed to help me aim. All the time

I was clearing, I was aided by a totally different sense of touch than I had ever had, and it occurred to me that I must have developed it on the cliff. I seemed able to tell the exact shape and weight of anything at first touch, and had to put out no extra strength to break or strip off any part of the tree I wanted to. Being alive in the dark and doing what I was doing was like a powerful drunkenness, because I didn't believe it. There had never been anything in my life remotely like it. I felt the bark next to me with the most intimate part of my palm, then broke off a needle and put it in my mouth and bit down. It was the right taste.

Reflections

1. Place a check mark over each sensory image in the passage.
2. Identify the sense each image makes an appeal to.
3. Which senses does Dickey tend to favor? Which does he omit?
4. What are your favorite images in this passage?
5. Did Dickey's description remind you of any of your own experiences, whether directly related to his scene or not?

Point of View and the Senses

The sensations you notice reflect your *point of view*. If you are angry, you will focus on things in your environment that make you angry. If you are in a pleasant mood, you are more likely to focus on pleasant sensations. A French chef will notice the edible mushrooms on a nature walk. An environmentalist will notice how pollution bleaches the bark on sycamore trees.

In this excerpt from her essay "Selective Hearing," Suzann Ledbetter offers her humorous point of view on this most human tendency.

As any wife and mother knows, husbands and children are experts at the art of Selective Hearing. In the animal world, this malfunction is comparable to the ostrich burying its head in the sand and believing itself invisible to predators. Fortunately, for most husbands and kids, mothers are seldom aggressively predatory…just frustrated.

When a woman marries, there's no mention of Selective Hearing in the "for better or for worse" and "in sickness and in health" parts of the ceremony she vows to take that man in spite of.

From that day forward, Hubby will always hear a friend whisper a Saturday afternoon tee time, your quiet confession to Mother that the grocery check bounced, or disparaging remarks detailing his character (or lack thereof) at frequencies previously detectable only by United States Navy radar. But he will *never* hear distinctly enunciated requests for milk or bread to be picked up on the way home, the sounds of toddlers being sick in the middle of the night in the middle of the living room carpet, teenagers arriving home two hours later than curfew, or the dog whining to go out. The same man who can hear his wallet being opened in another room is deaf to the thunder of an approaching garbage truck.

Once children come along, a mother realizes that they, too, can filter key words and phrases through their ears, and begin doing so at a surprisingly tender age.

Of course, Mother's auditory antennae can scan all familial frequencies, at all times, and without fail. From a spoon clinking against a bowl of "I-said-not-before-dinner" fudge ripple ice cream to an infant's quiet whimpers to hissed threats of impending sibling massacre, a mother's ear is never out of range. A house may be filled to the rafters with a dozen children and their father, but only Mother will hear and respond to the ringing telephone or buzzing doorbell.

Children *will* respond to certain words such as: *candy, cartoons, toy store, pepperoni pizza, swimming pool, yes, play,* and *go.* And if Mom has stashed the last box of chocolate mint Girl Scout cookies for her own well-deserved reward, any child over the age of five can hear and accurately identify the r-i-p of their wax-paper packaging, and appear at the scene with Olympic speed. Kids can hear Mom wearily running water for a desperately needed, take-me-away-please bubble bath, or paperback pages gently turning in the bathroom, and will scream an urgent need to use the toilet.

Teenagers hear checks being cashed at the bank, gas tanks filling at a self-service station, and new credit cards with higher user limits sliding into the mailbox.

Simultaneously, the words *lawn mower, homework, shut, clean, flush,* and *no* cannot be comprehended. And sentences beginning with "I want you to...," "You can't...," or "You already owe me..." don't register either.

Selective Hearing is the reason most mothers eventually become Yellers. They erroneously believe if the volume is raised, Spouse and children cannot deny hearing them. Though logical, this solution does not address the underlying problem and is akin to a chocoholic giving up broccoli as a weight-reduction technique.

Since point of view determines how you sense the world, it is placed at the center of the model of the senses in Figure 6.1.

Explorations

Each person tends to favor some senses over others, depending on her or his physical constitution, culture, and training and the purpose at hand. The following Explorations invite you to notice which senses you favor and to develop senses you may have ignored.

1. *Solo.*

   a. Go to a place that is significant to you in some way—it could be a room, a natural setting, a store, a restaurant, a laundromat, a library, a sports area, a transportation depot, or even your writing classroom. Draw the sense star on a page. (See Figure 6.1.) Choose a sense you tend to ignore. First, collect images for that sense. Then record other images that occur to you for that or any other sense. Use more paper if you need to. Here are some places and activities that may stimulate the three senses people tend to ignore:

      Smell: Place yourself in a busy bar or restaurant, garden, bus depot, or hospital, or by a river or lake.

      Hearing: Sit where you can eavesdrop on conversations and write or record exactly what you hear, including nonhuman sounds. Or describe the sounds in a nightclub, at a ballgame, in a library, or in your car as you drive.

      Body Sensations: Moving at a tenth of your usual speed, tie or untie your shoes, brush your teeth, or comb your hair. Record what it feels like to lift a particular weight, hit a tennis ball, take a ride in an amusement park, or knead dough.

   b. Freewrite in your journal about the experience. What did you notice that you hadn't noticed before? How does focusing on your senses and looking for images affect what you actually experience? What lesson can you learn from this Exploration about finding what you need?

   c. Write an essay about your chosen place or activity, focusing on some human interest. Give your reader a you-are-there experience.

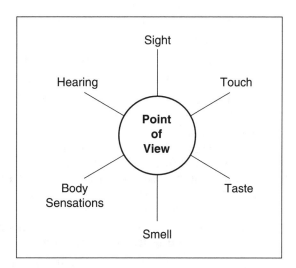

FIGURE 6.1   The Sense Star

2. **a.** *Solo.* Write two sets of directions from school to your home for the purpose of directing your choice of two different audiences: a child, a physically or perceptually disabled adult without a car, a teenager with a car, a trucker, a helicopter pilot.

    b. *Together.* Read and discuss your descriptions with each other. Use the following suggestions and questions:

    •   Point out sense cues that the writer offers.

How to Collect Sensations

1. **Cluster.** Draw the sense star in the center of a piece of paper. (See Figure 6.1.) As you observe, record sensations for each of the senses at the appropriate rays.

2. **Brainstorm** sense impressions. Whenever possible, with someone else, observe the subject you are trying to describe. Another point of view may help you become aware of images that you take for granted.

3. **Draw.** Sketch your subject. This is an effective way to stimulate your memory.

4. **Prime your senses.** Don't try to remember sensations. Get your subject in front of you. Go to the place you are describing.

5. **Use prompts.** If you can't prime your senses directly, use photographs and audio and video tapes. Collect objects that can help you recall sensations.

- To which senses does the writer appeal?
- Which sense does the writer favor?
- Compare and contrast directions offered to different audiences.
- Are the directions tailored to the needs of the chosen audiences?
- Take the point of view of these audiences and ask questions to help clarify the routes.

   c. *Solo.* On your way home, stop to observe your route closely and make notes. When you were looking for cues, what did you notice that you had forgotten or not noticed before? What did you learn about your perceptions from consciously observing your route home? Revise your first draft, or write new directions using as many sense impressions as you can.

      Variation: Write a route to a certain place using only one sense (e.g., a smell route or a touch route).

3. *Solo.* Following Dickey's close attention to and use of sensory details (pages 131–132), describe a significant experience you once had. Use the suggestions offered in the sidebar on how to collect sensations to help you to give your readers a *you-are-there* experience.

4. *Together or Solo.* Following Ledbetter's humorous insights into selective perception (pages 132–134), write an essay in which you describe some frustration you have experienced because others perceive differently than you do. You may focus on any of the senses— for example, discussing how someone else does not see what you see while driving on a certain road.

Showing and Telling

Anton Chekhov, one of the world's greatest playwrights, once said, "If you bring a cannon onstage, you have to fire it." In early drafts, you might find yourself *telling* your readers about your subject instead of *showing* them your subject. The benefits of telling your reader about your subject are these:

- Telling helps you to clarify your feelings and attitudes.
- Telling helps to focus your reader on your point of view.

But when all you do is tell about your subject, you ask your reader to read your mind and do the work of filling in the details for you. This is a sure way to bore your reader and to find yourself misunderstood. You also bore yourself and hurt your writing, because you are just stating what you already know and feel. This is like bringing a cannon onstage and letting it rust.

Telling only superficially engages you and your reader. *Showing*—focusing with sense images—engages and empowers everyone.

Instead of just telling you about the difference between showing and telling, I'm going to show you the difference between two descriptions of the relationship between a mother and daughter. Consider the following paragraph:

> Mothers and daughters experience many daily activities together that help them to create a bond. My mother and I were very close. She did everything for me as a child, and I will always be very grateful to her.

Notice that this paragraph is very general. Almost anyone could have written it, and therefore it is not especially interesting. There is no sense appeal being made, and readers' attention will drift off. They certainly do not experience a you-are-there involvement.

Now read the following passage from author Audre Lorde's autobiography *Zami:*

Sitting between my mother's spread legs, her strong knees gripping my shoulders tightly like some well-attended drum, my head in her lap, while she brushed and combed and oiled and braided, I feel my mother's strong, rough hands all up in my unruly hair, while I'm squirming around on a low stool or on a folded towel on the floor, my rebellious shoulders hunched and jerking against the inexorable sharp-toothed comb. After each springy portion is combed and braided, she pats it tenderly and proceeds to the next.

I hear the interjection of *sotto voce*° admonitions that punctuated whatever discussion she and my father were having.

"Hold your back up, now! Deenie, keep still! Put your head so!" Scratch, scratch. "When last you wash your hair? Look the dandruff!" Scratch, scratch, the comb's truth set my own teeth on edge. Yet, these were some of the moments I missed most sorely when our real wars began.

I remember the warm mother smell caught between her legs, and the intimacy of our physical touching nestled inside of the anxiety/pain like a nutmeg nestled inside its covering of mace.

°sotto voce: whispered.

Showing and Telling

To recognize the difference between showing and telling, ask these questions of your own and others' writing:

1. How many sense details are offered? (Sense details tend to *show*.)
2. Which words and expressions carry evaluations and preferences? (Evaluations and preferences tend to *tell*.)
3. Does the writer make any claims without illustrating them? (That is, does the writer tell and not show?)
4. Will readers know what is meant without having observed what the writer observed?
5. Are any of the sense details irrelevant?

The radio, the scratching comb, the smell of petroleum jelly, the grip of her knees and my stinging scalp all fall into—*the rhythms of a litany, the rituals of Black women combing their daughters' hair.*

Using the sidebar on showing and telling to guide you, compare and contrast the paragraph above, which merely tells of mother-daughter relationships, with Lorde's passage, which shows what they can be.

*E*xplorations

1. *Together.* Consider the following pairs of statements. Which of each pair tells more than shows? Which of each pair shows the reader what the writer has in mind? To which senses is the writer appealing in the "show" statement?

   Pair A

   Nursing homes are sometimes run by people who care only about money, not their clients' comfort.

   The cafeteria in Shady Rest Nursing Home reeked of urine and disinfectant.

   Pair B

   Twenty-five people linked arms in front of "Girls, Girls, Girls" to bar businessmen in gray suits from entering the nude show.

   Lots of people dislike nude shows.

Pair C

My roommate is a terror.

Old styrofoam cups with moldy food in them, socks that trip me like puppies, weird music squealing from his headset at night, and magazines with leather and chains in them—my roommate is a terror.

Pair D

There is nothing worse than taking a class you don't want to take, with a teacher you can't understand, in a subject area that has nothing to do with your major.

I took the last open gym class, Fencing, with Mr. Zsolt, who sounded like Count Dracula and made me wonder what pushing a sword in someone's face had to do with studying nursing, my major.

2. *Solo.* Following Lorde's strategies (pages 137–138), describe a person who is important to you for some reason—pleasant or unpleasant. Be clear as to why this person is important to you. Show your reader why you feel as you do. Let your reader experience this person in detail, using as many senses as seem appropriate to support your point of view.

3. **a.** *Together.* Read papers in progress to each other. Point out statements that, like rusty cannons, tell without delivering. Suggest ways in which the writer can show the reader what's happening by using sensory images.

   b. *Solo.* Revise your paper to show more of what you mean. Use the sense star in Figure 6.1 and the sidebar on page 135 to encourage yourself to use sensory images.

Subjective and Objective Modes

To focus your writing and your reader's experience of it, you have to discover and relate what your subject means to you. In other words, you have to *make sense* of your subject:

- Why is it important?
- How do you feel about it?
- What questions do you have about it?
- How do you evaluate it?
- What do you need to do with it?

The answers to these questions reveal your *subjective* attitude toward your topic.

Recognize that you will tend to choose images that reflect your purpose, attitudes, ideas, intuitions, and experiences; the audience you anticipate; and your emotional states—in short, you will reveal your point of view. Unless you consciously strive to take another point of view, you will tend to ignore images that don't reflect your current point of view.

For example, think of a red rose. Most people think of it as a symbol of love. If you limit yourself to the popular point of view, you won't notice that it can mean many more things. You can look at the same red rose and have many different reactions at the same time. You may feel despair because the rose reminds you of the funeral of a loved one. You may feel proud because you grew the rose from a bush you revived. You might be fascinated by the pattern of the rose's petals as you analyze it for a botany class.

The writing process gives you an opportunity to become aware of many points of view and to sort out what each means to you. It also gives you an opportunity to recognize other points of view. Learning how to take other points of view can help you grow as a person and thinker.

Your point of view may be relatively subjective or objective. An *objective* collection of sensory images is meant to avoid biases and prejudices. Objective statements are often used to illustrate and support subjective statements. Notice the differences between these three descriptions that education major Amy M. Puzzo wrote about a high school class she observed:

> *Objective:*   The students were calling out answers to the teacher's questions as soon as she asked them. Many students answered without raising their hands. The teacher did not pause but proceeded from one question to the next as soon as the correct answer was given.

> *Subjective (positive):*   The students were eager to respond to the teacher. They obviously wanted to please her. Many of them were so eager that they answered without raising their hands. The lesson was energizing.

> *Subjective (negative):*   The students in this class were anxious about their grades. They competed for the teacher's attention and competitively cut each other off. It was a tense class.

The relatively objective description avoids emotional and evaluative terms such as *eager, please, energizing, anxious, competitively, cut each other off,* and *tense.* The objective description focuses on describing events that anyone would agree upon, no matter what attitude, feelings, biases, or prejudices the person may bring to a situation.

However, it is possible to write descriptions that *seem* objective but that leave out important details that the writers either don't recognize or don't want to recognize because of their particular attitudes or biases. For example, the following two descriptions may *seem* objective—others would see the same details—but they show a biased attitude:

The sky was filled with bright flashes of lights against a red sky.

The bombs were bursting over the burning city.

Both of these sentences seem to objectively describe events, and most viewers on the scene would agree that both descriptions are accurate. However, the first description, if taken alone, shows the bias of someone who may be glad that a city is being bombed. The details the writer chooses sound much like the details that someone would choose during a beautiful fireworks display at sunset. The second description, if taken alone, is more likely to be made by someone who mourns the events. The details focus on violence and destruction. Your choice of images determines the relative objectivity or subjectivity of what you write as much as your choice of words does.

Here are some relatively objective and subjective statements:

Objective	Subjective
The bus went 60 mph.	The reckless driver pushed the school bus to go 60 mph on the dirt road.
The governor wrote the budget.	The governor slashed public programs to cut taxes and please the voters.
Only women bear children.	Women are the best caretakers of children.

Neither objectivity nor subjectivity is, in itself, better than the other. A subjective statement may, in the long run, be far more accurate and true than a seemingly objective one. An objective statement may take things out of context and miss the larger scope of what is being described. It is important to describe situations objectively, in ways that others can also perceive them. However, much can be said for the subjective hunch, felt sense, gut feeling, or intuition that often precedes and inspires breakthroughs in human endeavors. The more you develop your senses, the more accurate your intuition will become and the more fully you will be able to support your subjective reactions with objective observations.

Using the Reflections suggestions listed below, compare the following two starts of student Leslie Cox's paper on the homeless:

First draft

```
    There are three homeless individuals who sleep in
the train station depot in our town. One is a man with
long gray hair and a beard who smokes cigarettes. Another
is a lady who pushes a Big Deal shopping cart. Then there's
a tall skinny man who talks to himself and walks back and
forth on the platform all day. Something has to be done to
offer them a decent place to live. They are causing problems
in the station.
```

Second draft

```
    No one seems to care about the three homeless individuals
who sleep in the train station depot in our town. One of
them is a gentle man who looks a lot like Santa Claus
with long gray hair and a white beard. He looks so lonely
sitting on the bench, looking at all the children who go
by. I tried to talk to him once, but I got scared. He
started to talk in a language I didn't understand.
Then he reached his hand out to me. I felt like screaming
and crying at the same time. I didn't know what to do. He
looked into my eyes. Then he just slid away on the bench and
walked to the next one. I felt terrible.
```

*R*eflections _____

1. As a whole, which draft is relatively more objective? Which is more subjective? Why?
2. Which draft do you prefer? Why?
3. Consider the first draft. Point to specific words, phrases, and sentences that are relatively more objective. Point to portions that are relatively more subjective.
4. Consider the second draft, using instructions in Reflection 3.
5. What purposes and audiences would best be addressed by the first draft? The second draft? Why?

Finding Meaning and Purpose

A common problem students experience in writing for sense appeal is they feel they offer too many irrelevant details that will soon bore their readers. Unless others find some *human interest* in your work, you will not engage them. Whenever you describe a person, place, event, or experience, always ask yourself, "What does this mean to me? Why would anyone else be interested in this?" Strive to appeal to strong and true emotions and needs.

Read author Allen Lacy's description of a bird from his book *The Gardener's Eye and Other Essays.* Using the questions in the sidebar on finding meaning and purpose, reflect on how Lacy writes with both sense and human appeal.

The best way to enjoy birds in a garden, I believe, is just to live alongside them, recognizing that you owe them a lot. Some of them eat insects

Finding Meaning and Purpose

As you answer the following questions of your readings, point to particular words, phrases, and sentences to support your claims. Consult your dictionary for further insights into both familiar and unfamiliar words.

1. What does this piece of writing mean to me?
2. Why would this piece of writing interest any other reader?
3. What statement or statements capture the meaning and purpose of this description?
4. What attitudes, feelings, and opinions are stated or implied in this piece?

Use one of the following methods for finding meaning and purpose in what you write:

5. a. *Explorer's approach:* Collect your sensory images and notice what you choose. Discover what these images mean to you, in the process. Then you can start your next draft with a thesis statement that embodies your subjective mood, attitude, or meaning.

   b. *Planner's approach:* Write a thesis statement about how you already feel, and collect sensory images that illustrate your statement.

that left uneaten would eat my plants. Even if I had only vegetarian birds, they still would bring the pleasures of their songs, the interest of their constant movement, and, in the cases of blue jays and male cardinals, the brilliant colors of their plumage. They also are a constant reminder of the wild nature that humans sometimes forget, some might say to the peril of their souls.

Early summer is a crucial time for birds, often fraught with danger or tragedy. A robin's egg on the ground is one less robin in the garden. Feral cats and other animals (including, I'm sorry to report to anyone who shares Walt Disney's view of nature, birds) destroy nests and nestlings. Fledglings fall to the ground somewhat prematurely. My own garden has been an anxious place for the past two weeks, as some starling parents and one catbird have tried to herd their precocious offspring into the protection of the shrubbery.

I have made it a practice not to intervene by going to the aid of a young bird, but I made an exception one late spring night. As I was moving a hose, I heard the fluttering of wings and some distressed cheeps in a clump of phlox at my feet. Then something pecked me hard on the toe, right through my sandals.

I reached down and scooped up a young cardinal with dripping-wet feathers. It protested vigorously, but I decided that I would save it if I could, so I brought it inside to the bathroom. I called a friend who knows a lot about birds. She said to feed it tuna fish, or cooked ground beef, impaling the food on a plastic straw when I proferred it to the cardinal's gaping conical beak.

I took the bird in one hand, the straw in the other. My avian guest had a lusty appetite. It also had a fiercely independent eye, a sign of spunk. My wife was watching, and I told her that the bird would live, that I thought it could fly, and that it no longer seemed afraid of me, as its pounding heart was beginning to calm down.

No sooner had I made this observation than I made another. I had a handful of dead bird in my hand. I also had a heavy heart. My best intentions of helping a fellow creature of the garden had resulted in a tragedy—a small one, but a tragedy nonetheless. I buried the bird and began to brood. It was clear: I had scared the cardinal to death by an act of tender mercy.

By way of example, here are some thesis statements that embody the meaning and purpose of some other writers' works. Notice that sometimes more than one sentence is needed.

A great majority of our nine million college students are not in school because they want to be or because they want to learn. They are there because it has become the thing to do or because college is a pleasant place to be.

—*Caroline Bird, "College Is a*
Waste of Time and Money"

I don't know what I would do if I didn't have my car. It's better to me than any friend.

—*Guy Percy, Student*

Men's individual consumption of magazines such as *Playboy* and *Penthouse*...is apparently very dependent upon looking at such pictures as if the women in the photographs are less real than the men's sexual feelings.

—*John Stoltenberg, "What Makes*
Pornography 'Sexy'?"

For even the humblest Cuban woman, being meticulous about beauty is never frivolous.

—*Gigi Anders, "The Violet Hour"*

If Ebonics is allowed to evolve without any national standard, the only language the next generation would have in common is body language.

—*Bill Cosby, "Elements of Igno-Ebonics Style"*

*E*xplorations

1. *Together.* Compare the following sets of statements. Decide which statement in each set is relatively more objective or subjective. Which subjective statements are more positive or more negative? Which statements could serve as thesis statements? Which statements could serve as illustrations of the thesis statements?

   a. Winter is the cruelest time of year.

      In New England, snow can fall from October to April.

      Other people may dislike winter, but for me it is a wonderland for sports and parties.

   b. His lips quivered and his upper lip sweat.

      The president looked agitated and guilty.

      His speech was full of passion and sensitivity.

Focusing Your Senses

1. **Choose your subject.** To focus your mind, be sure to choose and design situations that will help you to keep focused on your subject. (Review suggestions for collecting sensory images on page 135.)

2. **Clear your mind.** To focus your senses, clear your mind of static. Sit comfortably and focus your eyes on a spot in front of you. Take a deep breath. Without moving, notice three sights, then three sounds, then three body sensations. Notice how your breathing changes, and notice whether any tensions release. Then notice two more sights, sounds, and body sensations. Next, notice one more sight, sound, and body sensation. Close your eyes for a few minutes. Return to your project by opening your eyes and stretching. Be receptive.

3. **State or show your meaning and purpose.** If you *state* your meaning and purpose, use either the explorer's or the planner's approach to formulate a subjective statement of what your topic means to you. If you *show* your meaning and purpose, choose your images carefully so that your readers will know exactly what your subject means to you. Develop and maintain a mood.

4. **Develop human interest.** Whenever possible, include human interactions in your descriptions so that your readers can identify with what is happening.

    c. Sampras wound up his racket and fired a bomb.

    Once again, Pete was slamming at the ball.

    The serve was clocked at 120 mph.

    d. The police nearly bludgeoned the man to death.

    The police restrained the perpetrator.

    The police hit the man with a club.

2. *Together.* Consider the following collections of images. For each, name the feeling, mood, or attitude of the writer who collected these images. Write a subjective thesis statement that the writer could use to show the meaning and purpose in the images.

    a. This baby never stops screaming, crying, whining, demanding. Then there are all those smells, mostly from the diaper, but also the spit-up. And you never saw such squirming in your life. He's always snatching at everything, breaking dishes, crawling around things, kicking people, and yanking off their jewelry.

    b. Black tubes hang from the wall of the auto repair shop. They look like elephant trunks. Next to them are hammers, wrenches, and screwdrivers carefully arranged like trophies. In the corner is the old dog, grease on his paws and muzzle, always sleeping. In the background, the radio is usually mumbling. With all the clanking and drilling and all the engines growling or screaming, it's hard to make out any music.

c. This ring is nearly 150 years old. The band is 18-karat gold with filigree carvings. The diamond in the center is round and multi-faceted. Exquisite ruby chips surround it. It was made for my great-great-great-grandmother's wedding.

d. First I get to the parking lot about ten minutes before my class and choose a particular aisle. I stop my car and wait. The trick is to look at people coming toward the lot. If they look like they're trying to see their car, get ready. Notice the direction their bodies are turned to as they walk. But don't be fooled. Unless they start fumbling for their keys in their pockets or have them in their hands, they're probably just going to the next building. The worst, of course, is when you are all set to take a space and the person is just getting something from the car.

3. a. *Solo.* Write a description of a child you know well. Write it from one of the following points of view:

- A loving grandparent
- A stressed parent
- The child itself
- An artist
- A jealous sibling
- A dentist
- Your special relationship (e.g., as a neighbor)

Be sure to relate your subjective experience of the child. Write a thesis statement and/or relate your feelings with images that clearly carry your attitude. Enliven your description by appealing to all the senses. In addition, relate how the child talks, and quote him or her.

b. *Solo.* Write another description of the child, using a different point of view.

c. *Together.* Read and compare your pairs of descriptions.

- What does the child mean to the writer in each description?
- How does the writer relate these subjective attitudes?
- Which senses are favored in the descriptions?
- How do the selections of sensory images relate the writers' points of view?
- How could the writer revise these descriptions to more fully reflect the intended meaning?

Variations. Do Exploration 3 using either of the following subjects:

  a. Write about a pet or a neighborhood animal.

  b. Write about a television or movie personality.

4. a. *Together.* Bring papers in progress to class. Read each aloud. Help each other discern what the subject means to the writer. Ask questions offered in the sidebar "Finding Meaning and Purpose." Help each other formulate some subjective thesis statements for each paper.

  b. *Solo.* Revise your paper with a clear focus on what your subject means to you. Choose and create more sensory images that will clearly relay your attitude to your readers.

Organizing Sensations

So far in this chapter, you have explored how to collect, focus, and find meaning and purpose through your senses. In order to keep your readers' interest and to most effectively present your observations, you will have to organize and develop your work. Notice the difference between student James Wong's two descriptions of his roommate:

First draft

```
              My Room...mate

    I am in my dorm room. The room is square, white, and made
of cinder blocks. There are two closets. The floor is made
of linoleum. There is a bathroom that we share with another
room. There are two windows. The room used to be tidy. That
was before my roommate settled in. My roommate is a sloven.
He infested our room with his junk. He possesses some basic
characteristics one would expect from a college roommate,
such as laziness and untidiness. He is a chemistry major.
His father owns an automobile shop. His mother sends him
food. He also has some of the most unusual bad habits I have
encountered.
```

In this first draft, James focuses on how his roommate treated their living quarters. Early on, he clearly states his attitude and collects images to show what he means. But James jumps from one idea to another, one sense to another, and one area to another. Although his peers found his essay humorous and engaging, they also found it somewhat hectic to read. So, James decided to reorganize his description:

Second draft

                        My Room...mate

        I am in my dorm room. The room is square and white, and
it used to be tidy. That was before my roommate settled in.
My roommate is a sloven. He infested our room with his junk.
He possesses some basic characteristics one would expect
from a college roommate, such as laziness and untidiness.
He also has some of the most unusual bad habits I have
encountered.
        We shall start with his laziness. He seldom washes his
laundry, so you can imagine the exquisite foul smell of his
clothes, especially his socks. They smell like rotten eggs
even if I'm ten feet away from them. Pheew!
        As for untidiness, his clothing is all over the place. I
almost can't walk anywhere without stepping on them, since
they're all over the floor. Luckily, I still have my bed and
desk or else I wouldn't be able to sit.
        Some of the bad habits my roommate possesses are that he
enjoys sleeping with his shoes on and he has a tendency to
keep bottle caps in his pocket. Other bad habits of his are
that, in the bathroom, he leaves his razor and shaving gel
on the shower floor or in the soap dish. Someone is going to
slip and get hurt one of these days. He also uses everyone's
soap and shampoo when he showers.
        Whenever I get back to my room, I feel like I just entered
the city dump. That's what our room looks like. If I tidied
the place today, tomorrow it would turn into a dump again.
I think nobody can get a worse roommate than mine.

Reflections _____

1. Point to specific transitions in James's first draft that seem illogical or abrupt.

2. How did James reorganize his paper for his second draft?

3. Mark the sensory details in James's second draft.

4. How did reorganizing help James find more sensory details to include in his description?

5. Could James reorganize or expand his essay? If so, how? If not, why not?

Just as you can take either an explorer's or a planner's approach to focusing, so, too, you can take either approach to organizing:

1. *Explorer's approach:* Collect your sensory images and notice how you are starting to organize them. Then you can decide on a strategy for organizing and revising. As you revise, you will collect more images to fill in the skeleton structure that your strategy provides.

2. *Planner's approach:* Decide on a strategy for organizing your paper. Write a thesis stating how you already feel. Collect sensory images to fill in the skeleton structure your strategy provides.

As always, strive to be flexible. You might write your first draft using a planner's approach, only to decide that you want to loosen up with a free-write. As you freewrite, you might find another strategy that will be more effective for organizing your observations.

After reading the suggestions in the sidebar on how to organize sensations, do some of the Explorations that follow.

*E*xplorations

1. **a.** *Together and Solo.* Describe the drawing of the woman in Figure 5.1 (page 97) for a reader who hasn't seen it. Choose an organizing strategy that will help engage your reader and accurately describe what is happening and how it feels to you.

   b. *Together.* Read your descriptions aloud. For each paper, notice:

   - The organizing strategy
   - Which sensory details were included or ignored
   - How the writer felt about the picture
   - How aware the writer was of the reader.

   In your responses, point to particular words, phrases, and sentences the writer used.

2. **a.** *Solo.* Choose an interesting and unusual object. List sense images about it, *or* freewrite your observations. Discover what

How to Organize Sensations

1. ***Start and end*** your work with the most interesting images that will engage your audience and fulfill your purpose, and/or start and end your work by stating what your subject means to you: your attitude, feeling, or purpose. Use human interest.

2. ***Shape*** your description of the object, place, person, or event to best orient your reader and relate your sensations. When appropriate, tell your reader which strategy you are using. Use one of the following strategies:

   Thesis and Support. Make a claim about your subject and support it with sensory detail. If you make *additional* specific claims about your subject, support these claims as well, preferably one at a time.

   Spatial. Use *one* of these strategies: top to bottom *or* bottom to top; left to right *or* right to left; one corner to the other; clockwise *or* counterclockwise; here and there; in relation to a point.

   You-are-there. Give your readers a you-are-there feeling by leading them through an experience as it happened.

   Before and After. Describe your subject as it was before and after a significant event.

   Senses. Describe your subject by appealing to one kind of sensation. Then describe it again using another sense.

   Chronological. Relate an experience as it happens or happened in time.

   Comparison or Contrast. Compare or contrast your subjects by describing one completely and then the other. Or compare or contrast your subjects by zig-zagging between them on each point of comparison or contrast.

the object means to you. Choose an organizing strategy and describe the object in writing. Use as many sense details as you can. Engage your readers' interest with sense appeal, so that they will want to own such an object as well.

   b. *Together.* Bring your descriptions to class. Bring your objects in a *closed bag or box.* Read the descriptions to each other in small groups. Then reveal your object. Discuss details that might have been included in the written descriptions to better engage readers. Were the organizing strategies effective?

3. *Solo.* Describe a person or a relationship between two persons. Be clear about your feelings and point of view. Show us the person(s) in

action and use quotes. Focus on sense appeal. Organize your essay so as to engage your readers.

4. **a.** *Solo.* Choose an event or activity in which you plan to participate in the next few days, such as a particular concert, sport, theater event, dance, or hobby. Referring to the sense star in Figure 6.1 (page 135), take careful notes either during or soon after the event. Freewrite about the event to explore what it means to you. Choose an organizing strategy. Write a description of the event or activity, using sense appeal.

   b. *Together.* Read your descriptions to each other. Point to your favorite words, phrases, and sentences. Discuss the organizing strategies. Ask questions to help each other revise.

Comparisons and Clichés

How do you describe the taste of coffee to someone who has never tasted it, or the colors in a sunset to someone who has always been blind? How do you describe a pain to the doctor who could never feel your pain? How do you describe a knock in your engine to the mechanic if your car just won't make that sound when you're at the service station? The best way is to compare what you experience to something that someone else can experience too. Drawing comparisons enlivens your writing and engages your reader.

Read student Lydia Gordon's description of a trip to a hamburger restaurant. Notice how she uses comparisons to relate and enliven her experiences for her reader:

```
                    Never Again

     Going to Burger Barn was a disgusting experience for me.
As soon as my sister April and I walked to the door, the
smell attacked us. It smelled like an old underground subway
station that hadn't been cleaned for years. I wanted to turn
around and get out, but my sister grabbed me by the arm and
insisted that I stay until she ordered.
     As I waited, I looked around at my surroundings and felt
my nose and lips curl as if someone were shoving cod liver
oil at me. It was terrible. There was a length of toilet tis-
sue curled on the floor like a snake that had been wrestled
to death by a hungry lion. The floor itself was supposed to
be white (as it was under one of the tables) but instead it
was yellowed like a set of rotting teeth. Ketchup was
```

smeared on the walls as if someone had tried to wipe his or her hands on it. There was dirt and tartar sauce on the tables that reminded me of soap scum in a polluted pond. I don't know how April could put up with the smell, either. I think she was too hungry to care.

When we entered, I had also been struck by the noise inside. People around us were arguing either among themselves or with the cashier. The phone was ringing and babies were crying.

April received her order and sat next to me. I told her, "It took long enough." She took the burger out of the box and felt it. She asked me to touch it. It was soggy and felt like the grease was stuck to the bread, making it look like pink dough. She wanted a refund, but I wouldn't let her get it. I didn't want to spend another moment in there.

April finally tasted it. From the expression on her face I knew it wasn't good. I laughed and asked her for a bite. I spit it back into the plate. It tasted like the dog food I once tried on a dare. It was half cooked, the meat still red, the grease oozing out, and it stuck to my hands. I lost my appetite. Burger Barn is a great place to start a weight loss program.

*R*eflections _____

1. What is Lydia's main purpose in writing the paper? What mood is she trying to create? How does she communicate this?

2. To what senses does Lydia tend to appeal? Point to particular images in Lydia's paper.

3. Are there any parts of "Never Again" that could be expanded to appeal to the senses that Lydia doesn't emphasize?

4. Underline portions of Lydia's paper where she uses comparisons to communicate her experiences. Are they fresh and new, or have you heard them before?

5. Are there any questions and suggestions you would offer Lydia if she were to revise "Never Again"?

Many comparisons—such as "white as snow"—have lost their zest because they have been overused. Overused expressions are called *clichés* after the sound made by a stereotyper (a printing machine) as it moves monotonously back and forth: *cliché, cliché, cliché.* Because they are too general, clichés do not help you either to develop your senses or to communicate your purpose to your audience. Clichés may feel safe and familiar: "Everybody knows what I'm saying." But clichés suggest lazy thinking by the person using them. Thoughtful listeners and readers lose respect for someone who relies on clichés.

Take, for example, "white as snow." Snow can take on many shades of color from blinding white to slush brown. Because most people have heard it before, the expression is an invitation for them to tune out. Compare "white as snow" with "white as a drift of new snow against a red barn." The contrast of the snow against the specific red barn focuses the mind and offers something you can imagine. Or consider the phrase "white as the skull of a dead vampire." The comparison is startling and humorous, so it forces you to form a picture in your mind. By either giving more details or forming fresh, new comparisons, you enliven your mind, engage your readers, and communicate your purpose.

In Chapter 13, you will have opportunities to write extended essays in which you compare and contrast. Here are some Explorations to help you start enlivening your work with fresh, new comparisons.

*E*xplorations _____

1. *Solo or Together.* For the next week, collect at least twenty-five comparisons from what you read or hear. Note that comparisons are often signaled by words and expressions such as *like, as, reminds me of,* and *as if.* Country and rock songs, especially, are filled with them. Bring these lists to class and consider which comparisons offer vivid, new images and which are overused and clichéd.

2. a. *Together.* Add some overused expressions to the following list of clichéd comparisons that refer to qualities. Use adjectives and nouns.

Smooth as silk	Cold as ice
Quick as a wink	Stiff as a board
Green as grass	Quiet as a mouse

   b. *Solo or Together.* Choose adjectives from the list of clichés you develop, and either revive them with specific details or write vivid, new comparisons. As you write, note the kinds of audiences that your comparison would engage, the attribute it could communicate, and the purpose it could satisfy.

3. **a.** *Together.* Add to the following list of clichéd comparisons that refer to activities and experiences:

Work like a dog	Sweat like a pig
Sing like an angel	Run like the devil
Sleep like a baby	Walk like a man
Feel like a wreck	Look like death

   b. *Solo or Together.* Choose verbs from the list of clichés you develop and either revive them with specific details or write vivid, new comparisons.

4. *Together and Solo.* Review for sense appeal some of the essays you are writing. Discuss whether any of your descriptions might be enlivened with comparisons. Revise the essays, incorporating fresh, new comparisons. Identify and replace clichés.

Reading for Sense Appeal

As you answer the following questions about your readings, point to particular words, phrases, and sentences to support your claims. Consult a dictionary for further insights into familiar and unfamiliar words.

1. Why is this subject meaningful to the writer?
2. What are some purposes the writer might have had in writing this piece?
3. Does the writer use a thesis statement?
4. To which senses does this writing appeal?
5. To which senses does this writing *not* appeal? Would it improve the paper to add more sense appeal?
6. Does the writer tell too much without showing?
7. Is the writer relatively more subjective or objective?
8. How does the writer organize sensations?
9. Does the writer enliven the work with fresh, new comparisons?
10. How might the writer have improved the sense appeal of this piece?

*E*xploration_____

Together and Solo. Using the sidebar on reading for sense appeal, reflect on the following passages from the works of professional writers. Then choose your favorite from these selections and write your own essay in response. Focus on a subject that resembles either the topic or style of the author you chose. Strive to create sense appeal. Then discuss your essays, using the same sidebar.

READING FOR SENSE APPEAL

From *Feel No Pain*

John Seabrook

In anticipation of the 1996 Olympic games in Atlanta, John Seabrook, a staff writer for The New Yorker, *wrote an article on one of the sporting events, rowing. In this passage, he describes the felt experience of competing in this sport.*

The paradox of rowing is that this most physically demanding of sports is about eighty per cent mental, and the higher you rise in the sport the more important mental toughness becomes. Rowers have to face the grim consequences of starting a two-thousand-metre race with a sprint—a strategy no runner, swimmer, cyclist, or cross-country skier would consider using in a middle-distance event. Since rowers race with their backs to the finish line, the psychological advantage of being ahead in the race—where you can see your opponents but they can't see you—is greater than the physiological disadvantage of stressing the body severely so early in the race. If you get behind, something like "unswing" can happen: the cumulative effect of the group's discouragement can make the individuals less inspired. Therefore, virtually every crew rows the first twenty or thirty strokes at around forty-four strokes a minute (which is pretty much flat out) before settling down to around thirty-seven for the body of the race.

As a result of this shock to the system, the rower's metabolism begins to function anaerobically within the first few seconds of the race. This means that the mitochondria in the muscle cells do not have enough oxygen to produce ATP, which is the source of energy, and start to use glycogen and other compounds stored in the muscle cells instead: they begin, as it were, to feed on themselves. These compounds produce lactic acid, which is a major source of pain. In this toxic environment, capillaries in the hardest-working muscles begin to dilate, while muscles that aren't working as hard go into a state of ischemia—the blood flow to them partially shuts down. Meanwhile, the level of acid in the blood continues to rise. Mike Shannon, a sports physiologist who works at the new Olympic training center, outside San Diego, told me that the highest levels of lactic acid ever found in athletes—as measured in parts per million in the bloodstream—were found in the blood of oarsmen, about thirty parts per million. "That's a tremendous amount of pain," he said.

Marathon runners talk about hitting "the wall" at the twenty-third mile of the race. What rowers confront isn't a wall; it's a hole—an abyss of pain, which opens up in the second minute of the race. Large needles are being driven into your thigh muscles, while your forearms seem to be splitting. Then the pain becomes confused and disorganized, not like the windedness of the runner or the leg burn of the biker but an all-over, savage unpleasantness. As you pass the five-hundred-metre mark, with three-quarters of the race still to row, you realize with dread that you are not going to make it to the finish, but at the same time the idea of letting your teammates down by not rowing your hardest is unthinkable. Therefore, you are going to die.

In a sense, all the training you do as an oarsman is to prepare you for this critical moment in the race, which is extremely dramatic, though it doesn't show up on television. But heavyweight oarsmen are famously laconic by nature, and they almost never talk about pain; it's a taboo subject. The feeling is that if you talk about pain you might begin to fear it, and the fear will get into your head in funny ways, both in the specific dread of racing and the long-term dread of training, like a psychic version of repetitive-stress injury. When I asked Redgrave about the pain, he said, "What pain? There's no pain," as though he didn't even know what I was talking about.

From *Of Wolves and Men*

Barry Lopez

A naturalist, Lopez has devoted his life to observing and closely describing the lives of wild animals. Here is a short excerpt of his book-length description of wolves.

It is now late in the afternoon. The wolf has stopped traveling, has lain down to sleep on cool earth beneath a rock outcropping. Mosquitoes rest on his ears. His ears flicker. He begins to waken. He rolls on his back and lies motionless with his front legs pointed toward the sky but folded like wilted flowers, his back legs splayed, and his nose and tail curved toward each other on one side of this body. After a few moments he flops on his side, rises, stretches, and moves a few feet to inspect—minutely, delicately—a crevice in the rock outcropping and finds or doesn't find what draws him there. And then he ascends the rock face, bounding and balancing momentarily before bounding again, appearing slightly unsure of the process—but committed. A few minutes later he bolts suddenly into the woods, achieving full speed, almost forty miles per hour, for forty or fifty yards before he begins to skid, to lunge at a lodgepole pine cone. He trots away with it, his head erect, tail erect, his hips slightly to one side and out of line with his shoulders, as though hindquarters were impatient with forequarters, the cone inert in his mouth. He carries it for a hundred feet before dropping it by the trail. He sniffs it. He goes on.

From *Lollapalooza, No Longer So Ambivalent About Bigness*

Jon Pareles

In the following paragraph from a review, music critic Pareles offers a dynamic description of some metal bands featured on the Lollapalooza tour.

Among metal bands, Lollapalooza chose well. Metallica snarls and thrashes while Soundgarden broods, but both bands demonstrated once again the profound affinity between stadiums and power chords. Hefty, uncluttered riffs and booming drums resonated like acts of nature. Metallica's set was a 90-minute sing-along punctuated by flashpots and fireworks; Soundgarden's made depression sound muscular. Screaming Trees, a long-running Seattle grunge band, has finally found melodies that are worthy of both its grinding riffs and Mark Lanergan's husky voice.

From *Dead as a Dollar*

James Gleick

In the following selection, columnist Gleick introduces his article on how electronic currency is changing our experience of money.

Cash is dirty—The New Jersey turnpike tried to punish toll collectors recently for wearing latex gloves (thus giving the driving clientele a "bad impression"), but who can blame them? Cash is heavy—$1 million in $20 bills weighs more than you can lift, and drug dealers have been disconcerted to note that their powdered merchandise is handier for smuggling than the equivalent money. Cash is inequitable—if you are one of the 50 million Americans poor enough to be "unbanked," you pay extortionate fees to seedy, bulletproofed check-cashing operations (even more extortionate than the fees charged for automatic teller machines, which are often up to 1 or 2 percent and rising). Cash is quaint, technologically speaking, unless you're impressed by intaglio-steel-plate-printed paper with embedded polyester strips (meant to inconvenience counterfeiters). Cash is expensive—tens of billions of dollars drain from the economy each year merely to pay for the printing, trucking, safekeeping, vending, collecting, counting, armored-guarding and general care and feeding of our currency.

Cash is dying.

From *One Writer's Beginnings*

Eudora Welty

In her autobiography One Writer's Beginnings, *Welty often writes about her experience of words themselves.*

In my sensory education I include my physical awareness of the *word.* Of a certain word, that is; the connection it has with what it stands for. At around age six, perhaps, I was standing by myself in our front yard waiting for supper, just at that hour in a late summer day when the sun is already below the horizon and the risen full moon in the visible sky stops being chalky and begins to take on light. There comes the moment, and I saw it then, when the moon goes from flat to round. For the first time it met my eyes as a globe. The word "moon" came into my mouth as though fed to me out of a silver spoon. Held in my mouth the moon became a word. It had the roundness of a Concord grape Grandpa took off his vine and gave me to suck out of its skin and swallow whole, in Ohio.

Berry Treasure

Molly O'Neill

In her weekly column on food that appears in The New York Times Magazine, *O'Neill often offers delicious descriptions of specific foods. Here is her essay on raspberries.*

Most spring foods symbolize renewal, but raspberries are different. Their drama, though perennial, is not a simple one. Rather, it's all about sweetness hard won—the triumph of tenderness over adversity.

Anyone familiar with the prickly tangle of a rambling raspberry bush knows of what I speak. Harvesting raspberries is a lot like cutting roses: hands and limbs bear scratches that last longer than the taste of the fruit or the scent of the rose. And yet, while the bushes scrape and scar, the berry itself demands a soft, gentle hand. Lazy picking, a careless toss in the bucket, and you've got jam.

But there is nothing jamlike or cloying about a raspberry, indeed nothing sentimental at all. A raspberry's sweetness is veiled by a musky, almost bitter perfume. The lesson here is one of authenticity. The fruit is no less sweet because its sweetness is slow to be revealed.

Tuck into a bowl of raspberries and cream, and the soft, pliant body of the berry and its velvety jacket seduce immediately. Still, the tough little seeds hiding in the drupelets can be a rude wake-up call. And there is the additional betrayal of coming upon a bitter berry, plucked from the same bough as a half-dozen others bursting with sweet perfume.

A native of eastern Asia (where there are more than 200 varieties), the raspberry can be used to give an exotic sweet and sour tone to lamb or duck, the necessary astringency to a marinade or a flowery note to vinegar for salads. Raspberries are synonymous with jelly and jam, sorbet and tarts, and vibrant dessert sauces. A dash of raspberry vinegar in water over ice, or a splash of raspberry liqueur (like Chambord) in Champagne can be the equivalent of an oasis on a turgid afternoon.

Having grown up on homemade raspberry jam, I can't imagine mornings without it. But for me, it's equally difficult to actually plan whipping up a batch. Only after the tempestuous little critters threaten to rot, and I've eaten my fill of them fresh, do I consider warming and sugaring them. Which, of course, happens on a fairly regular basis from late April to early June.

The sight of a cardboard crate filled with raspberries makes me greedy for their flavor, which can be relied on to be unreliable: exhilarating one bite, confounding the next. Thus the raspberry paradigm—difficult, fragile, complicated. That raspberries are all these things and still sweet makes them endlessly compelling. For as long as there has been spring, people have been inspired by them.

As Waverley Root wrote: "There is a harmony among all things and the places where they are found." He was simply echoing an unnamed poet from the crusades who rhymed: "Raspberries grow by the way, / With pleasure you may assay."

*C*hapter Review

1. *Solo.* Choose three specific strategies from this chapter that you want to remember, such as using the sense star (Figure 6.1). For each strategy, do the following:

   a. Record the strategy at the top of a page.

   b. Describe the strategy.

    c. Write about why this strategy is important to you. Offer examples from your own writing to show how you have experimented with it.

    d. Using your own words and insights, write advice to a new writer on how to use this strategy.

    e. Wherever it is appropriate, quote directly from *The Flexible Writer.* Acknowledge your source and use proper punctuation.

2. *Together.* Share the results of review question 1.

Chapter 7

Organizing

This chapter offers opportunities to

—Explore the dynamics of **organizing**

—Write **leads, titles,** and **endings**

—Learn when to use **thesis** and **topic** statements

—Develop your work for **coherence** and **unity**

—Learn how to **shape** and to **outline**

—**Organize** writing to satisfy different purposes

> Good form is whatever keeps the
> reader feeling at home.
> —*Martin Joos, Writer*

The Dynamics of Organizing

Cartoonist Gary Larson drew a "boneless chicken farm" with chickens draped on stones, fences, and the ground, as if they were rags and not fowl. A chicken without bones is just not a chicken. A human without a skeleton can't survive. A building without beams and girders is just a pile of rubble. So, too, each piece you write needs some *structure* to keep you and your readers focused and secure. You create the structure of what you write by *organizing.*

Applications and other forms are structured to direct you to do specific things such as record your name, list previous jobs, and offer references. How a piece of writing is formed or structured directs your audience in how to read and what to do in response. If a letter of application is well written, for example, it directs your audience to offer you an interview. If the letter is carelessly written, it directs your audience to set your letter aside.

In this book you know when a new chapter is beginning because the words begin lower on the page, there are summaries of what to expect, and there is a quote or two. You come to know that the words *Chapter Review* signal that it's time to stop, reflect, review, and perhaps take a breather from reading. At the end of this book there is an index. You would not read through the index from beginning to end the way you would a chapter. You just dip into it when you want help in finding a certain topic in the book.

Chapter breaks and the index are only two examples of the organizational structures that help establish relationships between a writer, her topic, and her readers. Organizing devices steady the flow of ideas and support your learning. This chapter outlines many more strategies that help you organize short as well as long pieces of writing.

Organizing and the Writing Process

Organizing, Focusing, and Coherence

As you focus a piece of writing, you need to develop an organizing principle that you and your audience will experience as *flow*. The technical terms for this flow are *unity* and *coherence*. When a piece of writing has unity, all the parts work together to maintain the focus of the piece. If any details or information were introduced that didn't help maintain the focus, it would be clear that something was irrelevant. When a piece of writing has *coherence*, the *arrangement* "holds together" the whole piece, just as glue adheres two pieces of paper. If any given part were taken out, something would clearly be missing.

Chapters 5 and 6 help you to understand how to create unity in your work. This chapter offers you strategies for developing coherence. You will learn how to begin your writing, structure its body, and create transitions leading to an effective ending.

Organizing and Collecting

When you organize your writing, you may discover that you have not collected enough information or ideas. For example, suppose you were writing about the effects of the Vietnam War on a particular veteran and decided to organize your essay in chronological order. If you were missing information on the year following the veteran's discharge, you would want to interview him about that time. Or suppose you decided to write about your experiences working through an injury and organized your essay to represent the full range of your experience from positive to negative. If you had forgotten to write about negative experiences or had written only about the pain and not the lessons you learned, you would want to collect more experiences to fill the gaps in your structure.

Organizing, Consulting, and Revising

Different readers may notice different patterns in your writing. When you consult with others, note carefully the parts of your essay that confuse or disorient your readers. You may need to reorganize your work or move back to another phase of the writing process. Revise your work with your purpose and audience in mind.

When to Organize

Some writers prefer the planner's style and organize their ideas and information *before* they begin to write. Other writers prefer the explorer's style and freewrite until they notice a plan developing *through* their writing. Most writers combine both styles, sketching a plan, writing, identifying an emerging structure, reorganizing, and so on. You will develop your own strategies for when to organize any given piece of writing.

Leads

Newswriters call introductions "leads." This term reminds us that introductions are meant to *lead* the reader to read on. Effective leads—in any kind of writing—focus the reader's mind as quickly as possible by offering something familiar and something new. Especially in a world where television pictures flicker away in five seconds, you need to find ways to sustain your own and your reader's attention. Effective leads do four things at once: (1) focus, (2) familiarize, (3) interest, and (4) immerse your reader in your writing. In addition, writing effective leads helps you to focus, familiarize, interest, and immerse yourself, as the writer.

Fourteen Strategies for Leads

There are many ways to focus yourself and engage your reader. Here are fourteen of the most-used strategies for doing so. Writers often combine them. To show you how flexible these strategies are, one subject has been chosen to illustrate them.

Leads that familiarize

1. Illustrating.   To familiarize your reader, you can focus on particular examples that illustrate your topic. Here is the lead from Ellen Goodman's article from the *Boston Globe*, "Checks on Parental Power." In it, she considers a law that allows parents to put children into mental hospitals:

> First, consider the stories.
> An eleven-year-old retarded boy was brought to a mental hospital with a teddy bear under his arm. His parents were, they said, going on a two-week vacation. They never came back.

In her lead, Goodman offers a clear illustration of the topic of her essay. Similarly, the lead for Chapter 8 of this book, "Consulting," illustrates what a writing community is like. Both give you a you-are-there experience.

2. Imaging.   A picture, a sound, a taste, a smell, a touch, or a movement can give your readers a you-are-there experience that leads them to read on. The image of the boy with a teddy bear under his arm makes a strong impression on Goodman's readers. Student LaDonna Kiley began her paper on child abuse with a strong image:

> My friend Shelly and I heard a moaning, like a cat, coming from the old boarded-up building we found. We thought maybe we could find a kitten to take home. When we found the door where the crying was coming from, we didn't know what we would see. We opened the door. A terrible smell came out, like a bathroom that's never been cleaned. There on the floor was a little child, naked, with his hair all matted against his face. His hands were tied to the corner of the bed with a piece of clothesline. Around his wrists were all these bite marks. He had been trying to get free.

In this lead, LaDonna offers us detailed sensory images to involve us as her readers. She kept the most powerful image for last.

3. Quoting.   A time-honored way to begin academic essays is to quote an expert in the field. You will notice that each chapter in this book begins with such quotes. Included, as well, are quotes by students like yourself, with whom you may identify. The purpose of quoting is to lend authority to your writing. Using effective quotes shows that you are familiar with others who have spoken well on the topic. Therefore, you are already a part of the community to which the audience wants to belong. Your quote may be from known people, books (such as the Bible), or the news. If your source is not likely to be familiar to your audience, offer some indication of the person's credentials. This is how a student began an essay about children's rights:

> In her essay "Checks on Parental Power," Ellen Goodman states: "Parents obviously have and must have a wide range of decisions over their children's lives. But they don't have absolute power and never have."

It is also effective to quote persons *about* whom you are writing. This gives your reader a feeling of knowing the person, too. So, for example, if you knew a child who was hospitalized unjustly, you could quote her or him. If you were writing about a grandmother, you could quote her favorite piece of advice to you.

4. Stating Your Thesis. Writing a thesis statement—a statement of your main point—is *only one* of the ways to begin an essay. Usually, this is the strategy used in essay exams, legal documents, news reports, business memos, and other pieces of writing in which the purpose is to quickly relay information or argue an interpretation. (This strategy is further explored in Chapters 5, 12, and 13.) The following lead states the thesis of a student paper:

> All children should have lawyers to protect their rights, even against their parents' wishes. Today, the judicial system in the United States is allowing parents more rights over their children's lives. This means that parents can put their children into a mental institution even if there is nothing wrong with the children. Children, in turn, have taken their parents to court.

5. Stating Your Purpose. You may find it helpful to state your purpose in writing. Sometimes you will leave this statement in the final draft. Sometimes the purpose of your writing will be so clear from your lead that there will be no reason to state that purpose. Here is an example of a lead that states the writer's purpose and method:

> In this paper I will argue that children have the right
> to decide where they want to live. By considering several
> situations, I will show that parents who don't respect this
> right are being abusive.

6. Defining. The word *defining* literally means to show the limits of a word, subject, or problem. The purpose of defining words and expressions is to establish a common understanding with your reader and to clarify your position on a subject. You can define your subject by what it is or by what it is not. Here is one possible way to define the expression *children's rights:*

> We can define children's rights according to the United States Declaration of Independence as the right to life, liberty, and the pursuit of happiness. Parents who do not honor these rights for their children are breaking the law.

7. Telling a Story. Humans are, by nature, storytellers. Children love bedtime stories, and gossip is all too popular. Telling a story can be a very effective way to focus yourself and involve your readers. Notice how this strategy is used in the following example:

> When I was a child, my father always told me to stick up for myself. However, there came a time when I had to stick up for myself with him. It was a Saturday morning and I had an extra soccer practice; my father had other plans for me. He expected me to clean out the inside of his car for him because he was going to Penn Station to pick up an important client that day. This was the beginning of an ongoing battle in my teens that culminated in our landing in court one day.

8. Showing Relationship to the Subject. To give readers a reason to read your paper, show them what it means to *you:*

> The most difficult thing a parent can ever do is to place his own child in an institution. Soon after my older son turned sixteen, I took him to a county hospital that would be the first stop on a long journey for both of us. For him it was almost a relief. He knew what was happening; nevertheless, I was filled with fear and anxiety. Even now as I write I can feel the tightness in my chest that I felt when I saw him standing in the corridor as I walked away.

You can also show relationship to a subject by *reflecting on your current writing process,* as the father who wrote this excerpt does.

9. Offering History. You can help orient your reader to your topic by offering historical background:

> In ancient Greece when a child was born with a deformity or if the child was an excess female, the child would be placed on a mountaintop to die. Throughout history, children have been forced to do work that even adults found difficult. Child abuse, in some countries, has been considered to be the best way to discipline the child. It is only in this century that we are coming to understand the need to legally protect children's rights.

10. Using the News. Student Jill Minor was very concerned about child abuse. She started her essay by reporting a current local news event:

> On March 14, 1987, Susan Greenville from Somer, New Jersey was stabbed 23 times in the upper chest and received a fractured skull from a 33-year-old man. Susan Greenville was a four-year-old child. The 33-year-old man was her father. This occurred after repeated beatings that nobody reported. My argument begins here. How could the people living near the Greenville family have let such a thing happen?

Leads that surprise

11. Asking Questions. Asking a question, you invite your readers to read on for the answer. Asking a question, you inspire yourself to discover an answer through writing—a strategy that is further explored in Chapters 5, 12, and 13.

Especially in academic settings, it is appropriate and helpful to begin essays with a question or questions, as student Dina Singer does in her essay "For Our Children's Sake?":

> ```
> Are we going back to previous times when children had no
> more rights than cattle? Some migrant children still work
> fourteen hours a day picking fruits and vegetables on farms.
> Can we afford to spend money on putting people into space?
> Countless children live on the streets with no place to call
> their own.
> ```

The questions do not have to be asked in the first lines of the essay but may be asked after some other introductory remarks. Notice how Dina Singer works her title as a question and uses questions in her lead, as well.

12. Stating Something Controversial or Contradictory. Dina considered starting her essay by saying something controversial:

> Let's take food from homeless children and with the money saved, send another person to the moon. That's what the government seems to be saying every time they make cuts on food budgets for children. But children have a right to expect to be fed so that they can grow into healthy adults.

13. Surprising with Statistics. Student Adam Joyner used startling statistics to rivet his readers' attention:

> This year over 40% of the homeless are under the age of eleven. Of these children 30% won't reach the age of eighteen, and 70% will have had experiences with drugs and/ or prostitution.

14. Using Humor. Put your readers at ease *and* encourage them to read on by leading with a joke or a touch of humor. Of course, not all topics lend themselves to humor. The following is a humorous lead to an essay about everyday negotiations between a parent and child:

> When I was a child my father would punish me by telling me he would put me in a Macy's bag and return me. Whenever I complained he said, "So, sue me." Well, I just received my law degree, and guess what my first case is going to be?

Writing Leads

Leads are written first and they are written last. With practice and luck, you sometimes devise a lead that works the first time. Most of the time, however, you will revise your lead many times, often finishing it last.

Writers have problems with leads during the writing process for two reasons: (1) they adhere too much to early attempts, or (2) they overdo

---

Writing Leads

1. Find a lead.
2. Choose a strategy.
3. Cross out false leads.

Fourteen Strategies for Leads

1. Illustrating
2. Imaging
3. Quoting
4. Stating your thesis
5. Stating your purpose
6. Defining
7. Telling a story
8. Showing relationship to the subject
9. Offering history
10. Using the news
11. Asking questions
12. Stating something controversial or contradictory
13. Surprising with statistics
14. Using humor

strategies. Leaving in failed attempts or freewrites is like having dancers do their warm-ups during a performance on stage or like tossing the leaves and vines in with the tomatoes for sauce. Overdoing a familiarizing strategy can bore or irritate the reader. For example, telling the twentieth-century reader that William Shakespeare wrote plays is giving too much background information to readers. Overdoing a surprising strategy can confuse or turn away the reader. Several jokes in a row can wear thin, for example, and saying something too controversial can make you sound unreliable. Here are three strategies to help you write and revise your leads:

1. *Find a lead.* Working as an explorer, find your favorite sentence or paragraph from a freewrite or early draft, and bring it to the top of your piece. Repeat this in your next drafts as often as necessary until you commit yourself to a final draft.

2. *Choose a strategy.* Working as a planner, choose a strategy from the sidebar above on leads. Create several leads using that strategy, and choose the best.

3. *Cross out false leads.* A true lead engages and interests both the writer and the reader. A false lead gives the writer and reader the feeling that the writer is running in place, getting nowhere. A humorous image of this is cartoon character Fred Flintstone trying to drive off in his car: he spins his feet and goes backward before he takes off.

   One of the most useful ways to find a true lead is to learn how to cross out chunks of early attempts. Writers often cross out two and three pages of writing to get to a lead that is right. Three chapter-length attempts at the first chapter of this book were set aside in favor of the current version.

You may have to freewrite and draft several times before you find a suitable lead. The lead for this chapter, describing Gary Larson's cartoon, didn't occur to me until four years after I first started writing the first edition of this book.

You may feel reluctant, at first, to let go of false leads. There is a certain amount of satisfaction in completing a project. But experiment. Cross out false leads. Place that later paragraph up front. You can always reorganize and reincorporate the dropped portions in another part of the paper or in another paper. Crossing out false leads will improve your writing and give you greater freedom and flexibility.

*E*xplorations _____

1. *Together.* Most writers combine strategies in a given lead. Return to the examples listed for the fourteen strategies (pages 165–170). For each, notice whether the writer is combining the strategy with another. Which leads both familiarize and surprise the reader?

2. *Solo and Together.*

   a. Read through a magazine or a newspaper. Choose three leads that interest you from three separate pieces of writing. Choose three leads that you find *uninteresting*. Bring all six to class.

   b. In small groups, read your leads and discuss how they affected you and why. As a group, choose one lead that you all find very effective. Which strategies does the writer use? Read the favorite leads to the whole class. How did the writers offer something familiar and new at the same time?

The purpose of Explorations 3 through 5 is to develop flexibility in writing leads.

3. *Together.* Consider the following beginnings of student papers. For each one:

   • Decide whether you think the writing is effective.

   • Cross out false leads or parts of the leads that seem to be leading nowhere.

   • Either find a better lead in the paper itself or write a new one.

   • Experiment with different strategies or combinations of strategies for leads.

   a. Living on campus compared to living at home is different in many ways. There are advantages and disadvantages when you are living on campus. The same holds true when you are living at home. In this paper I will discuss the different aspects of living on campus and living at home with your parents.

When you are dorming you have freedom that you never had when you were staying home. You can basically do what you want when you want to.

b. "The more things change the more they stay the same." Last semester at Kean College parking was virtually impossible and this semester, as expected, the situation has not changed.

My first day at Kean College in the fall semester I found out that parking was going to be a problem. I thought if I came early I would get a parking space right up front. Apparently everyone else had the same idea....

c. Snow is one of nature's weapons in fighting excessive heat waves. It is not found in every part of the world. My country in particular sees no snow even though the temperature remains comparatively low. Some months of the year are hotter than others.

Between September and March, Nigeria is crossed by the northeast trade winds. During this time, dusty winds blow from and across the Sahara Desert bringing dusty winds and sand throughout the inland.

My first experience with snow didn't come until I came to the United States from Nigeria. What I saw was a dream come true.*

d. "Union is strength." We witness this constantly throughout our everyday lives from the machinists of Eastern Airlines, to the anti-apartheid movement in South Africa; from the teamwork of athletes on the gridiron, to the cohesiveness of a championship basketball team on the hardwood floor. Two experiences I have had which truly demonstrated the power of a union to me were in the United States Army, and a speech delivered by the Reverend Jesse Jackson.†

e. Happiness and anger is in one's inner self. It is the personality that makes me a person. Happiness in my opinion brings out joy that is held in my feelings as well as the anger that lies deep inside me.

Happiness at one point can bring laughter among myself and others. It is a sign of a smile. Being happy doesn't mean having everything like money, houses, and cars. There's a saying, "Money can't buy happiness." But happiness is the feeling of enjoying.

Anger is one aspect of my personality that brings the devil out of me. There are many times I have gotten angry at myself and others. Muscles flare, body tightens, and my body temperature rises. I can remember getting into a particular fight recently.

4. *Together.* In small groups, choose one of the following topics and develop a series of possible leads. Use as many of the fourteen strategies for leads as you can, either singly or in combination.

---

*By student Edem Ikurekong.
†By student Alan T. Russell.

    a. Can prisons rehabilitate criminals?

    b. Is joint custody good for children?

    c. Who should decide which artists should be supported by federal grants?

    d. Should women be in combat?

    e. Would it be worth letting go of some luxuries for a while to reduce dependence on nuclear energy and fossil fuels and to transfer over to solar, wind, and hydroelectric power?

5. *Solo or Together.* Read over the leads of papers you are writing. Develop different possible leads. Use the instructions for Exploration 3.

Titles

Titles must do in a short space what leads do: both familiarize and interest. Whether the stress is on familiarizing or interesting readers depends on your purpose and audience. The chapter titles in this book are designed to help you find specific aspects of the writing process that you want to explore. For example, instead of being called "Landing the Helicopter"—a title that might have surprised and amused you—Chapter 5 is called "Focusing I: Strategies." This reflects a main purpose of this book: to help you to find what you need for yourself. If the chapter were an article for a writing magazine, the title "Landing the Helicopter" might cap-

---

Ten Strategies for Titles

Strategies for titles are similar to those for leads.

Naming your topic: Children's Rights

Quoting: Suffer the Little Children

Stating your thesis: Children Have Legal Rights

Addressing your audience: Save the Children

Showing relationship to subject: My Son's Life in an Institution

Offering history: Child Abuse: From Ancient Sparta to New York

Asking questions: For Our Children's Sake?

Stating something controversial: Let's Starve Our Children

Surprising with statistics: Forty Percent of the Homeless Are Children

Using humor: Bagging Dad

Writing Titles

1. **Brainstorm** as many possible titles as you can, preferably with the help of others.

2. **Choose** for your title a favorite phrase or sentence from a freewrite or draft.

3. **List common or popular expressions and quotes** that relate to your topic. Adapt the language of your choice expression to suit your purpose and audience. For example, "Suffer the little children" is from the Bible. Check reference books of quotations, such as *Bartlett's Familiar Quotations*. The book is organized according to topics and authors.

4. **Use** one of the **ten strategies for titles.**

5. **Model your title** on ones you find in books, magazines, and newspapers. To prime yourself, do some browsing.

6. **Revise** your title. Make it brief and specific.

ture the reader who is more interested in being entertained than having an easy reference.

Writing Titles

Some authors wait until they are finished with their stories, poems, essays, chapters, or books to title them. In the writing process, though, you should always have a *working title*. The process of writing and rewriting a title helps remind you of your focus, purpose, and audience. As you develop your title, more ideas may occur to you for the body of your piece, as well.

Explorations

The purpose of these Explorations is to help you become aware of the characteristics of effective titles.

1. *Together.* Read the following titles and decide which ones interest you and why. Discuss whether each title is meant to familiarize or to surprise the reader. Which titles do both? Name the strategy or strategies the writer uses. What does each title suggest about the nature of the piece it heads? Which titles are not engaging, and why? How would you revise them? What do you learn about yourselves as readers from this Exploration?

Mother	Challenging My Fears
Crocodile	Ducks on Corrigan's Pond
How to Cram	Jealous
College Is a Waste of Time and Money	Dusk in Fierce Pajamas
But What If I Need It Some Day?	Living with Death
When Nice People Burn Books	Amusing Ourselves to Death
Write On	

2. *Together.* Bring your favorite magazines to class. In small groups or as a class, collect and record titles that interest you. Discuss them, using the suggestions offered in Exploration 1.

3. *Solo.* Choose your favorite title from Exploration 1 or 2. Freewrite for fifteen minutes in response to it. If you find you are engaged, develop this freewrite into an essay.

4. *Solo and Together.* Choose some papers you have been writing and develop titles for them. Use strategies suggested in the sidebar on writing titles. Discuss how your sense of your paper changes with different titles. Revise your paper to reflect your best one.

Endings

A tightrope walker steadies her eyes and her steps by focusing on a point at the end of her rope. Similarly, you can keep yourself focused during the writing process by keeping your eyes on a *working ending.* A working ending not only steadies you, it helps you decide what you need to reach your goal. Once you reach that goal, you will have a certain sense of completion and satisfaction. So will your reader.

The purposes of effective endings are (1) to leave a lasting impression on the reader, (2) to frame the paper for a sense of completion, and (3) to keep you focused in the writing process.

Eight Strategies for Endings

1. Use a Lead. In general, the same strategies that work for leads work for endings. In some cases, you may choose to use an ending from an earlier draft as the lead in a later one, and vice versa.

2. Full Circle. By referring to the lead, you fulfill the purpose of forming a frame for the whole piece. You can refer to the lead using the same strategies as Goodman does in her essay "Checks on Parental Power":

> Chalk one up for the folks who dropped off the boy with the teddy bear.

3. Resolution. You can solve a problem or answer a question that was posed in the lead. The father concluded his paper about his institutionalized son in this way:

> Today my thirty-year-old son is living in a group home with five other adults. He has a job folding boxes which he enjoys. He has always loved working with his hands on things he can do over and over again. Every day he goes to the pool and dazzles everyone with his 100 laps of perfectly smooth strokes. When I visit him, we go shopping for clothes just as we did when he was a little boy. But now when it's time for me to go, he's the one who walks away as I stand there in the corridor.

4. Meaning or Lesson. Formulate what your subject means to you. This will help you to better understand and revise your writing. It will also help to complete the experience of it for your readers. Here is how one student summed up the meaning of an essay:

> I learned that some things are more important than family pride. If a trusted parent is abusing a child, the child's pride must be saved first.

5. Quotation. You can offer your reader a short memorable quote or a phrase with which he or she may be familiar. This establishes a common bond at the end of a piece of writing. However, avoid overused quotations that seem clichéd (see pages 152–155 for further discussion of clichés). Write variations on them so they sound new. Here are several endings that would be appropriate for papers on children's rights. Some are direct quotes. Others remind us of quotes.

> Suffer the little children so they won't have to.
>
> The child shall be father to the man.
>
> Keep the cradle out of the trees.

6. Image. You can leave the reader with an image to remember, just as Goodman ends her essay with the image of the teddy bear and the father leaves us with the image of his son walking away.

> ### *Eight Strategies for Endings*
>
> 1. Use a lead
> 2. Full circle
> 3. Resolution
> 4. Meaning or lesson
>
> 5. Quotation
> 6. Image
> 7. Questions or problems
> 8. Summary

7. Questions or Problems.   Writing is a process not only of exploring questions but of posing new ones for further consideration. Many scientific papers end up with more questions than they started with. It's effective to end essays and papers with questions and problems. Here are two examples of such endings:

> Do we have a future if our children remain homeless?
>
> How can we identify at-risk children and the families that they come from? What can we do to help them heal?

8. Summary.   If your essay or story is long and your purpose is to clarify or stress your main points, sometimes it is appropriate to summarize them in your last paragraph. To summarize is to collect the main points that you want to remember or that you want remembered. This summary may take the form of a thesis statement.

Use this strategy *very carefully.* Readers may skim over it: they've seen the strategy before. In very short essays, avoid writing anything that sounds like "This is what I have just said." Here is an example of a summary ending:

> It is clear that there are many issues to be considered in deciding the line between children's and parents' rights. Not only safety and welfare are important but so is the quality of the life of the whole family. It is hard to develop a good balance. It must be adjusted daily, hourly in some families. In this paper I have considered some of the major court cases in recent history in which this delicate balancing either didn't occur or was too late and not enough.

Writing Endings

The clearer your lead is, the more easily you will be able to find a suitable ending. The best way to develop an effective ending is to fully write and

> ***Writing Endings***
>
> 1. ***Record*** attempted leads. The second choice for your lead may serve as your ending.
> 2. ***Choose*** and use a particular strategy for endings.
> 3. ***Repeat*** your actual lead with an interesting twist.
> 4. ***Signal*** your reader if you are ending with a summary by using an expression such as *in conclusion, to summarize, let's review, so then, reconsidering, essentially,* or *in sum.*
> 5. ***Focus on*** and ***revise working endings*** throughout the writing process.

revise the body of your paper. Use the strategies listed in the sidebar on writing endings to develop and leave a lasting impression on your readers.

*E*xplorations

1. *Together.* Choose a section from a chapter in this book or from one of the essays that are printed in entirety. Is the ending effective? What strategy is being used? Could the ending be more effective? If so, what strategy could the writer have used?

2. *Solo and Together.* Choose some papers you have been writing. Develop endings for them using strategies suggested to you in this section. Discuss how your sense of your papers changes with different endings.

3. *Solo.* For your next paper, develop a working ending to help you focus as you write the first draft. Revise the ending as new ideas develop in the process.

The Body

Depending on your purpose and audience, there are many ways you can develop the main body of your writing between your lead and your ending. The following is a discussion of ten main strategies of development. Notice that they all start with some focus. Each strategy also depends on certain transitional words that enable you to maintain coherence, guide your reader from one idea to another, and show your reader how your ideas are related. To save space, the examples used to illustrate the strategies are paragraphs. Whole essays and books are developed using these strategies either singly or in combination. The illustrations range over a variety of subjects.

Ten Strategies of Development

1. Chronological Order. When your purpose is to relate a series of events, whether personal or professional, you can follow them as they occurred through time—chronologically. Describe events *forward,* as they happened. Or, use *flashback:* start with an event in the present and reflect on events that led to it. The following two paragraphs (written by student Bruce Inge) use these strategies:

Forward

> During my early teens, cars were very attractive to me. I spent all of my time finding work so I could buy a red Oldsmobile two-door coupe. Once I bought it I spent all of my time washing it, caring for it, and riding it around the neighborhood.

Flashback

> As I sit in my new Mercedes-Benz 500E, I look back at all I've experienced in order to get where I'm sitting. Not only the past five years, but my whole life seems to have led to this. Five years ago I was driving my third red Oldsmobile two-door coupe.

Transitional words for maintaining chronological order include these: *first, later, finally, next, as soon as, suddenly,* and *earlier.*

2. Spatial Order. When your purpose is to familiarize your reader with how a place, an object, or a person looks or acts, develop your description focusing on space. You can describe your subject from *left to right, right to left, top to bottom, bottom to top, clockwise or counterclockwise, diagonally, to or from a particular focus,* or *from your particular perspective.* Here is student Loretta Durning's description of a sculpture for an art assignment. She uses a particular perspective to anchor her observations:

> One of Cuevas's works was of "wood, ceramic clay, found objects," which could describe the day-to-day acquisitions of these people wandering the streets, gathering discarded

treasures. There was a body made of clay, reclining on a bed
of wood. The eyes and mouth of its gaunt face were gaping
holes. A television mounted on the wall across the room
showed bright colors. The person on the bed looked away. A
chair stood in the corner, and hovering above it was a rope
knotted into a noose. It seemed as if the body on the bed
was so hopelessly depressed by his situation that he was
gathering the courage to end it.

Transitional words for maintaining spatial order include these: *under,
over, around, in, out, beside, next to, left, right,* and *through.*

3. Statement and Illustration. To engage your readers, illustrate
your claims. You can develop your entire essay by using a series of examples that amplify and elaborate on your statement. Here is a statement
supported by an example:

> The grading system of pluses and minuses has proved to be very dis-
> couraging to students. One student who received minuses on all his
> grades decided to switch out of his major. He said, "I always thought I
> was an 'A' student and that my professors in my major considered me a
> candidate for a scholarship. Now with all these minuses, I think I'm
> going to switch. I'm too discouraged."

Transitional expressions that link statement and example include these:
for example, for instance, as, such as, and *to illustrate.*

Your illustration may also take the form of sensory images, as in this
paragraph:

> My bedroom is a warm and cozy place. The soft rose-pink walls are
> complemented by a deep maroon and gold Persian rug. Large paisley and
> striped pillows nestle into the lofty goose down comforter. Bayberry pot-
> pourri scents the air. And if that doesn't beckon you in, the soft lights or
> the classical guitar music will.

Transitions for sensory images are most easily managed either by using
spatial development, by appealing to one particular sense, or by choosing
a variety of images to create a mood (as in the illustration).

4. Statement and Argument. If your purpose is to convince someone to adopt your point of view and to accept your claims, or if you want
to show your grasp of information, you can develop your writing by focusing on a series of statements followed by supporting arguments: reasons

why readers should believe you. This is a strategy often used in academics. Here is a statement supported with arguments:

> The college should not change the grading system to include pluses and minuses because it is unfair to those students who have been under the old system and haven't yet graduated. The change in calculating their grade point averages would put them at a disadvantage in comparison to students who will now be receiving pluses. You may argue that the pluses would be balanced out by minuses. However, in an informal survey of instructors, it was found that though they appreciate being able to award pluses, most of them are reluctant to add minuses. Students much prefer the clarity that whole grades provide. The old system also is a check on any unfairness in grading that may come from personality differences between instructors and students.

Transitional expressions that link statement and argument include these: *in order to, therefore, hence, because,* and *in sum.* Strive to anticipate others' disagreements and counterarguments. Use transitional expressions such as these: *you may argue that…, one objection could be…,* and *on the other hand….*

5. Question and Answer.   If your purpose is to question an issue or explore alternatives, you can develop your paper as a series of *questions and answers.* This is an especially effective strategy for developing and connecting ideas (as Chapters 12 and 13 show), because questions, by their very nature, lead you from one idea to the next. You can proceed in two directions (or move back and forth): *statements to questions* and *questions to statements.* For an example of this procedure, turn back to page 169 where student Dina Singer develops her lead with a series of questions and answers.

Transitional words for the question and answer strategy include these: *who, whose, what, which, when, where, how, why,* and *in response to.*

6. Problem and Solution.   If your purpose is to solve or propose a solution to a problem, you can organize your work by focusing on *problems and solutions.* You can state a problem, list possible solutions, explore the consequences of those solutions, and suggest further problems that may arise. Here is a statement of a problem with proposed solutions:

> Small rodents destroy crops and invade grain supplies. There are several approaches to solving the problem: poisons, traps, and natural forces.

Poisons are effective in destroying rodents but can affect the water supply and endanger other animals. Traps are not effective in handling a large infestation. In exploring the balance of nature, it has been found that a population of certain kinds of owls may be helpful in controlling rodents and protecting the environment at the same time.

Transitional expressions for the problem-and-solution strategy include these: *one solution is...; another approach to the problem is...; one way to think about...;* and *if this doesn't work, then....* You can also use process analysis and cause-and-effect transitions.

7. Process Analysis. When your purpose is to understand how something is done or should be done, you can focus your writing by describing or analyzing a process. Chapter 2, "The Writing Process," is organized as a process analysis.

Transitional words that help you develop process analyses include words for chronological and spatial ordering and words used to establish cause and effect.

8. Cause and Effect. When your purpose is to explain why something happened, you can develop your paper by focusing on the links between causes and effects. A cause is connected by time and space to its effect. Your task is to fill the relevant gaps in time and space. The distinction between a mere chronological or spatial development and one that establishes cause and effect is that the events have to be linked by logic and evidence. Here is a paragraph that links causes to effects:

> Sherlock Holmes proved that Beppo stole the rare, expensive pearl of the Borgias and hid it in a plaster bust of Napoleon. He proved this by showing that Beppo had all the resources for stealing and hiding it. A sister of a friend worked for the countess from whom the pearl was stolen. A cousin was a sculptor. Beppo's store sold plaster busts of Napoleon. The one in which he stashed the pearl was accidentally sold. He went around breaking these busts at customers' houses. He was the one who engineered the theft because he had the motive and the means to do so.

Transitional words for establishing cause and effect include these: *because, since, hence, therefore,* and *if...then.*

9. Classification. When your purpose is to more fully understand the differences and similarities between persons, places, objects, or events, you can develop your writing through classification. This chapter and this section classify types of organizing strategies. *Classification* is a process of finding different types within a group. For another example of classification, refer to Chapter 8, pages 209–211, which offers you a classification of different kinds of workshop personalities. To develop your classifications, use a comparison or contrast strategy.

Transitional expressions that help you classify include these: *There are _____ ways to categorize X, there are _____ kinds of X, and X is a type of _____.*

10. Comparison and/or Contrast.   When your purpose is to make connections or distinctions between two or more ideas, people, places, objects, events, or ideas, develop the body of your work by using strategies of comparison and/or contrast. When you focus on *similarities*, you write a *comparison*. When you focus on *differences*, you draw *contrasts*. You can devote a whole paper either to comparison or to contrast, or you can write a paper in which you both compare and contrast. For this strategy, begin by creating lists under your subjects that match points of comparison and contrast. Here is an illustration of corresponding lists comparing and contrasting cats and dogs as pets. In process, these lists will be much messier as you cross out and draw arrows to match points.

Cats	**Dogs**
Easy	Take time
Litter box	Need to be housebroken
Naturally clean	Need to be bathed
Food reasonably priced	Food expensive
Affectionate	Pals
Good lap sitters	Learn tricks

To develop your essay, use either the block or the zig-zag method. In the block method, you describe each subject fully before considering the next. In the zig-zag method, you move back and forth between the two or more subjects you are considering. The following paragraphs, contrasting cats and dogs as pets, illustrate the block and zig-zag methods:

Block method

Cats are the easiest pets to have and enjoy. Kittens can be trained to use a litter box in one or two days, and they are naturally clean. Supermarkets sell many cat foods at reasonable prices, so the cost of feeding them is low. Most cats are affectionate, just wanting to curl up with you and make you feel good with their purring.

Dogs are a lot of fun and a lot of trouble. They take patience and time to housebreak, and they need to be walked frequently, whatever the weather. Some of them are messy with food and water, scattering it all around their feeding bowls. As companions, they can't be beat. They love to run and play and greet you as soon as you come home.

Zig-zag method

Cats are the easiest pets to have, but dogs are more fun. All cats can be litter-trained in a few days; however, dogs can take weeks to house-break. While cats are naturally clean, dogs need regular baths or they smell terrible. Feeding a cat is easy and inexpensive. Dogs eat more than cats. Cats are good lap sitters, but dogs are more affectionate. There is no greater fun than running with a dog or throwing a stick for the dog to retrieve.

Transitional expressions that help you *compare* include *similarly, the same as, just as, also, not only…but also, like,* and *and.* Transitional words that help you *contrast* include *whereas, on the other hand, but, although, however, while,* and *although.* When you attempt to both compare and contrast in an essay, be especially careful to use transitions that clearly state when you are focusing on similarities and when you are focusing on differences.

For further discussion of comparison and contrast, turn to Chapter 13, pages 351–359.

Deduction and Induction

Even within a particular strategy for developing the body of your paper, you have different options for how you arrange your examples and evi-

Ten Strategies for Developing the Body

1. Chronological order	6. Problem and solution
2. Spatial order	7. Process analysis
3. Statement and illustration	8. Cause and effect
4. Statement and argument	9. Classification
5. Question and answer	10. Comparison and/or contrast

Matching Leads and Development

Some leads naturally call for certain kinds of development. Here are a few possible matches:

Lead	Development
Telling a story	Chronological
Offering history	Chronological
Imaging	Spatial
Quoting	Statement and argument
Stating a thesis	Statement and illustration
Stating your purpose	Problem and solution
Asking questions	Question and answer
Using the news	Cause and effect

dence. In this section you are offered seven shapes to help you structure what you write.* You can use the planner's style and decide on a shape for your writing before you begin, or you can use the explorer's style and develop your sense of the shape in process.

There are two directions from which you can develop the body of a piece of writing. You can state your thesis and provide illustrations of it or arguments for it. This is called *deduction.* Or, you can shape your essay by offering a series of examples concluding with a summary thesis statement. This is called *induction.* You can combine deduction and induction in a given essay as well.

Your thesis statement can come in different places in your essay:

1. The first sentence
2. The last sentence of the first paragraph
3. The first sentence of the second paragraph, following a description, example, or story told in the first paragraph
4. Part of your ending

Whether you use deduction or induction, and where you place a thesis statement, depend on your purpose, audience, and style. Experiment

---

*Note that each academic discipline has special formats for how to write reports, essays, proposals, memos, and other types of writing. Before beginning a writing assignment in any course, be sure to ask your instructor for guidelines on how you should structure your writing.

Deduction and Induction

Deduction

Options for the Lead

1. State the problem.
2. State your position (key or thesis statement).
3. State your purpose.
4. Define any key words.
5. Ask a question.
6. Establish common ground.*

Options for the Body

1. Present the first main point, example, or supporting evidence.
2. Continue to present more points, examples, and supporting evidence.
3. Anticipate and respond to possible objections.
4. Organize your supporting materials either from least important to most or from most important to least.

Options for the Ending

1. Restate the problem, your position, and your purpose.
2. Suggest further action or discussion.
3. Reestablish common ground.
4. Use a striking example.
5. Ask a question.
6. Summarize.

Induction

Options for the Lead

1. Engage your reader by providing a striking illustration of the issue or problem.
2. Establish common ground.

Options for the Body

1. Add more evidence and examples illustrating the issue or problem.
2. Anticipate and respond to possible objections.
3. Organize your evidence and examples from least important to most or from most important to least.

Options for the Ending

1. State the problem.
2. State your position (key or thesis statement).
3. Establish common ground.
4. Use a striking example.
5. Ask a question.
6. Summarize.

*For a discussion of establishing common ground, see pages 379–381.

with both deduction and induction. You may find that in revising a paper you will want to switch completely from one to the other. In either case, focus on the lead and the ending. These are strategic points for engaging your audience. The sidebar on deduction and induction shows some options you have.

Writing the Body

In the writing process it is helpful to keep a *working plan,* or outline. This outline may be as simple as a few words on a scrap of paper, noting what you want to include. Or, the plan may be as formal as the table of contents of this book. In general, the larger the work, the more planning there is. Hammering two boards together doesn't take much planning. Raising a house requires an intricate design. In any case, the plan often changes as you develop a piece of writing, just as your title, leads, and endings change in the process.

1. Collecting.   As you work, jot down points you want to cover. You can write on notecards, on pieces of paper, or, as some writers do, at the point in a computer file where you anticipate using an idea. You can shuffle your cards into piles for lead, body, and ending. Or you can divide a paper into three columns and jot down notes for lead, body, and ending in them. Plan and replan throughout the process: before (to help you focus), during (to help you keep track), and after (for final polishing).

2. Outlining.   An outline is an arranged list of topics and ideas that guides you through your drafting and redrafting. If you are working as a planner, list what you want to include in your paper *before* you start

---

Writing the Body

Use the following strategies singly or in combination:

1. *Collect* your ideas on notecards, on pieces of paper, and in computer files. Organize them before and during the drafting process.
2. *Outline* your topics and ideas before and during the drafting process.
3. *Analyze* strategies of development. Choose those that best apply to your current purpose and audience.
4. *Diagram* your work, using the shapes in Figure 7.1 on page 190.
5. *Pace* your writing by asking yourself the questions on page 191. Draw blocks to visualize your pacing.

drafting it. If you are an explorer, freewrite, experiment, and draft your paper. Then review what you have written and write an outline of it. Most often, you will find yourself working both as a planner and an explorer, as I did with this book. The first draft of this chapter was written to fill in this planned working outline:

    I. Leads

   II. Body

  III. Endings

As I wrote, I discovered and developed further ideas for how to detail each section. I rewrote my outline. Here is a more fully developed outline for leads:

    I.   Leads

        A. Fourteen strategies for leads

        B. Sidebars

        C. Writing leads

        D. Explorations

           ...

Because one of the purposes of this chapter is to offer you opportunities to discover ideas for yourself, this description helped me to check whether I was offering enough Explorations in each section. You may have noticed that this chapter includes comments on the process of writing leads, titles, endings, and bodies of papers. The idea to do this occurred to me while I was writing about leads. I wrote it into my working plan, which reminded me to offer such sections on the process of writing endings, titles, and bodies, as well. Putting "Sidebars" into the outline reminded me to formulate them for each section.

3. Analyzing. Review your work and decide which strategies of development are most appropriate for your purpose and audience. Experiment with drafting your paper using these strategies. Choose the one that provides the most unity and coherence of the topics you want to cover. Write a working outline. Revise it as necessary.

4. Diagramming. Writers who are visually oriented often find it helpful to diagram their work in process. Figure 7.1 illustrates some shapes your writing might take. The V shape, reflecting the funneling effect of collecting specific experiences, ideas, and information as examples to

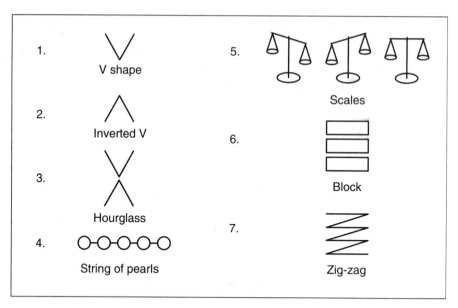

FIGURE 7.1   **Summary of Body Shapes**

reach a point, illustrates *inductive reasoning.* The *inverted* V, which starts with a general statement, theory, or rule and then offers examples, evidence, stories, and other illustrations to support it, illustrates *deductive reasoning.* The *hourglass* combines the strategies of the V and inverted V shapes.

If events and processes are told from beginning to end or in exact reverse order without any emphasis or distinction among them, it is as if the ideas are a string of matching pearls. Instead, you can organize your evidence and examples to show their relative importance. The scales stand for places in your paper where you can offer more or less important ideas, at the beginning or the end. When you use the scales to review the placement of your examples and ideas, focus on the purpose of your work. Maintain your readers' interest and make a lasting impression. Finally, the block and zig-zag shapes illustrate comparison and contrast.

5. Pacing.   Pacing is especially important in writing. Too much too soon, or too little too late, and you lose your focus and your reader. It's helpful to notice how long you spend on each section of a piece of writing. If you claim that your paper is a strong argument in favor of AIDS research but you spend only three sentences on it in a three-page paper, you will have to readjust. If you find that you only offer one brief focused

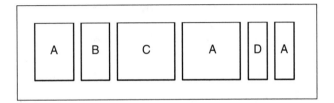

FIGURE 7.2 ***Drawing Blocks for Pacing***

example to support your point, you may want to add more. (Or you may want to revise your whole purpose and approach.)

To pace yourself, count your sentences, paragraphs, examples, and sometimes even your words in particular portions. Use these calculations to help you decide whether you could speed up or slow down your paper by subtracting or adding. So, for example, if you claim to be writing about the difference between poisons and medicines but don't devote equal space to them, you may want to readjust the balance. These are some questions that may help you in pacing:

- Am I trying to do too much?
- Could I spend more time on any parts?
- Do I spend too much time on things that are not important to my purpose or audience?
- Does the order make sense?
- Are there some sentences that belong to another paragraph?
- Do I try to cover too much in any paragraph?
- Am I leaving out any relevant steps?
- Do I get bored with writing any of the portions, myself? Why? How could I make it more interesting for me to write them?
- Should I remove any section?

Draw blocks to indicate the relative amount of space you devote to each idea or topic (see Figure 7.2). This will help you visualize your pacing.

*E*xplorations

1. *Together or Solo.* Select two essays from the readings at the end of Chapter 11, and discuss them using the questions in the sidebar on reading for organization.

2. *Together.* In the following paragraphs, the sentences have been placed out of the order in which the author arranged them. Reorganize them using these suggestions:

- Find what you believe would be a good lead sentence.
- Reorder the sentences so that they make sense to you.
- Decide what the purpose and audience could be.
- Decide which strategy of development your version follows.
- Decide which shape your version takes. Draw a diagram.
- If you work in small groups, compare the results as a class. How do different orders change the meaning?

a.   Perhaps a center will emerge. If that is not the final center, then go on to another way of writing. Keep up this burst of writing—this attempt to figure out what your writing is about—as long as you can. Keep this up for a while. If not, go on to the step of standing back and looking for a center. Give your writing more time in a drawer unlooked at. If this doesn't work, you may simply have to stop and rest. Some complicated and important reordering of things is trying to take place inside you. Anything that takes this long simply to emerge is probably important.

b.   But how much TV does one have to watch to qualify as a heavy TV watcher? Try to create a mental picture of what these phrases represent. Look closely at her reasoning. Also, what does it mean to overestimate the danger of physical violence, or to become desensitized? She argues that heavy TV watchers "overestimate the danger of physical violence in real life" and "become desensitized to violence in the real world." You can see that if you accept this writer's argument without requiring her to clarify these ambiguous phrases, you will not have understood what you agreed to believe. If you can't, the phrases are ambiguous.

c.   Not you. And although we're taught that it is bad to boast, that it is trashy to toot our own horn, that nice people don't strut their stuff, seek attention, or name-drop, there are times when showing off may be forgivable and may be even acceptable. No one is completely immune. Indeed everyone, I would like to propose, has some sort of need to show off.

d.   Helping women to disguise their pregnancy so that it will not interfere with "business" has itself become big business. This ensemble presumably provides her the male dress she needs to navigate in a man's world even while she manifests what Robert Seidenberg has called the irreducible of womanhood—pregnancy and birth. Working women who gather the courage to have families despite the culture's dismissal of mothering find themselves subject to corporate standards even in this female process. Here again women have been coerced by "male" values, the professional overtaking the personal and blotting it out. One of many

Reading for Organization

As you answer the following questions about your readings, point to particular words, phrases, and sentences to support your claims. Consult your dictionary for further insights into both familiar and unfamiliar words.

1. What is the purpose of this reading?
2. Who is the anticipated audience?
3. Does the title interest readers and effectively familiarize them with the topic? If so, by which strategy?
4. Does the lead focus, familiarize, interest, and immerse readers?
5. Which strategies does the writer use for the lead?
6. Which strategies does the writer use to develop the body of the work?
7. Does the writer use deduction or induction as a strategy?
8. Into what sections is this reading divided?
9. How does the writer shape and pace the work?
10. Does the ending leave a lasting impression and frame the paper for a sense of completion?

ads for stores with this intent, titled "Today's Maternity," pictures a woman dressed in a dark suit, complete with stiff white collar, "softened" by the usual corporate tie at the neck. Franchised chain stores with names such as "Mothers Work" specialize in supplying pregnant women with the obligatory corporate uniform.

3. *Together.* Choose a short newspaper or magazine article or a paper on which you are working. Cut it into paragraph segments and number the original order of each paragraph on the back of the paper with a pencil. Shuffle the paragraphs, and in small groups or as a class, decide the order in which you would put them. The group may have different ideas of the best order. You may decide that some paragraphs are not necessary. Then compare your version to the original order and note differences. (Resist the temptation to just fit the pieces back as if they were parts of a jigsaw puzzle.)

- Which order do you prefer, and why?
- What shapes would you assign to the different versions?
- Create a list of phrases describing what the author is doing in each paragraph.
- How does the meaning vary between versions?

4. *Solo and Together.* Choose a paper on which you are working either for your writing class or some other purpose. Photocopy it. In pairs or groups of three, help each other order paragraphs (or sentences), while reflecting on the purpose and audience of the paper.

5. **a.** *Solo.* Revise a paper you are writing, with special attention to coherence. Develop a working outline. Diagram the shape of your development. Notice whether you are using a planner's or explorer's approach. Decide whether to organize deductively or inductively. Monitor your transitions.

   b. *Together.* Read and discuss each other's papers, with special attention to organizing strategies.

Chapter Review

Together. Discuss how this chapter is organized, using the following questions and suggestions:

a. Read the table of contents for the chapter.

b. What are the major sections of the chapter?

c. For each section:
   - Outline what is included.
   - What strategy is used for the lead? Why?
   - What strategy is used for the title? Why?
   - How is the body developed? Why?
   - What strategy is used for the ending? Why?

d. What charts and diagrams are used?

e. Would you reorganize the chapter? If so, how and why?

Chapter *8*

Consulting

This chapter offers opportunities to

—Create a **community of writers**

—**Respond** to each other in **writing workshop**

—Become a better **reader**

—Turn problems into **opportunities**

> Company is better than will power.
> —*Amrit Desai, Artist and Educator*

> No passion in the world is equal to the
> passion to alter someone else's draft.
> —*H. G. Wells, Novelist*

A Community of Writers

You open the door to a noisy computer writing lab and hear bits of conversation: "I like..." "Maybe you could..." "Did you save..." "I meant...." Students are clustered in small groups of four or five with papers, dictionaries, and magazines spread out near their computers, on their desks, and on the floor. They are leaning toward each other, gesturing, pointing to each other's papers, and calling out. Several other students are writing by hand in a corner. In the middle of the classroom is a wastebasket; around it are crumpled papers that missed. In one group, two students are discussing what happened during a nationally televised court case: "You can't say the woman was guilty without evidence. It makes you sound sexist." In another group, there's a burst of laughter and someone says, "There I go. Can't stop talking about my favorite person: me." A student stands up to consult with another in the next group. "You're the comma expert," she says, pointing to a paper. "Do we or don't we put a comma here? Marsha says it weakens the sentence. I say it makes it clearer." An older man dressed in a suit (who seems to be the teacher) walks over to a group silently focused on the papers before them. "Come back later," says one of the readers. The man raises his hands and calls for attention. But people are just too involved to notice. He smiles and shrugs his shoulders. Welcome to a community of writers.

This scene may be different from what you have come to expect in a writing classroom. Perhaps you have written most of your papers with only teachers as audience. You would try to figure out what they wanted and write accordingly. They would mark and grade your papers. Maybe you would revise the paper once, just changing what was marked. That would be that. The teachers would end up doing *for* you what they were hoping you could do for yourself. You wouldn't feel as if your papers were your own.

In the real world of writing, writers consult frequently with other writers, colleagues, family, friends, and members of their prospective audiences. For example, writers of children's books regularly gather children to listen to readings of their work in progress. These children tell them what they like, both directly and indirectly. In response, the authors revise their own writing. Business executives consult with each other on proposals, and often their support staff will edit and reword memos for them. Scientists, journalists, and textbook writers—among others—often write together. Hundreds of people have been directly involved in giving suggestions and ideas for the development of *The Flexible Writer*. Some of these people are listed in the acknowledgments section in the Preface of this book and in footnotes.

One of the most important characteristics of practicing writers is that they know how to talk about writing. This chapter offers you a variety of ways in which you can develop your own community of writers so that you can discover how to talk about writing and revise your work.*

---

*For ideas that inspired this chapter, I am indebted to Peter Elbow, Pat Belanoff, Dixie Goswami, Nancy Sommers, Mimi Schwartz, and the New Jersey Center for the Study of Writing, which granted me a Fellowship for Research in the Classroom.

Writing Workshop

One of the most exciting parts of learning to write is consulting with others in *writing workshop.* In writing workshop, writers discuss their own and others' papers. Writers benefit because they get a broader and deeper range of responses than they would if only the teacher were "marking" their work. Teachers feel refreshed because they learn more about and from their students and are freed of having to be error-hunters. Everyone is in charge. A sense of belonging develops. As one student said at the end of a workshop session, "Wow! We're so great together."

The following are some practical considerations to negotiate with each other and your instructor as you discuss papers. Experiment to suit your needs and resources.

Names. Names on papers can be included, deleted, or replaced by made-up names. Remaining anonymous, writers may be spared some self-consciousness and can speak about papers as if they belonged to someone else. Writers can start out anonymously—to get comfortable—and can identify themselves at any point. The benefit of identifying yourself as the writer is that you can more fully discuss your work, ask questions, and request specific responses. You can guide the discussion toward issues that concern you. Often, you may not realize that the idea that seems too obvious or familiar to you is, in fact, very engaging and interesting to others. If you identify yourself as the writer, others can help you recognize the value in what you have to express.

Size. You can respond to papers as a whole group, in small groups of four to five writers, or in pairs. Workshop with the whole group helps you develop a common understanding and new points of view. You collect more responses to your paper, and you build on each other's ideas. Small groups can offer more freedom of expression and more time for more papers.

Choosing and Copying Papers. Ideally, all papers should be typewritten when you consult others about them. Although you may not want to consult over every paper, as part of the community you will want *some* of your work considered. In the beginning, you may want to entrust teachers to choose and copy papers anonymously. Later, you may be asked to bring in three or four copies of papers for small group workshop. If you bring copies for the whole class to share, one copy for every two persons is enough. If you are working in a computer lab, you can sometimes generate copies on printers.

For quick response in a regular classroom, you can use carbon paper to create multiple copies of first drafts that you can discuss in small groups right away. How much you will cover of any given paper may vary, too. Many of the most fruitful workshops are focused just on those important first paragraphs or first pages.

Timing. Decide how many papers you want to discuss in a given time and what levels of responses you want to give. Appoint a timekeeper whose job it is to make sure every paper is given a fair share of time. A half hour is usually enough for a one-page paper, although a focused fifteen minutes may accomplish as much.

Recording. Make a habit of writing comments on all copies of papers in workshop, for several reasons. First, writing on all copies protects the author's anonymity: if everyone is recording comments, questions, and corrections, the author is not singled out as the only one taking notes. Second, it's good practice to make adjustments in writing: You learn to write better. Third, writing workshop can be lively, and you don't want to forget your point by the time it's your turn to talk.

Sometimes one person will record all comments and read them back to the class as a review. This is a useful exercise in taking notes. Sometimes two people will record comments, and you can notice the differences in their perceptions. If identified, the writer may be the best one to tell the group what she or he has learned. The recorder gives the notes to the writer.

Order. If possible, arrange seating so that participants can face each other. For example, as a whole class, you can place your desks close to the walls to leave a central area open. In small groups, you can arrange your desks so that everyone is equally included: the front edges of the desks in a group of three will form a triangle, four will form a square, five a pentagon.

Responses can be managed by your instructor or a designated student. Above all, be *flexible*. You may want to open up your workshops so members can speak to each other without first raising hands. Sometimes there will be periods of silence while you consider your responses. That is perfectly all right.

Usually in writing workshop, a writer, if identified, will stay silent while participants discuss his or her paper. Later in the process, the writer may ask and answer questions. At that time, direct responses to the writer.

Reminders.   On bulletin boards and chalkboards, post photocopies of diagrams, charts, and sidebars from *The Flexible Writer.* Choose those that are most relevant to your needs and processes.

Networking.   Post papers and letters you would like to "publish" for others to read. If your class uses a writing lab, you can develop a mailing system. Partners can read and respond to papers in a file at their individual convenience. If, in addition, you are working with computer systems, you can leave electronic mail messages and responses concerning your papers and workshops.

Responding to Writing

Most students find writing workshop to be the most productive and enjoyable activity in their writing courses. But how you respond is important. Read the purposes of writing workshop listed in the sidebar. Writing workshop is a supportive, not a competitive, activity. The better reader you become of other people's writing, the better reader you can become of your own. Respond to writing first by looking for the person and purpose behind the words. Identify strengths. Then reach for ways to build on these strengths.

There is *no absolute sequence* for how to conduct a workshop, because each session is a unique—often surprising—experience with different people focusing on different things at different times. The following basic sequence, however, is designed to ensure that you notice writers' *strengths first.* It makes no sense to correct punctuation in a section of a paper that will be deleted because it doesn't fit anyhow. Skip certain kinds

---

Purposes of Writing Workshop

1.   To help each other find *meaning and purpose* through writing
2.   To be the *ideal audience* for each other
3.   To develop *flexibility* with phases of the writing process
4.   To develop *honesty and confidence* in both reading and writing
5.   To develop *commitment* to excellence

> ## *Workshop Reminders*
>
> 1. Find strengths first.
> 2. Be specific.
> 3. Point to words, phrases, sentences, and punctuation *in* the writing.
> 4. Suggest changes, but don't rewrite for others.
> 5. Skip certain kinds of responses until a draft is ready for them.
> 6. Be honest.
> 7. Writing workshop is supportive, *not* competitive.

of responses until a draft is ready for them. *You don't have to take every step for every paper every time.* For example, the discussion may focus on the issue of audience. Stay with what seems most relevant and helpful. *Always point to specific parts of the paper as you respond.*

Offer suggestions. Look at the model of the writing process (Figure 2.1, page 31), and suggest the phases to which the writer needs to pay more attention. Perhaps the writer hasn't collected enough information or needs to reorganize or refocus. Perhaps the writer is using words with unwanted connotations. Suggest models of writing you have read that the writer might find useful.

Offer alternative ways to write the paper, but don't argue them too strongly. Avoid the temptation to rewrite others' papers for them. Writers need to have final say on their own papers. Writers also need time away from workshop to consider suggestions.

For your first few workshops, you may want to respond to each other in the order in which the twelve responses to writing are offered in the next section, just to practice; then develop your own flexible procedures. As with anything else, the more you practice responding to writing, the better you will be at it.

Twelve Responses to Writing: A Model Workshop

To illustrate writing workshop, we will be considering a student paper on computers. George Lee decided to identify himself as the writer of the paper so that he could participate more fully in the workshop process. George wrote his paper in response to the question "How have computers changed our lives?"

First draft

```
                          Computers

    Computers are helpful in many places in life. Because
in school computers give information from library, in
work computers give much help for making money, in
medicine doctors can make tests with computer and save
people life.
    Personal computer bring much interest. I have this expe-
rience too. Because in my life their is a computer in my
room. For my birthday I got e-mail for my computer. I play
many fun games like Command and Conquer and make friends
with people on my dorm floor. Now they come to my room every
hour of the day and night. They come also to ask my computer
for homework and play many games. Computers are fun.
    Everybody want to use computer at home, at school, and at
work. Because computers are fun and very helpful. All of a
sudden everybody think computer save life. Computers also
make bad things. Because people forget what life is. People
use computer and sometimes forget other people have feeling.
```

1. Read Aloud. Someone other than the writer reads the paper aloud *exactly* the way it appears on the page. As a reader, read slowly. Don't add, delete, or otherwise correct as you read. When you read so precisely, you help the writer recognize what does and doesn't sound right. Where a reader hesitates, has trouble pronouncing a word, seems confused, or fumbles over whether to raise or lower the voice, there may be a problem with the writing. Circle those portions. In some workshops, you may decide just to read everyone's paper aloud without commenting. This is what authors do when they offer readings of their works at gatherings in libraries, schools, and other forums. You can learn much about writing just by listening and reading along without comment.

Read George's first draft aloud before you read further here. What do you notice?

When his paper was read aloud in writing workshop, George said he noticed that his paper was short. He also noticed how often he used the word computer: *fourteen times. The class laughed when the reader said, "They come also to ask my computer for homework." George realized that his sentence implied that his dorm mates came to his room to be given homework by his computer.*

2. Remember. Start your responses by saying what you remember specifically from the paper (without looking back at it) and why you remembered it. This will show the writer what "sticks." People tend to remember what they heard first and last, what they liked, and what caused them trouble.

Before reading beyond this paragraph, jot down what you remember of George's paper. This is a test of the paper, not your memory. Compare your list with the workshop list.

On first reading, workshop participants remembered these portions of George's paper:

- *E-mail (because some of the students didn't have it)*
- *Command and Conquer*
- *The use of computers in medicine (because of one student's health problems)*
- *Dorm friends (because many students felt used by theirs)*

3. Express Likes. Looking back at the paper, focus on what you like about it. Point to specific sentences, words, and ideas on the page. *Place check marks* by them as you notice them. Read them aloud. Or perhaps you appreciate the way the paper is shaped. Say so. Be sure to say *why* you like what you like so that the writer can understand how you are reading the paper. For example, if you like a paper because it's about a grandmother and you like your grandmother, say so. Understand, though, that this is not a reflection on the writing. The writer needs to know what the paper itself does for you.

Before reading on, place check marks and write about what you liked in George's paper. Then compare your reactions to those of George's workshop peers.

Students said they especially liked the way George showed how many different uses a computer has. Nancy, who was shopping for a personal computer, said she would be interested in his suggestions for how to get e-mail. Juan responded that George's paper was not about how to get e-mail.

4. Name Purposes and Needs. Name what may be the writer's purposes and needs in writing the paper. Was the paper written, for example, to

- Express a feeling? Name it.
- Argue a certain point? Name it.
- Clarify a problem? Name it.

- Find an answer?
- Cause trouble?
- Get an assignment over with?

Does the writer try to fulfill too many purposes at the same time?

Write down what you believe to be George's purposes and needs. Then compare them with the purposes and needs George's peers identified.

Most students thought that the purpose of the first paragraph was to name different places where computers are used. The second paragraph was meant to identify George's experience with his personal computer. No one was sure, reading this first draft, why George thought computers "make bad things." Some students felt that George's main purpose in writing the paper was just to fulfill his assignment to bring a draft to writing workshop. They felt this because he jumped from one idea to another without fully explaining himself. Nancy suggested that his second paragraph may have fulfilled George's need to complain about people in his dorm. Tiffany disagreed because George ends the paragraph by writing "Computers are fun," so he didn't seem to be complaining.

5. Assess Audience Appeal.   Discuss who the audience of the paper seems to be. For example, does the paper sound as though it's written to a government official or a next-door neighbor? Discuss whether a paper in progress pays attention to the needs of the audience. Does the paper offer enough information for you to understand what is happening? If not, what more do you need to know? Has the writer made an effort to make the paper interesting, engaging, and clear? How? What more does the writer need to do? What point of view is being taken? How much is the reader asked to fill in?

Write your reaction to George's paper. Were you engaged? If so, why? If not, why not?

Workshop members felt that George had anticipated a limited audience: the instructor. The first paragraph seems to be an attempt to quickly answer the question and get it over with. The second paragraph was more interesting because it included details with which readers could identify. Most students felt the paper didn't hold their attention because they already knew most of the things George wrote about computers. Readers who weren't interested in computers were not fully engaged by this draft. Readers who were interested in computers felt he could have written in much more detail.

6. Find Focus.   Identify the focus of the paper as a whole, and look for sentences that capture it. Help the writer identify whether she or he needs to further use any of the focusing strategies: choosing, specifying, quoting, illustrating, questioning, and/or stating. Are all portions of the paper relevant to the main focus? Are there shifts in the purpose and focus as the paper proceeds? Do these work? Help the writer decide what is the most promising focus and which portions throw the paper off center. Could the writer delete early portions of the paper and begin with ideas discovered later in the writing?

What do you think is George's main focus for the paper? Compare your response to the workshop responses.

Discussing George's needs, purposes, and audience, students wanted him to focus more clearly on what the computer meant to him. Some students were sure that George was in favor of computers. Some students felt George mentioned only the positive aspects because he thought that that was what was expected of him. Juan said, "Why don't you write about the bad side? We already know that we're supposed to like computers." As a whole, workshop participants recommended that George focus on the downside of computers because that would be a more surprising and interesting approach.

7. Ask Questions.   Ask questions *and record them* to help the writer further focus the paper. The writer doesn't have to answer right away. Use the question star from page 120 (Figure 5.4) to help you develop questions.

What questions do you have concerning George's draft?

Workshop members asked George these questions:

- *How do you get e-mail?*
- *Whom do you let use your computer?*
- *How can a computer help you make money?*
- *When can you show me how the library computer works?*
- *How do doctors use computers?*
- *Which games do you have?*
- *Do you have a math program?*
- *Do you surf the Internet?*
- *What bad things do computers do?*
- *What bad things happened to you?*
- *Did you ever see Data on* Star Trek?

- *What kind of computer do you have?*
- *Why can't I print a Windows file on a Macintosh?*

Not all of the questions were relevant to George's paper. Which ones were? Which ones were not, and why? In your workshops, list all questions on the board, whether or not they seem relevant. Then choose and discuss those questions that will help the writer further develop the paper. In the case of George's paper, most students were interested in hearing about the Internet and what bad things had happened to George because of his computer.

8. Assess Sense Appeal. Notice whether the paper has enough sense appeal. Does the writer use specific images that bring the focus to life? To what senses could the writer appeal to better engage the audience and fulfill the purpose of the paper? Use the sense star from page 135 (Figure 6.1) to help trigger ideas for imagery.

Does George's draft have enough sense appeal for you? If so, where? If not, where could he incorporate more images?

Workshop members felt that George missed opportunities for giving his first draft sense appeal. Here are some questions students asked to help George:

- *What does your room look like?*
- *How many people can fit into your room?*
- *What kinds of graphics can your computer do?*
- *Can you change the background color on your screen?*
- *What kinds of characters do you get in your games?*
- *Can you play CD-ROMs and music CDs?*

9. Describe Organization. Notice whether and how the paper is organized. Sketch an outline of the paper as it is now, naming what the purpose of each paragraph or portion seems to be. Draw a diagram of how the ideas are or aren't connected. Draw boxes to determine the balance and pacing of ideas. Discuss the effectiveness of the title, the lead, the body, and the ending. How is George's draft organized?

George's first draft shifted so much—from computers in general to his own computer and some vague mention of bad effects of computers—that students felt it was more important, at this point, for George to refocus and expand the paper than to organize it. Once George's purpose and focus were clearer, he could consider how to organize. The instructor recommended that George write a better working title to specify how the computer had changed his life.

10. Find Repetitions and Redundancies.   Note and circle repetitions of words and ideas. If you need to distinguish different kinds of repetitions, use other coding devices, such as squares, triangles, highlighting in various colors, or marking with stars, numbers, or letters. Do these repetitions help connect ideas, or are they distracting? Can the writer offer more variety to maintain the reader's interest? Sometimes the writer may repeat the same idea but with different wording. Distinguish unnecessary or uninformative repetitions from effective ones.

Workshop members noticed that George repeated the word com-puter four times in the first paragraph and fourteen times in three short paragraphs. He stated that computers are "fun" three times. He also repeated that computers are "helpful." Both repetitions seemed redundant because they didn't add new information.

11. Copy-edit.   Spend time silently circling portions of the paper where you have questions or concerns about grammar, punctuation, style, or spelling. Notice whether there is a pattern of difficulties. Look for repetitions and decide whether they are effective or distracting. Then, as a group, decide which parts deserve the most attention and how the writer might change these features of the paper.

What grammar, punctuation, and spelling changes do you think George needs to make?

Although it was clear that George would have to revise his paper substantially, students made the following comments and suggestions to help him clarify his writing:

- *Always make the word computer plural by adding an s unless you're talking about only one computer.*
- *Otherwise, put a or the in front of computer, if you are talking about one computer or the computer as a general idea. The same rule goes for other nouns.*
- *Computer and computers are correctly used several times in the paper.*
- *Their isn't the right spelling in that sentence. (George said he had used the spelling checker, and everyone smiled.)*

- *Omit the words* people life *in the first paragraph and write* save lives *instead.*

- *Finish all the sentences that started with* Because.

- *Everybody is a singular subject. Put an* s *on* want.

12. Reflect. To clarify and emphasize the benefits of writing workshop, summarize what you learned from discussing a certain paper. Discuss how the workshop went. Make plans for next time. What did you learn about yourself as a reader? If the writer has been identified, this is the time for her or him to respond, to say what helped, and to ask questions.

What did you learn about yourself as a reader of George's paper? How did your insights compare with those made by members of George's workshop?

George was eager to respond to what the other workshop members said about his first draft. He said that as he wrote, he knew he wasn't writing the whole story. As he listened to others speak about his paper, he felt more confident that they would understand his real story and that he was ready to write it. As he put it, "I think I know the audience now. You are my friends, and you help me a lot. You listen to me."

George started to talk about how he used the Internet to contact other people who were interested in boogie boarding. He said he had started to correspond with a young woman. The class hour was up before George could offer any further details. The instructor asked George not to talk away his experiences after class with other students but to write a new draft of his paper that focused on what had happened on the Internet.

Figure 8.1 shows George's own notes on his first draft. George's next drafts about his experience with computers are featured on pages 222–227 and 230–231 in Chapter 9, "Revising." Experiment with writing workshop yourself, using the following Explorations to guide you.

Twelve Responses to Writing

1. Read aloud.
2. Remember.
3. Express likes.
4. Name purposes and needs.
5. Assess audience appeal.
6. Find focus.
7. Ask questions.
8. Assess sense appeal.
9. Describe organization.
10. Find repetitions and redundancies.
11. Copy-edit.
12. Reflect.

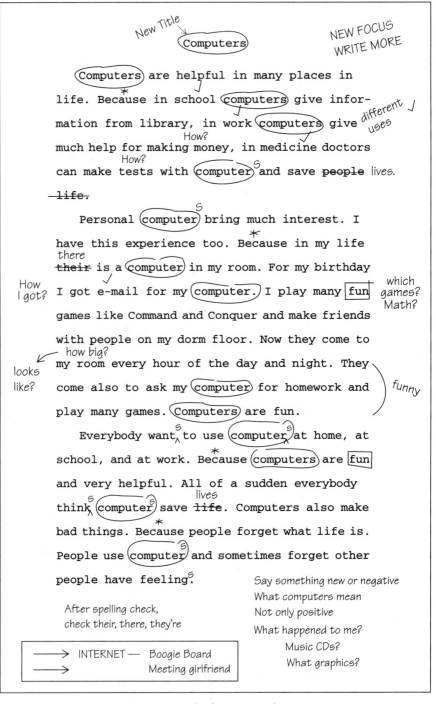

FIGURE 8.1 George's Marked First Draft

*E*xplorations _____

1.   *Together.* In turn, read aloud a choice of your papers in process, without making comments. Discuss your experiences of doing so. What did you learn about your own and others' papers?

2.   *Together.*
     a.   Conduct a workshop to discuss a paper. Use the twelve responses to writing in the order in which they are offered in this chapter. Or, develop your own flexible procedures.

     b.   List words you would use to describe your experience of this writing workshop. Why do these words describe your experiences?

     c.   Plan your next workshop. Discuss which phases of the writing process you would like to explore further, and refer to the appropriate chapters in Parts II and IV to refresh and refine your skills.

3.   a.   *Solo.* Before others respond to one of your papers, write a statement of your intentions: Why are you writing this paper? What are your purpose and audience for the paper? How do you hope specific parts of your paper will affect others? What questions do you have?

     b.   *Together.* Conduct a workshop on these papers. After others respond, read them your statement of intention. Compare it to their responses. What could you change in your paper to better reflect your intended purpose? Would it be more satisfying to adopt a different purpose or audience?

4.   *Together.* One way to develop a sense of how to write is to read and reread models of writing that you admire. Choose a piece of writing from this book that you admire, and discuss it using the relevant steps in the list of twelve responses to writing. Suggest how the writer could revise the piece to tailor it to you as a reader.

Workshop Personalities

In writing workshop, you will find yourself at different times defending a point, cleaning up, wondering, questioning, appreciating, laughing, and puzzling. You may have a preferred approach to workshop. From time to time, step back and notice what role you are playing, and think about whether it is helpful. The difference between someone who is new and someone who is practiced in writing workshop is that the *practiced* person can move flexibly among different roles. In a workshop, these are the roles that people may assume at different times:

The *Judge* is interested in following rules and what she or he interprets as "correctness." The Judge asks important questions about whether something makes sense, contradicts itself, or is true. This can be very helpful when you are editing and proofreading and keeping a piece of writing organized. But the Judge may be too impatient and hard on a piece of writing that is still in an early draft and may try to rewrite the paper for the writer prematurely. You can tell when the Judge is overdoing it because people will tense up, and the writer will become very unhappy.

The *Free Spirit* is very energetic in brainstorming and creating new ways of looking at a topic and will often discover strengths that others may not see. The Free Spirit is fun in a workshop and may offer interesting and valuable points of view. But the Free Spirit may also pull the discussion too far away from the paper and onto something that may turn out to be irrelevant. You can tell when the Free Spirit is overdoing it because no one will be looking at the paper in question or writing anything down.

The *Social Worker* wants peace, good will, and cooperation. Often the Social Worker will be the one negotiating between opposing viewpoints. However, the Social Worker may try to force everyone to agree on everything. One of the best features of writing workshop is that you realize that there are many points of view and many ways of reading a paper. The writer has to decide what will serve the purpose of the paper. You can tell that the Social Worker is overdoing it when people stop being willing to disagree.

The *Doer* is very helpful in organizing the workshop so that it runs smoothly, papers are thoroughly reviewed, and the focus stays on how the paper is actually written. But the Doer may be so task-oriented that he or she forgets that sometimes going off on a tangent may be helpful to the writer and that laughter and flexibility smooth the process. You can tell that the Doer is overdoing it when people look distracted, uninvolved, or overwhelmed.

The *Rebel,* unlike the Social Worker, doesn't like to be just "one of the crowd" and may resist the whole process of group interaction or try to undermine it. This resistance may show up in two extremes: sullen silence, withdrawal, chronic lateness, and absence; or active objections, distractions, griping, and hostility. The Rebel can be a very important member of a community, pointing out problems that need to be addressed. It's often the Rebel who initiates positive change. After all, the United States has developed into the nation it is because it allows for opposing viewpoints and styles. However, if the Rebel is disruptive or is too much of a damper on the group process, she or he will have to negotiate with the group about whether to stay. Someone will have to address the Rebel directly. Keep in mind that rebellion may be temporary and minor—at some point, everyone feels like withdrawing because of fear, hurt, or just having a bad day.

The *Silent Partner*, rarely talking or interacting with others, may seem to be a Rebel. The difference is that the Silent Partner listens carefully and is alert to group process. The Silent Partner offers support by his or her presence and is a welcome balance in a group of talkers. Often the Silent Partner is the one who formulates *the* insights for which others are grappling aloud. However, the Silent Partner may recede so much that he or she seems bored or judgmental, which reduces the group's energy. When the Silent Partner gets too silent, draw the person out by asking, "What do you think?"

The Checklist for Writing Workshop can help you assess how you are working together in writing workshop.

Problems and Opportunities in Writing Workshop

To revise your writing is to revise your language. To revise your language is to revise your beliefs and yourself. Revising may, at times, be uncomfortable and embarrassing. Most of the time it is empowering and energizing. The more you notice how others respond and the more generous you are in responding to others' writing, the more *flexibility* and *strength* you develop as a writer. Here are some problems you may encounter in response to writing workshop and ways you can turn them into opportunities:

Problem: You don't understand the response.

Opportunity: Ask your responder to rephrase the comment and point to more specific examples in your paper.

Problem: You disagree.

Opportunity: Restate the purpose and audience of your paper as a basis for discussing how the paper is written. If your responder still disagrees, consult with other readers.

Problem: You don't know how to change.

Opportunity: Ask for suggestions. Consult with resources such as this textbook and handbooks. Reread examples of writing that you admire.

Problem: You get conflicting responses.

Opportunity: Ask your responders to further clarify the reasons for their comments. Evaluate for yourself who you believe (1) has more relevant experience (this may be a peer instead of your instructor), (2) understands your purpose and audience best, and (3) is the kind of reader you are most interested in capturing.

Problem: You feel resistant to change.

Opportunity: Take time off from your paper until you can gather the proper resources to return to it. Reconsider which phase of the writing process you may have neglected, and relax with Exploratins in the relevant sections of this book. You may find a way to

Checklist for Writing Workshop

On a scale of never (0) to always (5), rank yourself and/or your group on the following kinds of participation:

The Writing Process

_____ Read aloud

_____ Remembered

_____ Expressed likes

_____ Identified purpose

_____ Assessed audience appeal

_____ Helped find and create focus

_____ Pointed to specific parts of papers

_____ Asked questions

_____ Helped develop sense appeal

_____ Suggested ways to organize

_____ Noticed repetitions and redundancies

_____ Discussed grammar, punctuation, style, and spelling

The Workshop Process

_____ Found and supported strengths

_____ Acknowledged others' ideas

_____ Offered honest reader reactions

_____ Voiced disagreements

_____ Involved quiet members

_____ Listened to suggestions

_____ Kept the group focused on writing

_____ Monitored time for papers

_____ Reflected and summarized particular lessons learned

Workshop Personalities

_____ The Judge

_____ The Free Spirit

_____ The Social Worker

_____ The Doer

_____ The Rebel

_____ The Silent Partner

maintain your approach in a way that other readers can accept, you may figure out how to use their responses in a way that satisfies you, or you may be satisfied with others' not accepting your paper.

Problem: Others won't take your suggestion.

Opportunity: Find another way to state your suggestion. Refer to the purpose and audience and point to specific parts of the paper to support your claim. Point out what you like and be encouraging about the strengths of the paper. If someone still won't listen to you, ask why, or drop the issue. The person may need some time to reflect. You may be missing something yourself.

*E*xplorations

1. *Together.*

   a.   To sharpen your awareness of the dynamics of workshop personalities, choose six people who feel they tend to (or would like to) assume one of the roles described above. These people will form a workshop group (either at the front of the classroom or in the middle of a circle formed by the rest of the class) and conduct a workshop on a paper. The rest of the class will take notes on what the different personalities do and say.

   b.   Discuss:

   - Which personalities people assumed
   - Whether people changed personalities in process
   - What kinds of words and expressions different personalities used
   - What did or didn't work
   - How the workshop could have been more effective

   Allow the discussion to develop its own direction. What role did you assume in the discussion of the workshop?

2. *Solo.* Write a journal entry discussing which workshop personality you tend to assume, what your special contributions can be, and how you could use your tendencies to learn more from working with others. In your journal entry, discuss the roles you take in other classes as well. How do you expect to be the same or different in your writing class? Why?

3. *Together and Solo.* Conduct a writing workshop (either as a whole class or in small groups) and evaluate your involvement, using the Checklist for Writing Workshop.

4. *Together or Solo.* Discuss or write a letter about any problems you have with writing workshop. How could you turn these problems into opportunities?

Five Variations

The benefit of conducting writing workshop as a whole group is that more people can offer a greater range of perspectives and insights. However, working as a whole group can be time-consuming. Fewer papers can be reviewed, and not everyone will be able to say all that she or he wants to say. Some people feel more comfortable talking in small groups of peers than talking with a whole class (including the instructor). Here are five variations on writing workshop that will enable you to respond to more papers, more often, and to become more familiar with the work and development of particular writers. Most important, these variations will help you to become more confident in your ability to read and revise your own work.

1. Self-review.   Before you submit a draft of a paper, do a workshop of it yourself. Fill in the form offered in the sidebar on letters and cover sheets, or write a letter to your instructor or workshop members answering the suggested questions. Workshopping your paper for yourself is an effective way to take a reader's point of view. Writing a letter or cover sheet further attunes you to purpose and audience.

Often you may write something in your letter or cover sheet that you could have written into your paper. Your instructor and workshop members can encourage you to use that idea. Also, by practicing self-review, you learn to revise your own writing and speed your development.

Here is the letter George wrote about his paper on computers. Notice how some of what he says in his letter anticipated comments and revisions in the model workshop.

```
Dear Readers,

    I am writing this letter to you. Because I like computers
a lot. I am very happy with computer. Computers do so many
different things. It is hard for me to say. Every time I
think something something else comes. Because I did not know
where to start my paper took me a long time. There is a prob-
lem I still think. There is a lot more I want to tell you
but I do not know how to get it all there.
    I hope you will see that computers are important.
    Thank you for being my workshop.

    George
```

2. Writing Partners.   Exchange papers with your partner. Note parts you like, circle areas of concern, and then write a letter to your partner about his or her paper. Then read the letters, make adjustments, and discuss them. If others (such as your instructor or tutor) have already commented on your paper, show these responses to your partner. Discuss what changes to make and how to make them.

3. Networking. Develop a system by which you can support each other through a network. Two different sections of writing courses can respond to each other. Or perhaps you might want to develop a letter-writing relationship with some members of the community, such as seniors or schoolchildren. Respond to each other's letters, saying what was helpful and what you need clarified.

If you have a writing lab, arrange for a file system by which you can review each other's works at convenient times. If you have a computer networking system, you can respond to each other's works on disk and leave e-mail messages. As always when working with computers, make back-up copies in case of technical failures.

4. Power Groups. Studies have shown that, more often than not, students who succeed work and study together. Students who isolate themselves slow down their progress toward joining the language communities to which they want to belong. Create a writing power group with other students and meet regularly. Do timed freewriting together and workshop the results. Discuss papers in process. This is how many professional writers develop and refine their skills.

5. Conferencing. Plan to work with your instructor or tutor regularly. Prepare by reviewing and reflecting on your own paper. Choose which aspects of it you want to discuss *specifically.* Your instructor or tutor will negotiate with you when and for how long to conference. After a conference, share what you learned with your writing partner, network, or power group.

Acknowledgments

Acknowledge each other's contributions to papers, especially when submitting them for grade evaluations. Practicing writers know that they are a part of a community of writers, whether in person or through reading. As a member of a workshop or network, each of you has committed time and energy to others' papers, as others have to yours. Always express your thanks when receiving help. Write your acknowledgment of workshop members, name them, and say exactly how they helped you. (Your instructor might want you to submit earlier drafts and some of your

Letters and Cover Sheets

For each submitted paper, write a letter or cover sheet on the following points. Use as much space as necessary.

Why did you write the paper?

Who is your audience?

What benefits did you experience in the process?

What do you like about your paper? (Highlight, checkmark, and quote directly.)

How did you organize your time, your collecting activities, your writing space, and your writing tools?

What specific problems in your paper do you want others to address? (Circle these portions. Ask specific questions in the margins. Refer to phases of the writing process.)

How have you developed as a writer while writing this paper?

letters and notes.) Showing your appreciation in this way shows that you know how to belong to an academic community. Not to acknowledge others' support can result in what is called *plagiarism*—stealing others' ideas. Plagiarism places you outside the community of thinkers and writers and may have serious consequences, such as expulsion.

Exploration _____

Together and Solo. Plan a system for consulting with others regularly. Develop a power group or a network for the term.

Chapter Review _____

Together.

1. Write a one-page manual about the writing process for new writers. Choose the ten points from this chapter that you feel are most important. One benefit of this project is that it provides you further practice in consulting with each other and negotiating decisions. Another benefit of discussing this chapter is that in the process, you will rehearse and thereby better remember it.

2. Reflect on the problems of writing this one-page manual and on how you created opportunities and benefits in response.

Chapter 9

Revising

This chapter offers opportunities to

—**Revise** your own papers

—**Help others** to revise

—Distinguish **revising** from recopying, readjusting, and copy-editing

—Develop **strategies for copy-editing** your papers

Error marks the place where education begins.
—*Mike Rose,*
Author of Lives on the Boundary

When you revise, the writing
becomes good to you.
—*Kyle Davis, Student*

Excellence is millimeters and not miles.
From poor to good is great.
From good to best is small.
—*Robert Francis, Poet*

Why Revise?

The word *revise* means to "see again," to "have a new vision." To revise means to use others' comments on your work to inspire you to develop new ideas. Revising means taking charge. It is an act of generosity. When you revise you not only change your paper according to what others suggest, you also take the risk of trying out ideas that occur to you as you return to your current draft. You develop and relate your own new "vision." You find new and better ways to change what you write so that you can better reach your audience and fulfill your purposes. Many writers claim that they learn the most and enjoy their writing best while they revise.

In practical terms, when you revise you reconsider which phase of the writing process you need to reenter. Perhaps you have to refocus your beginning or reidentify your purpose and audience. Perhaps you need to reorganize or to collect more materials. In some cases, you may decide to start all over again. The biggest breakthrough is being willing to let go of a large portion of your work in the service of expanding on that *one* sentence that really matters. Revising takes courage, work, humility, flexibility, and a sense of humor.

Revising Strategies

When you revise, you follow some of the same procedures as you do when you consult with others.

1. *Read aloud.* Throughout the drafting and revising process, read your paper aloud as often as you can. Voicing the words will help you notice for yourself what you want to keep and what you want to change.

2. *Mark your own paper.* Using colored pens, cross out what you want to delete; draw arrows to reorganize the order of words, sentences, and paragraphs. Check or underline main points and favorite passages.

Purposes for Revising

- To learn more about your purpose and how to satisfy it
- To further sensitize yourself to your real or anticipated audience
- To discover and create meaning
- To enjoy the benefits of creating something new
- To develop courage and generosity in the writing process

Cut anything that distracts from them. If you want to add something, note it and place a wedge (/\) where you want to insert the additions. Circle portions you are unsure of.

3. *Pace yourself.* Time is one of the most important factors in revising. You need time off between drafts to let ideas surface, to collect more information, to write other pieces—in short, to distance yourself from identifying with your paper. Sure, those are your words. But you aren't your words. That's why it is so important to start writing projects early enough to give yourself the necessary time and space to explore, experiment, and have enough work from which to harvest your best. It's like this—the larger the school, the better the basketball team, because the larger school has more candidates from which to choose the best. The more you write and the more time you have to write, the better your final product will be. You will have more to choose from.

4. *Be efficient.* Sometimes using scissors and tape in the revising process is easier than recopying. Cut out large sections of your paper that don't belong. If you need to expand, either tape the additions to the side of the paper or cut your paper where the addition needs to be taped in. You can also reorganize by cutting, reshuffling, and taping sections.

If you are working on a computer, learn and use commands that let you add, delete, insert, and move letters, words, phrases, sentences, and paragraphs. Be sure to open a new file and copy in your previous version. This will let you save versions so you can choose portions that best satisfy your purpose.

5. *Be organized.* Use a revision to-do list or a writer's journal (both described below) to help you benefit the most from others' responses and make the most effective revisions.

Revision To-Do List

If you know exactly how to start revising, just go to it. Continue to mark your drafts during workshop and when ideas occur to you. But when you're at a stopping point, you may want to create a revision to-do list. A *revision to-do list* helps you focus on and remember suggestions offered by others. It helps you develop a plan for revising. You can organize this list in several ways. The first is to organize your list by referring to the phases of the writing process. Here is an example of such a revision to-do list. George compiled it, using the responses he recorded on his paper featured in Chapter 8. Note that George is already incorporating suggestions about plurals, articles (a and the), and verb forms.

```
                        Computer

1.  Purpose. Write what computers mean to me. Why the com-
    puter is bad.
```

2. Audience. <u>Write so my readers will be interested in computers</u>.
3. Focus. <u>Answer questions the workshop asked</u>.
4. Collect. <u>Go to the computer and write down things that happened to me</u>. <u>Do not talk it away with other people</u>.
5. Organize. <u>After making a focus, make a list</u>. <u>Write a new title</u>.

Another way to write a revision to-do list is to list all the questions you and others ask about your paper. To guide his revision process, George used the list of workshop questions on pages 204–205.

*E*xploration _____

a. *Solo.* Choose a paper to which you have received responses from your instructor, your peers, or both. Write a revision to-do list focusing on phases of the writing process. Then write another revision list in the form of questions.

b. *Together.* Read these lists in small groups with the purpose of expanding or shortening the lists. Pay special attention to purpose and audience.

Writer's Journal

Your writer's journal helps you discover how to revise. If you write even a short note about a draft, you are already experiencing what student Michelle Willabus calls "semi-revision." Other students have mentioned these benefits of reflecting on their own writing:

- It opens a door.
- It develops a relationship with your first reader—*yourself.*
- It gives you ten times more confidence.
- To think and talk about writing is to start revising.

George developed ideas for revising his paper while writing in his writer's journal. Here is one of his entries:

Today people did my paper in workshop. First I was unhappy because they did not think it was good. But it was too short. I do a lot with my computer. I did not want to

talk about what bad thing happened to me. I learned a lot
because other people think different from me.

This time my workshop helped me because I did not tell my
story. They had a lot of questions. Now I will show them that
the computer is like life because it is good and it is bad.

*E*xplorations

1. *Solo.* Write in your writer's journal about a paper that you have been
   revising or that you plan to revise. Include all your concerns and
   develop your plans.
2. *Together.* Read to each other from your writer's journals and discuss
   what you learned by writing in them.

George revised his paper, taking the advice of his workshop:

Second draft

Computers and Surfing

Computers help in many places in life like school. Computers give information from the library. In work computers
give much help for making money in the stock market. In medicine doctors make tests with computers to save lives from
heart attacks, cancer, and other diseases.

Personal computers bring much interest. I have this experience too. In my life computers are important in my room. I
surf the Internet with a modem for my computer. I found a
newsgroup for surfing because I like boogie boarding. For my
readers, I will write what the boogie board is. A boogie board
is small surfboard made of styrofoam. You bring it into the
water and lay on it. You wait for waves. I can surf and I can
roll over with my boogie board. The boogie board is fun.

I lurk the surfing newsgroup on the net. When I lurk it
means you read messages but not post messages. One day I send
a message to a person who writes about boogie board party.
I will not write the name because I protect the innocent.

The person was a young woman and we went to boogie board
party. We had more date. Boogie board people have much fun
on the beach. Then it was winter and she went away to school.
I wanted e-mail for my birthday because I wanted to write my

new friend. We did e-mail and I was very happy because we
were boyfriend and girlfriend. So now you know why everybody
wants a computer.

One day I got e-mail from this girlfriend she send to
somebody else. People sometimes make a mistake and send
e-mail wrong. My reader will be kind to read the message was
to boyfriend who was not me. In message she say bad things
about me. She make fun of me.

I stop to write this mean person. I was very lonely.
Because e-mail was so bad to me I play computer games. I play
many fun games like <u>Command and Conquer</u>, <u>Myst</u>, and <u>Civili-
zation</u> and make friends with people on my dorm floor. Now
they come to my room every hour of the day and night. Ten
people can fit at one time. They come also to ask my computer
for help because they have homework and play games. I
make charts for them and pictures they need for papers.
I play CD-ROM games. I meet many young women and have new
friends.

My experience with computers is it brings people to
friendship and fun. Like life, the computer is good and bad.
People use computers to hurt people. My girlfriend did not
tell me to my face how she felt. She made a stupid mistake.
Maybe she did because she is a coward.

Reflect on George's second draft, using the following questions and
suggestions.

*R*eflections _____

1. Read George's second draft aloud. What do you notice?
2. What do you remember without looking back at it?
3. What do you like about George's second draft?
4. Is George's purpose clearer? What does the computer mean to him?
5. Has his audience appeal improved? Are you better engaged? If so,
   where in the paper does he engage you?
6. What specifics does George mention in this draft?
7. Where does George make a sense appeal in this second draft?
8. What statement(s) might serve as a thesis?
9. Does George place his thesis statement(s) in an effective place? If not,
   where could he place it?

10. Is George's title effective? Does it both familiarize and surprise his audience?

11. Are there ineffective repetitions or redundancies?

12. Circle any problems with grammar, punctuation, spelling, or style.

Copy-editing Strategies

To copy-edit is to adjust grammar, punctuation, spelling, and typing. As the Handbook chapters (15 and 16) in this text show, grammar and punctuation are crucial to the creation and communication of meaning. Often copy-editing leads to deeper revisions: reformulating purpose, readdressing audience, refocusing, recollecting, reorganizing. Notice whether copy-editing leads to deeper revisions for you.

George's class did a workshop of his second draft, addressing questions you were invited to consider above. They had some further concerns about focus and organization, which he addressed in writing a third draft.

In reading George's second draft, you may have noticed, as he and his classmates did, that there were problems with grammar, punctuation, spelling, and style. So, at this point, when George had better established his purpose, audience, and focus, students offered copy-editing suggestions he could incorporate into his next draft. The eight strategies that follow will help you to copy-edit your own writing:

1. Read Backward.   You can look at your own work for so long that it's hard to see it after a while. One sentence leads to another, and the flow of ideas takes over. When you read aloud forward, you might introduce punctuation with your voice that is not on the page. So one of the most useful strategies for editing your paper is to read aloud backward, sentence by sentence. This strategy helps you to recognize grammatical structures, punctuation, and spelling.

2. Mark Your Paper.   Use these symbols:

Insert ∧	Transpose ∪∩	Connect ⊂
Cut ⟋	New paragraph ¶	Space ⧣
Capitalize ≡		

Circle any parts of the paper where you feel uncertain about something or wonder whether a punctuation mark is needed. Write a question mark if you don't understand something or a word is missing. If you have an idea of what to do, write it in. Circle and/or number repetitions. Use the following helpful abbreviations (keyed to Chapters 15 and 16) for grammar, punctuation, style, and spelling concerns:

Fragment frag	Comma splice cs
Misplaced modifier mm	Parallel construction ‖
Run-on RO	Verb tense Vt
Subject-verb agreement S-V	Verb shift V-sf
Pronoun agreement pro	Missing plural pl
Pronoun shift P-sf	Spelling SP
Word choice W	Redundant red

Make up your own symbols as you discover patterns of concern in your work or in that of others. Sometimes a particular portion can be marked with several editing notes. However, remember this: *You don't have to name what's wrong to be able to copy-edit a portion of your paper effectively. If you know what to change, just change it.*

With the help of some of his classmates, George circled and marked parts of his paper that he needed to copy-edit for grammar, punctuation, spelling, or style. George and his group focused on editing his paper so that his meaning would be clear to his readers. The marked version is shown in Figure 9.1.

3. Make Easy Changes First. If you know how to edit a particular portion of your paper, do so right away. There is something satisfying about reducing the task of editing in this way. So George corrected his spelling, quotation marks, and typos first.

4. Experiment. Consider portions of your paper that need more careful attention. These will include phrases or sentences that are difficult to understand or that contradict what you want to say. Experiment with different ways of rephrasing or punctuating these portions.

George tackled his lead because he wanted to establish exactly what computers meant to him. This had been his first lead:

```
                          Computers

     Computers are helpful in many places in life. Because in
school computers give information from library, in work com-
puters give much help for making money, in medicine doctors
can make tests with computer and save people life.
```

(continued on page 228)

Marked second draft

(1) Computers and Surfing

(2) Computers help in many places in life like
school. (3) Computers give information from the
library. (4) In work, computers ~~give much~~ help ~~for~~
~~making~~ money in the stock market. In medicine∧
doctors make tests with computers (5) to save
people
~~lives~~ from heart attacks, cancer, and other
diseases.

(6) Personal computers bring much interest. I
red have this experience too. In my life computers (7)
are important in my room. I surf the Internet
(8) with a modem for my computer. I found a
newsgroup for surfing because I like boogie
boarding. ~~For my readers, I will write what the~~
~~boogie board is.~~ A boogie board is∧small   *red*
                                         a
surfboard made of styrofoam. (You) bring it into
                              w
the water and lay on it. (You) wait for waves.
repetition (I can) surf and (I can) roll over with my boogie
board. The boogie board is fun.

I lurk the surfing newsgroup on the net.
                      P-sf   *?*
When I lurk it means you read messages but not
                          Vt
post messages. One day∧I send a message to a
person who writes about boogie board party. I
                                  ?
will not write the name because I protect the
innocent.

    ?   The person was a young woman and we went to
boogie board party. We had more date. *Pl* Boogie
                          w
board people have much fun on the beach. Then

FIGURE 9.1   George's Marked Second Draft

226

it was winter and she went away to school. I
wanted e-mail for my birthday because I wanted
to write my new friend. We ~~did~~ e-mail and I
was very happy because we were boyfriend and
girlfriend. So now you know why everybody wants
a computer. ⑨

One day I got e-mail from this girlfriend
she send to somebody else. People sometimes
make a mistake and send e-mail wrong. My reader
will be kind to read the message was to
boyfriend who was not me. In message she say
bad things about me. She make fun of me.
I stop ~~to~~ write this mean person. I was
very lonely. Because e-mail was so bad to me I
play computer games. I play many fun games like
<u>Command and Conquer</u>, <u>Myst</u>, and <u>Civilization</u>
and make friends with people on my dorm floor.
Now they come to my room every hour of the day
and night. Ten people can fit at one time. They ⑪
come also to ask my computer for help because
they have homework. I make charts for them and
pictures they need for papers. I play CD-ROM
games. I meet many young women and have new
friends. ⑫

My experience with computers is it brings
people to friendship and fun. Like life, the
computer is good and bad. People use computers ⑭
to hurt people. My girlfriend did not tell me
to my face how she felt. She made a stupid mistake. Maybe she did because she is a coward.

227

> Personal computer bring much interest. I have this expe-
> rience too. Because in my life their is a computer in my room.

George realized that his first paragraph was not focused on his specific concern, so he dropped it. George also realized that the first two sentences of his second paragraph were redundant. Instead of trying to
reword them, he dropped those two sentences as well. He decided to
begin his paper with *I surf the Internet,* which is direct and focused and
uses surprising language. George revised his lead paragraph as follows:

> I surf the Internet with a modem for my computer. I found
> a newsgroup for surfing because I am an excellent boogie
> boarder. I take my boogie board to the ocean and surf the
> waves. Everybody know me as the best able person to roll with
> my boogie board in the waves. Because of the boogie board I
> am very strong and have handsome muscles.

When George showed this version to the other students in his workshop, they agreed that he had made a breakthrough. Instead of starting his
paper with uninteresting remarks about computers, he, as Tiffany put it,
had "zoomed in" on why computers were important to him. He was no
longer just repeating that he liked computers. His lead promised to show
his readers why.

5. Make a Checklist.   All writers have habits that they need to
develop or break. Identify comments and suggestions that people often
make in editing your papers. From these, create a *checklist* of notes on
grammar, punctuation, spelling, and style that apply particularly to you.
Keep it on the inside cover of your writer's journal where you can easily
refer to it or on a sheet tacked up in front of you where you write. On this
list, record those things you want to double-check for yourself. Organize
your checklist according to grammar, spelling, punctuation, and style.
Use the sidebar to format your own copy-editing checklists.

6. Use Spelling and Grammar Checkers.   If you can use a computer
for your writing, you may find that spelling and grammar checkers are
valuable learning aids and time-savers.

7. Reread Changes Aloud.   Do so to ensure that you don't leave both
old and new versions in your papers, especially if you use a computer. If
you change a sentence in any way, read out the whole sentence. If you add

new sentences or paragraphs or reorganize larger portions, read the new versions in the context of what precedes and follows.

George compiled a checklist of the particular copy-editing concerns his workshop members noted:

Copy-editing Checklist

```
Grammar
```

- Verbs--every sentence must have a verb.
- Verb tenses--check past tenses.
- Fragments--check for sentences starting with <u>because</u>.
- Pronoun shifts--check for <u>I</u> and <u>you</u> in the same sentence.
- Articles--check all nouns for <u>a</u> and <u>the</u>.

Copy-editing Checklist

Make a checklist for yourself, including the types of errors you tend to make most often.

Grammar

- _____
- _____
- _____

Punctuation

- _____
- _____
- _____

Spelling

- _____
- _____
- _____

Style (including repetitions and redundancies)

- _____
- _____
- _____

Punctuation

• Commas after introductory phrases.

Spelling

• <u>Their</u>, <u>there</u>, <u>they're</u>

Style

• Count how many times I use the same word in a paragraph or a paper.

George then referred to Chapters 15 and 16 to explore ways to further develop his style with regard to grammar and punctuation.

8. Revise Your Work Yourself.   Don't feel that you must always rely on others to help you revise. The purpose of writing workshop is to help each other so that you will be able to read and revise your own work more independently.

Third draft

Computers and Surfing

I surf the Internet with a modem for my computer. I found a newsgroup for surfing because I am an excellent boogie boarder. I take my boogie board to the ocean and surf the waves. Everybody know me as the best able person to roll with my boogie board in the waves. Because of the boogie board I am very strong and have handsome muscles.

I lurk the surfing newsgroup on the net. When I lurk it means I read messages but do not post messages which means to send them. One day, I sent a message to someone who has the e-mail name merMAID. We went to a boogie board party and I met her.

This person, who I will not give the real name, went on more dates with me. What we did on our dates was boogie board, go to Red Lobster because she likes shrimp, and many times we walk on the beach because we were boyfriend and girlfriend. She was very beautiful with long black hair all the way down. She had a beautiful body because she was a boogie boarder. What I like is merMAID was a boogie boarder and not many girls do that. I am a man who likes equality with the woman.

Then it was winter and she went away to the University of Hawaii which is far away from San Diego, California, where I live. I wanted e-mail for my birthday because I wanted to write to my new friend and e-mail has spelling checker. We e-mailed every night for a long time and I was very happy because we were boyfriend and girlfriend. One day I got an e-mail from merMAID. This is what she said in the message:

> I am so happy to have found you. There is nothing as beautiful as spending a day in the waves with you, kissing underwater, racing our boards, feeling the heat of the sun on our backs. I am so lucky to be able to walk with someone as handsome and built. I am the envy of all of the girls on my floor.

When I read the message I thought it was very strange because she was so far away and we had never kissed under the water. Then I read more:

> I want you to know that guy in San Diego was just a blip. We've been e-mailing each other because I needed him to help me with my computer programming class. Also, I am going to ask him to give me copies of his computer games, which I'll give to you when I see you. He's a nerd and he can barely speak English. All my love.

That woman made a mistake and posted that message to the newsgroup. I was friends with many people in that newsgroup. She broke my heart. She made fun of me in front of my friends. Many people in the surfing newsgroup e-mailed me how mean merMAID was. She made me look like a thief. I did not pirate games for her.

My experience with computers is they bring people friends. Like life computers are good and bad. People can use computers without care and hurt other people. merMAID did not tell me to my face how she felt. Here is the last e-mail message she sent me. Read it and what do you think of her?

> You are such a computer expert and I understand why you don't want to give me copies of your games but I really need one to help me relax because I am so upset about how you overreacted and how the group trashed me. I really think we can still be friends and you would really like to meet Paul.

Copy-editing Strategies

1. Read backward.
2. Mark your paper.
3. Make easy changes first.
4. Experiment.
5. Make a checklist.
6. Use spelling and grammar checkers.
7. Reread changes aloud.
8. Revise your work yourself.

Reflections

In addition to helping George copy-edit his second draft, students in his workshop asked him questions and offered suggestions for deep revision. Compare George's marked second draft (Figure 9.1, pages 226–227) and his third draft. Answer the following questions for each draft. Point to specific parts of his papers to focus your Reflections.

1. Which draft do you like better, and why?
2. How has George further revised so that his third draft might have greater audience appeal?
3. What purposes and needs does George's third draft satisfy that his second draft did not?
4. Which focusing strategies does he use in his third draft?
5. How does he organize his third draft?
6. What changes has George made in grammar, punctuation, spelling, and style?
7. Are there any suggestions you would offer for revising or copy-editing George's third draft?
8. What questions do you think the other students in George's workshop asked in order to help him revise his second draft?

Explorations

1. *Together.* Copy-edit a classmate's paper as a whole class or in small groups. Use the first five copy-editing strategies. Notice how different people focus on different aspects of the paper. Discuss what you learned about yourself and others as editors.

2. *Together.* Team up with someone who has copy-editing strengths where you have weaknesses and vice versa; or, create groups where a student expert in some aspect of writing presides. Copy-edit papers together, and notice what you learn.

3. *Together and Solo.* Copy-edit one of your own papers. How does copy-editing alone differ from doing it with others?

Levels of Changes

Many people use the word *revise* to talk about different ways you can change your writing by cutting, adding to, or reorganizing it. In the process of making changes, you will find yourself moving among four levels: (1) recopying, (2) readjusting, (3) copy-editing, and (4) revising, the most satisfying level. Revising and copy-editing have already been discussed in this chapter. This section distinguishes revising and copy-editing from recopying and readjusting so that you will not mistake one level of change for another.

Recopying

The purpose of recopying is to create a clean reading copy. A paper cluttered with marks and changes can be overwhelming. Furthermore, a typed paper is easier to revise than one that is handwritten. A clean paper is an act of respect to yourself and your readers and a first way of establishing good writer-audience relations. If you write with a computer, you will find it much easier to generate clean copies.

Remember that recopying is not *revising.* When you recopy, your main concern is neatness and typos. These are surface concerns, and anybody can manage them. Your attitude may be to "get it over with." That's no wonder. Humans need to be intellectually and emotionally engaged in their work to want to devote energy to it. Unless you enjoy typing or handwriting, recopying is not as satisfying as revising.

In early stages of writing your paper, sometimes it is more effective to use scissors and tape to reorganize and clean up your copy than to spend time recopying. *Don't avoid revising by settling for recopying.* Recopying is effective if it is your way of warming up for a writing session. If you find that recopying inspires you to revise, then start your revising sessions with recopying. Never avoid revising for fear of messing up a clean copy. Making changes shows that you know how to read and to revise.

Readjusting

The purpose of readjusting is to satisfy the readers who have responded to your work. Readjusting your work is responding to only specific comments others have offered. Sometimes this may be enough on a given paper. However, in readjusting, others are still guiding your process. The most satisfying way of changing your work is to use others' comments mostly as springboards for developing new ideas. Never settle for merely doing what others say: be your own person.

Revising in the Writing Process

Keep the following ten points in mind as you perform different levels of revising:

1. Make a Commitment.   Commitment is most important in the revising process. *Sometimes a piece of writing seems to get worse before it gets better.* The more you develop as a writer, the higher your standards for yourself will become. There may be a period when you are not satisfied with what you have written, but you haven't yet found a better way. If you give up at this point, you may be shortchanging yourself. Remember that there's a valley before every mountain. If you are discouraged, give yourself a specific amount of time to feel discouraged: "I'll feel bad about this until noon." Then, move on. Consult with others. Experiment. Use the strategies offered in *The Flexible Writer* to keep going.

2. Choose Your Level of Changes.   Be aware of which level of change you are performing. Don't settle for recopying, readjusting, or copy-editing when you have opportunities to revise.

3. Don't Revise Too Soon.   Be aware that you may need more time and space to collect ideas, focus, draft, organize, and consult before you revise.

4. Revise as Many Times as Necessary.   Someone once said that you don't finish a piece of writing, you abandon it. Writers report doing anywhere from 0 to 600 revisions of poems, stories, leads, articles, plays, memos, proposals, and so on. Most practiced writers will look at their own published work and want to change it. If you feel there's more you want to do, do it. But, at some point, something—a deadline, the end of a semester, a new writing project—will signal that it's time to let go. Know this: every bit of writing you do, whether you save it or not, helps make the next bit of writing better.

5. Let New Ideas Emerge at All Stages of Revising. It's tempting to settle for recopying or readjusting. It may be frustrating to finish copy-editing only to find more ideas and insights that might help you more fully *revise* your paper. But ideas come as a result of making changes. Note the new ideas, take a break, and revise when you can.

6. Keep a Clean Copy. As you move from one level of the revising process to another, a clean copy invites you to develop new ideas and make effective changes. Whenever possible, create a clean copy of your paper. Using a computer can help you to do this easily. Mark several copies in different ways. This will help you experiment with ways of revising and reorganizing your work.

7. When You Can't Solve a Problem, Come Back to It Later. Sometimes you may not be able to solve a particular problem right away. Leave it, even if for only a few minutes, and turn to some other task; in the meantime a solution for the first problem may emerge.

8. Study Writing Strategies You Need to Learn. Sometimes you can't solve a problem in revising because you don't know what to do. In the revising process, you will discover which phases of the writing process and which points of grammar, spelling, punctuation, and style you need to focus on. Use this book to help you develop the strategies you need to learn. Refer to the index and the table of contents and consult with your instructor and peers to find the sections of the book that address your particular needs. Post photocopies of sidebars from *The Flexible Writer* that respond most specifically to your writing concerns. Post your revision and copy-editing checklists.

9. Develop Your Own Copy-editing Style. Just as some writers prefer to compose according to a plan, and other writers compose by exploration, different writers follow different copy-editing procedures. You may prefer to copy-edit your papers line by line. Or, you may prefer to address a particular problem throughout your paper before turning to another problem. You may switch between the two styles.

10. When in Doubt, Try Without. If you struggle and struggle with a particular portion of your paper but never seem to get anywhere, try

Revising in the Writing Process

1. Make a commitment.
2. Choose your level of changes.
3. Don't revise too soon.
4. Revise as many times as necessary.
5. Let new ideas emerge.
6. Keep a clean copy.
7. When you can't solve a problem, come back to it later.
8. Study writing strategies.
9. Develop your own copy-editing style.
10. When in doubt, try without.

crossing out that phrase, sentence, or paragraph. Maybe it just doesn't belong. Read your paper without that troublesome part. Are you still making sense? If so, and the paper is better, you have successfully revised. If not, try writing a whole new replacement. Developing the ability to cross out what doesn't work will give you freedom and strength in the writing process. Why hang on to false starts and stubborn words that get in the way?

Reflecting on the Revising Process

To monitor your progress, use the Progress Review Checklist on page 93. Check the points of process, grammar, punctuation, and style on which you most need to focus.

Just as writing about early drafts helps you to prepare for revising, writing about the revising process helps you to name and understand what you learned *through* revising. In turn, writing about revising can prepare you for further revisions. Here is what George wrote about revising his paper in response to the question "How do computers affect our lives?"

```
     When I was revising my paper "Computers and Surfing," I
had to get focus about my own time with the computer. I
looked at suggestions of my workshop (who did two on me) and
```

decided it was OK to write about my experience with merMAID.
My workshop would not let me stop until I said what happened.
I was very happy because they listen.

Once I got what the computer mean to me, I remembered
many parts of it. Before I wrote this paper I never knew how
much I could write. What I know for myself is more important
than to say what everybody else knows. Then we worked on my
grammar, punctuation, spelling, and style. Then my paper got
better again.

The benefit of revising is that I know I can do it. I
never did any better on my papers before. Now I know I can.
I am not a computer nerd. I am a person who knows how to
learn.

*E*xplorations

1. *Solo.* Revise a paper to which you have had responses. Write a letter reflecting on the changes you have made. You may want to respond to the following questions and suggestions:

    a. How did you actually organize your time so that you could revise?

    b. What problems did you have?

    c. What were the benefits of revising your paper? You may want to start with expressions such as these:

        "I realized…"

        "I remembered…"

        "Before I wrote this paper I never knew that…"

        "I see _____ in a whole new way."

    d. Draw arrows to portions of your paper you want others to notice. Your instructor may want you to highlight portions in your revision that represent changes.

2. *Together.* Read your revisions to each other, and reflect on them. What improved? What more could you change?

3. *Together.* Discuss what makes you proud about your revisions. For example, students report being proud of noticing what they needed to change on their own, having revised a paper three times, or even having placed a specific semicolon. Discuss what more you could do with your paper.

Chapter Review _____

Together.

1. Write a one-page manual for new writers, choosing the ten points from this chapter that you feel are most important. One benefit of this project is that it provides you further practice in consulting and revising with each other. In the process of discussing this chapter, you will rehearse and thereby better remember it.

2. Reflect on the problems of writing this one-page manual. How did you revise it in the process?

Chapter **10**

Writing to Remember

This chapter offers opportunities to

—Develop your **memory** skills

—**Write** to remember

—**Find meaning** in past experiences

—Create **personal and family histories**

> The version we dare to write is the only truth, the only relationship we can have with the past. Refuse to write your life and you have no life.
>
> —*Patricia Hampl, Novelist and Educator*

> You have to own it before you can leave it.
>
> —*Carletta Joy Walker, Writer and Broadcaster*

The Dynamics of Memory

Writing helps people survive in the minds of others. William Shakespeare captured this idea in a sonnet he wrote to his beloved:

So long as men can breathe, or eyes can see,
So long lives this, and this gives life to thee.

239

As long as people can read Shakespeare's sonnet, his loved one will live through their readings. As long as people read his works, Shakespeare, as the writer, survives as well.

Writing memories not only helps you survive—it also helps you to understand and therefore live your life more fully. Richard Rodriguez captured the essential need for remembering in the title of his memoir, *Hunger of Memory.* We all need to remember, to tell and be told stories, to learn and to teach through them. Before there was writing, traditions and knowledge were passed down through storytelling and singing. But if you have ever played the game of telephone or found yourself at the wrong end of gossip, you know that stories can change with each telling. Writing brought a new dimension to storytelling. Because the written word is a physical object—like a painting or an arrowhead—it can outlast the writer. We are still deciphering and enjoying the memories that ancient civilizations carved into stone thousands of years ago.

Most people are unable to retain more than four things in their conscious minds at the same time. Through writing, you can access thoughts without having to strain to keep them in that narrow corridor of consciousness. By turning thoughts, feelings, and ideas into solid objects—written words—you can inspect your thoughts, arrange and rearrange them, and hold a conversation with yourself. You can communicate with people in the past and those in the future. You can, in short, own your life.

This chapter focuses on accessing and finding meaning in personal and family memories.* Chapters 11 through 14 offer you further strategies for accessing the memories of the community that are embodied in books, newspapers, tapes, and other documents.

Meaning and Purpose

The purpose of writing memories is not merely to record them but to make sense of them—to discover why those flowers or that first car were important to you, why the groom was chewing on his cuffs during the wedding, or why you weren't wearing a cap at your graduation. When you read through your memoirs, you can discern patterns in your life and recapture or discover meaning. At the very least, if you record your memories, others might be able to discover these meanings for you.

Writing to remember may mean different things at different times. You might write about a hand injury, sustained from computer use, to

---

*For ideas that inspired this chapter, I am indebted to Morton D. Rich of Montclair State University.

learn a spiritual lesson from your body. Or, you might write about the injury to help put safety regulations on computer design into the law. In a play or a poem, you might write about your injury to make, as one poster put it, "lemonade out of lemons." These purposes are, respectively, self-expressive, interpersonal, aesthetic, or a combination of these.

Some general *self-expressive* purposes for writing to remember include the following:

- For relief
- To relive an experience
- To own your life
- To learn life lessons
- To make sense of, come to terms with, or find reasons for what happened
- To savor good times and find strength from them
- To ask important questions
- To formulate plans of action
- To create at least one sympathetic reader: yourself

Some *interpersonal* purposes for writing to remember include the following:

- To be heard
- To gain sympathy from your audience
- To help you forgive and forget
- To reach out to others
- To create changes
- To inform
- To connect with the past
- To create a record for future generations

Some of the *aesthetic* satisfactions of writing memories are these:

- To fit pieces of your life into a meaningful whole
- To create an order that distills meaning and purpose from your experiences
- To move others with emotion
- To make something beautiful

Finding Meaning and Purpose in Memories

1. *Choose* topics that are meaningful to you, that carry emotion, drama, conflict, or surprise.

2. *Assume a sympathetic audience.* The more you anticipate being heard without judgment, the more honest and thorough you can be.

3. *Strive for balance.* Few people are all good or all bad. Add dimension to your work: consider different angles.

4. *Find humor* in what you are writing, whenever you can.

5. *Connect memories to the present.* Note changes in your own and others' attitudes, personalities, and expectations.

6. *Ask questions* to help you focus on meaning. Here are some that you might find helpful:

   - Why is this important?
   - How did I feel it about it then? How do I feel now?
   - What am I learning by writing this memory?
   - Who would benefit from reading this memory? Why?
   - What would my audience want to know?
   - How can I win the sympathy of my audience?
   - What does this memory mean to my life?
   - How did this experience shape my life?

Deaths, accidents, illnesses, divorces, abuse, and other losses—these are events in your life you may want to forget. But they are often the events that hold the most meaning. Therefore, we will start our exploration of memories with these more difficult experiences. Often you can't leave them behind unless you express and learn lessons from them. As Carletta Joy Walker puts it, to leave them you have to *own them.*

*E*xplorations _____

These Explorations offer you opportunities to write about experiences for which you want to discover new meaning. Each time you do one of these Explorations, reflect on what you have learned and gained.

1. *Together.* Using the sidebar titled Reading Memories (page 264), discuss the passage on pages 332–333 from Paul Monette's memoir on

AIDS, *Borrowed Time*. Notice how he uses sense details to recapture the last moments of his friend's life.

2. *Solo.* Write about a difficult experience in your life, such as an accident, a death, an illness or injury, a divorce, a lost relationship, an incident of abuse, a troubling sight, or a "close call." Describe what life was like *before* this event and *during* and *after* the event. How is your life affected by it *now*? What does it mean for you to be writing about the experience?

3. *Together.* Write a letter to a person in politics, sports, entertainment, or education. Choose a person for whom you have some strong feelings. Address the person directly, clearly state the events to which you are reacting, and express your collective response. State the purpose of your letter and ask any questions that arise. Discuss whether to send the letter. If you decide to do so, would you change it? Why? How?

4. *Solo.* Write a personal letter to someone (alive or dead) saying, at last, what you have needed to say. This letter may express grief, curiosity, fear, anger, love, regret—whatever. Notice whether there are any changes in you as you write. Reflect on what it means to you to write this letter. What have you learned? Consider how it might affect your writing if you anticipated that the person would read it. You may want to write more letters to this person and see if there are changes from letter to letter. Freewrite in your journal about the experience of writing each letter.

5. *Solo.* Describe a recurring nightmare. What do you learn about yourself from having written about it?

Focusing Memories with Statements

A memory can become meaningful to both you and your readers by the mere act of stating clearly why it is or was important to you. Notice how focusing these statements are:

> It was the worst experience of my life.
>
> My first kiss changed me forever.
>
> I never want to do that again.
>
> My last conversation with my father was very moving.

Such statements of meaning are like magnets that invite you to write more. They draw readers to you—engage and interest them. Notice how the following paragraph by student Sandy Freeman is transformed from the first to the second draft when she clearly states what her father's restaurant means to her:

Focusing with Statements

1. *Choose* topics that are meaningful to you, that carry emotion, drama, conflict, surprise, or humor.

2. *Specify.* Write about particular events and particular times.

3. *State* what your subject means to you. Here are some sample formats with examples that can help you focus:

    "I [feeling verb] [subject]."

    > "I feel disgusted with Burger Barn."

    "My [adjective] [subject] was _____."

    > "My favorite baseball game was the Little League match between the Cubs and the Jays one summer."

    "The [subject] is just like a [noun]."

    > "During the holidays, the convalescent center is just like a carnival."

4. *Commit* yourself to strong words and statements that clearly capture what your subject means to you.

5. *Illustrate* your statement. Show what you mean by offering specifics, quotations, examples, and sensations. Use the question star (Figure 5.4 on page 120) and the sense star (Figure 6.1 on page 135) to ensure that you have included all significant details.

6. *State* at the end of your paper what it was you learned through writing your story. Here are some formats to help you focus:

    "From this experience I learned that _____."

    > "From this experience I learned that sometimes it's better to stay silent than to say what you're really thinking."

    "I'll never [action] again because _____."

    > "I'll never ski in muddy snow again because the price Jane paid for doing it will always haunt me."

    "I'll always remember [subject] because _____."

    > "I'll always remember Mimi because I never want to lose a friend that way again."

First draft

Upon entering our family's restaurant, I can see its title in big blue letters "The Dolphin." Once inside the restaurant, the first thing I notice is a forty gallon fish tank. The tank was recently added in mid-August. My father and grandfather thought it would be attractive for the res-

taurant. The tank has many tropical fish with decorations of
plastic weeds and different color rocks. The next thing I
can see is that one side of the wall is covered by mirrors
that run the length of the restaurant. The mirrors make the
restaurant look larger and reflect the fish tank. It looks
like there are fish all around and you are in the water.

In this first draft, Sandy describes the setting without offering her
subjective point of view. She doesn't tell us what the setting means to her
or why we should be interested in it. In her second draft, she finds a focus
by stating what the place means to her and her family:

Second draft

My father's restaurant, The Dolphin, has meant different
things me. He has made it beautiful as an ocean with a fish
tank, works of art, mirrors, and blue lights. But the place
sometimes felt like a pool of sharks to me with all the problems that are involved when you work in a busy restaurant.

When Sandy stated that the restaurant sometimes felt like a pool of
sharks because of problems, she not only focused her discussion but also
engaged the interest of her readers. They wanted to know more about
how the restaurant was beautiful. They also wanted to know how it felt
to work in the restaurant and what problems Sandy had.

Fires, accidents, sudden lights, strange sounds—people tend to gather
around the unusual. Strong words and statements, problems, conflicts,
fears, feelings, surprises, and unusual things and events capture attention
like a couple bungee jumping at their wedding. Whenever it is appropriate, endeavor to engage your readers with striking statements.

The following Explorations are designed to help you trigger and interpret memories using strong words, phrases, and statements. The Explorations assume that you create who you are—your identity—by what you
favor and what you choose.

*E*xplorations _____

1. *Together and Solo.* Emotion is usually a signal that something is
   meaningful to you. Fill in this blank to create a working title for an
   essay: "A Time I Felt Most _____." Here are some feelings from
   which you might choose:

Embarrassed	Shy
Angry	Loving
Afraid	Joyful
Frustrated	Confused
Surprised	Harassed
Silly	Amused

Create a working title and start writing. State your subject clearly and show what it means to you. Be sure to illustrate your discussion with significant details, quotations, examples, and sense impressions. Write so that your audience will empathize with you. What purpose does it serve you to write, and others to read, this piece? State what you learned from your experience. Share and discuss your essays.

2. *Together and Solo.* You are reflected in what you choose and what you favor. Therefore, your favorite things are meaningful to you. List some ways to fill in the blank in this working title for an essay: "My Favorite _____." When something inspires you—start writing. Here are some favorites that others have used to fill in the blank:

Uncle	Car
Ice Cream	Mall
Sweater	Beach
Pastime	Book

Notice as you write who your likely audience(s) might be. Write so that your audience will appreciate what you favor, as well. Share and discuss your results.

3. *Together and Solo.* First impressions, first romances, first times at most anything are significant. Brainstorm some ways to fill in the blank in this working title for an essay: "My First _____." When something inspires you—start writing. Here are some "firsts":

Basketball Game	Failure
Day at School	Childhood Memory
Date	Car

Be sure to offer your audience a you-are-there feeling. Formulate what this "first" means in your life. How does this experience affect you today? Share and discuss your results.

4. *Together and Solo.* Last impressions can be the lasting ones. Brainstorm ways to fill in the blank in this working title for an essay: "My Last _____." Here are some "lasts" that may inspire you:

Time with My Sister   Cigarette
Day in High School   Child
Skiing Trip   Hamburger

Choose a lasting last event and start writing. Why will this event be the last one of its kind for you? How has this event affected you in the past and today? How do you project it will affect you in the future? Share and discuss your results.

5. *Solo.* Write an essay with the following working title: "I'll Never Do That Again." Follow this format to get started:

   • State what you did.

   • Explain why you did it.

   • Report the results.

   • Clarify what the event meant to you.

   • State why you won't do it again.

Collecting Memories

You have probably had experiences in your life that you want to relive and savor. So you may photograph or videotape weddings, graduations, and other important events. Perhaps you save objects:

   • Statues

   • Postcards

   • Printed buttons

   • Dried flowers from wreaths or corsages

   • Letters, cards, and other documents

   • A hood ornament from an old car

   • An old baseball glove

Such objects are called *memorabilia* or *souvenirs*. Memorabilia and souvenirs are memory aids. But what they mean—just like whispered messages—can change and be distorted over time. As *you* change, your memories can change, too. It's fascinating to collect memories and see how their meanings vary over time.

Because photographs and videotapes are such powerful aids to memory, we will focus on how to use them to collect memories. Most of the same principles will apply to how to use other objects, as well. In the

---

Collecting Memories

1. **Collect** memorabilia, souvenirs, and photographs to help you recollect meaningful events and feelings.

2. **Visit** significant places and participate in activities that will help memories surface.

3. **Brainstorm, freewrite, and cluster.** Your basic source of information and meaning is you.

4. **Draw** pictures of your topic. This will help you to visualize and recall details.

5. **Interview** other people who can remember with or for you. (For guidelines, turn to the sidebar on page 86.)

---

following passage from his memoir *Parallel Time,* journalist Brent Staples uses photographs to help him focus on the death of his brother Blake. Blake had been shot and killed by a man that Blake, himself, had previously shot. Read Staples's description through twice, the first time for the experience, the second to notice how Staples works with the photographs.

From *The Coroner's Photographs*
Brent Staples

My brother's body lies dead and naked on a stainless steel slab. At his head stands a tall arched spigot that, with tap handles mimicking wings, easily suggests a swan in mourning. His head is squarish and overlarge. (This, when he was a toddler, made him seem top-heavy and unsteady on his feet.) His widow's peak is common among the men in my family, though this one is more dramatic than most. An inverted pyramid, it begins high above the temples and falls steeply to an apex in the boxy forehead, over the heart-shaped face. A triangle into a box over a heart. His eyes (closed here) were big and dark and glittery; they drew you into his sadness when he cried. The lips are ajar as always, but the picture is taken from such an angle that it misses a crucial detail: the left front tooth tucked partly beyond the right one. I need this detail to see my brother full. I paint it in from memory.

A horrendous wound runs the length of the abdomen, from the sternum all the way to the pubic mound. The wound resembles a mouth whose lips are pouting and bloody. Massive staplelike clamps are gouged into these lips at regular intervals along the abdomen. This is a surgeon's incision. The surgeon was presented with a patient shot six times with a large-caliber handgun. Sensing the carnage that lay within, he achieved the largest possible opening and worked frantically trying to save my brother's life. He tied off shattered vessels, resectioned the small intestine, repaired a bullet track on the liver, then backed out. The closing would have required two pairs of hands. An assistant would have gripped the two sides of the wound and drawn them together while a second person cut in the clamps. The pulling together has made my brother's skin into a corset that crushes in on the abdomen from all sides. The pelvic bones jut up through the skin. The back is abnormally arched from the tension. The wound strains at the clamps, threatening to rip itself open. The surgeon worked all night and emerged from surgery gaunt, his greens darkened with sweat. "I tied off everything I could," he said, and then he wept at the savagery and the waste.

This is the body of Blake Melvin Staples, the seventh of my family's nine children, the third of my four brothers, born ten years after me. I know his contours well. I bathed and diapered him when he was a baby and studied his features as he grew. He is the smallest of the brothers, but is built in the same manner: short torso but long arms and legs; a more than ample behind set high on the back; knocking knees; big feet that tend to flat. The second toe is also a signature. It curls softly in an extended arc and rises above the others in a way that's unique to us. His feelings are mine as well. Cold: The sensation moves from my eyes to my shoulder blades to my bare ass as I feel him naked on the steel. I envision the reflex that would run through his body, hear the sharp breath he would draw when the steel met his skin. Below the familiar feet a drain awaits the blood that will flow from this autopsy.

The medical examiner took this picture and several others on February 13, 1984, at 9:45 A.M. The camera's flash is visible everywhere: on the pale-green tiles of the surrounding walls, on the gleaming neck of the spigot, on the stainless steel of the slab, on the bloody lips of the wound.

Blake was a drug dealer; he was known for carrying guns and for using them. His killer, Mark McGeorge, was a former customer and cocaine addict. At the trial Mark's lawyer described the shooting as a gunfight in which Blake was beaten to the draw. This was doubtful. Blake was shot six times: three times in the back. No weapon was found on or near his body. Blake's gunbearer testified that my brother was unarmed when Mark ambushed and gunned him down. But a gunbearer is not a plausible witness. A drug dealer known for shooting a rival in plain public view gets no sympathy from a jury. The jury turned back the prosecution's request for a conviction of murder in the first degree. Mark was found guilty of second-degree murder and sentenced to seven years in jail. Five years for the murder. Two years for using the gun.

Blake is said to have cried out for his life as he lay on the ground. "Please don't shoot me no more. I don't want to die." *"Please don't shoot me no more. I don't want to die."* His voice had a touch of that dullness one hears from the deaf, a result of ear infections he suffered as a child. The ear openings had narrowed to the size of pinholes. He tilted his head woefully from side to side trying to pour out the pain. His vowels were locked high in his throat, behind his nose. This voice kept him a baby to me. This is the voice in which he would have pleaded for his life.

· · ·

...My brother Bruce called me with the news. "Brent, Blake is dead," he said. "Some guy pulled up in a car and emptied out on him with a magnum. Blake is dead." I told myself to feel nothing.... I skipped the funeral and avoided Roanoke for the next three years. The next time I visited my family I went to see the Roanoke Commonwealth Attorney and questioned him about the case. He was polite but impatient. For him, everything about the killing had been said. This, after all, had been an ordinary death.

I asked to see the files. A secretary brought a manila pouch and handed it to the Commonwealth Attorney, who handed it to me and excused himself from the room. The pouch contained a summary of the trial, the medical examiner's report, and a separate inner pouch wrapped in twine and shaped like photographs. I opened the pouch; there was Blake dead and on the slab, photographed from several angles. The floor gave way, and I fell down and down for miles.

After they read Staples's essay, students developed the following guidelines for "reading visuals," such as pictures, photographs, paintings, drawings, and videos:

- Ask yourself what emotional state or attitude you bring to the picture or photograph. (You can figure this out as you see what ideas come to you as you read along.)
- Relate the sense data to human events at the time of the photograph, before and afterward.

- Reintroduce motion, smell, taste, and touch in whatever way you can.
- Notice what significant person or thing is left out.
- Treat all "errors" or "irregularities" seriously.
- Treat every detail as significant.
- Use your imagination.
- As you read, notice how you feel in relation to the picture or photograph. Notice what you learn and what it means to you.

In working with their own photographs, students added further guidelines:

- *Notice faces.* What are the eyes doing? Blot out different portions on a face and notice whether the expression of the eyes matches the expression of the mouth. Notice the differences between upper and lower portions and left and right sides of faces. Is the person putting on a false face? What feelings are being expressed?
- *Notice relationships.* How are people relating to each other? In what positions are they relative to each other? Who's touching and who isn't? What attitudes are you noticing and from what details?
- *Notice perspective.* What attitude or position is the photographer/artist taking? (This is especially interesting and sometimes humorous when you look at photographs taken by professionals who are strangers to the persons they are photographing.)
- *Notice who or what is left out* of the photograph.
- *Notice the attitudes* people in the photograph have toward the photographer.

*R*eflections

1. What did the photographs mean to Staples?
2. What might Staples's main purposes have been in writing the essay?
3. Who would be included in Staples's chosen audience for the essay? Who might not?
4. Find specific portions of Staples's essay that illustrate the guidelines students developed.
5. Formulate further guidelines for reading and writing from photographs.

*E*xplorations _____

The purpose of Explorations 1 through 3 is to practice using photographs and objects to recollect memories. The purpose of Explorations 4 and 5 is to practice writing for different audiences and purposes.

1. *Together.* Compare and contrast Paul Monette's description of his dying friend (pages 332–333) with Brent Staples's description of his brother's death. Consider subject matter, purpose, audience, sense impressions, and insights.

2. **a.** *Together.* Bring photographs of family and/or friends to class. In small groups, discuss these informally. What do other people discern about the relationships they see in your pictures?

    b. *Solo.* Freewrite about a meaningful event or relationship the photograph(s) bring to mind. You can write about something in the photograph or something else that you remember as you look at it. Apply some of the guidelines developed above.

    c. *Together and Solo.* Read some of these freewrites to each other, and discuss what you learned. If you find an inspiring focus through freewriting, plan to write an essay from it. Help each other notice interesting focuses for further writing. Be clear about what purpose you want to serve in writing about your chosen topic. Discover and state what your memory means to you.

3. *Together and Solo.* Bring a treasure to class—an especially important object that you could never discard (and that you can carry into the classroom). Talk with each other about what these objects mean to you. When you find yourself focusing on some meaningful event or relationship that this object represents, start freewriting. Some of the objects that have inspired others are these:

    •   A mouthpiece from a saxophone
    •   An heirloom ring
    •   A membership card
    •   A personal Bible
    •   A teddy bear

4. **a.** *Solo.* Choose a paper you are writing about a memory. Think of an audience (a family member or friend) who would find it difficult to read what you wrote. Revise the paper so that this new audience would be able to read it. What do you change? What do you leave out? What do you introduce? How does the purpose of your paper change? How do you feel about making the changes?

    b. *Together.* Discuss the differences that occur when you write for different audiences. How do purpose and meaning change as a result?

Focusing Memories with Sense Appeal

1. *Choose* a meaningful memory.
2. *Specify* particular people, actions, events, and objects related to your memory.
3. *Draw the sense star.* Cluster sense images related to your topic around each ray (see Figure 6.1 on page 135).
4. *Prime your senses.* Use souvenirs to stimulate sense memories.
5. *Offer a you-are-there description* for your reader.
6. *Appeal to the sense of smell* whenever appropriate, to help both you and your reader experience your memory most fully.

---

5. a. *Solo.* Choose a paper you are writing about a memory. Revise it for one of the following audiences:

A doctor	A psychologist
A lawyer	A film director
A member of the clergy	A banker

b. *Together.* Do Exploration 4b for this exploration as well.

Focusing Memories with Sense Appeal

Seeing a photograph of a forgotten friend or touching the worn leather of a baseball glove can trigger a whole range of memories. Sometimes even a simple sensation like a few notes from an old song or the smell of mothballs is enough. In one episode of television's *M*A*S*H*, Hawkeye relives the whole experience of his cousin's drowning when he smells mildew. His cousin had smelled of it when they pulled him out of the water.

A research study reported in *The New York Times** showed that college students who smelled chocolate while studying and again during the test were better at remembering their answers than others who did not use the chocolate smell to help trigger their memory. The article also suggested that smell could be a more powerful trigger for memories than could any of the other senses. We will focus on the sense of smell in this chapter on remembering. Many of the insights you gain apply to other senses, as well.

---

*"Memory: It Seems a Whiff of Chocolate Helps," *The New York Times*, July 10, 1990, p. C2

Features reporter Gigi Anders started an essay by focusing on the smell of violet water. It triggered a series of memories she wrote into an article that was published in *Latina Style* magazine. Read this excerpt and reflect on it, using the sidebar on page 264.

From The Violet Hour

Gigi Anders

As Latinas in America, we straddle two cultures. In our dualistic world, the past lingers on in the present in sometimes subtle but distinct ways. Our feminine traditions in particular tend to distinguish us from other women. This story is about how one who considers herself a modern Hispanic woman living in the New World finds a sense of beauty and memory, home and comfort—in a bottle of Cuban hair tonic. We each have our memories. We all have our stories. This one is mine.

For even the humblest Cuban woman, being meticulous about beauty is never frivolous. What a non-Latina might consider self-indulgent—washing with imported soaps, always wearing perfume and body lotion from head to toe—is for us imperative. So much so that we cannot maintain self-respect and well-being unless we are scrupulously clean and with soft and sweet-smelling skin.

The mere thought of having foul body odor or dirty hair is unthinkable; either state could putatively lead to social disgrace and the loss of self, of feminine identity. In my Cuban culture, femininity, like its counterpart machismo, begins with external rules and works its way into the psyche gradually, step-by-step. This is a defining philosophy, whose aromatic effects begin early, virtually from the day we are born.

That was the day my own initiation began. In fact, I emerged into the pretty world of *La Habana* with a head full of curly, black hair. This unlikely feature was a source of pride and intense excitement for my glamorous mother, who got to send for the *Agua de Violetas* at once. Rule number one of the Cuban beauty mystique had officially commenced: Hair is good, but hair with *Agua de Violetas* in it is better.

Agua de Violetas. Violet water, in Spanish. A topaz-colored eau de cologne for the hair. Its exotic name is only somewhat misleading; while violets are the fundamental ingredient, 30 essential oils commingle to create its subtle, citrusy bouquet. Even today, a whole continent and three-and-a-half decades later, *Agua de Violetas* is my Proustian madeleine. The smell involves an immaculate, unforced sensuality, like a hand-stitched white cotton nightgown billowing in a breeze. As my elegant grandmother had done for her, my mother would sprinkle the unction on my hair every morning of my childhood after my bath. I was just 3 years old when my family and I fled Castro's Cuba, but I still remember it was streaming in cool rivulets down my scalp, flushing the air with the fragrance of cut oranges.

That smell has been an enduring comfort, especially welcome during times of loss, which the displaced often feel. For Mami, the smell is a remembrance of the old life before Fidel, of home. All her girlfriends wore it when they were growing up in the '40s and '50s, and when they had their babies, they'd give a bottle of Violetas as a shower gift. You'd see them piled up on the mothers' beds.

Back then, it was known as *Violetas Rusas*, Russian Violets. And the lettering on the labels of the bottles was done in 24-carat gold leaf. That was customary. Yet it wasn't expensive: about $2 for a 5-ounce bottle. A Havana perfumer named Agustin Reyes created it in the 1920s and it became an instant, permanent hit all across the island. It wasn't only for babies' hair, either. Men used it as cologne; women sprinkled their bed linens with it. It was an integral part of living. It would be there forever.

What few Cubans considered would be there forever, on the other hand, was the communist revolution. We took it to be a political psychosis, a fleeting aberration, treatable by the powerful drug known as military intervention. As people by the thousands fled their homeland in waves, the collective mind-set was one of temporary flight, six months at the most. Along with my birth certificate, a stuffed toy lamb and some clothes, Mami packed a dozen bottles of *Agua de Violetas* in my lone suitcase. She figured two bottles a month ought to see us through....

As my twelve slim bottles of *Agua de Violetas* dwindled, and the Castro dictatorship wore on, the golden solution became more precious. Concurrently, so did the time I had alone with my mother. Her attention span and disposition were diffusing, atomizing like a fine spray I could sense but not grasp. It was necessary to go to work, she explained to me, because we needed the money. Okay, I replied, but you still have to do my hair every day, and you definitely, definitely have to put the *Agua de Violetas* in there. By then I had cultivated specific needs, thanks to her, and I was onto things, especially the endings of things. Diminishing supplies of hair cologne, of mother or of the hope of returning to Cuba notwithstanding, I had to have what I needed in order to feel normal.

What's worse for a little Cuban girl who feels like a castaway? The absence of a mother or the absence of *Agua de Violetas*? Rule number two of the mystique takes hold here: Mother and smell are the same, womanliness and home and safety—are all the same. Today I can secure my own *Violetas* at the local mercado Latino, run by a Hispanic couple. I asked them recently how any woman can manage to live without it.

"They just live," the husband said. But Latinas, we always crave memory and delight, the kind you can smell. It matters to us. That's not the same thing as living. That's BEING ALIVE.

*E*xplorations

The purpose of these Explorations is to help you stimulate memories through sensations.

1. *Together or Solo.* Do you agree with the claims of *The New York Times* article that smell can be a more powerful trigger for remembering than the other senses? Refer to specific smells and their effects on you.

2. *Together and Solo.* Brainstorm two lists of specific smells—one of pleasant smells, the other of unpleasant. Choose one smell that is particularly meaningful to you, and freewrite about the memories it stirs for you. Share these freewrites. If a freewrite inspires you, write a memory essay from it.

3. *Solo.* Spend a day recording smells you perceive in your environment and how you feel about them. If any particular smell stirs a memory, freewrite about the memory.

4. *Together and Solo.* Do a choice of Explorations 1 through 3, focusing on either the sense of touch or the sense of hearing.

5. *Together and Solo.* In small groups, discuss freewrites or essays you are writing in order to remember. For each paper, refer to the sense star (Figure 6.1 on page 135).

    *   To which senses does the writer appeal? Where exactly is the appeal made in the paper?

    *   To which senses does the writer *not* appeal? Would it enliven the paper to appeal to these senses? Where?

    *   Does the writer offer a you-are-there feeling? If so, how? If not, how could it be done?

Organizing Memories

You have access to an enormous store of memories. But most memories lie in clutter in the mind. By organizing memories through the writing process, you gain greater access to them, just as organizing objects in an attic helps you to retrieve them when you need them.

Personal and family histories are exciting to organize and write. In exploring and writing personal and family histories, you can connect not only with past but future generations as well. Because memories and histories are meant to last for a long time, you will want to fill in all the missing pieces you can and to anticipate questions that may be of interest to future readers. Also, you will want to polish drafts to show your writing to its best advantage. Bind your memories and histories in attractive covers, and include photographs and drawings where appropriate.

Organizing Memories

1. *Lead* your essay with a clear focus, using one of these strategies:

   - State your memory and what it means to you.

   - Tell a story.

   - Describe a person, place, object, or event.

2. *Develop* your essay with special attention to time. Use one of the following organizing strategies:

   - *Chronological.* Report your memory as it happened through time.

   - *Flashback.* Start with some present event and then show how events led up to the present.

   - *Before and after.* Focus on a significant event that created changes. Show how conditions were before and after the event. Show how the event created the changes.

   - *Zig-zag.* Move back and forth from the present to the past.

   - *Backtrack.* Start with some present event and move backward in the exact order of events to the first event you want to consider.

3. *Create transitions* that show how events are related.

4. *Avoid* details that are not relevant to either fulfilling your purpose or showing what your memory means to you.

5. *End* your essay using one of these strategies:

   - State what your memory means to you.

   - State what changed.

   - State what you learned.

   - Describe a person, place, object, event, or image that best sums up the experience.

6. *Construct* a special album in which you collect photographs, memorabilia, notes, ideas, and essays.

Personal History

When you construct a personal history, you develop a sense of order or meaning. To write a personal history, you need to divide the task into smaller sections so that you don't end up saying something so general that it can be the history of *any*one and so *no* one.

Notice how film director Akira Kurosawa writes a personal history of his babyhood. He focuses most of this memory on one experience in a washtub. To organize this passage, he starts with the technique of flashback and ends by linking an earlier to a later experience.

From *Babyhood*
*Akira Kurosawa**

I was in the washtub naked. The place was dimly lit, and I was soaking in hot water and rocking myself by holding on to the rims of the tub. At the lowest point the tub teetered between two sloping boards, the water making little splashing noises as it rocked. This must have been very interesting for me. I rocked the tub with all my strength. Suddenly it overturned. I have a very vivid memory of the strange feeling of shock and uncertainty at that moment, of the sensation of that wet and slippery space between the boards against my bare skin, and of looking up at something painfully bright overhead.

After reaching an age of awareness, I would occasionally recall this incident. But it seemed a trivial thing, so I said nothing about it until I became an adult. It must have been after I had passed twenty years of age that for some reason I mentioned to my mother that I remembered these sensations. For a moment she just stared at me in surprise; then she informed me that this could only have been something that occurred when we went to my father's birthplace up north in Akita Prefecture to attend a memorial service for my grandfather. I had been one year old at the time.

The dimly lit place where I sat in a tub lodged between two boards was the room that served as both kitchen and bath in the house where my father was born. My mother had been about to give me a bath, but first she put me in the tub of hot water and went into the next room to take off her kimono. Suddenly she heard me start wailing at the top of my lungs. She rushed back and found me spilled out of the tub on the floor crying. The painfully bright, shiny thing over head, my mother explained, was probably a hanging oil lamp of the type still used when I was a baby.

*Translated by Audie E. Bock.

This incident with the washtub is my very first memory of myself. Naturally, I do not recall being born. However, my oldest sister, now deceased, used to say, "You were a strange baby." Apparently I emerged from my mother's womb without uttering a sound, but with my hands firmly clasped together. When at last they were able to pry my hands apart, I had bruises on both palms.

I think this story may be a lie. It was probably made up to tease me because I was the youngest child. After all, if I really had been born such a grasping person, by now I would be a millionaire and surely would be riding around in nothing less than a Rolls-Royce.

*R*eflection

Together.

1. Using the sidebar on reading memories (page 264), discuss Kurosawa's "Babyhood." How does Kurosawa organize his essay?

2. Using the sidebar on reading memories, read Siu Wai Anderson's "A Letter to My Daughter" (pages 267–269). How does the strategy of letter writing affect the reader?

3. How does the difference in their anticipated readers affect the way Kurosawa and Anderson write?

*E*xplorations

1. **a.** *Together.* List some ideas for filling in the blank in the working title "A History of My _____." Some ideas that others have used include these:

Name	Hair
Soccer Career	Strudel Recipe
Shoes	Jobs
Illness	Writing

   b. *Solo.* Create a working title by filling in the blank in "A History of My _____." List crucial events or scenes that you would want to include in the history. If you prefer, create a cluster around the title. Organize the events you want to write about by using one of the strategies offered in the sidebar on organizing memories.

Focus on one event at a time, and enliven your essay with sense impressions, quotations, and examples. These questions may help you to draw meaning from this history:

- What do you learn about yourself as you write?
- What do the events mean to you?
- How did events in this particular history affect other aspects of your life?
- Who would be your likely audience(s)?
- Who would *not* be a likely audience, and why?

2. *Solo.*

   a. A turning point in your life is when you go through a significant change. This change may be as simple as starting to wear makeup or taking a road test, or as complex as going through a divorce or moving to a different country. Because turning points bear so much meaning, they provide a strong focus for memories. Choose a turning point in your life and create a cluster around it (for instructions on clustering, see pages 83–85). Include the following:

Sense impressions	Events	Persons
Objects	Places	Feelings

   Choose one item from your cluster to start a freewrite. As you develop an essay on this topic, consider these questions:

   - What did your turning point mean to you?
   - Who would be your likely audience for this essay?
   - How did your turning point change your life?

   b. Create a personal history by writing an outline for a series of papers about other turning points. Create transitions between the papers by finding similarities between events and changes.

3. *Solo.* Imagine that you could change something that happened in your life. Rewrite some special aspect of it. In developing your paper, use any of the following questions that you find useful:

- What would you change?
- Why would you change it?
- How would you change it?
- What do you regret?
- To whom would you like to make amends?
- What would you gain or lose in the rewritten life?
- Who would you want to read your revision of your life?
- What do you think the likely response would be?
- What do you learn from rewriting your personal history?

Interviewing for Family Histories

1. *Review* the instructions for interviewing on pages 85–87.

2. *Interview older people* when possible, because they are such valuable resources for family histories. If you can, interview family, friends, and other people who know the family, such as doctors and merchants.

3. *Ask focused questions.* Here are some questions that are especially helpful in interviewing people directly. (Revise them if you are speaking about others. For example, "When was *she* born?"). Think of your own questions, as well.

   - When and where were you born?

   - How were you named, and what is the significance of your name?

   - With whom did you live as a child?

   - Where did you live, and what were your accommodations?

   - What was the most important turning point in your life, and what did it mean to you?

   - What was the most difficult time in your life, and why?

   - What was the happiest time in your life, and why?

   - What was (*name another family member*) like as a child or teenager?

   - What kinds of foods did you eat as a child?

   - What were holidays like for you? (Choose a specific one that reflects your culture or religion.)

   - What are the most important changes in technology, culture, or the economy that you've experienced? How did they affect your life?

   - Who was the most important person in your life, and how did she or he affect you?

   - Am I like anyone else in my family? Who? How?

   - Do you have any regrets?

   - What advice would you give me?

To get started, you might want to fill in this sentence: "If I could change one thing in my past, it would be _____." Organize your paper by using strategies suggested in the sidebar on page 257.

4. **a.** *Solo.* Using Sui Wai Anderson's letter on pages 267–269 as a model, write a letter detailing your personal history to a specific family member. Then write a second letter to a different person (in your family or otherwise).

> **b.** *Together.* Read and compare the pairs of letters you wrote. How does the anticipated audience affect the details you choose?

5. *Together and Solo.* Consult each other with special attention to how you organize your papers on personal history.

Family History

To know where you are going, you have to know where you have been. Becoming more aware of your family patterns can help you practically, emotionally, financially, physically, and spiritually. For example, it can be very encouraging to you to learn that—although your family may be experiencing difficulties now—you had a courageous great-grandmother who single-handedly raised ten children. Knowing the history of family illnesses can save your life: you can monitor yourself for warning signs. In constructing a family history you may discover relatives who can become a resource to you emotionally. And so on.

Many of the strategies for writing personal histories apply to family histories, and vice versa. An essential tool for constructing family histories is the interview. When you interview someone, you hold a conversation—much as television talk show hosts do—to learn more from and about another person, a time, an object, or an event.

For example, here is a passage from an essay in which Dennis Folly reports an interview with his family about favorite phrases and expressions family members commonly use.

From *Getting the Butter from the Duck: Proverbs and Proverbial Expressions in an African-American Family*

*Dennis W. Folly**

When I interviewed my great-grandmother and mother, my sister, Angie, and my brother, Levi, joined us as we sat in the livingroom, warmed by the crackling wood stove. The informality and spontaneity that characterized our usual gatherings prevailed. The simple mention of many of the proverbs prompted gales of warm-hearted laughter from my

---

*Since this work was published, Folly has changed his name to Sw. Anand Prahlad.

mother and great-grandmother. They laughed not only at the proverbs themselves, but at the memories they brought forth.

Sewed Up in a Salt Sack

GRANNY: *That's a saying ah, just like Angie at times, she gets her mother to believe just like all children do. Sometimes they are doing things they don't want their mother to really know they're doing 'em, and they will put off a front. Tell you different things, tell you something different. They won't come right out and say. They're trying to fool you.*

Lots of people say, "She just got her mother sewed up in a salt sack 'cause her mother believe everything she says. She ain't doing nothing but foolin' her to death."

JEAN: *Basically, though, it's somebody taking advantage of you, fooling you.*

. . .

Getting the Butter from the Duck

Perhaps because my family kept ducks, there are numerous expressions which utilize the duck imagery. This one is my favorite. My great-grandmother learned it from her mother, and the expression is still used by several relatives. When I asked about it, my mother and great-grandmother burst into laughter, mainly because of my well-known, longtime interest in the phrase. I have attempted to use this expression on several occasions, sometimes embarrassing myself by substituting "goose" for "duck." "Dennis is certainly anxious to get that one," my great-grandmother laughed this time.

I first remember my great-grandmother saying this when several of us were splitting wood to take in and keep the next few days' fires going. When my mother had just finished splitting a particularly difficult piece and breathed a deep "whew!," my great-grandmother, who was sitting nearby said, "Boy, that done got all the butter from the duck now!"

JEAN: *You have to realize that a lot of these sayings are interchangeable things. They happen to mean something different to any given situations. I first heard it I think when people were cutting wood, and you come upon a tree that was really hard to get down. You know when he was able to get it down, or whatever the job accomplished, he would say, "I tell you that thing really got the butter from the duck!"*

See the fat on the inside of the duck doesn't come away easy. You can't pull the fat from the duck like you can from a chicken, or the other fowl. I think the older

> ### *Reading Memories*
>
> As you answer the following questions about your readings, point to particular words, phrases, and sentences to support your claims. Consult your dictionary for further insights into both familiar and unfamiliar words.
>
> 1. What purpose and meaning do you believe the writer discovered in creating this piece?
> 2. Who was the anticipated audience for this piece?
> 3. How does the writer feel toward the subject?
> 4. What feelings arise in you as you read this piece? How does the writer engage you in these feelings?
> 5. What do you find most memorable about this reading?
> 6. What do you learn about the writer and about her or his family and community?
> 7. Where and how does the writer use the following focusing strategies: choosing, specifying, stating, illustrating, questioning, quoting?
> 8. How does the writer use sensory images to focus and enliven experiences for the reader?
> 9. How does the writer organize the reading: lead, body, transitions, and ending?
> 10. Does this reading remind you of any similar experiences? What?

people associated their everyday activities with these animals and what not. It's between the skin and the meat, see? And sometimes you even rip the skin trying to get that fat out of there. But it's so rich and fat it's just like butter. You can use it in cakes and all those kind of things, just like you would use butter.

GRANNY: *Yes, Lord, my momma used to use that one. 'Cause she used to go in the woods and cut wood. And sometimes when she'd get through cuttin' she'd be sweatin' and going on. And she'd have to set down, and she'd say, "Ah Lord, y'all go ahead chillun, that thing done got all the butter from me."*

Although I've never plucked or cooked a duck, this proverb has become a part of my repertoire. It retains a special place in my feelings for several reasons. Besides its poetic appeal, it reminds me of a moment of special warmth and closeness to my mother and great-grandmother. It also links me to my family history, and to experiences of my childhood when ducks and other farm animals were about.

Explorations

1. **a.** *Together.* Using the sidebar on reading memories (page 264), discuss Folly's interview with special attention to how he quotes and reports on the people he interviews.

   b. *Solo.* Interview some family members about favorite family phrases and expressions used either currently or in the past. As an example of what you expect, read Folly's essay to them. Then write a report on your interview.

2. *Solo.* Write a tribute—a statement of gratitude, respect, and admiration—to a significant family member. To balance your tribute, write not only about positive traits but about how this person managed difficulties, problems, and personal flaws. Collect information by interviewing.

3. *Solo and Together.* Look through family albums and discover people that you don't know. There are often family members or friends of whom little or nothing is spoken. Interviewing different family members and family friends, construct a history for the person. Direct their attention to photographs, using the strategies on pages 250–251. Note any resistance. Reconstruct this person's life, and write about some specific turning point in it. Record and write about any mysteries that surround this person.

4. *Solo and Together.*

   a. Choose a relative or family friend whom you would like to interview. Select three questions you would like to ask. Star the one question you want answered most. Conduct an interview at this person's convenience. Start with your selected questions. Allow other questions to emerge in the process.

   b. Choose the most interesting portion of the interview and write it down. Write about why it is useful or meaningful to you. Organize it so that it will engage other readers. Write about how you benefited from interviewing and writing about your family memory. What more do you want to learn about your family, and why? Do you think you can get this information? Why or why not?

   c. *Variation.* Ask a relative to show you his or her treasured objects. Interview him or her, asking, "What memory does this object hold for you?" or "What stories does this object have to tell?"

5. *Solo.* Family members have different—often conflicting—perspectives on family stories. Choose a family story that you have heard from different points of view, and try to sort out the different versions on paper. What accounts for the differing points of view? How do they agree and disagree? Whom do family members remember with affection? Toward whom do they express negative feelings? What is your sense of what is true? What further information would you need to settle the story better? How could you find this information?

*E*xplorations

1. *Together and Solo.* Read the following memoirs and family histories. Choose what you believe to be the most effective or interesting one. Discuss what makes it so for you. Ideally, classmates will disagree. This will provide you not only with an intellectual challenge but also with the opportunity to discuss how your choices reflect your particular points of view.

2. a. *Together.* Choose one reading to discuss at a time. Use the questions in the sidebar on reading memories (page 264) to guide the discussion of your chosen reading. Be sure to point to particular words, sentences, and ideas to support your claims.

   b. *Solo.* Write a letter to the author of one of the readings you discussed in class.

3. *Solo.* Using your favorite reading as a model for writing to remember, create a memory piece of your own.

READING MEMORIES

A Letter to My Daughter

Siu Wai Anderson

Siu Wai Anderson, a fiction writer, was born in Hong Kong and raised in the United States. In the following letter, she offers her daughter a family history.

August 1989, Boston

Dear Maya Shao-ming,

You were born at Mt. Auburn Hospital in Cambridge on June 6, 1989, an auspicious date, and for me, the end of a long, long travail. Because you insisted on being breech, with your head always close to my heart, you came into the world by C-section into a chilly O.R. at the opposite end of the labor and delivery suite where, exhausted yet exuberant, I pushed out your brother in a birthing room nearly four years ago.

I couldn't believe my ears when your father exclaimed, "A girl!" All I could do was cry the tears of a long-awaited dream come true. You are so beautiful, with your big dark eyes and silky black hair. Your skin is more creamy than golden, reflecting your particular "happa haole" blend. But your long elegant fingers are those of a Chinese scholar, prized for high intelligence and sensitivity.

You are more than just a second child, more than just a girl to match our boy, to fit the demographical nuclear family with the proverbial 2.5 children. No, ten years ago I wrote a song for an unborn dream: a dark-haired, dark-eyed child who would be my flesh-and-blood link to humanity. I had no other until your brother came. He was my first Unborn Song. But you, little daughter, are the link to our female line, the legacy of another woman's pain and sacrifice thirty-one years ago.

Let me tell you about your Chinese grandmother. Somewhere in Hong Kong, in the late fifties, a young waitress found herself pregnant by a cook, probably a co-worker at her restaurant. She carried the baby to term, suffered to give it birth, and kept the little girl for the first three months of her life. I like to think that my mother—your grandmother—loved me and fought to raise me on her own, but that the daily struggle was too hard. Worn down by the demands of the new baby and perhaps the constant threat of starvation, she made the agonizing decision to give away her girl so that both of us might have a chance for a better life.

267

More likely, I was dumped at the orphanage steps or forcibly removed from a home of abuse and neglect by a social welfare worker. I will probably never know the truth. Having a baby in her unmarried state would have brought shame on the family in China, so she probably kept my existence a secret. Once I was out of her life, it was as if I had never been born. And so you and your brother and I are the missing leaves on an ancestral tree.

Do they ever wonder if we exist?

I was brought to the U.S. before I was two, and adopted by the Anglo parents who hail you as their latest beautiful grandchild. Raised by a minister's family in postwar American prosperity and nourished on three square meals a day, I grew like a wild weed and soaked up all the opportunities they had to offer—books, music, education, church life and community activities. Amidst a family of blue-eyed blonds, though, I stood out like a sore thumb. Whether from jealousy or fear of someone who looked so different, my older brothers sometimes tormented me with racist name-calling, teased me about my poor eyesight and unsightly skin, or made fun of my clumsy walk. Moody and impatient, gifted and temperamental, burdened by fears and nightmares that none of us realized stemmed from my early years of deprivation, I was not an easy child to love. My adoptive mother and I clashed countless times over the years, but gradually came to see one another as real human beings with faults and talents, and as women of strength in our own right. Now we love each other very much, though the scars and memories of our early battles will never quite fade. Lacking a mirror image in the mother who raised me, I had to seek my identity as a woman on my own. The Asian American community has helped me reclaim my dual identity and enlightened my view of the struggles we face as minorities in a white-dominated culture. They have applauded my music and praised my writings.

But part of me will always be missing: my beginnings, my personal history, all the subtle details that give a person her origin. I don't know how I was born, whether it was vaginally or by Cesarean. I don't know when, or where exactly, how much I weighed, or whose ears heard my first cry of life. Was I put to my mother's breast and tenderly rocked, or was I simply weighed, cleaned, swaddled and carted off to a sterile nursery, noted in the hospital records as "newborn female"?

Someone took the time to give me a lucky name, and write the appropriate characters in neat brush strokes in the Hong Kong city register. "Siu" means "little." My kind of "wai" means "clever" or "wise." Therefore, my baby name was "Clever little one." Who chose those words? Who cared enough to note my arrival in the world?

I lost my Chinese name for eighteen years. It was Americanized for convenience to "Sue." But like an ill-fitting coat, it made me twitch and fret and squirm. I hated the name. But even more, I hated being Chinese. It took many years to become proud of my Asian heritage and work up the courage to take back my birthname. That plus a smattering of classroom Cantonese, are all the Chinese culture I have to offer you, little one. Not white, certainly, but not really Asian, I straddle the two worlds and try to blaze your trails for you. Your name, "Shao-ming," is very much like mine—"Shao" is the Mandarin form of "Siu," meaning "little." And "ming" is "bright," as in a shining sun or moon. Whose lives will you brighten, little Maya? Your past is more complete than mine, and each day I cradle you in your babyhood, lavishing upon you the tender care I lacked for my first two years. When I console you, I comfort the lost baby inside me who still cries out for her mother. No wonder so many adoptees desperately long to have children of their own.

Sweet Maya, it doesn't matter what you "become" later on. You have already fulfilled my wildest dreams.

I love you,

Mommy

Mary Nina

Valerie Kack-Brice

Kack-Brice, a clinical social worker for more than twenty years, is the editor of a collection on grandmothers, For She Is the Tree of Life, *from which one of her own personal contributions follows.*

She was the first one to teach me about guilt. That, of course, was only a small gift from this grandmother. There were other things like permission to follow one's heart, like she did to marry my grandfather, out of the tuberculosis ward, out of the convent. It wasn't a big guilt she taught me, just enough for a four year old to sting a little. Mary Nina probably weighed over three hundred pounds and on her small frame, she looked more round than a peach. I was fascinated by her form. It dominated my experience of her. More so than the porcelain madonnas she painted in sky blue and white lace. More so than the black 1932 Model T she drove to get eggs.

What I wondered one day when she cared for me while my little sister was being born, was what she wore *under* her big round black skirts. Surely they didn't make pink polka dotted panties like I wore in her size. And surely, the white bras my mother wore couldn't be nearly enough to harness those huge face-crushing breasts. Did she wear diapers like my little sister would wear? Being a clever four year old, I figured I was entitled to know.

I schemed to catch her unaware and called her to look out the window at some unimportant detail I had identified to distract her. I dropped my rubber doll and kicked it under the sideboard and naturally had to get down on the floor to retrieve it. This required reaching way under. I had to turn my head (so I could see up her skirt). I was scared and ashamed, and only glanced upward then grabbed the arm of my doll and quickly pulled her out. Once standing, to my dismay, I realized I didn't know what I had seen. There were folds of cloth under there, but no true, clearly defined form of anything that looked like panties.

Though what I later learned to be guilt was nudging at my consciousness, I waited a day and plotted another research expedition. This time, I attacked from below while she prepared the biscuit dough at the kitchen table. Sitting under the table, I could feel the shame rising to my face but was compelled to finish what I started. Although she was still a stranger to me, I knew she loved me. That deserved some kind of loyalty.

Halfheartedly, the ball rolled out of my hands and rested against the edge of her shoe. Perfect. I stared at it a long time. My mind fought to connect that foot to the folds of…something which was connected to my grandmother, the peach. I don't believe anyone ever taught me that it was impolite to look under a woman's skirt, but somehow, I knew that what I was doing was wrong.

My ball rocked against her foot as she stirred and kneaded. I watched it roll away a little, then back again. I felt sad. Only later was I to understand that my wickedness was probably more about missing my mother and my fear about who would be coming home with her to take my place. Then, I only knew I hurt from having to harness my curiosity with the sting of betrayal. In my mind, what I was doing had gotten complicated too by my remembering that she had been a nun. What I felt was surely the pinprick of God's wrath.

I couldn't do it. I reached for the ball without looking up, and said, "Grandma, can I help you make the biscuits?" I could. We did. And until she died, I remained only slightly curious and then, a little jealous of the undertaker. He was a real stranger and knew more about her than I ever would.

A Still Pose

Student Marta Cuervo

*Much inspired by how photographs can stir memories,
Marta Cuervo, then a student at Montclair State University,
wrote this piece for her developmental writing class.*

It's incredible how so many memories can be recorded in one still pose. I have a photograph of myself that I treasure. When I look at it, I can remember the exact moment when it was taken. The details are still vivid in my mind. Even a quick glimpse of the image has the ability to transport me to a wonderful moment in time.

Looking at the picture I can still hear the music of Vivaldi's *Four Seasons.* The crescendo sound of the violins consumed the space. We were thirty-two dancers on that huge stage. Our bright-colored costumes appeared to be swirling out of control. We were leaping, twirling, running, and swaying. As the tempo of the music increased and the sounds of the violins became louder, we danced faster and stronger. I could hear the dancers around me breathing hard. We were stomping the floor with our feet and slashing the air with our arms. In essence, we were trying to devour the space with our bodies. The kinetic energy of the group made it feel as though we were all one body, with one connecting heartbeat. That one shared beat had the driving force to keep us united in motion.

Then, in one nanosecond, it happened. Thirty-one dancers exited the stage, all at once. The music was replaced by complete silence and the bright-colored lights gave way to total darkness. Everything seemed to stop. I had been left alone.

What happened next took place in thirty seconds. However, the details I remember make it seem as though the moment lasted an eternity. On a very high and sustained musical note, I stepped into a lit spot on a dark stage. This light came from a huge computer-operated flashlight in the back of the theater. In the business we refer to it as a "spotlight." As I stepped into the circle of light, my body froze in a position I had executed many times before. My arms went up in the air to create a V formation. One of my legs extended itself behind me, in the air. The other leg was on the floor, balancing me. My foot was inside a pointed shoe that was drilling an imaginary hole into the floor. My four limbs were reaching in four different directions. I felt like a marionette being held up by a set of strings. I was experiencing the peacefulness and serenity of perfect balance.

As I held this position I became aware of many things that were occurring in and around me. I remember being aware of the pounding beat of my heart. The only other sound, which seemed faint and in the distance, was that of a soft note from a violin. My eyes had been fixed on the beam of light coming from the back of the theater and basking me with glorious warmth. If I looked hard enough I could see the dust particles in the ray of light. They too seemed to be giving me energy.

In the midst of all this, I heard a loud snap. It was then that I realized that a picture had been taken. I knew instantly what the eye of the photographer had captured. This moment would be imprinted in my mind for the rest of my life.

Chapter Review

Solo or Together, respond to the following:

1. If you were an instructor of writing, what five points from this chapter would *you* stress in teaching student writers? Why?

2. Which strategies offered in this chapter were either new to you or made clearer?

3. Which strategies do you need to further develop? How do you plan to incorporate them into your writing process?

4. What are the benefits, drawbacks, and challenges of writing to remember?

Chapter 11

Writing to Bridge Cultures

This chapter offers opportunities to

—Explore how **cultures** work

—Discover the dynamics of **language** and **dialect**

—Practice taking different **points of view**

—Understand what it means to be an **outsider**

—Focus on issues concerning **ethnicity, gender,** and **age**

—**Bridge cultures** through writing

If we are to achieve a richer culture, rich in contrasting values, we must recognize the whole gamut of human potentialities, and so weave a less arbitrary social fabric, one in which each diverse human gift will find a fitting place.

—*Margaret Mead, Anthropologist*

What Are Cultures?

The word *culture* comes from a Latin word that means "to work the soil." You are who you are—to a great extent—because of the culture that offers you the physical, emotional, mental, and spiritual soil from which to grow. This culture, or environment, is made up of people, food, shelter, clothing, objects, customs, laws, and language.

The word *culture*, when used in reference to human culture, most often refers to ethnic or national cultures such as the Japanese, Hungarian, or Jamaican cultures. The United States in the 1990s has within it diverse *national* cultures including, among many others, Navajo, Puerto Rican, Ethiopian, Chicano, Chinese, Greek, and Creole cultures that each have special things in common. In this book, the word *culture* is used more generally to refer to any group of people who have something important in common. So, for example, in the *popular* culture of the United States today, we have things in common that distinguish us from people of the United States in the 1890s, such as CNN, *Star Wars*, McDonald's, Nikes, Madonna, and the Internet.

Some cultures cut across national lines. Women of all national cultures have things in common that distinguish them from men. Parents share experiences that their childless children don't. Those who were born eighty years ago have lives that are different from those who were born twenty years ago. If your culture has been shaped by slavery, war, or certain illnesses, you will be different from people who haven't been so oppressed.

Finally, there are many smaller cultures, such as those defined by clubs, your workplace, the corner store, a popular eating place where you tend to see the same people, your neighborhood, your place of worship, the recreation hall you frequent, your school, and your writing class. The way people interact with others, the customary way to dress, and the rules of what is or is not appropriate will vary from culture to culture.

This chapter invites you to explore similarities and differences between human cultures, especially those that include people who are different by virtue of ethnicity (nationality, religion, race), gender, and age. Begin with the following Explorations, which help you appreciate how many cultures you already live in every day and how these cultures shape you and your values.

*E*xplorations

1. **a.** *Together.* List the different environments, or cultures, in which you live in a typical week. Name them specifically: writing class,

skating rink, father's kitchen, mall, school cafeteria. Notice whether there is a culture within a culture in a particular place. For example, a recreation center might have different cultures, such as those of weight lifters, swimmers, runners, or spectators.

b. *Together.* Choose two cultures (such as the writing classroom and the school cafeteria) in which most of you participate: one in which you feel comfortable and one in which you feel less comfortable. Create two columns, and list the dos and don'ts that define each culture and that make each different from the other. What rules are the same for each? Are the rules different for different people?

c. *Solo.* In writing, compare and contrast your particular experience of two different cultures. Focus on rules, spoken or unspoken, that significantly affect you. Organize your essay by using the block or zig-zag strategy for comparing and contrasting. (See pages 184–185 and 351–359 for guidelines.) Ask yourself the questions in the sidebar Writing to Bridge Cultures (page 278).

2. **a.** *Together.* Using the sidebar Reading to Bridge Cultures on page 286, discuss Jo Goodwin Parker's essay "What Is Poverty?" (pages 292–293). Pay special attention to how economic factors separate people into different cultures.

b. *Solo.* Write an essay in which you discuss how economic issues determine the culture in which you currently live. As you write, consider how different your life would be if your financial status suddenly changed.

3. **a.** *Solo.* Your values are cultivated by the environments in which you live and grow. Read the following list of values. Place a mark along the continuum (the line) to indicate the importance of each value to you.

	Least	Somewhat	Most
	←——————————————————→		
	Continuum of importance		
Ambition	_____		
Cheerfulness	_____		
Cleanliness	_____		
Creativity	_____		
Generosity	_____		
Honesty	_____		

	Least	Somewhat	Most
	←		→
		Continuum of importance	

Intelligence   _____

Love   _____

Obedience   _____

Openmindedness   _____

Patience   _____

Politeness   _____

Responsibility   _____

Self-reliance   _____

Successfulness   _____

   b.   *Solo.* Write an essay about your top three values. State your three values. Illustrate each value by describing an incident that shows how you learned the value and from whom. For example, if honesty is your top value, you might illustrate how telling a lie got you into serious trouble as a child.

4. a.   *Together.* Many television programs feature members of special ethnic and regional cultures, such as African Americans, Hispanics, Japanese, and Appalachians. List some of these programs. Choose an episode from one of them. If possible, watch a taped version of it together. Discuss how you relate to the portrayals of the cultural group.

   b.   *Solo.* Describe, in writing, a television program that bridges cultures. Your audience has never seen it. Argue that you believe the program offers worthwhile insights into language habits and bridging cultures. Focus on specific characters, events, and episodes to illustrate and support your case.

Why Bridge Cultures?

Bridging cultures can be as sensitive and difficult as it can be powerful, enriching, and fun. Therefore, it is important to (1) be clear about the purpose of your explorations and (2) know your audience. Here are two lists of purposes to consult during the writing process:

Empowering purposes

- To find meaning in difficult experiences
- To appreciate different points of view
- To enjoy new experiences
- To stretch your world view
- To assert your needs
- To clarify problems
- To negotiate solutions to problems
- To develop compassion
- To develop common values
- To create new cultures that include more people

Destructive purposes

- To stereotype
- To blame without negotiating
- To oppress
- To diminish others
- To pity yourself without dignity
- To inflate yourself at others' expense

By committing yourself to empowering purposes, you discover ways to bridge cultures and grow.

Develop your sense of audience by writing from several points of view. Find values you hold in common with your anticipated readers. Pay special attention to how language embodies attitude.

Language and Culture

Languages are storehouses of shared experiences. To know a language is to know a way of life.[*] For example, Inuit peoples of Alaska, Canada, and Greenland have many words that refer to different kinds of snow and ice. To know an Inuit language is to realize that the native speakers of the language depend on being able to distinguish different traveling and hunting

---

[*]From Ludwig Wittgenstein, *Philosophical Investigations* (New York: Macmillan, 1953), p. 88.

Writing to Bridge Cultures

As you write to bridge cultures, ask yourself these questions:

1. Why am I writing this? Is my purpose empowering or destructive?
2. What is my point of view? What other points of view are there?
3. Who is my audience? Do I need to adjust my approach?
4. How can I best focus my essay?
5. What point(s) do I hope to make?
6. What sensory images can I use?
7. How can I best illustrate my point(s)?
8. How can I best organize this to fulfill my purpose?
9. What questions do I anticipate others might ask?
10. What am I learning or gaining from writing this?

conditions. To learn the language of a community is to take the most important step in becoming a member.

Language and life-style differences are reflected in the vocabulary, the grammar, the accent, the tone in which the language is expressed, the gestures that people use to support their communications, and the rules of writing. Languages can be vastly different from each other—both in oral and in written form. Notice how different the word for "woman" is in English, Japanese, and Greek—*woman*, 女 (pronounced *onna*), and γυνη (pronounced *gūnā*). Originally, people who spoke these languages were totally separated from each other geographically and culturally. Since these people had no reason to formulate lines of communication, their vocabularies, grammars, accents, and gestures—and therefore their ideas and experiences—were very different.

If people speak the same basic language, such as English, but live apart either geographically or socially, they may develop different forms of the same language, called *dialects,* with some shared vocabulary and grammar. The differences between dialects are often noticeable in accents and emphasis. For example, some American English dialects (as opposed to those of British English) are Chicano, Black, Creole, Southern American, and Brooklynese. These dialects differ from the standard English used in the popular culture determined by schools, television, newspapers, advertising, and other established communities. The different dialects show that the people who speak them have been separated from each other at some point. Whether you tend to say "I don't have any money," "I got no money," "I no have money," "I'm temporarily low on financial resources," or "I'm broke" depends on the cultures you frequent.

Language communities can be grouped according to professions and mutual interests, as well. These differences may be limited to vocabulary or grammar, and accents and gestures may not matter. For example, the dialects of computerese, legalese, militarese, and "writerese" have favored technical terms for *eliminate: trash, strike, terminate, delete.* But the accents in which these terms are spoken don't matter. Professional communities also have varied rules for written communications, as, for example, academic communities (considered in Chapters 12 and 13). Although many professional languages bind people together, they may also leave other people out. Luckily, there have been moves in different professions—such as law and education—to develop languages that will allow more people the opportunity to learn the terminology of these professions and so become empowered to use the resources of those communities.

Sometimes there are more specialized and even secret languages such as those that mark off a pair of lovers or twins, a club, or a spy ring. You may even have a special code just for yourself, as some people do for writing journals or notes.

Finally, cultures differ with respect to the gestures, or body language, that people in them use to support communication. In Greece, for example, nodding your head means "no." In the United States, nodding means "yes."

The more varied the community using a language, the greater are the gains made by bridging gaps, as can be seen in the case of air traffic controllers and international pilots, who are united all over the world by using English. And the more languages you know, the more easily you can move among different environments.

*E*xplorations

Try some of the following Explorations to discover how languages serve to either include you in or exclude you from a given culture.

1. *Together.* Using the sidebar on page 286, Reading to Bridge Cultures, discuss a choice of the following readings about language, which appear elsewhere in *The Flexible Writer:*

   Student Annie E. Lee's essay "Owning My Words" (pages 26–27)

   Dennis Foley's interview of his family in "Getting the Butter from the Duck" (pages 262–264)

Nancy Masterson Sakamoto's essay "Conversational Ballgames" (pages 294–295)

2. **a.** *Together.* If the language or dialect you speak in your home community is different from the one you use at school, discuss how people at home react if you speak in academic English. How do people react to you in an academic setting when you speak in your home language or dialect? What is your experience of trying to move between your different language communities? If you normally speak academic English, how do you react to people who don't?

    b. *Solo or Together.* Write a basic instruction manual teaching others how to communicate in your home language or special dialect. Focus on a few phrases, words, grammatical habits, and gestures. Include a list of dos and don'ts. Write what it means to you to be relating these codes of language to an outsider.

3. *Together and Solo.* Silence, or absence of words, can speak as powerfully as words themselves. Discuss experiences in which silence was used in a particular culture to include or exclude you or someone else. Focus on one such experience as an illustration. Describe how silence is interpreted in your home community.

4. *Solo.* Between friends, relatives, lovers, club members, and spies, there are often secret codes or "in" languages. Write about a secret language or gesture code that you had with another person or persons. Relate what these codes were, how they functioned, and what they meant to you. Illustrate with specific examples. Relate what it means to you to be revealing these codes now. If you presently have such a code, write about that—if you are willing.

5. *Together.* In the late-twentieth-century United States, television is a prime medium to which most people have access. List some programs that most of you favor. What words, expressions, gestures, and ways of communicating do they teach us? Which ones have you adopted? Why?

Points of View

People tend to find what they look for, that is, to interpret events in ways that support what they need to believe. When you meet someone who is different from you, who *you* are becomes more obvious by contrast. For example, if you were always with people who are the same height as you, you wouldn't much notice it. However, meeting someone much taller or much shorter will make you aware of the other person's height and your own as well. Having to question the belief that most adults are the same height might be difficult for you. Questions might arise from both points of view: Will this very big person hurt me? Will people ignore me because they don't like craning their necks to look up at me? Am I inferior because I can't walk as fast with my short legs? Won't I seem clumsy in this small conference room?

Meeting someone with a different point of view, who makes you question who you are and what you believe, can elicit many reactions: lack of interest, mistrust, fear, curiosity. Lack of interest may be insulting. Mistrust and fear can lead to anything from rejection to war. But curiosity may lead you to learn more about others and therefore yourself. That tall person and that short one may be able to benefit from their differences. One can sink the baskets while the other runs defense. One can dust those higher shelves while the other does the lower. One can see over the hill while the other can see details closer to the ground. Through writing, you clarify the differences between cultures and learn to take others' points of view. By finding what you have in common, you can learn to honor and appreciate differences, as well. You move more comfortably between environments and don't feel so fragmented. Ultimately, by bridging cultures we create a global culture whose purpose is the survival and enrichment of all. (To support you in this process, you may want to review "Audiences for Writing," "Audience Appeal," and "Denotations and Connotations" in Chapter 3.)

Being an Outsider

If you feel comfortable in a particular culture and have all your needs met, it is easy to ignore or mistrust those who are outsiders. One way to shut others out is to stereotype them. To *stereotype* someone is to make snap judgments about a person because of race, religion, sex, clothing, physical features, or any other clichéd excuse. To stereotype someone is to be locked into old myths about people who may be different from you. It is to be *prejudiced.* When you stereotype someone, you deny the person's individuality and therefore freedom. You lock yourself into your contrasting role. You forfeit your own freedom to learn and grow.

A first step to bridging cultures is to appreciate that everyone has—to a lesser or greater extent—been an outsider. To further appreciate the dynamics of what it means to be an outsider, read writer Delia Ephron's account of being an outsider. As you read, highlight or underline portions to which you have strong reactions.

I Am the Green Lollipop: Notes on Stepmothering

Delia Ephron

Lisa and Alex, ages six and three, were standing in a fountain in the middle of the Santa Monica Mall. I insisted they get out. They refused. Again I insisted. Lisa put her arm around her brother and drew him closer to her.

This is what happened the first time I was left alone with my future stepchildren. I insisted they get out of a fountain that did not have water in it. I have given this act of mine considerable thought. At the very least, it indicates a certain amount of panic on my part. A tendency to over-react. Certainly a lack of playfulness. I could have gotten into the fountain with them. I also could have ignored the whole business, waited for their father to return, and let him deal with it or not. But I couldn't wait. I had to seize an opportunity, any opportunity, to assert my authority.

My claim to authority at that time was tenuous—I was not yet their stepmother. I must have wanted to prove just how tenuous it was. Why else would I try to stop two children from doing nothing? Naturally they refused to obey me. But more was at stake here and we all knew it—our futures. Lisa and Alex were seizing an opportunity themselves: They were taking a stand against me, the intruder. It is one of the few moments in their lives when they have been in agreement. And I, in my muddleheaded way, con-tinued to insist, "Get out," when what I really meant was, "Let me in."

...

I am the cause of [Lisa's] pain, whatever it may be, perhaps because she blames me for her much greater hurt, that her parents are no longer married. I am not the reason they are divorced, but I am evidence of it, as well as being a hindrance. How can they get back together if I'm here? I am also privileged to be the adult that Lisa can most risk being angry with or, put another way, that she can most afford to have angry with her. Life is less secure than it used to be and she isn't taking any chances. So when Lisa feels mistreated, she thinks of me.

The only problem with her point of view from my point of view is this: How can I be her persecutor if I'm her victim? For I *am* her victim. My identity as a stepmother is amorphous at best, and if she takes this away from me, what will I have left? Consider:

Larry and his first wife got divorced. Both stayed involved with their children so Lisa now has two mothers—two mothers because she has her regular mother and she has her father. Now that he sees the children alone, Larry is doing a lot of mothering—feeding, soothing, bathing, reading, setting limits (well, sort of...). Then I arrive and suddenly Lisa has three mothers.

Two were difficult enough. Lisa is in the peculiar position of being overloaded with mothers and deprived of family. And she is possessive and protective of her father, feeling vulnerable to losing him altogether now that the family has fallen apart. And how do I fit in? Who am I, as far as Lisa is concerned? Unwelcome and unnecessary. Unfortunately for her, I am also unstoppable—though that won't keep her from trying.

When I first arrived, I checked out the territory. I wanted to participate. I wanted to be helpful. Well, truthfully I wanted most to become indispensable. To Larry, not to Lisa, who, at least in the beginning, was simply a means to an end. So what did I seize upon? Cooking and chauffeuring. (And one other task—criticizing....)

Even if I had known I was cooking my own goose, I would have taken on these jobs; they were the only ones available. The problem that developed was this: When I cooked my own goose, Lisa wouldn't eat it. Because I can cook all I want, but I can't feed. Feeding is what mothers do, and here Lisa drew the line. "I'm not hungry," she said, or something equally upsetting, like, "I just feel like eating yogurt tonight." It was her way of saying, "You can't mother me." So, at least in part, my efforts were thwarted. I was getting little payoff for my hard work. Though I succeeded in becoming indispensable to Larry, I wasn't satisfied. I wanted love. Lisa's love. I wanted this even before I loved Lisa myself, for its symbolic meaning—that I belonged in the family. Oh, what an unreasonable expectation. The self-centeredness of it. Of course, I might have settled for gratitude or respect, but good luck to me.

So the inevitable took place. I began to feel used. The rest of the world may see me as a wicked stepmother, but I see myself as Cinderella in a fairy tale that goes something like this: Once upon a time, there was a handsome prince who fell in love with a beautiful princess (me). He took her away to his castle to live with him and his two children from a previous marriage. Here things quickly went to pot, and the princess became known, at least to herself, as Cinderella. Now she could have given up cooking and driving the coach-and-four, but then she wouldn't have been Cinderella. And what would she be?

A problem, you see, of options.

It happens, however, that there is another role, besides that of victim, that is available to me: the outsider. The problem is, Lisa has a stake in this identity too. She feels driven out by my relationship with her father, while I feel doomed never to be allowed full membership in the club. It occurs to me that one of the unappreciated side effects of all this uncoupling and recoupling is the endless opportunity it offers all participants to feel sorry for themselves. I was at the door of our house one day having a conversation with my husband's ex-wife. She complained about having to miss *The Jewel in the Crown* on television that night. I said we were going to miss it too. "Oh, but you can tape it," she said. "Why don't you?" I asked, falling into the trap. "I don't have a tape machine," she said mournfully.

This conversation wasn't about a television show. She was actually saying, You have more money than me; life is so much harder for me; I am the victim. Well, let me say this about that: Hands off my role!

---

*E*xplorations

The following Explorations help you to explore what it means to be an outsider.

1. **a.** *Together.* Using the sidebar on page 286, discuss Delia Ephron's essay "I Am the Green Lollipop: Notes on Stepmothering." Focus on her experiences of and strategies for coping as an outsider.

    b. *Together or Solo.* List the different possible points of view represented in Delia Ephron's essay. Write an essay about the events she reports—from a different point of view. Present the point of view either compassionately or in order to expose its limitations. If you write these essays solo, read and compare them. Use the sidebar on page 278 to guide your discussion. What do you learn?

2. **a.** *Together.* The following chart lists some kinds of prejudicial stereotyping and the division into dominant and subordinate groups they create. Complete the list of subordinate groups. Can you think of any other kinds of stereotyping?

Stereotyping	Dominant group	Subordinate group
Sexism	Males (in some cultures)	Females (in some cultures)
Classism	Professionals, wealthy	_____
Ageism	21- to 50-year-olds	_____
Racism	Whites (in some cultures)	_____
Physicalism	Body types featured on magazine covers	_____

Stereotyping	Dominant group	Subordinate group
Fashionism	_____	_____
_____	_____	_____
_____	_____	_____
_____	_____	_____

b. *Solo.* Write an essay about the benefits you have gained from being a member of a dominant group. Write about some of the problems and drawbacks. Focus on specific events to illustrate your experiences. Use sense appeal. Organize your paper by writing first about benefits and then about drawbacks. End your paper by relating what you have learned about being a member of a dominant group.

c. *Solo.* Write an essay about the difficulties you have experienced from being a member of a subordinate group. Record any benefits. Illustrate your paper with specific examples. Relate strategies you have developed to cope.

3. *Solo.* Write an essay about a stereotyping belief you formerly held. Relate some incidents that contradicted that particular stereotype. Who was involved? What did you learn about others? About yourself?

4. *Solo.* Write an essay about an experience in which you were (or are) an outsider. This may include being part of a smaller culture, such as a club; or a larger national, racial, economic, or religious culture. Respond to these questions:

- How were you different from the other people?
- What particular experience best illustrates how you were (or are) an outsider?
- How were you treated?
- How did you treat the insiders?
- How did you feel?
- Did you put on a social mask—changing your facial expressions, language, gestures, or actions—in order to belong?
- Did a common understanding develop? If so, how? If not, why not?
- What beliefs did you formulate from the experience?
- What, if any, were the benefits of being the outsider?

Variation. Describe an experience in which you were an insider and a newcomer arrived into that particular culture.

Reading to Bridge Cultures

As you answer the following questions about your readings, point to particular words, phrases, and sentences to support your claims. Consult your dictionary for further insights into both familiar and unfamiliar words.

1. As a reader, with which part of this reading do you identify with most? Why?
2. What is the purpose of this reading? Is it empowering or destructive?
3. What is the writer's point of view and attitude toward readers?
4. How does the writer either engage or disengage readers?
5. On what interests or problems does the writer focus?
6. What sense appeal does the writer make?
7. Which aspects of the organization of this piece support the writer's purpose, and how? Title? Lead? Body? Transitions? Ending?
8. Does the writer seem to better understand or bridge cultures because of writing this piece?
9. Have you had similar cultural experiences?
10. How does this reading affect your approach to cultural differences?

The next part of this chapter contains a series of Explorations to help you bridge cultures through writing. The points of view represented by differences in ethnicity, gender, and age were chosen because they are general enough to encompass the concerns of all people, regardless of race, economic class, or religion. While considering issues of ethnicity, gender, and age, you will be able to focus on those issues of race, economic class, and religion that are important to you.

Ethnicity

The word *ethnicity* comes from a Greek word meaning "nation" and is usually used to refer to cultural groups that are defined by religion, race, or nationality. Because the United States is so rich with diverse ethnic groups, you can travel the world while staying at home. Your own sense of yourself and your origins deepens as you compare and contrast ethnic differences.

Satellites, air travel, high-speed information networks, and sophisticated television and telephone systems have united the world into a global community. If we can use these systems to bridge cultural differences, perhaps we will eliminate the misunderstandings and wars that belong to a divided world.

Explorations

1. a. *Together.* Using the sidebar Reading to Bridge Cultures on page 286, discuss Dahlia Aguilar's "Behold Her Blackness" (pages 295–297), with special attention to questions of race and cultural origin.

   b. *Solo.* Write an essay in which you discuss how your own ethnic roots either complement or conflict in your experience. You might focus on issues of religion, race, and economic status. To keep focused, ask yourself the questions in the sidebar Writing to Bridge Cultures (page 278).

2. a. *Together.* Create a list of the ethnic groups—religious, racial, and national—represented by members of your class. List some special events, holidays, and ceremonies in which these ethnic groups participate. Describe your favorite events to each other and what they mean to you.

   b. *Solo.* Choose one special event and write in depth about a most memorable occasion of it.

   c. *Together.* Read your essays to each other. If class members choose some of the same holidays to discuss, compare and contrast how different ethnic groups celebrate them. What have you learned about yourself and each other?

3. *Together and Solo.* One of the most satisfying and instructive ways to learn about other ethnic groups is to explore food habits. Create a list of foods that are typical of your ethnic group. In writing, describe a special meal, how it is prepared and eaten, and any special ceremonies or meanings associated with the food. Assume your audience is from a different culture. Include any special memories you associate with the food. (You might want to have an international potluck meal together.)

   Variation. Adapt this Exploration by focusing on clothing instead of food. Wear or bring costumes to class.

4. a. *Together.* People of different cultures have varied ways of coping with emotions. In some cultures, it is inappropriate to express emotions, and there are complex ways in which people are stopped from doing so. In some cultures, emotions are freely and openly expressed. Consider your own cultural background. Compare notes with each other on how the following emotions are dealt with, in your experience. Consider which facial, bodily, and verbal cues are permitted and how these are either encouraged or discouraged, in different circumstances.

- Anger

- Parental affection

- Romantic interest

- Fear

- Confusion

- Inadequacy

- Envy and jealousy

- Grief

- Sadness

- Mistrust

Write a group essay comparing how a particular emotion is expressed by different cultures. Use either a block or zig-zag organizing strategy (see pages 184–185 and 351–359).

b. *Solo.* Write an essay describing an occasion when you did not follow the rules of a community in expressing an emotion. How did other people treat you? What did you learn about yourself and others?

5. a. *Together.* Find newspaper articles that address ethnic issues and cultural clashes either directly or indirectly. Share these articles with others in class.

b. *Solo.* Choose one of these articles. Write a summary of it for someone who hasn't read it. Then write your reaction to the events and issues raised in the article. Point out prejudicial and violent actions. Suggest solutions to problems and how you would bridge the clashing cultures.

Variation. Do this Exploration by focusing on a television program or film.

Gender

Cultures determine what roles females and males should have and what is feminine and masculine. These roles and rules determine a person's gender. *Sexual* differences are biological. *Gender* differences are social. Gender roles are meant to define and control a person's activities and sexual preferences.

Gender roles are defined by many cultural influences, including religion, race, ethnicity, economy, geography, age, and historical era. For example, people who insist upon conventional family gender roles for everyone may disapprove of others who prefer careers without parenthood, interracial marriages, or homosexual relationships. People with alternative life-styles may, in turn, be hostile to those who try to impose conventional values on them. The following Explorations provide opportunities for you to discover such variations in gender expectations and the complications they may produce.

*E*xplorations

1. a. *Together.* Using the sidebar Reading to Bridge Cultures (page 286), discuss Sydney Harris's essay "Why Men Should March for Women's Rights" (page 298–299). Consider whether Harris's argument applies to current marches by particular groups of people.

    b. *Solo.* Write an essay in response to Harris's argument in which you either agree with him, offering your own illustrations of his point, or disagree with him, offering your counterarguments. Ask yourself the questions in the sidebar Writing to Bridge Cultures (page 278).

2. a. *Together and Solo.* Using the sidebar Reading to Bridge Cultures (pages 286), discuss John Stoltenberg's essay "What Makes Pornography 'Sexy'?" (pages 299–301). In light of his work, consider the following controversial statements about pornography. Write and compare papers on response.

    *   There's nothing wrong with prostitution or pornography. Women get well paid for their services, and they enjoy it.

    *   Pornography is free speech: squelch it and you squelch the Constitution.

    *   Pornography keeps men from straying.

3. *Together and Solo.* Discuss one or more of the controversial statements listed below. For each statement you discuss, brainstorm two lists, one in favor of the statement and one against it. Then write an essay agreeing or disagreeing with one of the statements. Describe particular individuals to illustrate your point of view. Directly address points that are opposed to your position and argue against them.

    *   Women should stay at home to raise their children.

    *   Date rape is usually the woman's fault.

    *   Wives should be loyal to their husbands. If they are beaten, they've done something to provoke their men.

    *   Men are by nature more intellectual; women are more emotional.

    *   Playful comments and touches are not sexual harassment.

    *   Homosexuals shouldn't be teachers or parents. They will corrupt the children under their care.

    *   A man's success depends on his having a woman behind him.

- Men need more sexual variety than women and should therefore be allowed more freedom outside of marriage.

- Sex-change operations are a viable way to improve life-style.

4. *Together or Solo.* Discuss and write about how different cultures have different expectations regarding the roles of men and women. Consider such aspects of life as child care, health care, family income, food preparation, sexual habits, recreation, clothing, and access to intellectual and creative development. Who has it easier in your home community, men or women?

Age

Age is important in determining how you experience the world. Not only is your body different at different ages, but so are your experiences. Among many other factors, medical care, technology, social roles, economics, world events, and ecology have varied tremendously over time, especially in the last few decades. People born today know a different world from people born sixty to a hundred years ago.

Cultures vary on how they care for children and the elderly. For example, in some cultures, children are raised collectively in a small, close-knit community. In other cultures, children are sent to boarding schools. In still others, children have to fend for themselves, often taking care of younger siblings. Similarly, in some cultures, the elderly are revered and are always cared for in the family. In other cultures, the elderly are sent to nursing homes and institutions and youth is revered. In still others, elderly members are expected to retreat by themselves when they no longer feel they can be active members of the family.

The following Explorations provide opportunities for you to discover the cultural variations experienced by people of different ages.

*E*xplorations _____

1. a. *Together.* Using the sidebar Reading to Bridge Cultures (page 286), discuss Ann Domitrovich's essay "Thoughts on Aging" (pages 301–303).

   b. *Solo.* Regardless of age, we are all affected by the passage of time and changes in our physical strength and appearance. Write an essay in which you explore, as Domitrovich does, your own aging processes.

2. a. *Together.* Create two lists of what you believe parents should be able to expect from their children and what children should be

able to expect from their parents. Include such things as long-term care, educational support, and care of grandchildren. If you disagree with other members of the group, state your reasons for disagreeing. Describe particular people and situations to support your position. Notice how your cultural backgrounds influence your ideas.

  b. *Solo.* Write an essay stating what you believe parents and children should be able to expect from each other. Support your position by describing particular people and situations. You might want to relate a situation in which you were in conflict with your parents. To balance your essay, write a section describing what you believe parents and children should *not* expect from each other, and why.

3. *Solo.* List conflicts that you have (or had) with your parents over such issues as money, dating, household contributions, and education. Focus an essay on a particular conflict and any attempts that have been made to resolve it. Was this conflict determined by differences in age? What other cultural and generational gaps helped to create this conflict? How could this essay help you?

4. **a.** *Together.* Some senior citizens have had their rights and freedoms limited by mandatory retirement age, retesting for driver's licenses, discrimination in hiring, low income, medical and insurance inequalities, and nursing homes. Discuss examples of such situations.

  b. *Solo.* Choose a person you know who has had her or his rights and freedoms infringed upon because of age. Tell the story from two or three points of view. Discuss what you have learned from doing this Exploration.

5. *Together and Solo.* Discuss and write about different cultural customs and expectations for treating the elderly. In your individual writing, focus on how the elderly are treated in your home community. Is this treatment a reflection of the traditions of your ethnic origin? If so, how? If not, what cultural influences determine how the elderly are treated in your family?

6. *Variation.* Adapt Exploration 4 or 5 to children's issues and rights. Compare and contrast treatment of the elderly with treatment of children.

READING TO BRIDGE CULTURES

From *What Is Poverty?*

Jo Goodwin Parker

Wishing to remain anonymous, the author of "What Is Poverty?" has assumed the name Jo Goodwin Parker. This is an excerpt from what was first delivered as a speech.

You ask me what is poverty? Listen to me. Here I am, dirty, smelly, and with no "proper" underwear on and with the stench of my rotting teeth near you. I will tell you. Listen to me. Listen without pity. I cannot use your pity. Listen with understanding. Put yourself in my dirty, worn out, ill-fitting shoes, and hear me.

Poverty is getting up every morning from a dirt- and illness-stained mattress. The sheets have long since been used for diapers. Poverty is living in a smell that never leaves. This is a smell of urine, sour milk, and spoiling food sometimes joined with the strong smell of long-cooked onions. Onions are cheap. If you have smelled this smell, you did not know how it came. It is the smell of the outdoor privy. It is the smell of young children who cannot walk the long dark way in the night. It is the smell of the mattresses where years of "accidents" have happened. It is the smell of the milk which has gone sour because the refrigerator long has not worked, and it costs money to get it fixed. It is the smell of rotting garbage. I could bury it, but where is the shovel? Shovels cost money.

...

Poverty is staying up all night on cold nights to watch the fire knowing one spark on the newspaper covering the walls means your sleeping child dies in flames. In summer poverty is watching gnats and flies devour your baby's tears when he cries. The screens are torn and you pay so little rent you know they will never be fixed. Poverty means insects in your food, in your nose, in your eyes, and crawling over you when you sleep. Poverty is hoping it never rains because diapers won't dry when it rains and soon you are using newspapers. Poverty is seeing your children forever with runny noses. Paper handkerchiefs cost money and all your rags you need for other things. Even more costly are antihistamines. Poverty is cooking without food and cleaning without soap.

Poverty is asking for help. Have you ever had to ask for help, knowing your children will suffer unless you get it? Think about asking for a loan from a relative, if this is the only way you can imagine asking for help. I will tell you how it feels. You find out where the office is that you are supposed to visit. You circle that block four or five times. Thinking of your children, you go in. Everyone is very busy. Finally, someone comes out and you tell her that you need help. That never is the person you need to see. You go see another person, and after spilling the whole shame of your poverty all over the desk between you, you find that this isn't the right office after all—you must repeat the whole process, and it never is any easier at the next place.

You have asked for help, and after all it has a cost. You are again told to wait. You are told why, but you don't really hear because of the red cloud of shame and the rising cloud of despair.

···

Poverty is looking into a black future. Your children won't play with my boys. They will turn to other boys who steal to get what they want. I can already see them behind the bars of their prison instead of behind the bars of my poverty. Or they will turn to the freedom of alcohol or drugs, and find themselves enslaved. And my daughter? At best, there is for her a life like mine.

···

Poverty is an acid that drips on pride until all pride is worn away. Poverty is a chisel that chips on honor until honor is worn away. Some of you say that you would do *something* in my situation, and maybe you would, for the first week or the first month, but for year after year after year?

Even the poor can dream. A dream of a time when there is money. Money for the right kinds of food, for worm medicine, for iron pills, for toothbrushes, for hand cream, for a hammer and nails and a bit of screening, for a shovel, for a bit of paint, for some sheeting, for needles and thread. Money to pay *in money* for a trip to town. And, oh, money for hot water and money for soap. A dream of when asking for help does not eat away the last bit of pride. When the office you visit is as nice as the offices of other governmental agencies, when there are enough workers to help you quickly, when workers do not quit in defeat and despair. When you have to tell your story to only one person, and that person can send you for other help and you don't have to prove your poverty over and over and over again.

I have come out of my despair to tell you this. Remember I did not come from another place or another time. Others like me are all around you. Look at us with an angry heart, anger that will help you help me. Anger that will let you tell of me. The poor are always silent. Can you be silent too?

From *Conversational Ballgames*

Nancy Masterson Sakamoto

Nancy Masterson Sakamoto, born in Los Angeles, and a former English teacher in Japan, is co-author of Mutual Understanding of Different Cultures. *In this excerpt from her book* Polite Fictions, *she explores cultural differences.*

After I was married and had lived in Japan for a while, my Japanese gradually improved to the point where I could take part in simple conversations with my husband and his friends and family. And I began to notice that often, when I joined in, the others would look startled, and the conversational topic would come to a halt. After this happened several times, it became clear to me that I was doing something wrong. But for a long time, I didn't know what it was.

Finally, after listening carefully to many Japanese conversations, I discovered what my problem was. Even though I was speaking Japanese, I was handling the conversation in a western way.

Japanese-style conversations develop quite differently from western-style conversations. And the difference isn't only in the languages. I realized that just as I kept trying to hold western-style conversations even when I was speaking Japanese, so my English students kept trying to hold Japanese-style conversations even when they were speaking English. We were unconsciously playing entirely different conversational ballgames.

A western-style conversation between two people is like a game of tennis. If I introduce a topic, a conversational ball, I expect you to hit it back. If you agree with me, I don't expect you simply to agree and do nothing more. I expect you to add something—a reason for agreeing, another example, or an elaboration to carry the idea further. But I don't expect you always to agree. I am just as happy if you question me, or challenge me, or completely disagree with me. Whether you agree or disagree, your response will return the ball to me.

And then it is my turn again. I don't serve a new ball from my original starting line. I hit your ball back again from where it has bounced, I carry your idea further, or answer your questions or objections, or challenge or question you. And so the ball goes back and forth, with each of us doing our best to give it a new twist, an original spin, or a powerful smash.

And the more vigorous the action, the more interesting and exciting the game. Of course, if one of us gets angry, it spoils the conversation, just as it spoils a tennis game. But getting excited is not at all the same as getting angry. After all, we are not trying to hit each other. We are trying to hit the ball. So long as we attack only each other's opinions, and do not attack each other personally, we don't expect anyone to get hurt. A good conversation is supposed to be interesting and exciting.

If there are more than two people in the conversation, then it is like doubles in tennis, or like volleyball. There's no waiting in line. Whoever is nearest and quickest hits the ball, and if you step back, someone else will hit it. No one stops the game to give you a turn. You're responsible for taking your own turn.

But whether it's two players or a group, everyone does his best to keep the ball going, and no one person has the ball for very long.

A Japanese-style conversation, however, is not at all like tennis or volleyball. It's like bowling. You wait for your turn. And you always know your place in line. It depends on such things as whether you are older or younger, a close friend or a relative stranger to the previous speaker, in a senior or junior position, and so on.

When your turn comes, you step up to the starting line with your bowling ball, and carefully bowl it. Everyone else stands back and watches politely, murmuring encouragement. Everyone waits until the ball has reached the end of the alley, and watches to see if it knocks down all the pins, or only some of them, or none of them. There is a pause, while everyone registers your score.

Then, after everyone is sure that you have completely finished your turn, the next person in line steps up to the same starting line, with a different ball. He doesn't return your ball, and he does not begin from where your ball stopped. There is no back and forth at all. All the balls run parallel. And there is always a suitable pause between turns. There is no rush, no excitement, no scramble for the ball.

No wonder everyone looked startled when I took part in Japanese conversations. I paid no attention to whose turn it was, and kept snatching the ball halfway down the alley and throwing it back at the bowler. Of course the conversation died. I was playing the wrong game.

From *Behold Her Blackness*

Dahlia Aguilar

In this excerpt from her article for Latina Style *magazine, contributor Dahlia Aguilar examines racism in Hispanic communities.*

As the Hispanic community comes to terms with the institutional inequities set against it, Hispanics face an equally important task of examining the racism within their own community. The lives of black Latinas offer the community an opportunity to assess its own standards of fairness.

Cyndi Centeno is a Puerto Rican from New York and a 1993 graduate of Wesleyan University. She currently works with the Northern Manhattan Improvement Corporation where she organizes job training and development for people embarking on new careers, and welfare recipients transitioning into the work force. She says that blacks experience the same prejudices in the Hispanic community as they do in U.S. society as a whole, and believes that negative stereotypes are perpetuated by unfair representations of black Hispanics in the media.

Centeno, 24, notes that black Hispanics are virtually invisible on English-language television, and inaccurately characterized in the Spanish media. "In *novelas*, you find that black people are either associated with Santeria or Voodoo, or are cast as maids and house servants," she asserts. "There are no strong black characters. Even magazines like *Cosmopolitan* and *Vanity Fair*, published in Spanish, don't represent black Hispanics; you only see light-skinned models. There's a perception that whiteness equals rightness."

In her early school days, Centeno struggled to identity herself in the midst of these messages. "I experienced a lot of self-hatred," she says, "Every day I thought to myself how much easier my life would be if I was white."

She recalls taking steps, such as straightening her hair, to try and diminish the differences between herself and the Anglo majority. Now, she feels differently. "I'm very adamant about [many] Hispanics recognizing that they're part of the African diaspora, no matter how we look. We hear a lot of *'pelo bueno, pelo malo'* or 'she's pretty, but she's black.' While I am proud of my cultural and historical inheritance, it's impossible not to get the subliminal message."

Centeno adds, "I know people who are darker than I am who deny their African influence. I can understand how years of colonization has led people to equate blackness with ugliness and whiteness with beauty." She believes, however, that the media has a responsibility to eradicate some of its negative portrayals of black Latinas

···

Centeno sees the color complex at work in Latin America as well. She notes that "even in Latin American beauty pageants, semifinalists are generally light-skinned, and that's not just a coincidence." Centeno says that politics, too, are affected by the color strata. "In the Dominican Republic, where the majority of the population is black, there is a reluctance to elect candidates who are too dark."

Natalia Manan was born and raised in the Dominican Republic and recalls experiences similar to those described by Centeno. Manan, who now attends Spellman College, one of the foremost black colleges for women in the U.S., says, "When I lived in the Dominican Republic, I used to try to stay out of the sun. My friends and I always wanted to date whiter looking boys." She remembers her skin color influencing her self-image.

When she moved to the United States as a teenager, she recalls that her Dominican heritage did not insure her acceptance into the Hispanic community. While she got along with both Hispanics and Anglos, it was the black community which embraced her as their own. She felt the black community was more accepting of differences that her Latina friends could not get past. She feels her years at Spellman have made her view her history differently than many Hispanics.

Both Manan and Centeno strongly identify with their African roots. Centeno says, "I feel I have more in common with someone from Jamaica or Trinidad than with someone from Chile or Peru. Geographically, our islands look alike, and our music and food are similar."

Ruth Matteo, a U.S.-born first generation Dominican, gained a strong sense of her Hispanic heritage from her parents. When Matteo entered the school system, though, she was surprised at the impact her color had on her peers. She recalls that Hispanic friends in high school would often compliment her beauty, yet qualify it with statements about her skin tone. "They'd say 'She's pretty, but she's black,'" Matteo remembers. "There was so much focus on color, I thought I wasn't as good as other kids. I was always reminded that I was a minority and I felt inferior in school."

Matteo also recounts her difficult interactions with the black community at her college, which labeled her a "sell-out" for not joining their social circles. Even now, Matteo says people seem confused by her appearance. "I don't think people realize that Latinos come in a variety of colors," she says. Regardless of her appearance, Matteo says she feels stronger ties to her Hispanic heritage than to her black roots, although she acknowledges some similarities between the two cultures, and says she does not ignore her African roots. "I hate comments like, 'Oh, you're not *really* black,'" she says. "I am black and I am also Hispanic. I know my roots."

Why Men Should March for Women's Rights

Sydney J. Harris

*Sydney Harris—journalist, editor, and author—wrote a
weekly column for the* Chicago Daily News *and the* Chicago
Sun-Times. *Syndicated to approximately 200 newspapers,
these articles have also been collected into six volumes. In
the following essay, Harris argues that men should actively
support women's rights.*

I don't happen to think there is any virtue in agitating liberties on
your own behalf, as necessary as it may sometimes be. After all, everybody is for himself; everybody wants as much for himself as he can get,
whether it is justice, freedom, security, or Green Stamps.

And I don't think that such agitation will mean much—or have a
solid moral base—until each group begins doing it on behalf of other
groups, even more than for itself. This is what carries weight in the ultimate scale of democratic values.

Women should march for women's rights, but men belong there even
more, if rights mean anything as a principle. Gays should march against
the orange-heads of the world, but straights like me belong shoulder to
shoulder with them, and there should be more of us than of them because
there are more of us in the population.

Blacks and Jews and Latinos and all minority groups are little more
than vociferous special interests as long as they devote all their public
efforts to demanding justice and equality for themselves, badly as they
may need it.

What they need to demonstrate—what would really be impressive—
is their devotion to the same principles for everybody.

What do we have otherwise? Fragmented groups, each appealing to
the same sense of fairness on the part of the general public, but each
showing little sensitivity to or appreciation of the just needs and demands
of other fragmented groups. This is more like lobbying than crusading.

What would grip the imagination of the public at large, what would
drive home the democratic message, would be for each minority group—
whether sexual, racial, religious, or what have you—to give its time and
energy and passion toward the rectification of another group's legitimate
grievances.

This is genuine morality, in the deepest and oldest Judaic and Christian tradition. I am quite aware that Hillel said, "If I am not for myself,
who will be for me?" But the best way to be authentically for yourself is
to ally yourself with all those others who face the same problem on a different front.

Liberty and justice are indivisible, no matter what one's gonads, genes, or genuflections proclaim to the world. If you assure the good treatment of others, you are assuring your own, but if you ask for yourself only, you are doing no more than any scoundrel might. Only by each putting the other first can all achieve parity.

From *What Makes Pornography "Sexy"?*

John Stoltenberg

John Stoltenberg, co-founder of Men Against Pornography, and author of The End of Manhood *and* Refusing to Be a Man, *is a frequent speaker and workshop leader across the country. In this excerpt, he outlines his program for raising the awareness of people about the alienating effects of pornography.*

In August 1983 I was asked to help lead a workshop on pornography at a regional antisexist-men's conference at Hampshire College. Somehow a phrase from the WAP [Women Against Pornography] slide show flashed back to me—"Imagine men in these poses"—and I was inspired to bring along some magazines: a *Penthouse*, a *Playboy*, a *Hustler*, and several others. Something of my background in experimental theater must have come into play too, because I had an idea to conduct a theater-games–type exercise during which I would select several men at random out of the group, give each a magazine, and tell them to "do the pose" in a designated photograph. While these men were struggling into their assigned poses, I would invite the rest of the workshop participants to go from pose to pose. And I would urge the workshop participants to compare each pose to the picture it was based on and to call out comments about how to get the body position and facial expression more accurate.

...

During tryouts of The Pose Workshop concept at those early MAP [Men Against Pornography] meetings, I first discovered for myself a strange phenomenon: Whenever I was "doing a pose" I experienced a distinct discrepancy between the body position I was in and the facial expression that I had to "put on" in order to imitate the pose "convincingly." My face felt discordant with the physical experience of the rest of me. I would look at a photograph, get into the pose, turn and twist my body according to how I was coached by my fellow MAPers—but when I consulted the photograph again in order to match the facial expression just right, I found that the face I now had to "put on" had no coherent relationship to the sensations in my body below the neck. I found this out only when "inside" the pose, really doing it: I recall the feeling vividly, as though my head and face were detached from my body, as if I were severed at the neck. For me and the cofacilitators of The Pose Workshop, this recognition was one of the first personal tip-offs about the inauthenticity of affect, the internal dislocation of emotion, and the lack of bodily integrity that occur in the body of the woman who is posing before the camera....

Just *looking* at such a photograph—before pretesting any poses—I might never have observed or detected this "alienation effect." Over the years I witnessed many men obviously unnerved by the experience—in part, I suspect, because most men are not in the habit of enforcing, inside themselves, such extreme emotional and physical dislocations during sex. For most men, what their body is feeling shows up spontaneously in their expression, unmediated by the self-objectifying question "How does my face look now?" Thus for many men, including myself, "doing the pose" was a startlingly visceral introduction to the "self-splitting" that female models perform in order to qualify as "sexy" in a camera's lens. From the perspective of the camera—and hence male consumers' eyes—the face and body of the woman appear as a visual unity. But in the emotional and physical sensations of an actual human being "doing the pose," face and body feel split asunder. Once having experienced this split myself, I could better recognize when a poser was discovering the "alienation effect" kinesthetically for himself but unable to talk about it, and I could better help him name the experience for himself.

...

Men's individual consumption of magazines such as *Playboy* and *Penthouse*—as purchasers, as browsers, and as users during private episodes of masturbation—is apparently very dependent upon looking at such pictures as if the women in the photographs are less real than the men's sexual feelings. From repetitive personal experience—reinforced by the sensation of ejaculatory release—men learn that if what they desire is erotic stimulation from such published pictorials (to feel "turned on to pornography like a real man") they had better not perceive or conceive of the pictured women as being equally real people. For many men "hooked" on pornography, such pictures do not "work" as a turn-on if the woman is regarded as a real person. This, it turns out, is what makes pornography "sexy." And this dissociative way of looking seems also to result in dissociative feeling: conditioned to shut off or numb out in a relational context of actual intimacy and equality.

Conversely, when a man, even momentarily, looks at a pictured woman as if she is as real as himself—as if what is happening to her (in the photograph) is real and as if her feelings are real too—the photograph may lose its perceptual distance and hence its effectiveness as an erotic stimulus. This experience is self-evidently far more to be desired than dreaded, as The Pose workshop may prepare a man to realize. As he does so, he may find himself on the brink of a profound new personal discovery, with implications for all his relational life: He may learn not only to fully perceive the person he has feelings for but also to perceive that person as someone who need be no less real than he in order for him to feel.

From *Thoughts on Aging*

Ann Domitrovich

Ann Domitrovich describes herself as a high school graduate who, at age thirty-five, developed a deep interest in visual and verbal expression. In this excerpt, she explores both individual and cultural experiences of age.

I remember the first time it occurred to me that time was not always going to be my friend, and that I was getting older. I was 34 and I was leaning over a mirrored table in the ladies room of a restaurant and I noticed that the skin under my chin was not tight. It was loose. That startled me. It wasn't much of a change—just a tiny little bit, but I was very aware that the world had shifted for me, and there was the beginning of fear in that insight.

After that I don't remember thinking much about age at all one way or the other. The 30s are, I think, the best years for a woman. She looks strong and healthy and beautiful with the confidence of that age reflected in her eyes.

My 40th birthday didn't bother me much. I had heard so much about it I was prepared for a jolt but nothing happened. I didn't melt or disappear and I looked exactly the way I had looked the day before. As I recall, it was around 43 that the real fear of aging, and what that meant to me, began. It started to attack in so many ways. Physically I was noticeably not as strong. My flexibility, which was just something I took for granted because I had always had it, began to go. I remember I started to get up from my knees one morning when I was weeding my garden and I felt like an old woman. And I know that I moved and looked like one. God, it seemed as though it took 10 minutes to get to my feet. I couldn't believe that this stiff, creaky old body belonged to me. I also became aware that my body didn't feel like me any more. Arms and legs, once sturdy and firm, now were saggy and flabby. And even if I lost weight (which I considered better than winning the Irish Sweepstakes) I didn't want anybody to hug me or touch me anymore because I didn't want them to feel my body. It had betrayed me. I didn't like the way it felt to me, so I was sure nobody else would either. I was beginning to relate differently to other people because my body had begun to age. The isolation of being an older woman in this society had truly begun for me. The prejudice of our culture was working on me and I was just as prejudiced as anybody else. I feared and hated these outward signs of aging, maybe even more than some other women as I have never had a particularly good image of myself. So the loss of my youth and the protection that gave me left me even more vulnerable than before. One more defense down.

And then there was my face. Oh God, my face. The lines, the wrinkles, the sags and bags. Every few months it got worse. Makeup only accentuated it, and, unlike my body, I could not cover it up. Your face simply cannot be hidden. Your eyes, your smile, your expressions—all right out there for the world to see and react to. And the world began to react to this middle-aged woman. My status as a citizen of this world we all live in began to waver. Women are desired and accepted because they are young. Middle-aged women lose rank fast just because they are not young. They are tolerated if they are bright enough, successful enough, and—this is most important—if they do not *appear* to be middle-aged. A middle-aged woman can still exist with some dignity as long as she belies her existence. If she looks thin enough, pretty enough, young enough, she can still be accepted. As long as she doesn't look like what she naturally is. For all those who have yet to travel that road, it is very frightening because you know the next day can only bring more of the same. And it will be that much harder because nature is taking her course. You can never catch up. Never. But I continued the chase because I didn't know what else to do.

Then there is the issue of sexuality. I have always wanted to have a fulfilling sexual relationship and took it for granted that I always would. But the chances of that diminish as the aging process accelerates. That was very frightening to me: the thought of not relating on a loving, sexual level to another person for the last 20 or so years of my life because nobody would want me. That nobody would let me get close enough to them because I was too old broke my heart. It was devastating. Another area of being cut off, shut out.

So that was my experience with aging in my 40s. I'm almost 52 now. Much of my life has not particularly come together as a whole the way I would have liked. I still do not have the confidence I could have wished for myself and for other women who have reached my age. I am still terribly afraid of the future, still neurotic and insecure and cowardly about many things. But there are a few areas where I have come a long way, and these few areas sustain me for the most part and get me through another long night. One is the fact that just by staying alive in this world I have acquired a certain wisdom and acceptance of life in general. I can look back now and get a glimpse of how people become who they are, and understand a little of how they got that way and it's ok. It's also ok that there is so much I'll never understand. Life has so many questions and so few answers.

···

I will not apologize for my age. I will wear my hair hanging down my back if I want to just because it feels good. I don't worry anymore that some of the clothes I like to wear will be denied me because they are "too young" for me. If I like them and they make me happy and I'm not wearing them to try to appear younger, then I will wear them anyway. I will feel my feelings and think my thoughts and express myself as the sum total of my experience and my years. I will be who I am. And my looks will reflect that.

*C*hapter Review

Together or Solo. Write a response to the following questions:

1. What are the three most important things you learned about culture from working with this chapter?

2. What cultural stereotypes did you believe before working with this chapter? Have you modified your view? If so, how? If not, why not?

3. Since working with this chapter, how have you modified your view of yourself and the cultures in which you move?

4. What did you learn about the challenges and benefits of *writing* to bridge cultures?

5. How can you more actively work against ethnic, gender, and age discrimination at home? At work? At school? In your community?

Chapter 12

Writing to Learn I

Becoming a Responsible Thinker

This chapter offers opportunities to

—Identify traits of a **responsible thinker**

—Compare and contrast purposes and audiences **across the curriculum**

—Take **effective notes**

—Identify **key words**

—Distinguish different **kinds of questions**

—Write **thesis statements** for exams and papers

—**Summarize** for different purposes

> Writing is a learning process.
> —*Bruce Inge, Student*

The Need to Learn

Being human, you have a vast capacity for learning. You start to learn even while in the womb and may continue to do so for over a hundred years. Using your senses and intellect, you can design experiences so that you can name and meet your needs. You can store most, if not all of the experiences you have in the storehouse of your experiences—your unconscious. The trick is to recall and utilize information when you need it. Doing so is a matter of survival: the better you use what you know, the better your life can be. Ideally, if you don't know what you need to know, you can find a way to search for it, learn it, and store it.

Writing to Become a Responsible Thinker

If you are like most people, you are able to hold only a few things at a time in the corridor of your consciousness. This is a survival aid. If all you know were to flood your mind at once, you would be utterly confused. In writing, too, you can write only one thing at a time. But usually, as soon as you write something down, you clear the way for more thoughts to follow. Writing is ideal for helping you recall and use information, because, by its nature, writing focuses on and draws things from the storehouse of your unconscious.

Intelligence can be defined as the ability to make useful and creative connections between experiences. The more you write about what you experience and read, the more of these connections you will develop. The more connections you can make between ideas and experiences, the more quickly you will be able to trigger your memory. Writing helps you to see, organize, and make connections that may be too complex to manage in the small space of your consciousness. For these and other reasons, writing and reading others' writings are the foundations of formal education.

The model of the writing process used in this book and the Explorations in this chapter and the next are designed to help you become more conscious of your educational experiences and to develop the following three qualities of a responsible learner and thinker:

1. Sensitivity to purpose and audience
2. Ability to adopt or formulate standards for coping with different purposes and audiences
3. Ability to adjust and correct oneself*

---

*These three characteristics are adapted from Matthew Lipman's three criteria for critical thinking published in *Inquiry: Critical Thinking Across the Disciplines* 1(2), March 1988—the newsletter of the Institute for Critical Thinking at Montclair State University.

This chapter shows you two tools to help you focus your attention so that you can better learn and remember what you learn: note taking and summarizing. Chapter 13 offers you opportunities to write responses and essays so that you can engage more actively with the materials you study.

To begin your explorations into learning, participate in some of the following activities that are designed to help you become more aware of the need to learn.

*E*xplorations _____

1. *Together.* Read the following illustrations of people who used writing to help them satisfy a need to learn. Discuss how each person displays the three main skills of a responsible thinker. How did the writing process help each person to solve problems? Identify how each writer used specific phases of the writing process.

   a.   Ned, a writer, develops severe pains in his hands from typing. The doctors diagnose it as carpal tunnel syndrome and recommend an operation. But Ned has both personal and religious objections to such intervention. Using the skills he has developed as a writer, he researches carpal tunnel syndrome, consults with others who have the syndrome, and finds alternative ways to heal his hands. Ned writes an article that creates more interest in these alternative methods. Readers write him letters with questions and further suggestions.

   b.   Jocelyn finds herself getting involved in one destructive relationship after another. She decides to start writing a personal journal to notice what these relationships have in common. A course in human interactions leads her to books and articles about such relationships. Using her own experience and the theories that are offered in her readings, Jocelyn synthesizes a plan for developing healthier relationships.

   c.   After years of believing that he just can't handle mathematics, Mark decides to give it one last chance. He has wanted a college degree so he could teach high school sports, but he hasn't been able to fulfill his math requirements. The class that Mark takes is taught by a teacher who uses writing to help students learn. Writing about what he doesn't understand, formulating questions, and describing his process, Mark finds he is able to articulate the kind of help he needs from his instructor. Mark steadily breaks through one block after another. By the end of the semester he has gained enough momentum to earn a B. Also, he has come to recognize ways in which mathematics can help him better understand the dynamics of muscle development and how to design a training schedule for athletes. The confidence he gains is helping him to explore difficult new ideas in his physical education courses, as well.

2. *Solo.* Write about a time when you needed to learn something for personal, physical, economic, social, or educational reasons. What steps did you take? What frustrations did you experience? What did you learn? How would you approach the problem if it occurred now?

Purpose and Audience Across the Curriculum

Formal education is divided into different fields of learning called *disciplines.* Some of the current academic disciplines are mathematics, sociology, history, and fine arts. Every discipline is a culture or community defined by certain rules, questions, languages, and procedures. Even within disciplines there are smaller cultures. History, for example, includes the subdisciplines of ancient history, African history, and history of ideas.

Learning a new discipline is like entering a new country or social club. To survive and thrive you have to learn what others expect, what they know, how you can adapt to them, and how you can make them adapt to you. Throughout this chapter, you will be invited to compare and contrast different disciplines so that you can learn how best to achieve your purposes with specific audiences.

Points of View

The more points of view from which you can approach the world, the richer your experience will be. The various disciplines provide you with different points of view or perspectives. Much as looking at a statue from different angles will enrich your experience of it, evaluating a social issue from different points of view will empower you with a greater sense of your options.

How you view a subject will be determined by your purpose. Notice the wide range of points of view from which the subject of laughter can be considered, according to the purpose at hand:

*   A physiologist explains the functions of the human body. Therefore, a physiologist would explain laughter as rhythmic, repetitive, spasmodic exhalation controlled by the parasympathetic nervous system.
*   An anthropologist explores human cultures. So, an anthropologist could show us that laughter is used in some societies as punishment and in other societies as a way of becoming comfortable with strangers.
*   A linguist notices and accounts for language patterns and would collect a series of successful jokes to discern what patterns of vocabulary and grammar they have in common.

- An economist, who accounts for how people earn, spend, and manage money, may research how humor is used in television commercials and compare the sales generated by humorous commercials to those generated by more serious approaches.

- A management science expert, trained in organizing people in work settings, may explore how humor can be used in the workplace to enhance job satisfaction.

- A mathematician, trained in predicting numerical patterns, may tabulate how a certain comedian paces her punch lines.

Exciting new insights are gained when ideas from one discipline are adapted by another. So, for example, the management science expert can use the anthropologist's insights when organizing workers from different ethnic backgrounds. The physiologist can formulate further insights about the physiology of laughter by using the mathematician's tabulations of comic pacing.

To discover for yourself the points of view from which different disciplines approach the world, do one or more of the following Explorations.

*E*xplorations

1. *Together.*

   a. Review the discussion of purposes in education on pages 54–56.

   b. Divide yourselves into groups of four. Assign a different academic discipline to each group. If possible, bring textbooks to class from these other disciplines. (One group can be devoted to *writing* as a discipline and use *The Flexible Writer* as an example.) Look through the tables of contents and indexes for ideas. Modeling your discussions on the example of laughter, above, formulate how someone in a particular discipline would approach one of the following topics. Create a typical assignment in that course on your chosen topic.

Death	Hunger
War	Love
Racism	Aging

   c. As a class, compare the different approaches that academic disciplines take to your topic. Identify the main purpose of each academic discipline as reflected in your assignments: is it information, skills, interpretation, or experimentation?

2. *Solo and Together.* For the next week, notice when ideas from one course or discipline give you greater insights into others. Record these insights in your journal and write about their significance to you. Share what you wrote with each other.

Focusing: Taking Effective Notes

Concepts, information, observations, and memories cluster around key words, questions, statements, and sense imagery the way the spokes of a wheel radiate from its hub, the planets cluster around the sun, iron gathers to a magnet, and fans congregate around a rock star. By learning to identify and focus on key words, questions, statements, and sense imagery, you develop your ability to access what you need from the storehouse of your experiences.

Key Words

A *key word* can literally open the way to whole portions of the storehouse of your own and others' experiences. Learning the key words in a discipline allows you into the community of people who have chosen that way of viewing the world. For example, historians are people who know the various meanings of key words such as *democracy, socialism,* and *fascism.* Lawyers are people who know how to effectively use such key expressions as *tort, habeas corpus,* and *writ.* Knowing the meaning of key words in a discipline helps professionals save time. They don't have to waste energy constantly renegotiating basic ideas. That's why, when needed, professionals will devote so much time and effort to carefully defining and redefining key words to form a firm foundation for communicating with their colleagues.

Focusing on key words in a discipline will help you to learn, retain, and recall information when you need it. The first step is to identify key words. Here are some ways to do so:

- Your instructor or book repeats the word.
- Your instructor or book emphasizes the word. Key words are often used as chapter or section headings in books, just as the key words in this book include *Purpose and Audience, Writing to Learn,* and *Key Words.* They are often italicized, underlined, printed in bold type, or set between quotation marks.
- Key words may be collected in the glossary of a textbook.
- You keep noticing a word, *yourself.*

Learning Key Words

1. **Collect.** For each course you take, collect key words and concepts. Here are places to write them:
   - The inside covers of your notebook or textbook
   - A computer file
   - A bulletin board

2. **Define** key words and concepts you collect.

3. **Write** in a learning journal, using key words for your focus. Record relevant examples that illustrate each concept. When appropriate, note differences and similarities between how a word is used in one discipline and how it is used in another.

4. **Review** key words and concepts for exams and projects. Ask someone to quiz you.

Do one or more of the following Explorations to practice identifying key words.

*E*xplorations _____

1. **a.** *Together.* Each person responds to certain key words that trigger strong reactions. Create two lists of everyday words that are significant to you—the first of favorite expressions, the second of ones you dislike. For example, one person loves to use *relish* as in the expression "I *relish* reading mysteries." Another person feels irritated with the word *share.*

   b. *Solo and Together.* Choose a significant expression and write about what it means to you. Read some of these responses to each other.

2. *Solo and Together.* Underline key words or expressions in the following passages.* Identify the disciplines to which they may belong. Then compare your identifications.

_____

*These passages were drawn from the following sources across the curriculum: Joel R. Evans and Barry Berman, *Marketing,* 4th ed. (New York: Macmillan, 1990), pp. 61, 173; Robert J. Foster, *General Geology,* 5th ed. (Columbus, Ohio: Merrill, 1988), pp. 21, 97, 240; Larry Madaras and James M. SoRelle, *Taking Sides: Clashing Views on Controversial Issues in American History* (Guilford, Conn.: Dushkin, 1989), pp. 21, 79; and Charles P. McKeague, *Pre-Algebra* (Belmont, Calif.: Wadsworth, 1987), p. 316. The excerpts on page 318 of *The Flexible Writer* are also drawn from these sources.

a. The consumer may use extended, limited, or routine decision-making. This depends on the degree of search, level of prior experience, frequency of purchase, amount of perceived risk, and time pressure.

b. The fit of the continents on a map seems to be too good to be accidental. The fit is even better if, instead of the shoreline, the true edge of the continent, the continental shelf, is used. Later deformation or erosion does spoil the match at some places.

c. There aren't any broad moral principles of justice, charity, equity, or benevolence that can be discovered in the moral systems of all cultures. There is a much deeper question that we have not touched on yet. Even if there *were* universally accepted norms, what would that fact prove? Does everybody believing something make it right? Don't we need some justification for our moral convictions that goes beyond saying, "Everybody agrees with me"?

d. No matter how carefully a measurement is made, it is never exact. A vital part of any good experiment is an evaluation of the degree of uncertainty of the results. The evaluation of the probable range of error in an experimentally determined parameter is often almost as important as the numerical value of the parameter itself.

Questions

A question, by its very nature, invites response and gathers information to itself. That is why questions are so powerful in learning and remembering. By developing the habit of noticing and asking questions, you enhance the speed, quality, and quantity of your learning. The better your questions, the better the answers you'll find.

Writing allows you not only to relate what you already know but to learn in the process. You learn best by maintaining a curious mind, by constantly asking yourself questions. In turn, you can engage your readers by anticipating questions they will be likely to raise in response to your writing. If you wrongly assume that your readers will understand or agree with what you are writing, you might lose them in the process.

To develop the habit of asking questions, use question words to trigger them. The *wh* words in Figure 5.4 (page 120) are key words that help you to start formulating full questions. Questions can also start with words such as *do, can, are, is, were, if,* and *has,* but, as you will soon see, these questions do not generate quite the same kinds of responses as the *wh* words do.

To develop your skill in asking and responding to questions, it is important to notice differences between them. Five basic categories of questions that will help you discern these differences are (1) good questions, (2) unfair questions, (3) yes/no questions, (4) one-answer questions, and (5) rhetorical questions.

Good Questions.   "Why are our hearts on the left instead of the right?" "Why do supermarkets place toothbrushes at eye level and why don't they alphabetize canned soups?" "Is there a God?" "Why do some people become alcoholics?" "How can we save the ozone layer?" "What happened to Uncle Frank that made everyone in the family avoid talking about him?" These and other questions are good questions. Students notice that good questions meet some, if not all, of the following standards:

- They respond to some important human need.
- They are focused and specific.
- They make you think.
- They may question popular beliefs.
- They invite more than one answer. Some of these answers may conflict with others.
- They lead to other questions.
- They suggest how you would go about answering them.
- They lead to good answers.
- They aren't unfair.
- They give you an "aha" feeling.
- They may cause strong reactions.
- They may meet with resistance from others.
- They make you say, "That's a good question."
- They can lead you to work with others.

For example, the question "How can we save the ozone layer?" is a good question because it responds to an important human need—to save the planet. The question makes you think, has more than one answer, leads to other questions about the environment, and suggests that you need to consider practical measures. The question has led to good answers by people who are working together on the problem. It isn't a trick or unfair question. It leads people to say, "That's a good question."

Unfair Questions.   "Are you still beating your dog?" "What's the difference between a duck?" "How come someone says they saw you do it?" "You don't want another piece of my pie, do you?" "What is it like to be blown up by a bomb?" These and other questions can be seen as unfair. Unfair questions have some, if not all, of the following characteristics:

- They assume something that the responder may want to question.
- They are meant to trick responders into saying things they wouldn't want to say.
- They often lead to only one answer.
- They may have no answer.
- They may lead you to say, "That's not a real question."
- They may leave you confused as to how you would answer them.
- They antagonize the audience.
- They may undermine your purpose.

For example, the question "Are you still beating your dog?" is unfair because it assumes that the person beat the dog in the first place. The responder couldn't win. A responder who says "Yes" is admitting to beating the dog in the first place. A responder who says "No" is still admitting to beating the dog! The question may antagonize and confuse the responder. The question could undermine the questioner's purpose of trying to save the dog from abuse. A fair approach would be to first ask, "Have you ever beaten your dog?"

Some questions may be unfair because of the context in which they are asked. For example, it could be unfair and embarrassing to ask a person, "What is your real hair color?" at a formal dinner. But it can be entirely appropriate for a hairdresser to ask this question of a client while in a salon. How you phrase the question is crucial. The question "What happened to my Uncle Frank?" may be a good question to ask of a relative, whereas "What did you do to him?" assumes that the relative injured Uncle Frank. "What is it like to be blown up by a bomb?" is unfair because it can't be answered by one who has had the experience. The question "What's the difference between a duck?" doesn't normally make sense. But when a comedian asks it, the question isn't unfair—it's meant to be funny.

Yes/No Questions. "Is there an afterlife?" "Have you gone to the store?" "Are there moons around Jupiter?" "Do they make navy blue blinds?" "Will there be enough ozone layer left in the twenty-first century?" "Should there be an extra microphone for the event?" "Can you loan me money?" Such yes/no questions have some, if not all, of the following characteristics:

- They often begin with some form of the words *is, can, do, have, could/would/should,* or *will.*
- They do not invite collaboration.

- They limit the range of response.
- They may be too general.
- They can be unfair.

Because of the way they are phrased, these and other questions like them usually call for a response of "yes" or "no." Because the anticipated response is so limited, for the most part yes/no questions do not invite the kind of richness, elaboration, and collaboration that other questions do. Sometimes yes/no questions can be unfair because they assume that the topic can be dispensed with by a short answer. For many religious and nonreligious people, the question "Is there an afterlife?" is too general. The topic requires more discussion, elaboration, and interpretation. A good question about the afterlife would be more focused, as this one is: "How were the arguments that current Roman Catholic theologians offer in support of an afterlife developed?"

One-Answer Questions.   "How much is 2 + 2 in the decimal system?" "What was the cause of the Civil War?" "Who is the main character in Chaucer's *Canterbury Tales*?" "What is the most important trait of a responsible thinker?" "Would any sane person ever want to kill an innocent child?" Such one-answer questions have some, if not all, of the following characteristics:

- They assume that there is only one right answer.
- They occur most often in courses where the focus is learning information.
- They can create the atmosphere of a guessing game.
- They can be satisfying to answer "right."
- They may create a competitive atmosphere.
- They may lead a person to answer without questioning the question.

For example, the question "What was the cause of the Civil War?" assumes, by the use of the word *the*, that there was one and only one cause of the Civil War. If the question were posed by a teacher in class it could create the atmosphere of a "guess what the teacher's thinking" game. Some students would settle for the satisfaction of guessing what the teacher thought at the time, while others would compete to say it first. Students who aren't good at guessing could give up and feel defeated. If these kinds of questions were very frequent, students would not be able to feel the satisfaction of responsible thinking: asking and exploring good questions, entertaining different points of view and perspectives, formulating standards, reflecting, correcting their own thinking, and collaborating with others to find interesting and provocative answers.

Rhetorical Questions.   "Would you starve little children to death?" "How many people have given their lives in Bosnia-Herzegovina?" "What more could we have done to save them?" Sometimes answers to such questions as these are meant to be so obvious that the questions are not really requests for answers. For example, the question, "Would you starve little children to death?" was used in a student's speech on children's rights to make a point: *You are not paying attention to these children—if you were, you'd donate to this fund.* The obvious answer to the question was "No." The question "How many people have given their lives in Bosnia-Herzegovina?," if used in a speech or political paper, would not be a request for statistics. The obvious answer and the implied statement is "Too many people have died." Nor is the question "What more could we have done to save them?"—when used in this way—a request for a list of things to do. The obvious answer is "We have done all we could."

If a question is used not as a request for an answer but as a strategy to persuade an audience of a predictable answer and point, it is called a *rhetorical question.* The word *rhetorical,* in this context, means "meant to persuade."

Rhetorical questions have some, if not all, of these characteristics:

- They are asked in speeches.
- They are used to make a powerful impression on the audience.
- They are used to make a point.
- There is only one acceptable answer to each question.
- Listeners or readers know there is only one acceptable answer.
- They are statements in disguise.
- They are not meant to be answered.

Notice that context—purpose and audience—determines whether a question is used rhetorically or not. A villain might ask, "Would you starve little children to death?" as a request for strategies. A writer seeking details to support an argument against war might ask, "How many have given their lives for this cause?" And to a Red Cross volunteer, "What more could we have done to save them?" would be a good question.

Learning to Ask Questions

1. *Remind* yourself, "The only dumb question is the one not asked." Even an unfair question can lead to a better question, once the first one is addressed.

2. *Use the question star* (Figure 5.4, page 120) to help you trigger and generate questions.

3. *Collect* questions for each course that you take. Mark the questions that are likely to be asked on an exam or that may lead to reports or papers.

4. *Collect* questions for specific problems you want to solve, whether they are personal or social, financial or spiritual, academic or professional.

5. *Analyze* questions. Ask yourself:

   - What kind of question is this: good, unfair, yes/no, one-answer, or rhetorical?

   - What kind of response, if any, does this question require?

   - How could I revise this question to be a *good* question?

6. *Practice* answering anticipated questions for exams, business meetings, social conversations, and interviews. Write your questions down. Freewrite in response to them, one at a time. Revise them for your purpose and audience.

7. *Allow questions to emerge* throughout your learning process. Respond to the most relevant ones.

*E*xplorations

1. *Together.* Consider the question "What are the three traits of a responsible thinker?" Decide, from the way it is phrased, whether it is a good, unfair, yes/no, one-answer, or rhetorical question. How would you rephrase it so that it would more certainly be a good question?

2. *Together.* Analyze and discuss the following questions. Using the standards offered in the discussion above, mark the questions as being good (G), unfair (U), yes/no (Y), one-answer (O), or rhetorical (R). Do any fit into more than one category? If so, in which contexts?

   a. What is nuclear winter?

   b. How is modern-day television different from its early days?

   c. Does the president of the United States have too big a job?

    d. Was the decision in the Sacco and Vanzetti case cruel?

    e. Who led the fight against Hitler?

    f. What is family life like in Argentina as compared to family life in the United States?

    g. Well, baseball fans, what is the world's greatest sport?

    h. What are the comparative benefits of organic and synthetic fertilizers?

    i. How should cigarettes be advertised?

    j. Are the problems of single parents being adequately addressed by local and federal governments?

3. a. *Solo.* Choose a class that is important to you or one in which you are having difficulties. During a class meeting, listen for and record the questions that are asked in the class. Mark the following letters by them to note who asks them—(T) for the teacher, (S) for students, (B) for books or other written material. Then write about what you noticed.

- Which questions were repeated?
- Which questions did *you* feel were *good questions?*
- How were they handled?
- What did you notice about the source of the questions?
- What did you learn by focusing on questions?
- Are the questions being asked in this Exploration helpful to you?
- What other questions occur to you about, or in response to, the questions asked in your chosen class?

    b. *Together.* Compare the results of collecting questions from your classes. Analyze them, using the instructions from Exploration 2.

4. *Together and Solo.*

    a. Choose a topic that is puzzling you in a course you are taking. Using the *wh* words as triggers, ask as many questions about the topic as you can. Next, discuss which questions are good, unfair, yes/no, one-word, or rhetorical questions. Which questions will lead you to the answers you are seeking?

    b. Write an essay on the topic, using your questions to stimulate ideas and insights. Organize your paper into a series of paragraphs, each of which poses and responds to a question. Write so that one question-and-answer paragraph leads logically to the next question and answer. As you write, allow other questions to arise. Do not require yourself to give a complete answer, especially if you are posing new good or rhetorical questions.

    c. Read these essays to each other, and discuss what you learned from doing this Exploration.

5. *Together and Solo.* Listen to a debate or an interview on television. Record the questions. Discuss whether the person answers the questions. If not, how does the person "dodge" offering a direct answer to the questions posed?

6. *Together and Solo.* Turn to pages 119–120 in Chapter 5 and notice how questions help you focus in the writing process. Choose a paper someone in the class is writing, and ask questions to help the author write more effectively. List these questions and analyze them using the criteria developed above.

Key Statements: The Thesis

Questions invite answers, and key statements (also called *thesis statements*) invite further elaboration, evidence, and proof. They are called *key* statements because, like keys, they unlock your mind as well as your reader's. If you have not already done so, review the sections on pages 110–116, which provide you with an in-depth discussion of how to identify and use these key or thesis statements. Complement the work in that chapter with these examples of key statements from textbooks in three different academic disciplines:

> *U.S. history.* "Four predominant schools of thought have emerged in American history since the first graduate seminars in history were given at Johns Hopkins University in Baltimore in the 1870s."
>
> *Geology.* "Many of the materials that form the crust of the earth are useful to us."
>
> *Marketing.* "Strategic planning efforts must accommodate the distinct needs of marketing as well as the other functional areas in an organization."

These "thesis" statements embody the main or key ideas the authors want to relate. They are good thesis statements because they meet some or all of the following standards:

Standards for good thesis statements

- They lead to good questions.
- They lead to other statements.
- They are focused.

For example, consider the thesis statement in U.S. history: "Four predominant schools of thought have emerged in American history since the first graduate seminars in history were given at Johns Hopkins University in Baltimore in the 1870s." This statement invites questions such as these: What are the four predominant schools of thought in U.S. history? Why does the author name Johns Hopkins University as a starting point? What happened in the 1870s that made that decade a turning point in U.S. history? The thesis statement leads to a long discussion of the four schools of thought and what forces influenced them. The thesis statement is focused on a particular time and doesn't try to cover all possible theories.

In the writing process—whether for an exam, an oral report, or a term paper—the purpose of writing a thesis statement is to make a commitment to a key idea so that it will trigger your memory and guide you to collect and recollect whatever further evidence you need to support your claim.

Remember that thesis statements develop in the writing process. Start with a working thesis statement. Revise and refine it as you draft your paper. A thesis statement is like a roof: it appears at the top, but first you have to construct the building under it.

*E*xplorations

1. *Together.* Discuss this statement: "The statements of a responsible thinker are made in the spirit of preserving or bettering human relations and the environment." What are the key words in the statement? How would you define them? Is the statement weak or strong? Why? Is the statement responsible or irresponsible? Why?

2. *Solo and Together.*

   a. Collect questions and assignments from your textbooks and class notes. Using the sidebar offered on page 114 for writing thesis statements, practice turning these questions and assignments into thesis statements. Write the statements on the board one at a time and revise your statements until they meet the standards for good thesis statements. Adjust them to be appropriately strong.

   b. *Solo.* Write an essay in response to a key (thesis) statement you developed in response to an assignment.

Learning Through the Senses

From a drop of water a logician could infer the possibility of an Atlantic or Niagara without having seen or heard of one or the other.... By a man's fingernails, by his coat sleeve, by his boots, by his trouser-knees, by the callosities of his forefinger and thumb, by his expression, by his shirt-cuffs—by each of these things a man's calling is plainly revealed.

> —*Sir Arthur Conan Doyle, Creator of Sherlock Holmes* "A Study in Scarlet"

Part of the education process is to sharpen your senses and mind so that you can create new ideas from available input. Chapter 6 invited you to explore your senses in everyday experiences. This section offers some basic insights into how to develop academic thinking skills through the senses.

Whenever you are writing—whether it be a paper, report, proposal, essay, poem, or story—prime your senses by collecting pictures, audio recordings, objects, and documents and by putting yourself in a place where you can best gather sensations. Ask yourself the following questions:

What visual or object would be relevant for me to look at? For example, if you are writing a paper about political unrest in Colombia, find photographs or news broadcasts depicting people and events there. When you write, start by describing a photograph or film to provide your reader with immediacy. If you are reporting on the Berlin Wall, you might want to find a piece of it and describe what it feels like to hold it in your hand. If you are writing about hairstyles in eighteenth-century Paris, you can either find a book of pictures or ask your local video store for a movie set in that time. (Be aware, however, that movies are not always accurate or well researched.)

What audio would be relevant for me to listen to? For example, if you are writing a paper about a speech, ask your librarian for a recording of the speech made by the speaker. Or, a paper on a poem would be much enriched by your reflecting on a taped reading of it by the author.

Where can I get firsthand experience of what I am writing about? For example, if you are writing about the homeless, you may want to visit a shelter or city bus terminal where homeless people live so that you can better understand their problems. While you are there, if it seems appropriate, talk with some of the homeless. When you reach for such firsthand experiences, make sure you consider your own and others' sense of safety and dignity. If you want to know what conditions are like in a mine, you would want an escort; if you want to know what hang gliding is like, you would want some training (lots of it).

*E*xplorations _____

1. *Together and Solo.* List visual and audio material that would help you prime your senses for each of the following assignments in different areas of study. Design, as well, some possible firsthand experiences that would enliven and inform the experience of doing each assignment.

Learning Through the Senses

1. *Use the sense star* (Figure 6.1, page 135) to remind you to collect images for all the appropriate senses.

2. *Ask yourself these questions* when posed with an assignment:

   - What visual or object would be relevant?
   - What recordings could enliven my process?
   - What firsthand experience could support my learning?
   - How could I trigger my memory?

3. *Research documents,* such as newspapers, books, reports, financial papers, letters, and journals.

4. *Prime your senses* by taking notes as you review your visual or audio materials. Don't expect to remember all the relevant details without this support.

5. *Consult* with others. Observe your object, film, or subject together. What relevant images do others notice that you have overlooked?

a. *Environmental Studies.* Environmental catastrophes such as depletion of the ozone layer are jeopardizing human life and the life of our planet. Investigate your community for instances of environmental degradation. Write a paper detailing the problems and showing how the community is either coping with or ignoring them.

b. *Sociology.* Nursing homes can be difficult places for the elderly to pass their last years. Write a paper detailing the problems and possible solutions to them.

c. *Political science.* Compare television and newspaper coverage of an important current event. How do the two differ in terms of the time, space, and emphasis they give to different aspects of the event? How does your experience of watching a television report differ from your experience of reading the newspaper?

d. *Psychology.* Write a paper stating your position on whether or not television violence encourages violent behavior in children.

e. *Fine arts.* Write a paper showing similarities between two pieces of art shown in a local gallery this season.

f. *Mathematics.* How would you go about estimating the number of leaves on a tree, grains of sand on a beach, cars that pass through a toll booth, or hamburgers eaten at an average local diner?

g. *Literature.* What are five of the most frequent subjects of Robert Frost's poetry?

    h.   *Media studies.* What are five main points of view (angles) that the camera takes in current horror films to terrify audiences?

    i.   *Management sciences.* Write a paper either agreeing or disagreeing with the statement "Women tend to be treated differently from men in the workplace."

2.   *Solo.* Write a paper in response to one of the assignments in Exploration 1. Conduct your research by priming your senses and collecting notes on as many sensations as you can cover.

3. **a.**   *Together and Solo.* List the courses you are taking this semester. List projects, papers, and other assignments that you anticipate having to complete. In small groups, develop suggestions for visual, audio, and firsthand experiences that will help you prime your senses for the assignments.

    b.   *Solo.* Complete an assignment by priming your senses. Write a report on how this process affected both your experience of doing the assignment and the outcome of the assignment.

Summarizing

A summary is a concise statement—in your own words—of a longer piece of writing. Whereas writing a key statement helps you to focus what you *write*, summarizing in key statements helps you to focus what you *read*. In the act of summarizing, you connect what you read with whatever you already know. Since what you read then becomes connected to what you know, you are more likely to remember and understand what you read and to notice what questions you have about it. Good summaries meet some, if not all, of the following standards:

Standards for good summaries

- They are brief.
- They identify the author, title, focus, and context of the work.
- They relay the author's main points.
- They omit most supporting information.
- They capture and honor the author's purpose and intention.

The purposes and audiences for a summary vary, and it is important to note why you are summarizing a particular piece of writing and for whom. For example, if your purpose in studying an article were to prepare for an exam that tests your recall of information, you would summarize

How to Summarize

1. Carefully *read* the material you are summarizing, several times.
2. *Identify the purpose and audience* for your summary.
3. *Identify the author, title, focus, and context* of what you are summarizing. Notice, for example, how the following summaries are begun:

   > In his book *Amusing Ourselves to Death*, Neil Postman argues that in the modern world we are destroying our minds in the pursuit of pleasure.

   > Joseph Campbell illustrates, in his book *Transformations of Myth Through Time*, that there are common themes in the mythologies of cultures around the world.

4. *Choose words that identify the author's purpose* in the work. So, for example, to say an author "claims" something is to suggest that the claim can be questioned. To say an author "shows" is to suggest that you believe the author is successful in proving a point.
5. *Underline* or highlight *key words and statements.*
6. *Notice what the author emphasizes* in the title, section headings, table of contents, underlining or italics, bold print, and boxes. The author may cue you as to what is important to him or her by using expressions such as "It is important to note..." "The main point I want to make..." or "In this article I will show...."
7. *Exclude most supporting details* from your summary, except those that are necessary for clarifying your main points.
8. *Rephrase only what the author says.* Do not make statements stronger or weaker than the author would.
9. *Be brief.* Place a working limit on the number of statements or words you will use in a summary. This will force you to choose what's most important. The act of choosing, itself, will help you learn. For a test, attempt to fit your summary of main points on one sheet. The summary should be significantly shorter than the original writing.
10. *Quote* directly when the author writes a statement so clearly that it's best just to copy it into your summary.

the article, trying to guess what your instructor considers important. You would take careful notes in class, listening for points that your instructor repeats, emphasizes, likes, or dislikes. If the instructor agrees with the article, you would look for what the author emphasizes. If the instructor doesn't agree with the article (and you can often tell), you would look—in addition to what the author emphasizes—for points of disagreement.

If you were summarizing a chapter in this book in order to remember skills you personally need to develop, you would focus mostly on the parts of the chapter that were important to you, just as in a course where interpretation is important, you would focus the most on those parts of a poem, painting, or musical performance that support your interpretations.

The audience for your summary also determines how you proceed. Suppose you read an article opposing smoking. If you were summarizing the article for children, you would not stress technical language. If you were summarizing the same article for medical personnel, you *would* stress technical language.

Read the following paragraph from S. I. Hayakawa's book *Language in Thought and Action,* and then read the discussion of three attempts at summaries that follows.

> People who think of themselves as tough-minded and realistic tend to take it for granted that human nature is selfish and that life is a struggle in which only the fittest may survive. According to this philosophy, the basic law by which people must live, in spite of their surface veneer of civilization, is the struggle of the jungle. The "fittest" are those who can bring to the struggle superior force, superior cunning, and superior ruthlessness.

Summary 1

> S. I. Hayakawa thinks that people who think of themselves as tough-minded and realistic take it for granted that human nature is a struggle of survival of the fittest. The fittest are those who can bring to the struggle superior force, superior cunning, and superior ruthlessness.

Summary 1 is not brief: it is almost as long as the paragraph it attempts to summarize. It includes too many supporting details and doesn't identify the title of the work it cites.

Summary 2

> He thinks that some people are selfish and live like animals in a jungle.

This summary is brief, but it does not identify the author or title of the work to which it refers. It misrepresents Hayakawa, who does not claim that some people live like animals in a jungle. What he says is that those people who think of themselves as tough-minded and realistic think of life as survival of the fittest. He doesn't identify himself as being one of them.

Summary 3

> In <u>Language in Thought and Action</u>, S. I. Hayakawa states
> that, according to adherents of the philosophy of tough-
> minded realism, human nature is selfish. For them, life is
> the struggle of the jungle where the fittest survive.

This is the most balanced summary of the three. It cites title and author. It is brief. It excludes supporting details. It states what Hayakawa states without attributing to him claims that he did not make.

Read this excerpt from a speech given by poet and feminist Adrienne Rich at a meeting of the New Jersey College and University Coalition on Women's Education on May 9, 1978. Then reflect on the three student summaries that follow.

> In teaching women, we have two choices: to lend our weight to the forces that indoctrinate women to passivity, self-depreciation, and a sense of powerlessness, in which case the issue of "taking women students seriously" is a moot one; or to consider what we have to work against, as well as with, in ourselves, in our students, in the content of the curriculum, in the structure of the institution, in the society at large. And this means, first of all, taking ourselves seriously: Recognizing that central responsibility of a woman to herself, without which we remain always the Other, the defined, the object, the victim; believing that there is a unique quality of validation, affirmation, challenge, support, that one woman can offer another; believing in the value and significance of women's experience, traditions, perceptions; thinking of ourselves seriously, not as one of the boys, not as neuters, or androgynes, but as *women*.

Summary 1

> Adrienne Rich, in her talk "Taking Women Seriously," says
> we should do just that. It's time we stopped treating women
> students as if they should only have babies and take care of
> men.

Summary 2

> In this speech, Rich says either we force women to be
> passive or we take them seriously when we teach them.

Summary 3

> In her May 9, 1978, address to the New Jersey College and
> University Coalition on Women's Education, "Taking Women
> Seriously," poet Adrienne Rich argues against those who
> teach women to be passive and powerless. She wants teachers
> to educate women to believe in themselves.

*R*eflections _____

1. Rank the summaries of Rich's speech from 1 to 3, with 3 being the most effective.
2. Which of the ten strategies for summarizing does each of the summaries clearly illustrate?
3. Which strategies are not applied in each of the three summaries?
4. Revise the least effective summary using the strategies it missed.
5. Revise the other drafts to better represent the material being summarized.

*E*xplorations _____

1. *Together.* To help you develop a vocabulary that relates how an author approaches a topic, do Exploration 1 on page 52.
2. *Together.*
   a. Bring in newspaper articles and cut off or cover the headlines. In small groups, write headlines that serve as summaries of the articles whose headlines you didn't see.
   b. Discuss the differences between the original headlines and what you wrote. Which are more effective for what purposes and audiences?
3. a. *Solo.* Choose a reading from the end of this chapter. Write three different drafts of a summary for a person who hasn't read it. Improve your summary with each draft.
   b. *Together.* Using the suggestions and questions in the preceding Reflections, review your summaries in small groups or as a class. Discuss whether your current draft meets the standards for a good summary. Revise your summaries to meet the standards.
4. *Solo.* Before your next exam, create a one-page summary of the material on which you will be tested, using your instructor's outline, the table of contents of your textbook, or a list of key statements. In your journal, write about what you learned by writing this summary and how you did on the exam. What improvements, if any, would you make in writing a summary for your next exam? Discuss these insights with other students.

The readings in this chapter range over a variety of academic and popular points of view on one topic: AIDS. Use the following Explorations to help you compare and contrast the various points of view the authors take on this topic and the writing strategies they use to fulfill their purposes.

Reading to Learn

Use the following questions to delve into any of your academic and professional readings. Refer to particular words, sentences, and paragraphs to support and inspire ideas. Consult your dictionary for further insights into both familiar and unfamiliar words.

1. What are some of the main purposes of this reading?
2. Who would be a sympathetic audience? Why? Who would not? Why not?
3. How does the writer engage or disengage you as a reader?
4. What are some of the key words in this reading?
5. To what question or questions is this reading a response?
6. What are the key statements in this reading?
7. What evidence, examples, or imagery does the author use to support key statements?
8. How does the author organize the piece? Consider title, lead, body, and ending.
9. How would you summarize this reading?

*E*xplorations

1. *Together and Solo.* Read the following works on AIDS. Choose what you believe to be the most effective or interesting one. Discuss what makes it so for you. Ideally, you and some of your classmates will disagree. This will provide you not only with an intellectual challenge but also with the opportunity to discuss how your choices reflect your particular points of view.

2. **a.** *Together.* Choose one reading to discuss at a time. Use the questions in the sidebar Reading to Learn (above) to guide the discussion of your chosen reading. Be sure to point to particular words, sentences, and ideas to support your claims.

   b. *Solo.* Write a summary of an article you discussed in class for Exploration 2a.

   c. *Together.* Compare and contrast your summaries, with special attention to points of view.

3. **a.** *Solo.* Choose a topic from the column on the left and a point of view from the column on the right. Write a short essay focusing your topic from your chosen point of view.

Topics	*Points of View*
Food	Medicine
Transportation	Education
Children	Geography
Nature	Business
Recreation	Politics

b. *Together.* Read and discuss the essays you wrote in Exploration 3a, with special attention to the points covered in the sidebar on reading to learn (page 327).

4. *Solo.* Using your favorite reading from this chapter as a model for how to focus from a particular point of view, write on an issue that concerns you.

READING TO LEARN

From *Making Kitsch from AIDS: A Disease with a Gift Shop of Its Own*

Daniel Harris

In the following excerpt from his article published in Harper's *magazine, San Francisco writer Daniel Harris reports on a trend to commercialize AIDS.*

AIDS may be the first disease to have its own gift shop. Housed in the Workshop Building of the AIDS Memorial Quilt—the acres of fabric that commemorate the deaths of thousands of AIDS victims—Under One Roof is at the epicenter of the burgeoning industry of AIDS kitsch. Catering to an upscale clientele beaming with good intentions, the store, on Market Street in San Francisco's Castro District, peddles memento mori as shamelessly as tourist traps peddle souvenirs: "Cuddle Wit" teddy bears that sport tasteful red ribbons; Keith Haring tote bags; and T-shirts stenciled with the words "We're Cookin' Up L♥ve for People With AIDS." The boutique also sells a unique line of AIDS-related sympathy cards, including one picturing a seductive man leaning inconsolably against a tombstone angel. Inside an unctuous caption that smacks of an undertaker's condolences reads: "I wonder at times why some are chosen to leave so soon. Then I remember who has left, and I know. God must have wanted them home because he missed them." One of the store's best-selling items is a macabre coffee-table book of the Quilt itself, lavishly illustrated and presumably meant for bored guests to casually thumb through while ignoring the presentation of death as political knickknack.

Although Under One Roof donates its profits to a variety of AIDS-relief organizations, commercial businesses have not hesitated to wrap their products in the shroud of AIDS to promote their own merchandise. Benetton, in the early 1990s, placed in glossy magazines an ad that featured a skeletal male figure, obviously dying of AIDS. Stretched out in a hospital bed, beneath a print of Jesus Christ, he is attended by a sobbing father, who clutches him like a rag doll, and a grief-stricken mother, who sits crumpled in despair. In the ad's left-hand corner several words sit quietly in mourning, like unbidden guests maintaining respectful silence in the company of the family's anguish; they read, "United Colors of Benetton…For the nearest Benetton store location call 1–800–535–4491."

From *First Church of AIDS*

Jeff M. Sellers

*A freelance journalist based in Madrid, Jeff M. Sellers
received a diploma in Christian studies from Regent College
seminary in Vancouver, British Columbia. In this excerpt,
Sellers reports on a religious congregation formed by people
struck with AIDS.*

On the surface, the Betel Church, one of the two largest evangelical
churches in Madrid, Spain, seems like countless other young Protestant
faith communities recently planted around the globe.

· · ·

There is, for example, the persistent cough of pastor Raul Casto,
wearing a warm jacket and sitting in the front row. Occasionally, he gathers his strength to join his wife and two daughters in giving thanks to God
in spite of the AIDS epidemic that has visited his own household. Down
the row, where another family worships, the frail body of a two-and-a-
half-year-old girl gives silent testimony to the HIV that both she and her
parents carry. Overall, there is a spirit of unity among a people who
together in Christ have beaten the long odds against overcoming addic-
tions to heroin and other illicit drugs.

Fifty Percent with HIV

Betel formed as an outgrowth of a gospel-based drug rehabilitation program, which began ten years ago without psychiatrists, doctors, or meth-
adone. The rehab program was part of the ministry of missionaries with
Worldwide Evangelization for Christ International (WEC).

The missionaries who came to Spain were church-planters, not rehabilitation experts. The fruit of their labor is the transformed lives of those
who formed Betel Church—though heroin has left about 50 percent of the
church with HIV, the virus that causes AIDS.

"AIDS has made a family of this church," says Casto, 37, who was
rescued from heroin only to find, four months after marrying a WEC missionary from New Zealand, that he was HIV positive.

Of the 12 pastoral leaders (six couples) at Betel, five have tested HIV
positive, including Casto's wife, Jenny, though only Casto is suffering from
AIDS. He was the first convert in the nascent drug-rehabilitation outreach.

In the beginnings of the Betel residential treatment program, WEC missionary Lindsay McKenzie of Australia invited the destitute Casto into his
apartment. Casto, who had trafficked in drugs and was supporting his heroin
habit by burglary and robbing at knifepoint, was awaiting a court hearing.

Since that cold January night in 1986, some 15,000 people have passed through Betel residential programs in 60 locations throughout Spain, Spanish-speaking North Africa, and centers that have sprung up in missionary thrusts to Italy, Germany, Mexico, and New York City. The centers are largely self-supporting from sales of second-hand goods and the services provided by recovering addicts. Betel Center claims a 15 percent cure rate, double that of other rehab centers. Although there are countries with a more serious HIV problem than Spain, there have been 16,500 AIDS deaths here since 1981.

Betel Church represents both the hope and the oncoming darkness of incarnational ministry. "People here carry the sentence of death within them, so for them, Christianity is very real," says Betel leader Elliott Tepper, a married father of three. "You have to live for eternity—there's no sense in planning a long career or accumulating wealth."

From *Florida Dentist Accused of Intentionally Spreading AIDS*

John Allen Paulos

A professor of mathematics at Temple University, John Allen Paulos has written numerous articles and books to enlighten and entertain readers on principles of logic, probability, and mathematics. In this excerpt from his book A Mathematician Reads the Newspaper, *Paulos offers a mathematical perspective on some cases of AIDS infection.*

Everyone's heard of the Florida dentist who infected, possibly intentionally, six of his patients with the AIDS virus. An investigation of the story by Stephen Barr in *Lear's* magazine and an excerpt in a *New York Times* op-ed in March 1994 revealed a number of lacunae in the case against the dentist. It appears that some, if not all, of the victims had other risk factors that might have exposed them. And the test used to determine whether two strains of the virus are the same is still controversial and not widely accepted. Furthermore, the rate of HIV infection among the dentist's many patients was only slightly higher than the overall rate in the two counties where the patients lived. The dentist himself may have been victim of the irrational fear induced by the AIDS epidemic.

The philosopher Daniel C. Dennett, in his book *Consciousness Explained*, describes a party game that I think provides a somewhat unusual slant on this and other cases in which there is an element of self-fulfilling prophecy. A familiar variant of the game requires that one try to determine by means of yes or no questions an arbitrary number between one and one million. Why, incidentally, do twenty questions always suffice for this? In Dennett's more interesting game (which you might want to play if you have a friend you'd like to shed), one person is selected from the group. He will be asked to leave the room and told that, in his absence, one of the other partygoers will relate a recent dream. When the person returns to the room, he will attempt, through a sequence of yes or no questions directed to the group, to accomplish two things: reconstruct the dream and identify whose dream it was.

The punch line is that no one has related any dream. The revelers are instructed to respond either yes or no to the victim's questions according to some arbitrary rule; Dennett suggests having the answers be determined by whether the last letter in the last word of the question is from the beginning or the end of the alphabet. Any rule will do, however, and may be supplemented by a noncontradiction clause stipulating that no answer directly contradict an earlier one.

The surprising result is that the victim, impelled by his own obsessions, often constructs an outlandish and obscene dream in response to the random answers he elicits. He may also think he knows whose dream it was, but then the ruse is revealed to him. Technically the dream has no author, but in a sense the victim himself is. His preoccupations dictate his questions, which, even if answered negatively at first, will frequently receive a positive response in later reformulations. These positive responses are then pursued.

There is a body of experiment that seems to support the thesis that dreams and hallucinations can be explained in part by a variant of this party game.

· · ·

I suppose that a somewhat similar phenomenon takes place for larger groups of people as well. Societies do not possess minds, of course, but in times of crisis—war, stock frenzy, pestilence, riot—they do develop a primitive sort of cohesiveness, a quasi consciousness approaching perhaps that of a very retarded person in a deep, drug-induced stupor. Because of the stress it endures, such a society will have indefinite fears, hopes, or anxieties, and its contact with reality will be tenuous. News reporting during a war or other crisis tends to be, for a variety of reasons, deplorably shoddy. (Recall the coverage of the Gulf War or during the early days of the AIDS crisis.) What news the society does get is vague and generic, allowing ample room for the societal analogue of dreams and hallucinations to develop. Societies without a free press and a literate population are especially vulnerable. [One] example is Guatemala, where peasants have seriously injured Western women they thought were kidnapping their babies.

Another is Rwanda, where terrifying rumors and radio broadcasts inflamed and exacerbated an already nightmarish situation.

Ambiguity, randomness, and lack of information in response to obsessive questions and concerns can, on a group level, breed delusions and mirages in the same way that the party game makes an individual concoct his own chimerical fantasy. Informative, skeptical, fastidious reporting is most needed when it's least likely to be forthcoming.

From *Borrowed Time: An AIDS Memoir*

Paul Monette

Monette wrote about people dying from AIDS. In the following passage, he touchingly described visiting his friend Roger, who was dying in the hospital. Monette himself died of AIDS in 1995.

The nurse said Rog was comfortable and that he'd been communicative, but for the present he appeared too sick to notice I was there. In any case, I was madly scrambling around making calls...and ordering the intern to speed up the drug from the pharmacy. Finally the nurse realized who I was, and she was my right hand from then on. I'd been there a few minutes, setting up command, when Roger began to moan. It was the saddest, hollowest sound I've ever heard, and loud, like the trumpet note of a wounded animal. It had no shape to it, nothing like a word, and he repeated it over and over, every few seconds. "Why is he doing that?" I asked the nurse, but she didn't know. I assumed he must be roaring with misery and anxiety, and he hadn't had any Xanax since the previous day. I ordered a tranquilizer and told him everything I was doing. It wasn't till ten weeks later, on New Year's Day, that I understood the trumpet sound. I was crying up at the grave, and started to mimic his moaning, and suddenly understood that what he was doing was calling my name. Nothing in my life or the death to come hurts as much as that, him calling me without a voice through a wall he could not pierce.

Within fifteen minutes the intern came in with a shot to relax him, and right after that they began the ampho drip. I was on the phone to Jaimee constantly, the two of us gnawing our hearts as we waited to see if he'd have convulsions. Meanwhile the nurse taught me to communicate with Rog by telling him to blink when I asked him a question. *Can you hear me, Rog?* And his eyelids fluttered. It was such a stunning gift to have him back, tapping through the wall like that. Thirty or forty times in the next hour I made him do it again, lobbing him yes questions and cheering at the reassuring flutter of his eyelids. I kept telling him how much of the drug still had to go in. I talked and talked, excitedly declaring that we were home free. It was working. We were going to bring him back. I held the phone so Jaimee could talk in his ear, and he blinked to say he heard her.

I don't regret a syllable of our manic cheer. I wouldn't have wanted the last he heard from me to be moaning and grief. We were pulling through, as we always did. I asked a friend with a thousand nights' experience of young men dying, How much pain was Roger in that last twenty-four hours? I've heard all the tales of the tribe now about the pounding headaches of crypto. He said the harder thing for Roger than the pain would surely have been the consciousness of his final imprisonment and exile from me. I know he's right because it comes to me in nightmares over and over, the last claustrophobia, no way to touch your friend again or say good-bye as you spiral down. At least we had that queer and eloquent hour of the eyelids, and then he fell asleep.

From *HIV Wasting: How to Stop the Cycle*

Joyce K. Anastasi and Vivian Sun Lee

Joyce K. Anastasi is director of the AIDS program and assistant professor at Columbia University School of Nursing in New York. Vivian Sun Lee is infectious disease nutrition coordinator in the AIDS Center Program at The New York Hospital Medical Center of Queens. In this excerpt from their article, these researchers discuss one of the clinical concerns of AIDS patients.

Malnutrition and wasting apparently start early in HIV infection. Decline in body-cell mass and deficiencies in vitamins A, B_6, B_{12}, and E, riboflavin, copper, selenium, and zinc have been seen in asymptomatic patients.

HIV infection may put a chronic stress on the immune system that raises demand for certain nutrients, such as vitamins A, B_6, and C, needed to mount an immune response. Also, individuals with even early infection have elevated metabolism and energy demand, presumably mediated by the immune system.

What's more, HIV infects the gastrointestinal tract. Though it's not known whether and how the virus causes it, HIV-positive patients commonly display GI disease (labeled HIV enteropathy) for which no other explanation can be found.

Less directly, HIV-related fatigue can prevent the patient from preparing meals or even eating. Neurologic impairment may cause dysphagia.

Or dementia may leave the patient too forgetful, confused, or apathetic to eat on his own.

As opportunistic infections and other HIV-related illnesses develop, their clinical manifestations can contribute to malnutrition and wasting. Dysphagia and odynophagia (pain on swallowing) may result from infections or other conditions that cause lesions or plaques in the mouth or esophagus.... Herpes simplex, cytomegalovirus (CMV), hairy leukoplakia, squamous cell cancer, and Kaposi's sarcoma are other possibilities. Aphthous ulcers may also cause pain and difficulty in eating.

Numerous infections can cause anorexia.... Nausea and vomiting may result.... Infections as well as salmonellosis, giardiasis, and CMV infection can also cause diarrhea.

The prophylactic and therapeutic drug regimens used in HIV can interfere with nutrition as well. Patients are often taking several medications that may cause GI discomfort, nausea, vomiting, and diarrhea....

Dapsone (Dapsone), acyclovir, and pentamidine may alter taste, making food unappetizing. Patients taking pentamidine typically report a metallic taste. Both didanosine and zalcitabine (ddC; Hivid) can cause acute or chronic pancreatitis, impairing GI function.

From *Days of Grace: A Memoir*

Arthur Ashe and Arnold Rampersad

Arthur Ashe, a renowned African-American tennis player, died in 1993 from the AIDS he contracted through a blood transfusion. Shortly before his death, with the help of writer Arnold Rampersad, Ashe wrote a memoir expressing his views on race, education, politics, sports, and AIDS. The following excerpt touches on all of these subjects.

In general, the sex life of an individual should be nobody's business but his or her own. Nevertheless, the sexual behavior of a famous athlete, when widely publicized, may have a powerful and deleterious impact on young people in particular. Add the factors of AIDS and rampant unwanted teenage pregnancy into the equation, and the sex life of individual star athletes may become a matter of public concern.

Sexual promiscuity has often been a feature of the behavior of athletes, or at least of male athletes. In recent times, in keeping with our collapse of standards, or our increasing commitment to candor, we have had a better understanding of what constitutes promiscuity for some athletes. The former basketball player Wilt Chamberlain, in his autobiography, has numbered his sexual "conquests" at about 20,000 women. (I don't believe him about the number.) By comparison, Earvin "Magic" Johnson has been almost monkish, with a mere 2,500 partners, according to one estimate. Many women wanted him, he once explained with his beautiful smile, and he tried to "accommodate" as many of them as he could....

As much as I like Wilt and Magic, I must say I did not enjoy reading these accounts. I must also admit candidly that part of my reaction to Wilt's and Magic's revelations was a certain amount of racial embarrassment, an affliction to which I hope never to become immune. African Americans have spent decades denying that we are sexual primitives by nature, as racists have argued since the days of slavery. Then two college-trained black men of international fame and immense personal wealth do their best to reinforce the stereotype....

Of course, I also know from experience that men's professional tennis, for all its white, upper-class associations, is also a haven of promiscuity and easy sex, as perhaps all male professional sports are. Even in my day as a player, we had our camp followers. Top players traditionally stayed not in hotels but in the homes of local patrons of the sport, and our hostesses now and then gave us bed and board and insisted on sharing the bed with us. We had our Lotharios and Casanovas among the players, and group sex was not hard to come by, if that was your taste. It was never mine.

And, as I said, I did not enjoy reading about Wilt's and Magic's escapades. I felt more pity than sorrow for Wilt as his macho accounting backfired on him, in the form of a wave of public criticism. This admission (or exaggeration?) will probably haunt him for the rest of his life. He did not seem to understand that many people would find his behavior dehumanizing, or that it might lessen his attractiveness to women.... I was also uncomfortable watching Magic talk on television about his own sexual adventures, just after the publication of his book. With his insouciant smile, he seemed to be boasting about them, as at least one television reporter suggested to him; and yet Magic had also preached restraint as part of his laudable efforts at AIDS education....

Magic may have missed one opportunity in his commendable campaign to fight AIDS. Although he doubtless was caught up in the business of promoting his book (an obligation he certainly owes to his publisher), he probably went too far as a salesman. Unconsciously, no doubt, promotion of the book took momentary precedence over his sense of the dangers of promiscuity. In addition, while Magic is certainly a good, honest man, his discussion of promiscuity seldom had anything to do with morality or religion. As far as I can tell, nowhere in his book does Magic ever address the question of religion and morality in relationship to sex....

Facing the problem of young people as ignorant and as unprepared for sex as I had been, I want them to know the moral and religious aspects of sexuality. I want them to be familiar with the teachings of the Bible and with other religious doctrines. Because of AIDS, however, I am equally committed to the policy of giving condoms, as well as the bare, unvarnished facts about sex and AIDS, to students.

From *Stitches in Time*

Peter S. Hawkins

In this excerpt from his article, Peter S. Hawkins, professor of religion and literature at Yale Divinity School, describes an encounter with the NAMES Project AIDS Memorial Quilt.

In early August 1988 I found myself rushing through the San Francisco Airport, late to catch a plane back to the East Coast. Haste kept me from seeing very much beyond who or what blocked my path; but as I negotiated myself through the walkways connecting one terminal with another, it was impossible not to notice the patches of color displayed everywhere. Names, dates, inscriptions, photographs, memorabilia, all crowding together on cloth rectangles: this was my first exposure to the NAMES Project AIDS Memorial Quilt. Although feeling under some obligation to be reverent—these were, after all, memorials to the dead that I was running past—the sight of the panels within glass showcases and hanging high above the floor of the terminals left me with a puzzling mixture of annoyance and discomfort.

To begin with, what I saw reminded me less of traditional American quilting, often so elegant and austere, and more of the fabric hodgepodge found at a crafts fair, where good intentions in wool, cotton, and macramé so often unravel into kitsch. The snob in me wondered, couldn't they do better than this? Nor was my sense of embarrassment limited to aesthetics. I was also put off by the choice of a traditionally feminine art form to memorialize the lives of homosexual men: Why needles and thread, fabric, embroidery, pinking shears, sequins? Why play into the stereotype of effeminacy, of weak sisters sewing and weeping together, rather than make something more, well, masculine?

But in the end what truly upset me about the quilt—what kept me running through the terminals, my eyes fixed straight in front me—was quite simply that it came too close to home. My partner of six years was living with AIDS and had finally acknowledged that he was beginning to decline. The quilt panels I saw only out of the corner of my eye, in a colorful blur of other people's misery and courage, were reminders that the syndrome from which Luis suffered had no cure, that one day (and probably sooner rather than later) he, too, would be dead.

All these thoughts are, of course, a rueful reconstruction; at the time, I had only hurried impressions, a mild sense of irritation, a little fear. What happened next, however, remains an indelible memory, an image so clearly inscribed in my mind that even now, seven years later, it is no less substantial or present than a person standing before me. Making my way across the floor of the North Terminal building, heading for the gate that would lead me home, I was stopped in my tracks by the sight of a panel that was hung, as if by design, directly above my path. Unlike the others, which focused on an individual, this navy blue rectangle included two names instead of one, reminding me of those gravestones that do double duty by serving a couple who refuse to be parted in death. What took my breath away, however, was that one of the names was my own.

Wherever I travel, I always consult the local telephone directory to see if by chance there is a "Peter Hawkins" who lives there, with his own address and number, in a personal world that does not belong to me but that I share nonetheless, if only because we answer to the same name. But to discover a single Peter Hawkins in Rochester, New York, or four of us living in various parts of London, is one thing: the sign of a larger community of "me," some claim to intimate connection with perfect strangers. In contrast, this experience in the airport was something else, for what I saw hanging above the entrance to my gate felt like the proverbial handwriting on the wall—a sentence of doom scrawled across the biblical king's banqueting hall, to inform him that his mighty kingdom was at an end, that his days were numbered. Was someone trying to tell me something?

Crossing in Fog

Edwin Romond

Poet Edwin Romond, an English teacher at Warren Hills Regional High School, is the recipient of numerous writing awards, including one from the National Endowment for the Arts. In the following poem, Romond writes about visiting a friend with AIDS.

I hesitated
when Greg in a whisper begged me
to hold him. Greg, forsaken
by lover and family to suffer alone
the last lash of AIDS, asked for arms
around him and I remember

his breath, tiny as a baby's
on my face, when I lifted him
and squeezed death against my heart.

To cross a bridge in fog is to memorize fear
one step at a time, to believe in the danger
of life and water and the eternal
nothingness of one wrong turn.
To die in combat could be noble,
to die old among your children, beautiful.
But to die knowing those you love fear for their lives
leaves you only the clipboard care of masked strangers
in hospital white touching you with rubber gloves.

I left Greg early, my "appointment" a lie
I could live with as I rushed away
to the men's room for the scalding water
and stinging handsoap on my face.
In 231 a man who was my friend
would not see another summer,
would never know that I scrubbed my skin
raw, erasing all of him that I could,
my face red as shame in the fogging mirror.

From *U.S. Charges University with Firing Instructor for Having AIDS*

Scott Jaschik

In this excerpt from his article, Scott Jaschik, Deputy Managing Editor of The Chronicle of Higher Education, *reports that a college instructor was fired for having AIDS.*

In what may be the first case of its kind, the Equal Employment Opportunity Commission has sued Campbell University for discharging an instructor because he has AIDS.

The commission filed its action in U.S. District Court for the Eastern District of North Carolina, charging that the dismissal violated the Americans With Disabilities Act.

EEOC officials said they did not know of any other case in which the agency had sued a university on behalf of someone with AIDS.

A spokesman for Campbell said, "It is the university's policy not to make any comment at all on pending litigation."

Details of the case are murky, in part because the EEOC and the district court have agreed to keep the identity of the instructor secret. He is referred to in court documents as John Doe.

Access to Medical Bills

According to an EEOC statement, the instructor was relieved of all teaching duties and told not to return to the campus after the university found that he had AIDS. John B. Meuser, a senior trial attorney at the EEOC, said the university had discovered the condition because Campbell self-insures its employees and had access to the complainant's medical bills.

The instructor taught physical education and sports management.

The suit seeks the instructor's reinstatement as well as unspecified financial damages. The complainant worked at the university for more than two years, receiving good job reviews, before his condition was discovered, Mr. Meuser said.

He added that the instructor was healthy and anxious to resume work.

Mr. Meuser said that universities generally could not fire people for having AIDS. Under the Americans With Disabilities Act, he said, an employer could only remove someone who posed a physical danger to others. "With the manner of transmission of AIDS, you aren't likely to find that kind of danger in a university," he said.

While the instructor taught physical education, Mr. Meuser said his courses did not involve contact sports. The complainant taught weight training, aerobic dance, and classroom courses in sports management.

Universities "have to be very careful about what they do" with employees with AIDS, Mr. Meuser said. "At the very least, they need to be aware of the coverage of the Americans With Disabilities Act."

Chapter Review

1. *Together or Solo.* Summarize this chapter for a new college student. Your purpose will be to outline the basic skills this chapter offers. Limit the length of the summary to one typewritten page.

2. *Together.* Compare and contrast the summaries you wrote for Chapter Review 1. Revise your drafts to meet the standards for good summaries.

Chapter *13*

Writing to Learn II

Making Connections

This chapter offers opportunities to

—***Learn by writing***
—Use a ***learning journal*** with ***double*** and ***process entries***
—***Write essays*** to support thesis statements
—Write essays that ***compare and contrast***
—***Chart*** information
—Practice the skills of ***responsible thinking***

Writing, like life itself, is a voyage of discovery.
—*Henry Miller, Novelist*

If we knew everything beforehand,
all would be dictation, not creation.
—*Gertrude Stein, Writer*

Reason and Evidence

Academic disciplines based on reasoning are systems of connected statements. Some of these statements are claims and others are statements of evidence in support of the claims. Statements of evidence should be clear, relevant, and sufficient so that other people can see for themselves the truth of the claims your statements of evidence are meant to support. For example, if, in biochemistry, you claim that high-cholesterol diets may lead to heart attacks, you should be able to support your claim with evidence such as blood test results of heart attack victims. Other people should be able to review your evidence (or perform the same tests) and come to the same conclusions as you did. If, in literature, you claim that Shakespeare did not write all the plays attributed to him, you should be able to support your claim with evidence such as an analysis of writing style in particular plays. You would support your claim by using the theory that every person's writing style is as unique as her or his fingerprints. Other people should then be able to analyze your evidence—the writing style in the questionable plays—and come to the same conclusions as you did.

Chapter 12 offered you strategies for identifying key words, questions, and statements. This chapter offers you opportunities to further develop your ability to reason by connecting these key elements—supporting claims, ideas, and theories with evidence—as thinkers in different academic disciplines do.

Drafting: Writing, Itself, Helps You Learn

In Chapter 12, intelligence is defined as the ability to make useful and creative connections between experiences. The more you write about what you experience and read, the more of these connections you will develop. Repetition is one of the foundations of learning: the mere act of writing reinforces what you learn or already know because you are repeating it as you write. You are also connecting your inner world with the outer because writing transforms ideas and feelings into a form others can experience, as well. As you continue to write, you recall previous experiences, integrate them with new material, and create new connections. Because of all these reasons and more, it is important to make and find opportunities to *engage* with words on the page.

Learning Journal

In a notebook, you record what someone else says or presents to you. In a journal, you *engage* with what you record and *make it your own.* You respond, question, argue, wonder, interpret, experiment, explore, and evaluate. Your *learning journal* is one of the most helpful tools you can use to develop yourself as a responsible thinker. The journal becomes your companion, a safe audience with whom to develop your unique perspective. Your learning journal is a source of ideas for papers, discussions, presentations, creative projects, and social interactions.

Double entries

A *double entry* offers you the combined benefits of a notebook and a journal. That's why it's called a *double entry.* On the left side of your double entry, you record key words, statements, questions, quotations, and other stimuli, including drawings and diagrams. On the right side, you enter your responses to what you recorded on the left. You can create a double entry in several ways: draw a line down the middle of your notebook page; use a stenographer's pad, which already has a line down the middle; or keep notes on the left sheet in your notebook and write your commentary on the facing right sheet. Start with the divided sheet. For some purposes you may want to switch to left and right notebook pages. Leave plenty of space for your responses. One side of your double entry will usually look emptier than the other. Some students prefer to distinguish notes from responses by using different colored pens instead of separating notes on the left from responses on the right.

Here are a number of ways in which you can respond in a double entry:

Repetition. If there is a key word, idea, or statement you want to remember, either copy it out several times just as it is or restate it several times in your own words. Here is how student Melanie Patel used repetition in a double-entry response to a note taken in her earth science class:

Incinerator pollution

```
    The landfill used by the county incinerator is filled
with toxic chemicals and mercury and lead. People don't know
that dumping ashes from burning our garbage doesn't mean
that we are finished with the toxic stuff in it. Rain and
other chemicals from garbage combine and go into the ground.
From there it gets into wells and streams and then evapo-
rates and comes back down on all of us in rain.
```

Questions. If something puzzles you, ask good questions about it. Remember that the only dumb question is, literally, the one not asked.

Sometimes, just writing out a question triggers a connection in your mind, and you find you already know the answer. Start with the words *I wonder*. Here is how Melanie used questions in her double entry to continue exploring the impact of the county incinerator:

> ```
> I wonder what other ways toxic chemicals get to us. If it
> comes down in rain then it must be getting into plants and
> therefore our food. And that means that it is getting into
> chickens, and cows, and any other animals.
> ```

Authority Notes.   Suppose you encounter a topic that overwhelms you. Take time to record five key statements that you already know about the topic. Start with the words *I know that*. One idea will lead to another, and you will be able to proceed with more confidence. Sometimes you encounter a topic about which you know a great deal. Take time to write about the topic in order to recall and reinforce what you already know so that you can absorb new information more quickly. Here is how Melanie continued her notes on pollution:

> ```
> So okay, what else do I know?
> 1. Chickens make eggs and cows make milk.
> 2. The worst amount of toxins usually go into eggs and milk
>    just as a mother's milk shows up concentrations of her
>    body chemicals.
> 3. If a mother nurses her baby then the baby will get the
>    worst amount of lead and mercury and chemicals.
> 4. This pollution problem is worse than I knew.
> 5. There is a committee in my town working on this problem.
> ```

Evaluations.   You may find yourself disagreeing with the point of view of an instructor or writer. Use your double-entry journal to anticipate arguments and to justify your current position. Start with the words *I feel that* or *I believe that*. Melanie wrote this:

> ```
> I believe that the county officials must have had chemi-
> cal experts come in to measure the problems at the landfill.
> Professor Pradl says that the tests that they made were not
> adequate. But we didn't have time to talk about it in class
> because we had a fire drill. I need proof. I can't stand the
> idea that it's possible that my sister is poisoning my niece
> without even knowing it. Sometimes I wonder if knowing some-
> ```

thing is better than not knowing it. But then again, how else do big problems get solved? Anyhow I feel scared.

Connections. One of the most satisfying experiences in school is to make connections between what you learn in different courses. Look for and write out ideas from other courses that occur to you in response to an idea or statement. Start with the words *This connects with* or *This reminds me of.* Melanie continued to write about toxins in the environment:

> This connects with my sociology course. We are reading about how people believe things because other people believe it. This happened when people believed the world was flat and that the earth is the middle of the universe. Right now I believe in the people who watch out for health in my county. I guess it's because I never thought about it. And what do I know about chemistry? There's so much I have to do with work. Who has time? It's hard to go against people who are in power. Now I understand about the saying "You can't fight City Hall."

Process entries

The focus in a notebook is to record *what* someone else is offering you. A double entry focuses on *your responses* to what others offer. *Process entries* focus on your style of learning, thinking, and responding. In process entries you do some, or all, of the following:

- Describe how you currently approach a skill or problem.
- Write what occurs to you as you work through a problem.
- Notice patterns and relationships.
- Identify difficulties.
- Explain procedures in your own words.
- Develop new ways of solving problems.
- Record what happens when you "catch on."
- Pose clear questions.

When you keep a process journal you enjoy opportunities to:

- Learn how you approach information and skills.
- Write your way through problems.
- Develop insights into your own and others' processes.

- Develop new ways of doing things.
- Develop more confidence and pleasure in learning.

Writing is a powerful learning tool in all academic courses. You might think that a numbers-based discipline such as mathematics would be an exception. But notice how José A. López, a student in Arthur Powell's Developmental Mathematics I class at Rutgers University, used a process journal to help him pass the course. Here are some process entries he made as he worked through his mathematics problems. You don't have to understand mathematics to notice that José became clearer about exponents as he wrote about his process and that writing helped him to learn and to succeed.

> Today in class, I observed that when working with exponents, when I move to the right the value of the exponential number increases by 1. The reverse is true when moving to the left. Also, the number of multiplication steps is the same as the exponential number. When moving to the left, I take the reciprocal of the positive value I found when moving to the right. When multiplying numbers with the bases the same, but different exponential numbers, I can add these exponents. E.g., $5^3 \times 5^1 = 5^4 = 625$. When dividing numbers whose base is the same, but have different exponents, I can subtract the second exponent from the first. E.g., $5^3/5^1 = 5^{3-1} = 5^2 = 25$.

You may find, as you write in your learning journal, that you want to share your reflections with peers and instructors. Write a letter to a classmate or instructor when you need some questions answered, are excited about an idea, want to propose a project, or just need to test some reactions. Sometimes you can just photocopy a journal entry and add a note at the top saying why you are sending that entry.

E*xplorations*

1. *Solo.* Choose a course that is important to you and create a double entry for it in your learning journal. Try a different double-entry strategy for each of the next few meetings of the course, and notice which strategies work best for you. Write a letter to your instructor about what you have learned by writing and what more you want to learn.

2. *Solo and Together.* Contact a student or group of students in a course you are currently taking. Plan to meet once a week to discuss questions and insights that arise for you, or arrange to write each other letters.

How to Keep a Learning Journal

1. *Commit yourself.* Decide on a regular schedule for keeping your journal, such as coming to class five minutes early and leaving five minutes late so you can freewrite in your journal. Be flexible. Revise your schedule so you can honor your commitment.

2. *Choose writing tools* that best support your process: a spiral-bound notebook, a binder filled with typed pages, or a computer disk. You might want to combine strategies, such as including taped-in typed pages among your handwritten notebook entries.

3. *Focus* your entries on particular key words, statements, and questions. Tape news articles, quotations, and photocopies of excerpts into your journal for starters.

4. *Collect* ideas by freewriting, listing, brainstorming, clustering, or drawing in your journal.

5. *Organize* your entries with tabs, colored pens, or computer files.

6. *Describe* your learning processes, especially when you get stuck.

7. *Prepare* for class, exams, conferences with your teacher, or study sessions by writing in your journal.

You may want to introduce double-entry strategies to your study partners. After a couple of weeks, reflect on the benefits you have gained.

3. *Solo.* Keep a double-entry journal for your courses. Write your notes on the left side, and on the right formulate possible questions to which those notes could be responding. Writing these entries will help you to prepare for exams.

4. **a.** *Together.* Discuss some problems you are encountering in other courses or at work.

   b. *Solo.* Choose a particular skill or group of skills you use in another course. Write a process entry, using some of the suggestions listed above.

   c. *Together.* Share your process entries from Exploration 4b with your writing class or with the instructor or students in the course for which you are developing your process journal. With the help of your writing class, you may want to compose a letter to the instructor of the course for which you are writing the process journal, explaining your process notes, what you are learning from them, and what help you need. Even if you don't send the letter, you will learn from the process of writing it. Reflect on what you learned, together.

For further Explorations on process, refer to 1 and 2 on pages 36–37.

Writing Essays: Thesis and Evidence

One of the basic ways that connections are made in science and education is by writing essays. An *essay* is far more than just a set of notes. An essay is a written report or interpretation of information, ideas, and observations. An essay presents evidence and examples to support statements and a certain point of view.

When you write essays, keep your purpose and audience in mind. In academic writing, you will want to focus on transfer of information, development of skills, interpretation, or experimentation. If the purpose of your essay is to display how much information you have retained, then you will want to offer more examples and evidence. If the purpose of your essay is to show reasoning skills, then you might want to limit the number of examples and increase the discussion of them. If the purpose of your essay is to develop an interpretation, then you must clearly describe and evaluate what you are interpreting and support your discussion with relevant quotes and details. If the purpose of your essay is to report an experiment, you might need to summarize relevant research done by others and compare your results to theirs. In each course, you will learn the purpose of your essays and what counts as evidence for the kinds of statements made in that discipline.

Some of the main strategies for fulfilling the purposes of academic essays are to:

Analyze	Inform
Argue	Interpret
Classify	Narrate
Compare	Outline
Contrast	Question
Define	Reflect
Describe	Solve
Evaluate	Summarize
Explain	Theorize
Illustrate	

For each strategy there are different ways in which to organize your thinking and writing. Chapter 7 offers you a variety of these ways to develop your academic and professional writing. If you decide to work more as a planner on a particular writing project, you might want to adopt a structure and then work to fill it in. If you decide to work more as an explorer, you will delay organizing your work until you have discovered and created ideas through focusing and collecting.

Writing an Academic Essay

1. *Read* the assignment carefully.
2. *Decide on your strategy for a lead.* This may be a story, a statistic, an example, or a thesis statement. Revise this lead as you draft the essay.
3. *Develop a key or thesis statement,* adjusting its strength to your purpose. You may need to write a first draft of your essay before you can formulate this statement.
4. *Position your thesis statement* either at the beginning of your essay or at the end of your lead. In some cases, your thesis statement might be delayed for your ending.
5. *Support* or lead up to your thesis statement with appropriate evidence and examples. Ask yourself:
   - Is this the most relevant information?
   - Is this all the information I need?
6. *Organize* the essay so that the evidence and examples combine to most effectively support your thesis statement. Use the kinds of reasoning appropriate to the purpose and audience of your essay. Choose between a deductive and an inductive approach.
7. *End* your essay reflecting, in some way, on your thesis statement.

Remember that the final product, your essay, may be different from the process of writing it. You may have to freewrite, collect information, organize, reorganize, and revise several times before you settle on a thesis statement and evidence you want in the final version. *Avoid the temptation to settle for your first draft of an essay.* A benefit of the writing process may be the discovery of a better thesis statement. It's worth the extra effort to redraft your essay with the better thesis statement rather than to settle for a mere first attempt.

Melanie wrote the following paragraph in response to an essay question for her earth science class: "What are the effects of burying incinerator ash in landfills?" Notice how her writing journal helped her to develop ideas.

```
The landfills used by the county incinerator are loaded
with toxic chemicals such as dioxin and metals such as mer-
cury and lead which have very serious effects on our health.
These chemicals and metals are pollutants. Dioxin, mercury,
```

and lead have been known to cause birth defects, mental
retardation, cancer, and earlier death. Also, these pollutants get into our food supply. Fish get filled with the pollutants. If they become our food we get sick. If they die
because of pollution, our food supply is being hurt. This is
true for all our food because the pollutants get into our
rain, go into plants, and then go into animals that we eat.
The worst part of this is when you realize that it gets con-
centrated in the milk that cows give. We use this milk to
feed our children, who need milk and are at greatest danger
because of pollutants. Officials claim that there is no
proof that incinerator ashes in the landfills cause the
problems. But they don't listen to the tests that outside
chemists are making.

Melanie begins her paragraph with a thesis stating that landfills have very serious effects on health. She supports this thesis by offering examples. She further supports her thesis by emphasizing that children, who are most vulnerable, are most at risk. Notice that Melanie briefly entertains an opposing viewpoint. This strengthens her position because it shows confidence.

*E*xplorations _____

Do one or more of the following Explorations, which are designed to help you work with thesis statements and evidence. For further discussions, turn to pages 110–116 in Chapter 5 and pages 318–319 in Chapter 12.

1. *Together and Solo.* Review the material on thesis statements offered in Chapters 5 and 12. If you have not already done so, do a selection of the Explorations corresponding to those discussions.

2. *Together or Solo.* List some essay assignments you have in your courses. Write thesis statements in response to selected assignments. Practice writing an essay in response to one of the statements. What is the purpose of the essay? Are you using enough relevant examples and evidence to satisfy that purpose? If you discover a better thesis statement during the writing process, revise the essay, starting with the better statement.

3. *Solo.*

   a. To help you prepare for your next essay exam, find a key or thesis statement in a course you are taking. Using it as a beginning, write an essay in which you offer evidence to support the statement. On your first attempt, write without referring to your notes or books.

Be sure to follow the strategies on page 349. Ask yourself, as well, which of the four main academic purposes—learning information, skills, interpretation, or experimentation—the essay can satisfy. This Exploration will help you discover what you need to study or practice.

b. To help you prepare for your next essay exam, find or formulate five questions you anticipate will appear on the exam. Answer the questions by formulating and supporting thesis statements.

4. *Together and Solo.* Read the essays you wrote in Exploration 3 with special attention to whether the writers offer enough relevant evidence to support key statements. Notice which purpose or purposes the essays are meant to satisfy. Revise accordingly.

Comparing and Contrasting

Writing essays in support of thesis statements helps you to interpret and remember information. An essay strategy that is especially helpful in making connections between two or more ideas, people, objects, places, or events is to compare and contrast them. When you *compare,* you notice similarities. When you *contrast,* you notice differences. You can write a whole essay in which all you do is compare two or more subjects. You can write a whole essay in which all you do is contrast two or more subjects. When you both compare *and* contrast in a paper, you explore the balance of similarities and differences between your subjects. By comparing and/or contrasting, you learn new things, create new connections, and keep what you know clearly organized.

There are countless examples, in all disciplines, of how comparing and contrasting can help you learn, create, and organize your learning. Friedrich Kekulé discovered the chemical structure of benzene when he compared it to a coiled snake. Lewis Thomas realized how interconnected all inhabitants of this planet are when he compared earth with a single cell.

The process of learning, itself, used to be compared to an assembly line: first you learn this, then this next, and so on, with no consideration for different learning and thinking styles and needs. Much progress has been made recently, since learning is now being compared to more organic processes. For example, in his article "What True Education Should Never Do," Sydney J. Harris compares learning to the formation of a pearl around an irritant in an oyster.* For Harris, learning is a process

---

*Sydney Harris, "What True Education Should Never Do," *Chicago Daily News,* 1964.

Standards for a Good Comparison or Contrast

A good comparison or contrast meets many of the standards that a good question meets. A good comparison or contrast:

- Is clear
- Makes you think
- Helps you question your ways of thinking
- Helps you see different points of view
- Helps you learn more about each point of comparison or contrast
- Is new or generates new insights
- Helps you remember better
- Helps you formulate good questions

of using mistakes to create new knowledge and understanding. If you think of the writing process as an assembly line, you may not be motivated to write. Every time you moved away from the rigid assembly line model you would feel you were doing something wrong. If, however, you see the writing process as forming a pearl, then any move that may seem like a mistake on the assembly line model would be the grain of sand around which another "pearl of wisdom" can form.

Writing Comparisons and Contrasts

Charting.   When you need to collect information to compare or contrast two or more subjects, it is helpful to create a chart. You can divide a sheet of paper into as many columns as you have subjects. For example, if you were comparing and/or contrasting women in U.S. history, you could create a column for each woman that you want to compare. If you were comparing marketing strategies, you could create a column for each strategy you were considering. Your subjects are written at the head of the columns, and you generate lists of phrases and statements under the subjects. As you write an item on one list, you can write a *corresponding* note on the others. If you can't think of something to write in one of the columns, leave a space and come back to it. Your chart will change and develop throughout the writing process, and you can add or subtract from the chart whenever you need to. If it gets too messy, recopy it.

To further explore issues raised by incinerator pollution, Melanie created a chart in anticipation of comparing and contrasting incineration and recycling as two waste-management strategies:

Incineration	Recycling
Already in place	Needs to be built
Manages 80% of trash	Would manage 80% of trash
Needs to be paid off	Needs bonds for start-up
Toxic	Nontoxic
Cancer risk	Eliminates incinerator cancer risks
Birth defects	Doesn't threaten unborn
Permanent IQ loss	Provides educational opportunity
Infertility	Eliminates fertility threat
Future legal concerns	Avoids punitive damages
Wastes resources	Uses resources
Loses town revenues	Raises town revenues
Poisons water	Helps maintain water supply
Based on bad politics	Based on ethical grounds
Divides community	Brings community together

Starting Comparison and/or Contrast Essays. In your introductory paragraph, state your subject, the purpose of your essay, and its significance.

Here is the statement Melanie formulated through revision:

> Having a niece with a birth defect that might have been caused by our local incinerator, I want to strongly urge that recycling is a much better way of dealing with trash.

Just as there are strong and weak thesis statements, some statements of comparison and/or contrast are stronger than others. For example, to say a car *is like* a girlfriend to some teenage males is not as strong as saying a car *is* a girlfriend. To say that teaching is not like running a factory assembly line is not as strong as saying teaching should never be conducted as an assembly line. The sidebar on comparisons and contrasts lists some phrases that distinguish weaker from stronger statements. Replace *X* and *Y* with your subjects. These formats work for more than two subjects, as well. Use them to get started. Then revise your state-ment to reflect your own style and purpose.

Here are two of Melanie's earlier drafts of her thesis statement:

1. `The local incinerator might be causing birth defects.`
2. `Incinerator and recycling methods for trash control can be compared.`

Sentence 1 is not a statement of comparison or contrast; it is a statement of cause and effect. Sentence 2 is weak because it states only that the two methods of waste disposal can be compared; almost any two subjects can be compared, so this statement says nothing. Melanie's revised state-ment, however, not only states her two points of comparison and contrast but also incorporates her purpose.

Organizing

Looking at your chart, or reviewing a freewrite, notice whether your main purpose will be to compare your subjects' similarities or to contrast their differences. It is far easier to *either* compare *or* contrast your subjects. However, you might prefer to explore the balance of similarities and dif-ferences between your subjects. Once you have committed yourself to

Comparisons

Weaker Statements	Stronger Statements
X is like *Y*.	*X* is *Y*.
X can be compared to *Y*.	*X* is always like *Y*.
X is similar to *Y*.	*X* is better than *Y*.
	X is more…than *Y*.
	X is less…than *Y*.

Contrasts

Weaker Statements	Stronger Statements
X is not like *Y*.	*X* is not *Y*.
X can be contrasted to *Y*.	*X* is never like *Y*.
X is different from *Y*.	*X* has nothing in common with *Y*.
	X is…while *Y* is….

Transition Words for Comparison and Contrast

Comparisons	Contrasts
Both *X* and *Y*	Although *X, Y*
Just as *X, Y*	Even though *X, Y*
And	But
Also	Yet
Compares with	Contrasts with
Similarly	Conversely
	On the one hand...on the other hand...
	Whereas
	While
	However

your approach, choose from these three methods for developing your essay: zig-zag, block, or combination. If you choose the *zig-zag method*, you consider a point of comparison or contrast on one line under a column of your chart and compare or contrast it to a point on the same line under other columns. You then zig-zag back and forth, point by point.

Melanie considered both the benefits and drawbacks of incinerating versus recycling. She chose to begin with the relatively few benefits of incineration so she could eliminate them early on.

Having a niece with a birth defect that might have been caused by our local incinerator, I want to strongly urge that recycling is a much better way of dealing with trash. Except for the fact that we already have an incinerator that manages 80% of our trash and the plant hasn't paid for itself yet, there are no other reasons for using an incinerator. Even though a new recycling plant would involve a bond issue to find the money, it would pay for itself faster than incinerating. However, with incineration there are huge health risks such as cancer, birth defects, mercury poisoning, infertility, and brain damage. On the other hand, recycling offers many benefits. Most important, it does not threaten to kill us. Recycling would save more natural resources than just human beings and would bring the community together for everybody's benefit.

How to Write a Comparison or Contrast

1. *Choose* your subjects.
2. *Chart* similarities and differences.
3. *Choose* whether you want to focus on comparison or contrast or both.
4. *Write a thesis statement.* Present your purpose and method for the paper.
5. *Organize* your paper using either the block or zig-zag method. Either start with an outline or revise a draft using an outline you develop in process.
6. *Develop* your paper by illustrating your points of comparison or contrast with examples and sense appeal.
7. *Balance* how much you say about each subject. Draw blocks to represent the relative amounts of space you devote to each.

Notice the expressions Melanie used for her transitions between different points of comparison and contrast: *except for, even though, however, on the other hand.*

In the *block method* you discuss all the points about one subject before turning to discuss the other subject. The block version of Melanie's essay reads like this:

Having a niece with a birth defect that might have been caused by our local incinerator, I want to strongly urge that recycling is a much better way of dealing with trash.

The incinerator we already have in our town manages 80% of our trash. The plant hasn't paid for itself. So, it would be a benefit to continue using it. However, with incineration there are huge health risks such as cancer, birth defects, mercury poisoning, infertility, and brain damage.

A new recycling plant would involve going through a bond issue to fund it. The plant would pay itself faster than the incinerator. It would offer many benefits. The most important one is that it would not threaten to kill us. Recycling would save more natural resources than just human beings and would bring the community together for everybody's benefit.

In the zig-zag method, it is easier to make sure that all points of comparison or contrast are made. In the block method, you are freer to discuss each subject in more depth. Be careful to cover all relevant points of comparison or contrast by reviewing your blocks point by point. You will probably want to discuss the points in your blocks in the same order so that your reader can easily find the corresponding point of comparison or contrast in the other blocks. In a longer essay, you could use the *combination method,* zig-zagging at one point in the essay and using the block method when you want to discuss a point about one subject in more depth.

Writing essays that compare and/or contrast, you will discover and create more connections. Jot these onto your chart and incorporate them into your essay. As you reread your drafts and consult with others, count sentences or draw blocks to discern the relative amount of space you devote to each of your subjects. Strive for balance and equal time. In this process, you might discover that you favor one subject or point over another. You might need to collect more information and ideas. You may also find, as you write, that your original purpose and method change. Your subjects may be far more similar or different than you had at first

Reading to Make Connections

As you answer the following questions about the readings, point to particular words, phrases, and sentences to support your claims. Consult your dictionary for further insights into both familiar and unfamiliar words.

1. What is the writer's purpose?
2. Who is the anticipated reader?
3. If the writer uses a thesis statement, what is it?
4. What evidence and examples does the writer offer in support of the thesis?
5. Where and how does the writer use the following focusing strategies: choosing, specifying, stating, illustrating, questioning, quoting?
6. What new connections does the writer discover?
7. How does the writer organize the reading?
8. If the writer compares and/or contrasts subjects, what are they? Does the writer use the zig-zag, block, or combination method?
9. Would you say the writer is a responsible thinker? Why?
10. What new connections between ideas did this reading suggest or inspire?

believed. This is one of the main benefits of comparing and/or contrasting: it leads to new discoveries.

*E*xplorations _____

1. *Together or Solo.* Choose what you consider to be the most effective or interesting of the readings at the end of this chapter. Discuss what makes it so for you. Ideally, you and some of your classmates will disagree. Notice how your choices reflect your particular points of view and interests.

2. **a.** *Together.* Choose one reading to discuss at a time. Use the questions in the sidebar titled Reading to Make Connections to guide you.

    b. *Solo.* Write a short summary of the reading you discussed. Quote directly from it.

3. *Together and Solo.*

    a. For each of the following topics, create three categories. For example, you could say there are three kinds of restaurants: takeout, fast food, and sit-down.

Dates	Students
Doctors	Teachers
Movies	Athletes
Diets	Excuses
Ways of taking an exam	Ways of sleeping

    b. Choose one of the topics for which you created categories in Exploration 3a. Create a chart with three columns and brainstorm corresponding points of comparison and contrast. Decide whether you want to compare similarities, contrast differences, or both. Using the block, zig-zag, or combination method, write and organize an essay on your topic. Be sure to illustrate your points with specific examples and sense appeal.

    c. Read and discuss what you wrote, noticing the methods writers used. Suggest and make revisions for clarity and balance.

4. *Together.*

    a. In small groups, or as a class, choose one of the following topics. Generate two columns of at least ten corresponding points of comparison and/or contrast:

    Falling in love and getting the flu

    Treatment of the aged and treatment of the homeless

Language used about women and language used about animals and children

Life at age fourteen and life at age eighteen

b. In small groups, write an essay of comparison or contrast using the chart you generated together. Formulate a thesis statement. Decide whether to use the zig-zag, block, or combination method.

5. a. *Together.* Referring to textbooks, collect assignments that call for comparison and/or contrast. Help each other design the necessary charts for preparing to write about a choice of these assignments.

   b. *Solo.* Formulate a thesis statement in response to a selected assignment. Draft an essay of comparison and/or contrast using the zig-zag, block, or combination method.

   c. *Together.* Using the sidebar on Reading to Make Connections, read your essays to each other and make suggestions for revisions.

READING TO MAKE CONNECTIONS

From *The Protective Frame*

Deborah Tannen

Deborah Tannen is a best-selling author and a professor of linguistics. In this excerpt, she focuses on the complexities of communication between men and women.

A protective gesture from a man reinforces the traditional alignment by which men protect women. But a protective gesture from a woman suggests a different scenario: one in which women protect children. That's why many men resist women's efforts to reciprocate protectiveness—it can make them feel that they are being framed as children. These underlying dynamics create sense out of what otherwise seem to be senseless arguments between women and men.

Here is an example of a momentary gesture that led to momentous frustration. Sandra was driving, and Maurice was sitting in the seat beside her. When she had to brake suddenly, she did what her father had always done if he had to stop suddenly when Sandra was sitting beside him: At the moment she braked, she extended her right arm to protect the person beside her from falling forward.

This gesture was mostly symbolic. Sandra's right arm was not strong enough to restrain Maurice. Perhaps its main function was simply to alert him that she was stopping unexpectedly. In any case, the gesture had become for her, as it was for her father, automatic, and it made her feel competent and considerate. But it infuriated Maurice. The explanation he gave was that she should keep both hands on the wheel for reasons of safety. She knew she did not lose control of the car when she extended her arm, so they never could settle this difference. Eventually she trained herself to resist this impulse with Maurice to avoid a fight, but she felt sadly constrained by what she saw as his irrational reaction.

Though Maurice explained his reaction in terms of safety, he was actually responding to the framing implied by the gesture. He felt belittled, treated like a child, because by extending her arm to break his fall, Sandra was protecting him. In fact, Maurice was already feeling uncomfortable about sitting passively while Sandra was driving, even though it was her car. Many men and women who feel they have achieved equality in their relationship find that whenever they get into a car together, she automatically heads for the passenger seat and he for the driver's; she drives only when he is not there.

The act of protecting frames the protector as dominant and the protected as subordinate. But the status difference signaled by this alignment may be more immediately apparent to men. As a result, women who are thinking in terms of connection may talk and behave in ways that accept protection, unaware that others may see them as taking a subordinate position.

From *Awesome Women in Sports*

Ruth Conniff

A graduate of Yale University, Ruth Conniff was a varsity track team member there and now coaches high school track and cross-county. In this excerpt, she addresses the issue of how women athletes appear in the media.

Slowly, over the past several years, *Sports Illustrated* has begun to recognize the appeal of women's sports, and to present women as sports heroes, the way it has long presented men. In a recent issue of the magazine, there's a good story on a women's collegiate basketball game between rivals Vanderbilt and Tennessee. The game sold out weeks in advance, according to the article, and generated more attention than any game in the history of women's basketball. Even Vice President Al Gore felt compelled to comment.

On the other hand, the same issue contains a two-page photo spread of the Dallas Cowboys' cheerleaders, prone on a football field, white booties pointing skyward. On another page there's an ad featuring the Budweiser girls.

It's startling how slippery these images of women are. One minute you're a role model, the next you've been disassembled into body parts.

Last year, an old friend from high school came to the indoor city track meet, where I was watching my team. I was lost in the competition, getting nervous before the gun went off, taking times, chewing my nails. Then my friend started talking to me about the girls' bodies as they stood on the starting line. "Don't you think her arms are too big.... Her legs look fat.... *Those* girls have *great* bodies, though. Maybe I should have run track."

It took the wind out of my sails to listen to her. It's easy to forget, and so annoying to remember, even if you're an athlete giving the performance of your life, some people will still look at you that way.

From *Illness as Metaphor*

Susan Sontag

*Herself a cancer survivor, Susan Sontag frequently
writes on such subjects as illness, photography, and
life-styles. In this excerpt, she compares reactions to
tuberculosis and cancer.*

Two diseases have been spectacularly, and similarly, encumbered by
the trappings of metaphor: tuberculosis and cancer.

The fantasies inspired by TB in the last century, by cancer now, are
responses to a disease thought to be intractable and capricious—that is, a
disease not understood—in an era in which medicine's central premise is
that all diseases can be cured. Such a disease is, by definition, mysterious.
For as long as its cause was not understood and the ministrations of doctors remained so ineffective, TB was thought to be an insidious, implaca-
ble theft of a life. Now it is cancer's turn to be the disease that doesn't
knock before it enters, cancer fills the role of an illness experienced as a
ruthless, secret invasion—a role it will keep until, one day, its etiology
becomes as clear and its treatment as effective as those of TB have
become.

Although the way in which disease mystifies is set against a backdrop
of new expectations, the disease itself (once TB, cancer today) arouses
thoroughly old-fashioned kinds of dread. Any disease that is treated as a
mystery and acutely enough feared will be felt to be morally, if not literally, contagious. Thus, a surprisingly large number of people with cancer
find themselves being shunned by relatives and friends and are the object
of practices of decontamination by members of their household, as if cancer, like TB, were an infectious disease. Contact with someone afflicted
with a disease regarded as a mysterious malevolency inevitably feels like
a trespass; worse, like the violation of a taboo. The very names of such
diseases are felt to have a magic power.

From *On Societies as Organisms*

Lewis Thomas

*Dr. Thomas is well known for his popular essays, which
provide us with new insights into the beauty and mysteries
of science. In this excerpt, he compares insects and humans.*

...A solitary ant, afield, cannot be considered to have much of anything on his mind; indeed, with only a few neurons strung together by

fibers, he can't be imagined to have a mind at all, much less a thought. He is more like a ganglion on legs. Four ants together, or ten, encircling a dead moth on a path, begin to look more like an idea. They fumble and shove, gradually moving the food toward the Hill, but as though by blind chance. It is only when you watch the dense mass of thousands of ants, crowded together around the Hill, blackening the ground, that you begin to see the whole beast, and now you observe it thinking, planning, calculating. It is an intelligence, a kind of live computer, with crawling bits for its wits.

. . .

Although we are by all odds the most social of all social animals—more interdependent, more attached to each other, more inseparable in our behavior than bees—we do not often feel our conjoined intelligence. Perhaps, however, we are linked in circuits for the storage, processing, and retrieval of information, since this appears to be the most basic and universal of all human enterprises. It may be our biological function to build a certain kind of Hill. We have access to all the information of the biosphere, arriving as elementary units in the stream of solar photons. When we have learned how these are rearranged against randomness, to make, say, springtails, quantum mechanics, and the late quartets, we may have a clearer notion how to proceed. The circuitry seems to be there, even if the current is not always on.

Electronic or Pipe Organs

Student Frank Dos Santos

An avid musician who can always be seen with his personal CD player, Frank is constantly tuned in to Bach and Beethoven. Here, he contrasts electronic and pipe organs.

There are different types of organs: pipe and electronic. The electronic organ is much cheaper than the pipe organ. The old churches of Europe had and still have beautiful pipe organs. The modern church in America is turning to the electronic organ, because it is much cheaper to maintain and repair.

A religious service that has a pipe organ is much more beautiful than one with an electronic organ. First of all, the pipe organ is more elaborate than the electronic. It has a beautiful wood finishing and is decorated with pipes. The sound is much more real than the electronic one because it is produced from a pipe and not a speaker. Wind is blown from blower to blower into a leather housing where it is stored and pressurized until it is called for. The organist presses down on a key and the pipe that it corresponds to will speak. The sound of the organ changes by putting down different sounds called stops; putting them down changes the volume of the organ also.

The electronic organ is totally different: it doesn't have a blower or pipes. Instead it has a computer that reproduces the sound. Some electronic organs come very close to reproducing the sound of a pipe organ. This holds true for the Allen Organ. This electronic organ uses a sampler. That is, it records the sound of a pipe organ electronically and reproduces the sound whenever the key is pressed down. Although the sound comes close to the pipes, it still isn't the same. But the churches of America, because of a lack of money, are dealing more and more with the electronic than the pipe organ.

*C*hapter *Review*

Solo or Together respond to the following:

1. If you were an instructor of writing, what five points from this chapter would *you* stress in teaching student writers? Why?

2. Which strategies offered in this chapter were either new to you or made clearer?

3. Which strategies do you need to further develop? How do you plan to incorporate them into your writing process?

Chapter 14

Writing for Power

This chapter offers opportunities to

—Explore **the dynamics of power**

—Analyze **the power of language**

—Distinguish appeals to **emotion, status,** and **reason**

—Develop strategies for **writing for power**

—Identify and revise **faulty reasoning**

> The pen is mightier than the sword.
> —*Edward Bulwer-Lytton, Novelist*

The Power of Language

Every day you are confronted with billboards, television and radio commercials, newspaper and magazine advertisements, junk mail, packaging, fast talking, arguments, and other kinds of pressure by people trying to convince you to buy, act, think, do, and be what they want you to buy, act, think, do, and be. The first sentence of this paragraph, itself, is a kind of pressure: agree with me; here are all these many examples that you can't ignore. The difference between a billboard and this book is that here you have more of a choice about whether you will agree. This book offers you reasons to do and believe what it suggests. A billboard does not offer you reasons, because advertising is meant to limit, not to expand, your range of choices.

Power can be defined as the ability to choose what you want to do, and to be what you want to be. When what you want is compatible with what others want, there is no need to struggle for power. However, if there is a conflict, if there are limited resources (time, space, people, things, or energy), if there is confusion, fear, anger, or any other form of resistance, power has to be taken, relinquished, or negotiated.

Language is the most valuable tool we have for managing power. "Talk it out," "you have my word for it," "as good as her word"—these, and other expressions, remind us of the power of words without which we could be reduced to physical conflict. In fact, that's what happens between nations when diplomatic talks fail.

The word *propaganda* is often used to refer to the promotion of particular ideas and activities. Originally, all it meant was the dissemination of views. However, *propaganda* has come to mean deceptive or distorted messages in the service of immoral or self-serving needs. This chapter offers you opportunities to develop your awareness of how to use language to protect and assert your own power without having to resort to propaganda. You will be offered strategies and opportunities to persuade, to negotiate, to assert, to argue,* to propose—in short, to write for power.

The following Explorations will help you identify issues or problems on which you want to write for power. The rest of the chapter will guide you through different phases of the writing process as you develop one or more essays on the issues or problems that you identify here.

*E*xplorations

1. **a.** *Together.* List and then discuss experiences you have had in which someone convinced you to do something or act in a certain way you didn't want to—drinking alcohol at a party, talking with someone you would rather avoid, accepting a job, putting out a cigarette, or buying an object or service. Use these questions to stimulate your discussion:

    - Who was the person who convinced you?
    - What attracted you to or repelled you from doing or acting as the person wanted?

---

*In this chapter, different forms of the word *argument* are used to refer to reasoning aimed at proving the truth or falsehood of claims. These arguments are not necessarily fueled by disagreement, though they might be. Unless otherwise indicated, these words are not used to refer to angry interchanges.

- How did you comply?

- How did the person convince you to do or act as you did?

- What kinds of nonverbal pressure did the person use?

- How did the person use language?

- Looking back, how do you feel about what happened?

- Do you wish you had responded differently? If so, how?

- What, if anything, could you do now to reverse the results of that experience?

   b. *Solo.* Freewrite on one incident you identified in Exploration 1a. How does writing about the situation affect you now?

   c. *Solo.* Freewrite on a current situation in which someone is trying to convince you to do something or act in a way you don't want to. How does writing about this situation affect you?

2. **a.** *Together.* Name and discuss experiences in which you tried to convince someone else to do, think, feel, or act in a certain way, such as lend you a car or money, have a date with you, hire you for a job, or take sides with you against someone else. Use these questions to stimulate your discussion:

- What was the situation?

- Were you successful? If so, how did you accomplish it?

- What strategies and pressures, verbal and nonverbal, did you use?

- If you were not successful, why do you think you failed? How do you wish you had approached the situation?

- Successful or not, what have you learned from the experience?

- Have your interactions changed since then? If so, how? If not, why not?

   b. *Solo.* Freewrite on an incident you identified in Exploration 2a. How does writing about this incident affect you?

3. *Together and Solo.*

   a. Bring current newspapers and magazines to class. Using them for ideas, create a list of issues and problems in which power is being asserted, taken, surrendered, or negotiated. Include local issues such as homeless people sleeping in the corner park, national issues such as Megan's Law, and global political issues such as free immigration. Add to this list as you work through this chapter. Avoid broad, often-discussed issues such as abortion, drugs, capital punishment, or mercy killing unless (1) one of these issues specifically affects you or someone close to you, or (2) you have a fresh approach to it.

    b. List issues and problems of power that arise for you or others at home (such as quiet hours), at school (such as grades), at work (such as fair salaries), and elsewhere.

    c. Choose an issue that is important to you, and think of people—such as particular relatives, friends, and people in the news—with whom you would like to discuss the issue. Consider who would be the most appropriate person for you to approach.

    d. Write a letter about an issue identified in Exploration 3a, b, or c, trying to convince someone of your point of view on the issue.

    e. Write a dialogue between two parts of yourself or between yourself and someone else concerning a specific issue. What do you learn?

Appealing to Your Audience

In his *Rhetoric,* the ancient Greek philosopher Aristotle identified three kinds of appeals:

- Appeals to *emotion* (fear, anger, greed, sexuality)
- Appeals to *status* (character, expertise, believability)
- Appeals to *reason* (logic, evidence, proof)

Appeals to *emotion* focus on the emotional reactions of the *audience.* Appeals to *status* focus on the believability of the *writer.* Appeals to *reason* focus on the *words and statements* the writer uses. Appeals to emotion respond to the first four levels of need that psychologist Abraham Maslow identified: survival, security, power, and love. (See page 378 for further dis-

---

Knowing Your Audience

Ask yourself the following questions whenever you are writing for power:

- Whom do I want to reach?
- What does my audience know?
- What does my audience need?
- What is important to my audience?
- What is my audience's point of view?
- What language will trigger the response I want?

cussion of Maslow's theory.) Appeals to status respond to needs for security, power, and self-esteem. Appeals to reason respond to the highest-level needs: love, communication, self-esteem, and self-fulfillment.

Appeals to Emotion

When a commercial shows you a crumpled and shattered car and red ambulance lights flashing in the background, you are supposed to feel so much fear, anger, and helplessness that you won't drink and drive. When two healthy-looking people are pictured smoking cigarettes together and broadly smiling, you are meant to associate cigarettes with happiness, contentment, and love. These advertisements appeal to your emotions.

In writing, the television commercial against drunk driving or the billboard favoring smoking would be translated into vivid scenarios using strong language to appeal to your emotions. *Trigger* or *loaded* words and expressions are those to which a community has attached strong feelings. That is, they have provocative connotations. In an advertisement against drunk driving, you would expect expressions such as *kills, destroys,* and *every 15 seconds someone is involved in an accident with a drunk driver.* In an advertisement for cigarettes, you would expect expressions such as *Alive with pleasure; You've come a long way, Baby;* and *I'd walk a mile* (which is meant to remind some people of a line in a romantic song that is followed by the line "for one of your smiles").

Repetition is another strategy for making an emotional appeal. As discussed on page 100, people have powerful responses to repetition. Used effectively, it can turn a peaceful assembly of people into a screaming mob. Or, it can turn a distressed baby into a slumbering infant. Repetition most often is used to make a subliminal emotional appeal.

Appeals to Emotion

In deciding whether to use an emotional appeal, ask yourself the following questions:

- What is important to my audience?
- To which emotions do I want to appeal?
- What emotional appeal would be appropriate and responsible?
- What are some strong words or images that I can use to appeal to these emotions?
- How could I effectively use repetition or humor?

Humor is yet another way to appeal to emotions. Sometimes the most convincing strategy is to delight your audience with a joke or to induce them to laugh with you at something of which you disapprove. This is why so many how-to books on public speaking focus on the use of humor.

When emotional appeals take advantage of people's fears, misrepresent the truth, or try to manipulate people into doing what they would otherwise not choose, they are irresponsible. But if the commercial against drunk driving could effectively save lives, and if an appeal to the emotions of authorities could result in better care for the needy or the oppressed, an appeal to emotions is legitimate.

Appeals to Status

If Arnold Schwarzenegger tells you to drink Lookgood, you are meant to believe that, since he is so well-built and since he tells you to drink Lookgood, he must drink it too. Advertisers want you to believe that Lookgood is what makes Schwarzenegger strong and that if you drink Lookgood you will be like Arnold Schwarzenegger, too. Similarly, you are more likely to believe Sharon Berman, *M.D.*, on issues of nutrition than Sharon Berman, *M.A.*, because an M.D. is supposed to be better educated on issues of health. (Of course, a person with an M.A. degree may know more about the issue than a person with an M.D. But you would discern this by examining the evidence a person offers for claims, not the status of the person.) Other, more subtle ways to appeal to the status of a person include tactics that are used to convince you to do something because *everybody else does it* or because something's been done in a certain way for a long time.

In writing, appeals to status include expressions that indicate that the person who is writing and the persons being cited are believable. The Lookgood commercial might include terms such as *protein-rich, 30% more energy, vitality,* and *results in ten days.* A report on nutrition might include not only the same terms as the Lookgood commercial but also technical terms that indicate Dr. Berman's familiarity with medical science. Some of these terms and expressions could be *amino acids, enzyme activity, double-blind study,* and *standard deviation.*

Appeals to status that take advantage of people's respect and admiration for the powerful and successful, that try to manipulate and use people to act in ways that they wouldn't otherwise choose, are irresponsible. But you are wise to consider the advice of Sharon Berman, M.D., on nutrition because what she says is likely to be backed up by a knowledge of medicine. And if you can successfully find a believable authority to quote in an argument, then you are wise to do so. When you are writing or speaking, your audience will be considering whether you are believable.

Appeals to Status

In deciding whether to use an appeal to status, ask yourself the following questions:

- Who does my audience know?
- Who would my audience believe?
- How can I convince my readers that I know the best and most relevant information on this subject?
- Can I use stronger sources to support my arguments?
- Which words will show that I know what I am writing about?
- Could I use stronger or more technical language to gain the confidence of my readers?
- How can I raise questions about the competence of those opposed to my viewpoint?

Showing that you know how to draw on the expertise of others increases your status in the minds of your readers.

Another way to enhance your status and believability is to question the motives of experts and people in power. You then may seem more honest and knowledgeable by contrast. This appeal to status has to be carefully used so as not to merely attack people without just cause. If you are arguing the point only on the basis of who is involved, then you must show that to do so is relevant. (Read further on this issue on pages 99–100.)

Appeals to Reason

When you make an *emotional* appeal, you are trying to manipulate your readers to believe or to do something because it would *feel* right to them. When you make an appeal to *status*, you are trying to pressure your readers to believe or to do something because you or *someone else believes or does it.* When you appeal to *reason,* you are asking your readers to believe or to do something as a result of the *evidence and arguments* you offer. Because an appeal to reason allows your readers more freedom to make up their own minds, it is the most powerful appeal. If your readers adopt your point of view, they will do so because they freely choose to.

The writing process is ideally suited for reasoning. Focusing enables you to clarify your claims and evidence. Collecting enables you to find

---

Appeals to Reason

In deciding whether to use an appeal to reason, ask yourself the following questions:

- What does my audience know?
- What would my audience believe?
- What examples or evidence can I use to support my position?
- Which reasons are most relevant?
- What reasons contradict my position? How can I respond to them?
- How can I best organize my reasons?
- What expressions can I use to show the relationships between my claims and my evidence and examples?
- How can I raise pertinent questions?

---

support for your claims. Organizing enables you to develop connections both within your sentences and between them. Consulting enables you to develop your purpose and sense of audience. Revising gives you opportunities to deepen your understanding and your ability to communicate.

Appeals to reason include statements reporting personal observations or experiences, relevant examples, comparisons, contrasts, scientific reports, statistics, and other forms of evidence. In addition, appeals to reason are organized in a logical order to show how the evidence and examples prove claims.

For example, a tree surgeon may claim that the best way to manage contagious Dutch elm disease is to remove a tree at the first sign of infection. Suppose you have two beautiful elms in front of your house and one of them is showing signs of the disease. In order to convince you, the tree surgeon could appeal to reason by telling you about incidents in which alternative treatments were tested and failed. In addition, the tree surgeon could explain how the disease is spread and show you how your uninfected tree may be in danger.

Suppose you wanted to start a new child care program that employs the elderly in your community. You could appeal to the pity or guilt of the local authorities. You could have a celebrity adopt the cause and speak for you. Or, you could provide the authorities with arguments, reports, and statistics to show that communities with such programs have significantly reduced child care and nursing home costs.

Appeals to reason are often expressed in forms that link causes with effects, problems with solutions, evidence with conclusions, and prior events with results.

Here are two examples of appeals to reason using two of the options listed in the sidebar on forms of reasoning:

Because the carburetor was clogged, the engine could not turn over.

If the government doesn't cut back on spending, then we are sure to suffer from inflation.

Presented with statements such as these, readers are in a position to consider the reason offered (X) and decide whether it is adequate to support the claim (Y).

An additional way to make an appeal to reason is to ask provocative questions. Questions, in general, involve both the writer and the audience in the process of discovering answers. Specifically, rhetorical questions make a most powerful appeal to reason: they invite the audience to fill in the obvious answers and thereby to feel as if the answers were their own. (See pages 119–120 and 311–318 for further discussion of questions.)

Combinations of Appeals

The most powerful writing integrates appeals to emotion, status, and reason in a balanced way, and the same statement can be an appeal to all three. Read and reflect on author and environmental activist Anna Maria Caldara's op-ed piece on incinerator pollution. Focus on the combination of appeals she uses to make her points. Use the questions and suggestions that follow the essay to guide you.

Forms of Reasoning

Reasoning often takes the following forms in which X and Y can be replaced by statements:

If X, then Y.	Whenever X, then Y.
X only if Y.	If Y, then necessarily X.
X causes Y.	Because X, therefore Y.
Since X, Y.	Y is the result of X.

PCFA Gets F for Corrupting the Community Trust

Anna Maria Caldara

Appeal to emotion

When is the fine line between education and propaganda crossed? It is when the Pollution Control Financing Authority (PCFA) of Warren County sees an opportunity to promote its incinerator in the schools.

Appeal to reason

Consider the front page headline of last summer's "Waste Paper," a publication of the PCFA, overseers of the county landfill. "Students Introduced to Environmental Management," it read. Ten school districts participated in a "Junior Environmental Program" thanks to a N.J. Education Recycling Grant obtained by the PCFA. Recycling saves the materials (aluminum, glass, paper, tin) if the whole object cannot be recovered, thereby saving the energy of recreating it. Warren County has the lowest recycling percentage in the state because its garbage incinerator needs gigantic amounts of plastic, paper, etc., etc., to burn.

Burning recyclables, as the incinerator does, does not save them. It destroys them. By design, mass-burn incinerators destroy massive amounts of our future resources. Garbage is their fuel; garbage, that if it was separated, would become piles of glass, tin, cardboard, compostables, paper, or, as they are more commonly called, resources. The burning process also transforms recoverable materials into heavy metals, dioxin, and other dangerous emissions that contaminate the food chain for generations.

Appeal to emotion

Questioning status

Because the Junior Environmental Program was funded by an Education Recycling Grant, it seemed ironic that an accompanying photo showed students being instructed how to build a "mini trash incinerator." This is even more ironic since the goal of the program was stated as gaining "a new awareness of how to preserve our environment."

How did the college students that helped build the mini trash incinerator explain that burning our resources preserves our environment? Should an Education Recycling Grant be used to teach children it's okay to consume and throw away because a garbage-eating machine has to be fed? Or should we be telling them that the amount of aluminum cans discarded each year in the U.S. could rebuild the entire jet air fleet three times? Should we be telling them that mining for aluminum is one of the most environmentally destructive procedures on earth, so therefore we must recycle soda cans and insist that soda be filled in bottles? And should we be telling them that the first step in "preserving an environment" is to prevent harmful substances from entering it—substances like the fine particles of mercury that fly from the incinerator stack and land in our lakes, where they poison our fish, and in our lungs, where they poison our bodies?

The children even took a field trip—to the incinerator. After all, if the PCFA and student instructors Kelly Crabtree and Rebecca Rush don't mind endangering children's minds, why shouldn't they endanger their bodies? March them through the plant in defiance of major studies that show minute amounts of lead, cadmium, mercury, chromium and dioxin can cause irreparable harm to developing bodies. Recycling Coordinator/Education Specialist Dinah Rush pokes with pride at a recent freeholder meeting of these "school tours" she arranges. Does she not have the responsibility to educate herself on the documented dangers of inhaling fine particles of heavy metals? Perhaps part of the problem is that she is paid by the PCFA. Rebecca Rush, co-builder of the mini trash incinerator, is Dinah's daughter. It seems blind eyes run in the family. And, the Rushes live in Harmony, where reportedly the elementary school does not recycle. Shouldn't Dinah look into that?

The PCFA allows deception, nepotism, endangerment of youth, misuse of funds, and propaganda to protect the incinerator...all in the name of protecting the environment, in the name of spending grant money wisely, in the name of educating children. They deserve an "F" for corrupting the trust—and the resources—of the next generation.

Appeal to emotion

Appeal to emotion and reason

Questioning status

Combination of appeals

*R*eflections _____

1. Which parts of Caldara's article do you find most effective? Why?

2. What basic human needs are at issue in this article?

3. Who is Caldara's anticipated audience? Describe the typical person you believe she is trying to reach—age, gender, education, class, parental status, and so on.

4. Circle trigger words.

5. Do you agree with the way the marginal notes identify the different appeals? If so, say why a given portion is making the indicated appeal. If you disagree, name the appeal you believe Caldara is making.

6. How does Caldara use questions?

7. How does Caldara use repetitions?

8. Which appeals work most effectively for you? Why?

9. What purposes does Caldara have for the article? Are they mainly to connect with, separate from, or negotiate with her audience? What is she hoping to accomplish?

10. What are the different points of view on the incinerator? On what issues might proponents of these different views agree?

*E*xplorations _____

1. *Together and Solo.* Read the following examples. Mark appeals with one or more letters: *E* for emotion, *S* for status, *R* for reason. Discuss the examples, using these questions as guides:

   • Does it make an appeal? If so, go on to the following questions.

   • Which words and expressions make a strong appeal?

   • What kinds of appeals do these words and expressions make?

   • Which need or needs are being addressed?

   • Which kind of appeal is predominant?

   a. "Thanks, New Hampshire Institute of Photography. Since enrolling, I've opened my own studio and already grossed over $7000. I love it!" (A version of this was written in a magazine next to a photograph of a young woman holding a long telephoto lens.)

   b. "If you don't teach your children the facts of life, one day, AIDS may be a fact of life for you." (This statement was written especially for this Exploration.)

    c. "Andre Agassi and Michael Chang are the top-seeded players this year in the St. Jude Classic." (This statement was made on the sports page of a newspaper.)

    d. "In a study recognized by the American Medical Association, researchers found that a program of exercise, diet, and relaxation significantly lowered the cholesterol levels of heart patients. If you want to avoid heart attack, stroke, and other life-threatening consequences of a high-fat diet, start today to readjust your life-style." (This appeared in a community newsletter.)

    e. "The only way to end all wars is to strike hard and fast at all would-be Hitlers now!" (This statement was made by a citizen making an editorial statement on a news show.)

2. *Solo and Together.* Using newspapers and magazines, identify three examples each of appeals to emotion, status, and reason. (You may find that most of the material combines appeals.) Then apply the directions in Exploration 1 to one of these examples.

3. *Together and Solo.* Revise examples collected in Exploration 2 so that they appeal to reason.

4. *Together and Solo.*

    a. List television programs and movies that focus on court trials. Choose one episode, movie, or trial. Take notes in which you record the different kinds of appeals that attorneys and witnesses are using to support their positions. To help you in your note taking, use a different sheet of paper for each position. Mark appeals to emotion *E*, appeals to status *S*, and appeals to reason *R*. Of course, you may want to mark a given piece of evidence with more than one letter.

    b. Either in writing or in discussion, report what you observed and learned about the case and the appeals favored by the participants.

5. a. *Solo.* Choose a power issue you identified either in your own life or in the news. Decide whether you want to address an audience that agrees with you, disagrees with you, or is neutral on the issue. Ask yourself the following questions:

- Which need or needs am I addressing?
- How do I hope to affect my audience?
- What purpose or purposes do I have in mind?
- What changes in thinking, attitude, or action do I want to effect?
- Which appeal or combination of appeals will most effectively create the changes I want to make with my particular audience?

    b. *Solo.* Freewrite a draft of a paper on your chosen issue, addressing the purpose and audience you have chosen.

    c. *Together.* Discuss your drafts with special attention to purpose, audience, points of view, and appeals.

Power and the Writing Process

The writing process is ideal for developing and asserting power. Clearly stating your purpose, understanding your audience, focusing your mind and energy, organizing your strategies, collecting your resources, consulting with others, and revising and refining your reasoning all empower you and strengthen your position.

Establishing Needs

Psychologist Abraham Maslow ranked human needs in the following order, starting with the most basic:*

- Survival
- Security
- Power
- Love
- Communication
- Self-esteem
- Self-fulfillment

The most basic needs for survival must be met first: these include the need for food, shelter, and clothing. Human beings also need the security that a social structure can provide. A social structure includes provisions not only for those who are strong, independent, and healthy but also for children, the elderly, the ill, and the poor.

Humans need a sense of power to be able to realize what they need. The drive for dominance, money, and possessions, above and beyond basic necessities, reflects the need for power. The need for community and love is the next level of need. Animals also need survival, security, power, and social contact. But what makes humans unique is their ability to meet their needs through words, to create new ideas and systems, and to implement them. Human beings also have the unique ability to reflect on and value themselves and the world through language—to realize that people are both unique individuals and fundamentally like all other human beings. Whenever you write for power, reflect on the kinds of needs you are addressing and which ones are your priorities for a particular writing project.

---

*From Abraham Harold Maslow, *Motivation and Personality*, 2nd ed. (New York: Harper & Row, 1970).

Naming Your Purpose

Writing provides you with opportunities to do some, or all, of the following:

- Connect (flatter, yield, agree, accept)
- Separate (blame, insult, undermine, stalemate)
- Negotiate (propose, discuss, bargain, adjust)

If your purpose is to connect with and to be accepted by your audience, emphasize needs and purposes you have in common. This process is usually referred to as "establishing common ground." For example, if you were writing a letter of application for a job, you would decide which of your abilities corresponded to the job description. You would emphasize what you could bring to the job, because the job is the common ground between you and the employer.

If your purpose is to separate from your audience, you should project the consequences of how you try to separate. For example, if you wanted to resign from a job because of sexual harassment, you could write a scathing letter to your employer. This letter would serve the purpose of expressing your frustrations; however, the letter could also be used against you if you ever brought legal charges against your employer. You could write a letter in which you resign without explanation. This would serve your purpose and still provide you access to other employees and records should you want to press charges. But you would not be expressing your frustration. A third alternative would be to resign with a short statement citing sexual harassment as your reason.

If your purpose is to negotiate with your audience, assess, as fully as you can, what you have in common, what conflicts of interest you may have, and how you can both benefit from the negotiations. In both connecting and negotiating, it is crucial to establish a common ground of human needs that all parties can understand. You establish common ground first by becoming aware of how different people can view the same events. Read Table 14.1, in which some typical parent-child interactions are recorded. Notice the internal messages behind the spoken words (written in parentheses). Notice the common ground of needs the parent and child share.

In each of the sets of positions in the table, the parent and the child are disagreeing over some kind of need. The parent wants to control the child's time, for example, whereas the child wants the freedom to decide about time. However, in many disagreements you can find some common ground of needs with which all parties can identify. Establishing common ground helps you avoid nonproductive disputes and power struggles. In

TABLE 14.1   *Finding Common Ground*

Parent	Child
"It's correct for you to have an 11:00 curfew."	"You don't trust me."
(I'm really scared you're going to be hurt. I won't be free to relax if I have to worry about you.)	(I want to be free to decide when to come back. I won't be able to relax if I'm afraid of missing curfew.)
Common ground: Need for security and self-esteem.	
"When I was your age I wasn't even thinking about a car."	"Everybody in my class has a car except me."
(I feel insecure about the budget.)	(I feel embarrassed to ask for rides.)
Common ground: Need for power.	
"Get your feet off the coffee table."	"It's my house too."
(I need respect for my things.)	(I don't want to feel unwanted.)
Common ground: Need for security.	
"We have always gone to the shore as a family."	"I want to be with people my own age. Your friends are boring."
(I feel you are growing away from us and don't want to see you go.)	(I feel stifled.)
Common ground: Need for communication.	
"Sex is a beautiful thing, after your wedding day."	"But that's not what your generation did."
(I'm terrified of sexually transmitted diseases.)	(Why do we have all these terrible sexually transmitted diseases today?)
Common ground: Need for security and love.	

the case of time, both parent and child could recognize the need for safety and self-esteem and negotiate a way to ensure a pleasant evening for all.

*E*xplorations

1. *Together.* Two people can volunteer to enact a dialogue between a parent and child, using one of the interactions from Table 14.1 as a starter. The rest of the class can serve as directors. Follow these two steps:

    First, allow the parent and child to maintain their own positions without considering the other person's point of view. The directors can interrupt when either parent or child starts to "give up" her or his position.

As a class, discuss what is wrong between the parent and child.

Second, the parent and child start as they did before, but this time they try to discover their needs and establish common ground. The directors can interrupt when either the parent or child starts to retreat to a one-sided point of view.

As a class, compare this interaction with the first one. What do you learn? Can you apply any of the insights developed in this Exploration to your own life? If so, how? If not, why not?

2. **a.** *Solo.* Refer to the power issues you identified in doing the Explorations on pages 366–368. Choose an issue or think of others that are important to you.

    b. *Together.* Do the following for each issue:

Establish at least two points of view.

Create a chart, similar to Table 14.1, in which you compare the different points of view. Write statements that people would make from those perspectives and the inner messages behind the statements.

    c. *Solo.* Using your chart as a starter, write a dialogue between two people with differing points of view on your issue. Ideally, this dialogue should involve specific people.

    d. *Solo.* Referring to basic needs—survival, security, power, love, communication, self-esteem, self-fulfillment—establish some common ground between the two points of view.

    e. *Together.* Read these dialogues to each other and suggest ways to revise the dialogues so that the perspectives are clear and strong. *Notice opportunities for establishing common ground.* How did you benefit and what did you learn from writing the dialogues?

Naming Your Purpose

In formulating your purpose, ask yourself the following questions:

- Why am I writing this?
- Do I want to connect with, separate from, or negotiate with my audience?
- What is the point of view of my audience?
- What common ground do I share with my audience?
- How much can I hope to accomplish with this audience?

Focusing

There are many ways to focus yourself and your audience when you write for power:

- Choosing
- Specifying
- Quoting
- Illustrating

- Stating
- Questioning
- Using sense appeal

Which combination of strategies you use will depend on your style, purpose, and audience. However, when you write for power, it is essential that you state what you want to prove or accomplish, at least to yourself.

The process of stating will help you to decide how much to try to accomplish. Suppose you felt, as student Melanie Patel did, that students at your college were apathetic about their academic community. Here are some ways in which you could state the problem:

- Students are apathetic in this college.
- Biology students should be more aware of the effects of environmental pollution on their lives and careers.
- Biology students should act now to patrol campus garbage disposal areas for violations of recycling.

The first statement is much too general. It includes all the students in the college and all kinds of concerns about the academic community, ranging from dorm buildings to chemistry labs. The word *apathetic* has strong emotional force because it has connotations of powerlessness.

The second statement is more specific because it focuses on biology students. It is easier to address a smaller audience when your purpose is to involve others in an action. However, it is still unclear what Melanie might prove or accomplish starting with such a statement.

The third statement is far more focused. It specifies biology students and points out not only the problem of recycling violations, but also a direction that might be taken to help solve the problem. Focusing is a powerful way to assume power over a situation.

When you are attempting to formulate a statement of your problem and your purpose, you may find that you have to experiment and rephrase until you find a focus. Before you can settle on a working focus, you may have to collect information and ideas. You may find yourself interviewing and consulting others.

Focusing for Power

To help you focus, ask yourself the following questions:

- What exactly is the issue or problem?
- How can I most directly present the issue or problem?
- How much can I accomplish effectively with my current resources?
- Is my statement of the problem clear?
- Is my statement sufficiently strong for my purposes?
- Is my statement fair and true?
- Is all my supporting evidence relevant?

To benefit the most from the writing process, proceed both as a planner (formulating statements to get you started) and as an explorer (discovering statements and ideas as you draft your letter or essay). In your final draft, you may place your focusing statements in a variety of positions (see the sidebar on page 187).

*E*xplorations _____

1. *Together and Solo.* If you have not already done so, turn to pages 112–116 and read about the differences between strong and weak statements. Do one or more of the Explorations in that section.

2. *Together and Solo.* For each of the following sets of statements, decide which is most specific and which is most general:

   a. Pornography diminishes both men and women.

      Thomas Johnson should not have his contract renewed as gymnastics coach at Millstream College because he has accepted a contract to be a centerfold model in a pornographic magazine.

      The number of pornographic magazines published in the last ten years has increased 250 percent.

   b. The beef-growing industry is directly related to the destruction of the rain forest in South America.

      There is a delicate balance between the insects, plants, and animals in the rain forests.

      We are all responsible for the well-being of our planet.

   c. People should be able to learn and write in the language in which they were raised.

For a Mexican American, Spanish is the language of warmth and intimacy.

In order for students to learn computer programming, there has to be a language that all international communities can share.

3. **a.** *Solo.* Return to the power issue you have chosen to address. Phrase a statement of the issue or problem in at least three different ways, ranging from the most general to the most specific.

   b. *Together.* Read your statements to each other. Choose the ones that are the most specific. Revise the statements so that they are as strong or as weak as you want them to be for your purpose and audience.

Collecting for Power

To formulate and develop your position on an issue or problem, you need to collect information and ideas. Otherwise, you may be repeating old prejudices and beliefs and not taking the opportunity to discover and invent better ideas. Collecting, like other phases of the writing process, will be determined by the particular purpose and audience for which you write. The better you focus, the easier it will be to find the kinds of evidence, examples, and appeals you need to support your position. The better you conduct your collecting activities, the more empowered and successful you will be in fulfilling your purpose.

Melanie Patel wrote a proposal on the problem of violations of recycling agreements around her college campus. She used a variety of collecting strategies to support her cause. First she spoke with members of the biology club to elicit support. Together, they listed the different areas where recycling containers were already in use and where they should be introduced. They divided up the task of observing how often the containers were used correctly. Melanie interviewed the head of maintenance at the college to ask her about how the garbage was managed on campus. She learned that the college was spending a large sum of money hiring independent contractors to separate recyclables from other waste.

As part of her collecting activities, Melanie *anticipated objections and resistances* that her proposal might raise, including hostility and invasion of privacy. This is a crucial strategy for anyone writing for power. As you present your case and your arguments, your readers—especially if they are predisposed against your position—will be thinking of objections to your points. If you show that you know these objections and can maintain your position nonetheless, your argument will be much more effective:

> ### *Collecting for Power*
>
> For help in collecting what you need, ask yourself the following questions:
>
> - What evidence or examples would best help me to make the kinds of appeals I want to make to my audience?
> - Who can I ask for information?
> - What method of collecting could I use?
> - What is the most efficient way to collect what I need?
> - What objections or resistances do I anticipate from my readers?
> - How can I directly address and defuse objections and resistances?

- You show yourself to be thoughtful and reasonable.
- You show that you can identify with those who disagree with you.
- You create an atmosphere of cooperation.
- You use others' disagreements to strengthen your case.
- You reduce the number of objections others can make.

Here are some transitional phrases you can use in anticipating objections:

- "You might object that...."
- "Some people have argued that...."
- "I know what it means to have been on the other side of this issue."

When you present your counterargument, you can use expressions such as these:

but	nevertheless
even so	nonetheless
however	on the other hand

*E*xplorations

1. *Together and Solo.* Consider the issues you are exploring in writing for power. Using the questions listed in the sidebar on collecting for power, decide what information you need to fulfill your purpose and

to make the kinds of appeals you want to make to your audience. Choose from the following list of collecting strategies:

Listing	Brainstorming
Clustering	Charting
Observing	Experimenting
Interviewing	Firsthand experiences
Dialoguing	Researching written materials

2. *Together and Solo.*

   a. In small groups or as class, present objections to the points that might be raised in response to the essays you are writing for power. Offer examples to disprove objections. Anticipate how others might resist. Do this to be helpful: it's better to test yourself with your working partners than to encounter resistance from a true adversary.

   b. Choose the most difficult objections to each paper. Brainstorm examples and ways in which these objections can be quieted or disproved.

   c. *Solo.* Revise your paper, directly addressing anticipated objections.

Organizing for Power

Organizing, like other phases of the writing process, will be determined by the particular purpose and audience for which you write. The better you organize, the easier it will be for your audience to absorb and respond as you want.

Structures.   You can write for power using many different structures and forms. These include

- Letters of application and complaint
- Letters to editors and companies
- Résumés
- Legal documents
- Proposals
- Term papers
- Business memos and reports
- Newspaper, magazine, and journal articles
- Book-length discussions

- Speeches
- Scripts
- Lectures
- Debates

How you organize what you write depends on what form best suits your purpose. You wouldn't write a job application as you would a television script (unless you were applying for a creative position at a television station).

Shapes.   There are two directions from which you can present your case when you are writing for power. You can state your position and purpose and then provide your examples and evidence. This is *deduction*. Or, you can shape your presentation by offering a series of examples and evidence and then conclude by summarizing them into a key statement of your position and purpose. This is *induction*. The sidebar on page 187 charts some options you have in using deductive and inductive reasoning.

In combining strategies, you can move back and forth from stating a position and supporting it with examples and evidence to offering examples and evidence and stating your position on them afterward.

Whether you use deduction or induction depends on the effect you want to make and your personal style. Experiment with both. You may find that in revising a paper you will want to switch completely from one strategy to another. In either case, focus on the lead and the ending. These are the strategic points where you either engage your readers or lose them. The more cleanly you organize what you write, the more confidence your audience will have in what you say. In short, the way you organize is an indirect appeal to status: "See how well I write—I must know what I'm talking about."

Melanie arranged her proposal by using headings, underlining, and white space so that it looked official enough for her to be taken seriously by her audience. In addition, clear headings helped her readers to grasp her main purpose at a glance.

Melanie began her proposal by establishing common ground: she is a member of the college community, a dorm resident, and a biology major. In addition, she appealed to her readers by offering a description of the environment in graphic detail.

Melanie stated her purpose and outlined the problems that led to her proposal. She continued by stating the advantages and practical considerations of following her suggestions. Notice how Melanie considers the point of view of all the people concerned and anticipates practical

Organizing for Power

For help in organizing what you write, ask yourself the following questions:

- What title would familiarize my readers with my topic and interest them?
- What kinds of appeals should I use in my lead?
- What lead would clearly focus my reader's attention on my concerns?
- What formatting would help emphasize the points I want to make?
- What is the most effective order for my supporting examples and evidence?
- How much do I want to emphasize any given point?
- Is every point and example relevant?
- Where can I address possible objections?
- Do I provide smooth and reasoned transitions between ideas and examples? Between major points? Between paragraphs?
- What point do I want to emphasize in my ending?
- What tone is appropriate for my ending?

objections to her proposal. She ends her proposal on a personal note that reestablishes common ground and invites negotiations.

```
To: Members of the Biology Club
From: Melanie Patel, Member
Date: November 6, 1996
Subject: Recycling on Campus and Biochemical Hazards
```

The Problem

Since the new county incinerator was installed at Oxford Township, environmental groups, especially Women for a Safe Future, have been trying to get it shut down. Children have been getting tumors, on one block near the incinerator six families have recently had someone get cancer, and fish and frogs have been dying in nearby lakes in huge numbers. The incinerator gives out ash that carries mercury, dioxin, lead, and other poisons wherever the ash floats.

Why should we care? After all, it's not in our county. Well, the ash and the poisons affect at least a hundred miles in every direction. And we go to school sixty miles from the incinerator. Also, the people at the incinerator are trying to sell the ash to a paving company that is going to pave the new parking lot between the new dorm and the gym. Do you want to be poisoned?

We are biology majors. That means we care about the life of this planet. We are the future. But what can we do now?

The Purpose

I think that we should get involved with this problem. The reason we have an incinerator is because we are not recycling. Now 80% of our trash is burned instead of recycled. We could recycle 80% instead.

Let's start at home. There are recycling containers all over campus. But people are still throwing cans, bottles, paper, and aluminum into the trash. And the recycling containers get all sorts of mixed-in trash. Can't people read?

I propose that we start a campaign to step up recycling on this campus, our home away from home.

Advantages

If nothing else, we could use this project to fulfill our community service requirement. Also, the Biology Club has not done anything but party since Jamie and Collette got us to clean up the brook behind Willis Hall. That was two years ago.

Mrs. Jordan, the head of our maintenance department, tells me that the college pays enormous sums of money each month to have the recyclables sorted out. So a lot of the money that could be going toward other things at this college--for example, tuition--is being lost because people are being careless.

If we get to the people on campus maybe they will take home the message to their communities. That would be one of the best benefits of focusing on recycling. We could talk to people about the awful effects of the incinerator.

If we can get this project going, we can get the newspapers to cover it and we can get publicity. Then we can show the community that if we can do it, so can everyone else. It's a small step. But it's one that can lead to other ways to save our planet for the future.

Objections

Students don't like to be told how to act when they're
away from home. They want to feel independent. We've had an
awful lot of tension on campus lately. However, if we could
get everybody involved over a common enemy--incinerator
pollution--this could be another benefit.

Conclusion

Being in college is an opportunity to have free time to
learn. It is not a time to waste. The incinerator at Oxford
poses a death sentence to all the people in this community.
Let's take the first step toward a cleaner, safer future for
ourselves, our families, and our communities.

*E*xplorations

1. *Solo.* Consider the issues you are exploring in writing for power. If you
   have *not* already drafted a paper on the issue, use the questions and suggestions listed in the sidebar on page 388 to organize your strategies.
   Then draft an essay to fill in your structure. If you have already drafted
   your paper, create an outline of it to determine your organization. Reorganize your paper for clarity. Use headings, where appropriate. Refer to
   the guidelines for deduction and induction on pages 185 and 188.

2. *Together.* Read and respond to each other's drafts, with special emphasis on organization.

Consulting for Power

When you are writing for power, it is very valuable to present your papers
in process to those who can offer you a clear sense of what you are doing
and whether you are likely to reach a particular audience. If you are working in small groups, ask one person to completely support you in your
position, one person to disagree as much as possible, and one person to
help you to find common ground. The more you rehearse different points
of view in this way, the more likely you will be able to anticipate and
manage objections or resistance. In addition, you will benefit from
insights into human nature that others can offer you that would take you
much longer to formulate by yourself.

As you write, as you consult with others, and as you learn more
through writing, you will find ideas and create strategies to accomplish

what you want. Even if you have already given what you write to your prospective audience and have gotten a response, you may want to write further, retract some of what you wrote, add to it, or reinterpret it in some way. You can revise by directly incorporating your audience's response; then send it back to your audience.

Revising Faulty Reasoning

As you move back and forth between the phases of the writing process, identify and revise any faulty or irresponsible appeals that may undermine your purpose. The following are some of the most frequently used faulty appeals to reason. Often *faulty reasoning* is a misused appeal to emotion or status, masquerading as an appeal to reason.

Ad Hominem.   *Ad hominem* means "to the man" in Latin. In an ad hominem argument, the truth of a statement is judged not by whether the statement is valid but by who states it. It is an example of a misuse of appeal to status. Whether a well-known politician or your next-door neighbor tells you that Rocketcar is your best value, you have to judge the car by its own merits. Conversely, you can't judge the merits of your doctor's diagnoses by whether she or he agrees with your politics. The following are two examples of ad hominem reasoning:

> I wouldn't believe a thing she tells me about honesty and relationships. She hasn't had her own hair color for years.
>
> If Professor Singer says it, I'll do it.

Sometimes an ad hominem attack is buried in a rhetorical question, such as "How can an undergraduate understand a professor's point of view?" or "Who, if not a mother, can feel deeply for children?" The first question assumes that being an undergraduate makes a person unsympathetic to professors. The second question assumes that being a mother guarantees a love for children. Neither of the assumptions is true.

If you question the believability or honesty of someone as part of your reasoning, be certain that it is relevant to do so. Notice that in her op-ed piece against incinerators (pages 374–375), Caldara questions the decisions made by Rebecca and Dinah Rush. They seem to support the incinerator because they both are invested in it. In this case, Caldara is not arguing ad hominem. It is relevant to question the decisions of people who have special interests.

Be careful of abusing your own status. Don't expect others to believe you just because of who you are or what you have done. Saying things such as "I know because I'm older" or "Do it because I said so" not only shows your inability to reason but invites others to rebel.

Counteract ad hominem arguments by separating statements from the person making them. Ask yourself, "Is it true just because *X* says so?" "Do the person's other activities or traits make a difference to this point? If so, how?"

Mudslinging.   *Mudslinging* is an extreme form of ad hominem reasoning. Mudslinging is an aggressive attempt to discredit or attack a person's statement by attacking the person instead of judging the statement on its own merits. For example, suppose a male politician believed in supporting AIDS research. A mudslinger would state that the only reason the politician supports AIDS research is because he must have AIDS and if he has AIDS then he must be homosexual. Furthermore, the mudslinger might aggressively attack homosexuals and suggest that the politician be impeached.

Counteract mudslinging with these questions:

- What is your evidence for that claim?
- What is the source of your evidence?
- What difference do the person's other activities or traits make to this point?

Point out that overemotional appeals to status are confusing and destructive. Avoid mudslinging, yourself—it usually backfires.

Hasty Generalizations.   Be wary of claims that ask you to believe something is true for every person, place, time, thing, or event. If these generalizations are made in response to only a few examples, they may be *hasty generalizations.* Just because you have had a bad experience with one make of car doesn't mean that all cars of that make are faulty. Just because one person dies while playing a violin doesn't mean that all violins are lethal. Another expression for *hasty generalizations* is *jumping to conclusions.* Jumping to conclusions can damage friendships, strain marriages, cause political friction, and discredit you in your profession.

Know, however, that many generalizations—such as "The sun rises every morning" or "Unprotected sex enhances the likelihood of contracting AIDS"—are useful, if not necessarily true for all time. A time may come when the sun goes cold, but for now we must trust its cycles if we are to feel secure. A cure for AIDS may someday be found, but for now it's best to protect ourselves against the devastating disease. A counterexample to a generalization does not mean that there isn't some truth in the generalization, only that it is not true in all cases.

Counteract hasty generalizations by offering examples that discredit them: *counterexamples.* If someone says all Model Q cars are jalopies, you might point out the counterexamples of Model Q cars that are not jalopies. If someone says gardening is too much trouble (meaning that *all* gardening is too much trouble), you might point out the counterexamples of avid gardeners who thrive on planting and tending their crops.

Stereotyping. *Stereotyping* is making a judgment about a whole group of people based solely on a few traits the members have in common, such as gender, race, religion, or age. Stereotyping—whether stated in positive or negative terms—can be harmful. A stereotyping statement such as "Men are good at controlling their emotions" may seem complimentary, but it is problematic in many ways: the statement puts undue pressure on men to tamp down emotions; it depreciates men who are expressive; and, by implication, it depreciates women. Stereotyping others negatively may serve to make you feel more powerful in comparison with them, but it severely reduces your opportunities for meeting, learning, and connecting with people who may be different from you. Stereotyping limits your personal growth and can backfire. If you degrade others, part of you will also be fearful of the judgment of others. This fear will reduce your power.

Counteract stereotyping both in yourself and in others, by treating persons as individuals, not as categories. Be aware of stereotyping statements. Look for examples of people who don't fit the stereotypes. Offer counterexamples to people who stereotype. You will find that counterexamples of stereotypes are abundantly available. (For further discussion and work on counteracting stereotyping, turn to pages 280–285 in Chapter 11, "Writing to Bridge Cultures.")

Either-Or Fallacy. There are rarely only two sides to an issue—good or bad, right or wrong, yes or no—because there are many ways to present an issue. In fact, give someone only two options and you may invite resistance. "What do you mean we have only two options: war or economic devastation?" Also, an extreme either-or position is much harder to live up to, as in "Either you buy this product or you will go bald." Be wary of any claim that seems to suggest only two sides or ways of viewing a situation.

Counteract the either-or fallacy by devising further alternatives. Introduce your objection with expressions such as these:

"There are more than two sides to this question."

"We can synthesize a position somewhere in between."

"Let's create a compromise."

Evading the Question.   Do you ever notice when people change the subject or don't answer questions? For example, after ordering an attack on a foreign government's building, a politician was asked if her country was trying to assassinate the minister in charge of the building. She replied, "We are not targeting any individual." She was not answering the question. Her statement could imply that her government was targeting a group of individuals that included the minister. And if you read her statement emphasizing *any,* the statement could imply, "We're not targeting just *any* individual. We are targeting an *important* one." She was *evading the question,* a tactic that avoids reasoning about the issue at hand.

Counteract the problem of evading the question by frequently asking these questions:

- Is this person answering the question?
- Is this person addressing the issue?
- Is this response relevant and to the point?

Be sure to ask these questions of yourself, as well.

False Comparisons.   *False comparisons* are often used when a person is trying to overpower an audience in some way. Consider these two examples using comparisons:

> We must use force to make people accept our religion as the only true breath of life. We would force breath into a suffocating child to save her, wouldn't we?
>
> If there is a rotten apple in a barrel, remove it completely or it will ruin all the apples. A radical mastectomy is perhaps the only reliable procedure for breast cancer.

It is true that we would all want to resuscitate a suffocating child. It is not clear that imposing a particular religion is the only way to "breathe life" into a person. The comparison is questionable. Similarly, a tumor can be as ruinous to the body as a rotten apple is to other apples. But a breast is not significantly like an apple. Apples in a barrel are far more similar than different parts of a body are. Also, it is not clear that cancer works in the same way that chemicals in a barrel of apples do.

Counteract false comparisons by first noticing that a comparison is being made. Notice how the things being compared are alike. Are these similarities relevant to the issue being presented? If the things being compared are not significantly alike, show how they are significantly different.

*E*xplorations _____

1. *Together and Solo.*

    a. Identify faulty reasoning in the following statements. Which appeal or combination of appeals is each making: to emotion, to status, to reason?

        -   In response to the question of how many casualties we have sustained so far, let me say that we are in the process of reevaluating our reports from the field.

        -   How can John Updike write about women when he's a man?

        -   If you're not willing to write this memo regarding the promotions, then you aren't qualified to remain on this job.

        -   His mother was a drug addict, his father an alcoholic, and his uncle a thief. How can he possibly run a hospital?

        -   Women were born to bear children, not heavy responsibilities.

        -   Skiing is like jumping off a bridge: sooner or later you stop.

        -   Either you're with us or you're not.

    b. Revise and add to the statements in Exploration 1a so that they will form true appeals to reason. For example, the first statement would be more honest if the person said either "I don't know" or "We have found four bodies so far."

2. *Together or Solo.*

    a. Collect examples of faulty reasoning from newspapers and magazines, especially on editorial and op-ed pages and in letters to the columnists and editors. Listen for faulty reasoning in debates and speeches on television and radio and in person.

    b. Choose some examples of faulty reasoning. Revise the speech or piece of writing so that it is a true appeal to reason. What changes in the message? What would change for the persons who used the faulty reasoning if they had used your versions?

3. *Together and Solo.* Read the papers you are writing for power, and identify any statements or arguments that use faulty reasoning. Revise them into true appeals to reason.

Results

In order to effect changes through writing, it is important that you reach the right people. Write to individuals you know personally, to the editor of your local newspaper, to the manager of a television or radio station, to people in government (both local and national), to associations such as the American Medical Association, and to places of business and com-

Reading for Power

As you answer the following questions about your readings, point to particular words, phrases, and sentences to support your claims. Consult your dictionary for further insights into both familiar and unfamiliar words.

1. What need is motivating the person to write the essay?
2. What is the purpose of the essay?
3. Who is the writer's anticipated audience?
4. What issue is the writer raising? Is it embodied in a thesis statement? If so, is the statement appropriately strong?
5. What is the writer's point of view on the issue?
6. How does the writer connect with, separate from, or negotiate with the audience?
7. What appeal or combinations of appeals (to emotion, to status, or to reason) is the writer using? Which words or expressions are especially strong?
8. How does the status of the writer affect your reading?
9. Does the writer attempt to establish common ground with readers? If so, where and how? If not, should the writer have done so? Where and how?
10. Does the writer focus the essay with clear, specific, and relevant examples, images, quotes, or comparisons? Is the approach interesting?
11. Does the writer anticipate and address possible objections and resistances? If so, how?
12. How does the writer organize the essay? Discuss the title, the lead, the body, and the ending. Does the writer use deduction or induction?
13. Does the writer fall into any faulty reasoning? If so, name it.
14. Does this essay effectively convince you of its point of view? Why might it satisfy its purpose with other readers, or why might it not do so?
15. How would you argue for or against the position taken by the writer?

merce. Distribute what you write to people in your community, workplace, school, and wherever else is appropriate for your purposes. Be bold. Someone in power may respond as you wish. Write to become that person in power, yourself.

Explorations

1. *Together and Solo.*

   a. Compare and contrast Melanie Patel's two responses to incinerator pollution on pages 355 and 388–390. How do her purpose and anticipated audience affect the way she focuses, organizes, and makes her appeals?

   b. Compare and contrast Melanie's two pieces to Anna Maria Caldara's op-ed essay. How do Caldara's purpose and anticipated audience present a different challenge and therefore response from Melanie's?

   c. Read the essays at the end of this chapter. Choose what you consider to be the most effective or interesting one. Discuss what makes it so for you. Ideally, you and some of your classmates will disagree. This will provide you not only with an intellectual challenge but also with the opportunity to discuss how your choices reflect your particular points of view.

2. a. *Together.* Choose one reading to discuss in depth at a time. Use the questions in the sidebar on reading for power to guide your discussion.

   b. *Solo.* Write a letter in response to one of the writers that most affected you. What questions and suggestions would you offer the writer?

3. *Solo.*

   a. Write an essay in response to some idea that occurred to you while reading the essays in this chapter. It need not be on the same subject as one of the essays.

   b. Using your favorite reading in this chapter as a model for how to write for power, write or revise a paper of your own. Consider the questions in the sidebar on reading for power in regard to your own work.

   c. *Together.* Conduct a workshop using the sidebar on reading for power to discuss your papers. Revise accordingly.

READING FOR POWER

From *Dr. Death's Dreadful Sermon*

Peter J. Bernardi

Peter J. Bernardi, S.J., is a member of the religious studies faculty at Loyola University. He is the author of The Truth about Physician-Assisted Suicide.

Jack Kevorkian, M.D., a.k.a. "Dr. Death," pleads his case to legalize doctor-assisted suicide in front of a Sunday congregation at Saint Paul's Presbyterian Church in Livonia, Michigan. He is kicking off a ballot driver for a state constitutional amendment to secure this "right." The packed audience includes friends and relatives of most of the 20 people he has helped commit suicide since 1990 as well as the national executive director of the Hemlock Society, dedicated to suicide rights. The host pastor is an avid supporter.

Dr. Kevorkian implacably asserts what he sees as the bottom line: "the right not to have to suffer." "This is really a right that already exists, and we already have, but which we have to put in writing because of human irrationality. Every reasonable adult is going to have to realize that if he votes 'no' on this, he is throwing his right away."

Kevorkian's simple logic resembles the glare of a single unshaded light bulb hanging in a bare cell. The cell contains a solitary inmate in pain who wants to end it all. Once again, the complex texture of human life has been deceptively and insidiously reduced to the unthinking slogan, *right to choose.*

Who Greased the Slippery Slope?

Where have we heard this "reasoning" before? Derek Humphry, long-time activist for "suicide rights" and author of the recent bestseller *Final Exit* (a how-to-manual), was asked in an interview why the euthanasia movement had picked up momentum in recent years. (Since 1990, two referenda that would have legalized euthanasia were defeated in California and Washington by slim margins. Currently, euthanasia initiatives are also under consideration in Connecticut, New Hampshire, and Oregon.)

He responded that *Roe* v. *Wade* was the turning point. Even Derek Humphry, the high priest of suicide, notes the connection between the legal victory of abortion rights and the growing demand for suicide rights. For when the "right to choose" to kill unborn babies was enshrined in law, founded on the "right to privacy," the suicide-rights movement got new energy and legitimacy. A database search has turned up at least 34 termination-of-treatment cases that cite *Roe* v. *Wade.* The Circuit Court of Michigan in *Michigan* v. *Kevorkian* ruled that Michigan's statutory ban on assisted suicide was unconstitutionally overbroad because it interfered with the right to commit a "rational" suicide. The court relies heavily on *Roe*—which means there is a "slippery slope" leading from abortion rights to suicide rights.

"Slippery slope" is a moral argument used to oppose an action on the grounds that a principle is being conceded that has pernicious extensions and applications, perhaps not envisaged by its original proponents. Although the "slippery slope" argument can be misused, it is surely important to consider it: ideas and practices, after all, have logical consequences.

• • •

The suicide-rights lobby is trying to push us further down the slope. Once again the "hard" cases are trumpeted to attract sympathy, and the "right to choose" rhetoric is invoked as reason for legalization. Huge numbers of abortions have resulted from *Roe,* and it can hardly be alarmist to envision similar consequences if assisted suicide is legally based on the "right to choose." Just as most abortions now are no longer "hard case" but "lifestyle" abortions, so will the circle of candidates for assisted suicide inevitably increase.

• • •

White-Uniformed Professionals

Ultimately, the religious conviction that life is a gift from God that we are not free to end on our own terms is the most effective motive for remaining opposed to doctor-assisted self-killing. But what effect would that argument have on someone who does not believe in God?

It is possible, however, to argue against doctor-assisted suicide without using religious arguments. Reflective people ought to consider the "slippery slope" experience of abortion before they assent to Kevorkian's logic. The words Edmund Burke wrote in 1790 deserve reflection: "The effect of liberty to individuals is that they may do what they please: We ought to see what it will please them to do, before we risk congratulations, which may be soon turned into complaints."

If assisted suicide is legalized, then, in the not-too-distant future, clinics are going to open up in rather nondescript "professional" services buildings. Perhaps they will be adjacent to abortion clinics. In front of these clinics, orange-vested escorts with sympathetic faces will protectively shepherd their clients to the front door, keeping them at arm's length from those "anti-choice fanatics" who would question their "right to choose."

There will be suicide on demand, available in a clinically professional atmosphere where staff in reassuring, white uniforms are dedicated to your "choice not to suffer." One thing is certain: These staff persons won't have to deal with unsatisfied customers suffering from post-suicide trauma.

There will be a media campaign aided by linguistic censors to insure that religious "zealots" do not impose their moral categories. Euphemisms will be coined to eviscerate the moral content of assisted suicide. Humphry's euphemism "final exit" will not catch on. It conjures up the unfortunate "final solution." How about "termination-of-suffering" clinics, TSC's for short?

The suicide-rights lobby will keep the spotlight on liberation from unbearable suffering and on the right to choose. The secular media, claiming dedication to free speech, will suppress accurate information about the astounding breakthroughs in pain management and will largely ignore programs like hospice that offer support for the terminally ill.

The TSC's will network with nursing homes and organ-donor businesses. Indeed, Kevorkian favors an "auction" for the buying and selling of human organs. He considers the donation of organs one of the "positives" of assisted suicide.

Our society is indeed on a slippery slope. The "right to choose" is the slogan of the era. Morality has been made captive to such legality, and Dr. Kevorkian has a wide and sympathetic following. The culture of death bids fair to extend its domain.

R-Rated Child Abuse

Alvin F. Poussaint

Alvin Poussaint is a professor of psychiatry at Harvard University and has worked as a consultant for television shows.

The movie blazed with steamy sex scenes, bursts of gunfire and shouted obscenities. But the live drama in the row ahead of me, where a girl no more than 6 or 7 years old sat between her parents, was the real chiller.

At the sight of a character being shot in the face, the girl screamed in terror. Her comfort? The mother told her to "shut up" and gave her a stinging slap. After all, the audience had been asked in the pre-feature clips not to disturb others.

This was an R-rated film, which means that those under 17 must be accompanied by a parent or guardian. But the parental nonguidance I witnessed—not to mention the unsupervised, suspiciously baby-faced "17-year-olds" seated around me—showed how ineffective this system is in protecting kids.

No children under 13 should be admitted to an R-rated film, and theaters should be made to enforce the ban on unsupervised 13- to 17-year-olds.

Of course, the ratings system is run by the Motion Picture Association of America as part of an industry agreement to avoid Government oversight. But unless the association makes stronger rules and finds a way to hold theaters to them, Congress should give ratings the force of law.

Hollywood would likely balk at strong restrictions. The director Oliver Stone says that he allows his sons, 10 and 3, to watch such films because he feels that children can be taught to distinguish between reality and fiction. "I wouldn't want either of my children to see an obscene or dangerous movie they might not understand, unless I had the chance to explain it to them," he wrote in *Family Circle* magazine. But why would it ever be important for a 10-year-old to understand "obscene or dangerous" ideas meant for grown-ups?

Child development experts agree that there is no justification for making children "understand" adult films when the content is traumatizing. The American Academy of Pediatrics has found that repeated exposure to graphic sexuality and violence desensitizes children to violence and distorts their understanding of sexuality.

There is little society can do to protect that little girl in the theater from her parents' indifferences. But we can keep children from being exposed to what Dr. Victor Strasburger, the chief of adolescent medicine at the University of New Mexico, calls "electronic child abuse." Putting some teeth into the R rating would be a healthy start.

Fashionable Fascism

Richard Golsan

A professor of French at Texas A&M University who specializes in the history of fascism in France, Richard Golsan is editor of the book Fascism, Aesthetics, & Culture.

Is there a "fascism in us all, in our heads and in our everyday behavior," as philosopher-historian Michel Foucault once observed? Are we surrounded by images that draw their inspiration from a fascist aesthetics emphasizing a cult of virility, an obsession with primitive forms of purity, and an ideal of community based on a fraternity of "supermen"— a world from which women are excluded? Is fascism, as the German cultural historian Klaus Theweleit argues in his influential study *Male Fantasies*, merely the unbridled expression of male desire? One need not share the views of Foucault or Theweleit to recognize parallels between fascist art and contemporary advertising. Naked, muscular male bodies in heroic poses, raised above the level of everyday reality and aspiring toward the azure purity of the Ideal, recall the grandiose, larger-than-life figures of the official Nazi sculptor, Arno Breker, and the pristine images of the German Alps and Nazi athletes in the films of Leni Riefenstahl. The chiseled, jut-jawed faces of short-haired, impeccably groomed men standing side by side recall innumerable wartime propaganda posters for the German army and fascist youth organizations in occupied Europe. If fascism, as the Weimar-era critic Walter Benjamin asserted, was in essence an aestheticization of the political, then perhaps the legacy of fascism can be found in the inevitable politicization of the aesthetic.

Look in the pages of what we used to call fashion magazines. Naked bodies are everywhere, selling perfume. Perfume for her, cologne for him. The scent becomes the only piece of clothing on the otherwise naked body. There is often a disturbing neofascist glamour to the muscular, self-enclosed stolid figures.

Kenneth Clark, the eminent British art historian, distinguished between the "naked" and the "nude." The naked body is merely divested of clothes. The nude, on the other hand, is nakedness invested with social significance. The nude is an idea, an ideal, as in classical Greek art. The Chippendale's strip joints patronized by middle-aged women, on the other hand, specialize only in nakedness.

With nakedness has come a fetish for tattoos and for body piercing and theatrical muscles. People who undress in public suddenly display a need to clothe their bodies with cartoon designs or swirling lines, or the body is pierced or bejeweled, or at a Gold's Gym the body is loaded with layers and layers of muscle. It is as though Americans cannot stand our nakedness.

We yearn for clothing. We yearn for shadow, for secrets. The politicians in Washington tell us we yearn for family values. What politicians do not dare tell us is that the political life, by its very public nature, is unable to repair what ails us—the absence of a private life. Without a private life, we are surrounded in public by nakedness that, more and more, we do not bother to see.

America Has No Secrets Anymore

Richard Rodriguez

Best known for Hunger of Memory, *his memoir of growing up as a Mexican American, Rodriguez is an internationally acclaimed writer and lecturer.*

We have grown so accustomed to nakedness that we barely see the naked allure of the Calvin Klein ad on the side of the bus anymore. At a time when Americans have lost the gift of intimate life—embrace, secrets, touch—public exposure is all.

The other day I met a teenager, a street kid you'd call him. Seventeen years old, a boyhood in the projects, on the street by 11, living alone. He had no memory of ever being embraced. You hear comparable stories in the American suburbs. Children come home to large, empty houses to watch afternoon talk shows on which Americans tell secrets in public.

There are no secrets in America. There is only gossip. The love lives of Bill Clinton and Newt Gingrich. Hugh Grant on Sunset Boulevard. Roseanne told David Letterman the exact location of one of her private tattoos on late-night TV.

What was once the realm of the private has become only public. Several years ago, Madonna, the rock star made famous by her public reincarnations, appeared at the Cannes Film Festival wearing her underwear. It was a witty gesture, an ironic inversion appropriate to a time when celebrity is all, and there is no private life.

In large American cities and perhaps not so large ones, there are young people, gay and heterosexual, who have become citizens of the night. They frequent clubs and dance until dawn. They will tell you that promiscuity is easy. Sex with a stranger is easy. What is much harder for them to imagine is what they call "a relationship"—finding someone in bed in the morning.

---

*C*hapter Review _____

Solo or Together, respond to one or more of the following:

1. This chapter provides a variety of strategies for writing for power. Which five strategies do you believe are most important, and why?

2. What are you and your writing partners hoping to accomplish in writing for power?

3. Do you believe you will be successful in accomplishing what you set out to do in writing for power? Why or why not?

4. What more could you do in writing for power on your current project?

5. Which parts of this chapter do you anticipate reviewing in the future? Why?

Chapter **15**

Grammar and Style

This chapter offers opportunities to

—Develop *perspective* on grammar

—Experiment with *phrases* and *clauses*

—Connect sentences for *meaning* and *style*

—*Revise* fragments, run-ons, comma splices, and misplaced modifiers

—*Revise* for *pronoun and verb agreement*

—*Revise* your writing to comply with nonsexist academic and professional standards

> Grammar is a piano I play by ear.
> All I know about grammar is its power.
> —*Joan Didion, Fiction Writer*

> Learning to write is not a matter of learning
> the rules that govern the use of the semicolon
> or the names of sentence structures...
> it is a matter of making meanings.
> —*Ann E. Berthoff, Philosopher of Composition*

How to Use This Chapter

Here are some possible ways you can use this chapter:

1. Work through the whole chapter, doing selected Explorations as you proceed.

2. Focus on a particular point of grammar until you are satisfied that you understand it. Collect examples of it in your readings. Look for it in your writing. Focus on it when you consult with others during the writing process.

3. Go straight to the Explorations; if you get stuck, read what precedes them.

4. In a small group or solo, create a lesson on a particular point of grammar. Illustrate your lesson with examples you have collected, especially in your own writing and in the writing of other students.

5. Review Chapter 9, "Revising." Remember that you don't have to name every part of speech or every kind of grammatical usage in every piece of writing to write appropriately. However, if you have had difficulty with particular kinds of usage, it can be helpful to learn how to identify them by name in your own writing. Ultimately, as long as you learn to revise your own writing, whether or not you are a grammarian won't matter.

6. If you work with a computer grammar checker, identify patterns you need to change in your writing. Work with the portions in this chapter that address your concerns.

If you have used grammatical terms before, you may notice that, in some cases, this chapter uses different terms. For example, the word *and* is called a *connector* instead of a *conjunction. Connector* is a more common word that better describes what the word does. Words such as *however* and *therefore* are called *afterthoughts* instead of the more technical *conjunctive adverbs*, which can be confused with *connecting adverbs*. Charts will include traditional terms for those who are more comfortable with them.

Grammar, Purpose, and Audience

Grammar is a description of how the different parts of a language are organized. In some languages, the order in which you put words is not as important as it is in English. In English, there are vast differences in meaning between "She saw me through" and "She saw through me" or between "The dog bit John" and "John bit the dog." The differences are determined by the order and the relationships of the words—the grammar of the sentences.

What is considered "correct" grammar is determined by who is in power, who is teaching, and how people are currently using language in different situations. How the powerful speak and write is what will be taught to those who also want to be powerful in the same way. For example, it was much more fashionable at the turn of the century to write long, complex sentences in advertisements because people were used to reading and had the time and patience to do so. Read the following advertisement. Notice how long the sentences are:

> **Genuine Castille Emollient Soap for Ladies and Gentlemen.**   Within the boundaries of polite society, there are many ladies and gentlemen who prefer a soap that offers more amenities than those offered by the local general store. For this distinguished clientele that understands the advantages of a true emollient, we offer Genuine Castille Emollient Soap, imported directly to our Emporium, or to your local apothecary.

Radio, television, and other electronic mass media did not exist at the turn of the century. Today, written advertisements have to flash their messages much more quickly because people are used to instant visual messages. Therefore, advertisements are more likely to communicate today by short sentence fragments. The same advertisement, above, could be written this way:

> Castille soap. Natural and gentle. Back to basics. In finer stores everywhere.

More than likely, this ad would be accompanied by a picture or photograph that would imply a complete message. Or, if the words *Castille soap* appeared in places normally used for advertising—such as a billboard or on television—you would know that the implied message is "Buy Castille soap."

Sentence fragments are rarely acceptable in academic and professional writing (other than ads), partly because the messages in school and work are far more complex than just "Buy this today." Also, academic and professional writing is not normally accompanied by sufficient visual or audio aids to communicate complete messages, as advertising copy is.

Other forces, as well, determine what is considered correct grammar. If you come from a community that has historically had less political power, then your rules of how to use and organize language may not be favored by those who have more political power. As poet Robert Frost once said, "You can be a little ungrammatical if you come from the right part of the country." In other words, what is considered acceptable depends on who you are with and where you came from. In fact, the word *glamour*—which means "exciting," "ideal," or "glorified"—originally came from a mispronunciation of the word *grammar*. Teachers were the only people with advanced education in many communities. Grammar, and knowing rules of reading and writing, became associated with being the best, or the ideal. At some point someone heard the word *grammar* as *glamour*, and a new word was coined. The word *glamour* is now used to mean *ideal*. *

The grammars of spoken language are different from the grammars of written language, partly because gestures and tones of voice complete spoken but not written communication. Spoken language is often more economical than written language. For example, *ain't*, a word usually used in speaking, can mean "is not," "are not," "has not," and "have not." *Ain't* is a four-in-one word. However, *ain't* hasn't yet become acceptable in written language. Many other words and expressions are acceptable and very useful in spoken language but haven't yet been incorporated into most academic and professional writing.

This chapter outlines the elements of grammar as they are used in academic and professional communities today. How you speak and write in your home community (with friends and family) and the kinds of writing you see in advertisements, school, and the professions may be different—not better or worse in themselves.

Your Writing Style

Yet another factor in determining the grammar of a language is individual style. Style is like a fingerprint. In fact, some experts can identify who you are by the patterns they notice in your writing. But, unlike your fingerprints, your style can be developed and changed. So, as you write and experiment with writing, you may find your style changing for different purposes and audiences. There is no one right style, only different styles for different meanings.

Consider the differences between these three passages, which, in essence, use the same words but combine and organize them in different ways:

---

*William Safire discussed this word origin in his December 13, 1987, column, "On Language," in *The New York Times Magazine*. He, in turn, was citing W. V. Quine's book *Quiddities: An Intermittently Philosophical Dictionary* (Cambridge, Mass.: Harvard University Press).

A. Yes. I see your eyes. They well up in tears. You brush them aside. You use the back of your hand. You claim you have an allergy. I know you feel grief. Our president died.

B. Although you brush away your tears with the back of your hand, claiming that you have an allergy, I know that you feel grief because our president died.

C. Your grief at the death of our president is obvious to me. You can brush aside those tears and claim you have an allergy. But I know.

Reading these three passages, students first noted the difference in attitude each conveys. *A* is very businesslike. The eight sentences are short and seem, in this context, emotionally clipped. Except for the word *yes*, each sentence begins with a pronoun. The constant repetition of *you* is almost accusatory, making readers feel as if someone were jabbing a finger at them.

B seems much more compassionate because the one long sentence seems like a friend who won't let you go even though you feel too vulnerable to fully grieve. The word *although* and the *-ing* (participle) form of *claim* connect ideas and create an inviting flow.

C is less emotional than *B* but is not as cold as *A*. The three sentences combine ideas to soften the clipped quality of *A*. However, the sentence "But I know," coming as it does at the end and introduced by the connector *but*, seems to modify the focus on the *your* and *you*. Introducing the *I* seems to be a shift to compassion. If the comma were removed, it would be a shift to asserting that the person knows—a rebuff, in this context.

As you can see, the length of your sentences, what words you tend to use to begin sentences, and how you combine and punctuate ideas determine how you will be received by your readers and what purpose your writing will serve. Grammar is far more the creation of meaning than the following of arbitrary rules.

As you work with grammar, resist the temptation to settle for merely correct sentences. It is far easier to write short sentences with simple structures than it is to strive for more complex sentences that connect and interweave ideas in more meaningful and interesting ways. In the past, you might have resisted writing complex sentences for fear of making errors in grammar or punctuation. Know that if you are writing defensively, your readers will be able to tell, and you will weaken your presentation. Develop your mind by experimenting with different ways to combine ideas. By doing so you will participate in the most basic strategy of maximizing your intelligence. Remember the quote from Laura Silwones on page 29, "You have to try something harder to do better."

Understanding and developing skills that help you to use language for different purposes, audiences, and communities will empower you. You will gain the trust and confidence of more people and learn from them, in turn. Such flexibility in using language could even enable you to change others' ideas of what is grammatically acceptable. Remember, as you learn more about grammar, that *all* the elements of writing are meant to help you create meaning, express yourself, communicate with others, and get things done.

Developing Style

1. **a.** *Together.* Discuss your experiences with grammar, using the following suggestions and questions:

   - List words you would use to describe your previous experiences with grammar. Why would you use these words?

   - Are there cultural differences between how you speak English with friends and family and how you are expected to write for academic and professional purposes? What are some of the specific differences?

   - Do your experiences with grammar affect your perception of yourself as a writer? If so, how? If not, why not?

   - What reactions do you have to focusing on grammar now?

   - What do you hope to learn, specifically, by working with this chapter?

   b. *Solo.* Using insights developed in your discussion in Exploration 1a, write a letter to your instructor about your experience of grammar.

2. *Together and Solo.* Read the following examples and discuss which ones are standard academic, casual contemporary, or neither. With whom, when, where, how, and why would these expressions be appropriate? Revise those that are not standard and contemporary English into sentences that are. How do the meanings of the examples change as you revise them? In what situations would the nonstandard phrases be appropriate?

   a. Yes. I can understand why you feel that way. I really can.

   b. Having checked the catalog and the *Index to Periodical Literature*, she approached a reference librarian for assistance.

   c. Hungry am I.

   d. I mean, like, what 'm I s'posed to do, Miss?

   e. Whilst the spring doth come and the wind doth blow, thou wilt weep.

     f. Because she refused her position to concede, the council her rights removed.

3. *Together and Solo.* Discuss how the two sentences in each set differ in meaning:

     a. John cooked because Mary cleaned.
           Mary cleaned because John cooked.

     b. She saw me through.
           She saw through me.

     c. "John, won't you help me?"
           "John, you won't help me?"

     d. All dogs are animals.
           All animals are dogs.

     e. Should the bridge be mended, I will cross it.
           The bridge will be mended; I should cross it.
           The bridge should be mended. Will I cross it?

4. *Together and Solo.* Discuss the meanings of the following news clips, which can be read in different ways. Under some interpretations the sentences have unintended or humorous meanings because of word orders and omissions. Revise the sentences to make better sense.

     a. Droughts turn deer to crops.

     b. He was raised by his grandparents because his mother died in early infancy.

     c. Youths drink and rob baker.

     d. The town meeting talked garbage.

     e. Detective denies his suicide.

     f. Jury gets drunk driving case.

5. *Together.* List words and expressions that you or others use that are not acceptable in the academic or professional writing you have done. Define the expressions. Revise them so they sound more academic or professional to you.

PARTS OF SPEECH

To understand how language is organized, grammarians have analyzed and categorized words into different parts of speech. You probably learned to identify parts of speech in sentences. This section provides you with an overview of the most basic parts of speech. In addition, you will explore how different parts of speech affect your writing style.

The Purpose of Words

The sidebar presents you with a quick review of parts of speech. As you learn more about language and its subtleties, you will come to appreciate how much you already know. Here is a short discussion of the real-life purposes that nouns, verbs, and connectors serve.

> **Nouns.** The purpose of nouns is to help us to focus and slow down the rush of input. When we were young children, our caretakers helped us to focus on one part of the world at a time through naming. To name something is to have power over it. Although nouns help us to organize our experiences, they can load down a piece of writing that depends too heavily on them.

> **Verbs.** The purpose of verbs is to help us understand how elements of our world interact. They are about movement, action, and, in comparison, static states of being. To enliven your writing, favor verbs that vividly support your purpose. They are, by nature, more dynamic than nouns, pronouns, and adjectives.

Parts of Speech

Nouns (n): Names for persons, places, activities, things, e.g., *child, town, walking, pen*

Pronouns (pro): Noun substitutes, e.g., *she, whoever, themselves*

Adjectives (adj): Words that modify nouns and pronouns, e.g., *dazzling, red, legal*

Articles (art): Words that point to nouns, i.e., *a, an, the*

Verbs (v): Words for actions and states of being, e.g., *run, wonder, exist*

Adverbs (adv): Words that modify verbs, adjectives, and other adverbs, e.g., *slowly, next, there, only, why*

Prepositions (prep): Words that introduce phrases, e.g., *in, of, at*

Connectors (con): Words that join, e.g., *and, but, yet, while, which*

Interjections (interj): Words that exclaim, e.g., *yes, well, wow*

Connectors. Prepositions and conjunctions help us to understand the relationships between portions of our world and the ideas we project onto them. They provide us with opportunities to formulate more interesting and complex ideas about the world. Ultimately, they return us to a state where the world is complex again, as it was when, as infants, we could not filter out experiences; however, we return with an empowered sense of how to organize and control ideas.

The following Developing Style activities will help you to discover what your current choice of words indicates. Naming what you do is the first step to taking control of it.

*D*eveloping Style

1. *Together or Solo.*

   a. Turn a piece of lined paper sideways and write the nine parts of speech across the page on the red line. Under these headings, list the following words according to the parts of speech you believe they are. Test words in sentences if you are uncertain. Some words may belong under more than one heading.

one	inn	kind
lightning	because	gentle
light	without	purse
belonging	reflection	geography
lug	sold	near
magically	were	oh
outcry	make	pick
vault	only	

   b. Using a dictionary, add to these lists so there are at least ten words in each. The dictionary will offer abbreviations, such as the ones in the sidebar, to indicate which parts of speech a word can serve.

2. *Solo.* To become aware of the elements of your own writing style, use the questions and suggestions in the sidebar on page 414 to analyze something you have written.

3. *Together.* Using the instructions in activity 2, notice stylistic patterns in each other's writing. Revise your papers for more variety.

Style Notes: Analyze Your Writing

1. Which words do you repeat?

2. Do you tend to begin your sentences with certain words or parts of speech?

3. Are your sentences generally long or short?

4. Count up the words on a handwritten page (or half of a typewritten page). Mark what part of speech each word is, using the abbreviations in the list of the basic parts of speech in the sidebar on page 412. Count how many of each part of speech you have.

5. Do you use connectors?

6. Do you use more adjectives or verbs?

7. Do you often use forms of the verb *to be,* such as *am, is, was,* or *were?*

8. What parts of speech do you tend to use more than others?

9. What did you learn about your writing style?

10. What do you like about it?

11. What do you not like about it?

12. How could you develop your style for greater variety in parts of speech?

SENTENCES

Suppose you read the word *tree* in the middle of an otherwise blank page. A word written in such isolation has little meaning. You don't know why the word was written or what to make of it. To write, you need to know how to connect ideas into meaningful sentences. A sentence presents a *subject* for the reader to consider and a *verb* that tells the reader what to make of it, as in these two simple sentences:

> The tree stands alone.
> The tree is being removed.

Although you might not know which tree is being referred to, you start to understand why the word *tree* is written on the page. Meaning starts to develop. A sentence may also include phrases and other clauses that further modify (add to or change) its meaning.

Phrases

A *phrase* is a group of words that has a subject (a noun) but not a verb, or a verb (with or without an object) but not a subject. A phrase with a subject but no verb is started by a *preposition*. For example, *during the revolution* has a preposition and a subject but no verb. Prepositional phrases usually function as adjectives or adverbs, modifying the meaning of subjects, verbs, or objects in sentences. A phrase with a verb but no subject is started by the *participle* of the verb. *Fighting injustice* has a verb, *fighting,* and an object, *injustice,* but no subject. Verb phrases, when used as modifiers, usually function as adjectives.

Prepositional Phrases

Prepositional phrases are phrases introduced by prepositions, such as *at, below,* and *in.* Here are some well-known prepositional phrases:

After the fall	Between the acts
Into the woods	Of mice and men

Some of the most common prepositions are listed in the sidebar on page 416. Other phrases may be added to the simple sentences above to make them more meaningful:

> The tree stands in front of Town Hall.
> The tree is being removed from the lawn.

Some Prepositions

about	except	over
above	for	since
after	from	than
at	in	through
because of	inside	to
before	into	toward
below	near	under
between	next to	until
by	of	up
despite	on	with
during	out	without

Verb Phrases

A phrase may start with a verbal. A *verbal* is a form of a verb that is not used as the main verb in a clause. (Clauses are discussed on pages 420–428.) A verbal may be a present participle, a past participle, or an infinitive. If a phrase starts with a verbal, it is called a *verb phrase.*

The *present participle* is formed by adding *-ing* to the present tense of a verb. For example, *walking* is the present participle of *walk* and can introduce verb phrases such as *walking down the street* in the sentence "Walking down the street, the dog wagged its tail." Note that not all verbs ending in *-ing* introduce modifying phrases. Some verb forms ending in *-ing* function as nouns, as in the sentence "*Walking* is good for your health."

The *past participle* of *regular verbs* is formed by adding *-d* or *-ed* to the present tense. For example, *walked* is the past participle of *walk* and can introduce verb phrases such as *walked twice around the block* in the sentence "Walked twice around the block, the dog was satisfied." Notice that in the sentence "Walking down the street, the dog wagged its tail," the word *walking* refers to what the dog is doing. In the sentence "Walked twice around the block, the dog was satisfied," the dog is having something done to it: the dog is being walked.

The past participle of *irregular* verbs is not formed by adding *-d* or *-ed* to the present tense. The present participle of the irregular verb *stand* is *standing,* but the past participle is *stood.* Notice that in the sentence "Standing alone, the potted tree grew well in the sun," the word *standing* refers to what the tree itself is doing. In the sentence "Stood alone, the potted tree grew well in the sun," *stood* refers to what was done *to* the tree. To help you form verb phrases using past participles of irregular verbs, the sidebar on pages 418–419 presents a list of commonly used irregular verbs that includes the present tense, the past tense, and the past participle of each. If you are not sure of how to form the past participle of a verb, consult the dictionary. Unless it offers an irregular past tense or past participle, form the past participle by adding *-d* or *-ed.*

If *to* is followed by a verb in the present tense, *to* is not used as a preposition. *To* and a present tense verb together form an infinitive, as in this example: "Harry loves *to cook."* An infinitive may also be used as a noun, as in this sentence: "To cook is Harry's greatest joy."

*D*eveloping Style

1. *Solo and Together.* Collect twenty-five examples of prepositional phrases from *The Flexible Writer.* See if you can find at least one example for each of the prepositions listed in the sidebar on page 416.

2. *Together or Solo.* Form prepositional phrases with each of the words listed in the sidebar on page 416. To explore the meaning of the prepositions, use the word *tree* as the object. Notice how certain prepositions will not work with *tree.* For example, *between the tree* does not make sense because you need two objects with *between.* A more appropriate prepositional phrase would be *between the trees.* Add interesting adjectives to your phrases.

3. *Solo and Together.* Collect examples of verb phrases from a book you are currently reading for another class or purpose. Endeavor to find both present and past verb phrases.

4. *Together or Solo.* Form the present and past participles of each of the following verbs. If you are uncertain whether a verb is regular or irregular, consult the sidebar on regular and irregular verbs or a dictionary.

walk	break	be	type
draw	got	drive	burn

5. *Together or Solo.* Discuss each of the following groups of words. Which are prepositional phrases? Which are present tense verb

Some Regular and Irregular Verbs

Present Tense	Past Tense	Past Participle
am,* are, be,** is	was, were***	been
beat	beat	beaten, beat
become	became	become
begin	began	begun
bite	bit	bitten, bit
blow	blew	blown
break	broke	broken
bring	brought	brought
burn	burned, burnt	burned, burnt
burst	burst	burst
buy	bought	bought
catch	caught	caught
choose	chose	chosen
come	came	come
do	did	done
draw	drew	drawn
dream	dreamed, dreamt	dreamed, dreamt
drink	drank	drunk
drive	drove	driven
eat	ate	eaten
fall	fell	fallen
find	found	found
fly	flew	flown
forget	forgot	forgotten, forgot
get	got	gotten, got
give	gave	given
go	went	gone
hang (suspend)	hung	hung
hang (execute)	hanged	hanged
has, have	had	had
hear	heard	heard
hide	hid	hidden
hurt	hurt	hurt

Present Tense	Past Tense	Past Participle
keep	kept	kept
know	knew	known
lay (put)	laid	laid
leave	left	left
let (allow)	let	let
lie (recline)	lay	lain
ride	rode	ridden
ring	rang	rung
rise (get up)	rose	risen
run	ran	run
say	said	said
see	saw	seen
set (place)	set	set
shake	shook	shaken
sing	sang	sung
sit (be seated)	sat	sat
sleep	slept	slept
speak	spoke	spoken
stand	stood	stood
steal	stole	stolen
strike	struck	struck, stricken
swear	swore	sworn
take	took	taken
teach	taught	taught
throw	threw	thrown
wake	woke, waked	woken, waked, woke
wear	wore	worn
write	wrote	written

*Normally, *am* is used only with *I* as in *I am* in academic and professional writing.

**Normally, *be* is not used as a singular or plural verb in academic and professional writing. However, *being* is often used as a present participle.

***When verbs are formed with helping verbs such as *is, are, was, were, been, had, has, have, do, does, get,* and *got,* they are followed by either the present or the past participle as in *is forming, is formed,* or *have been forming* and *have been formed.* Note that other than the simple past tense, past tenses are formed with the past participle.

phrases? Which are past tense verb phrases? Which are infinitives? Which are none of these?

a. To the park

b. To go swimming

c. Swimming in the pond

d. Walked across the field

e. Because of walking

6. *Together or Solo.* Choose a paper you are currently writing, and circle the prepositional and verb phrases. Discover your writing style by using the questions in the sidebar titled Style Notes: Phrases. Revise your paper, either reducing or increasing the number of phrases you use. Challenge yourself by introducing the past participle of some irregular verbs. Discuss how these changes affect your purpose and audience appeal.

Clauses

A clause is constructed of a subject and a verb. Every sentence is a clause, but not every clause is a sentence. Only an *independent clause*, containing a subject and a verb, is a sentence. A *dependent clause* also has a subject and a verb, but a dependent clause functions as an adverb, an

---

Style Notes: Phrases

To analyze your use of phrases, first circle the prepositions and participles in one of your papers. Then ask the following questions:

1. Do you favor certain prepositions?

2. Do you tend to string prepositional phrases one after another?

3. Do you use too many or too few prepositional phrases?

4. Do you use present tense participles to introduce phrases?

5. Do you use past tense participles to introduce phrases?

6. How could you introduce more variety and meaning into your writing with prepositional and verb phrases?

Challenge yourself to introduce more variety and meaning into your writing with verb phrases. Experiment with prepositions and participles that you tend not to use.

adjective, or a noun. An adverb, an adjective, or a noun cannot function independently of a sentence. The meaning of a dependent clause *depends* on the main or independent clause into which it is incorporated.

Independent Clauses

An independent clause has two elements: a subject (what the sentence is about) and a verb (what the subject does, is, or has done to it). The verb may stand alone; or the verb may have an object, as, for example, the word *ball* in the sentence "Sam threw the ball." All sentences are or contain independent clauses. What makes a sentence a sentence is that it carries a *complete* message. Only a sentence that contains an *independent clause* is a sentence, because as its name implies, it stands alone.

A sentence can be as short as one word, as in the sentence "Write." *You* is the implied subject, and *write* is the verb. An independent clause with no attached dependent clauses is referred to as a *simple sentence*. The end of a sentence is marked by a period, a question mark, or an exclamation point—appropriately called *end marks*. Sometimes a word or a couple of words will be followed by an end mark without being a sentence. For further discussion of such "sentences," refer to pages 493–495.

Here are two *simple* sentences:

The diseased elm trees were removed from Linwood.

Trees in the neighboring towns were stricken with Dutch elm disease.

Trees are the subjects in these sentences; *were removed* and *were stricken* are the verbs.

A *compound sentence* is composed of two or more sentences connected by a comma *and* a sentence connector such as one of those in the sidebar on page 422. The two sentences above can be joined into a compound sentence by using a comma and a sentence connector:

The diseased elm trees were removed from Linwood, **but** trees in the neighboring towns were stricken with Dutch elm disease.

It is important that you choose the sentence connector that best expresses your meaning. If the word *so* were used in the compound sentence above, it would mean that the trees in neighboring towns became diseased *because* the trees were removed from Linwood. But the trees were removed *to save* neighboring trees. The sentence joined by *but* means that they became diseased *even though* the sick trees in Linwood were removed. Choose your sentence connectors carefully to create sentences that say what you mean.

CONNECTORS AT A GLANCE

Sentence Connectors

(Coordinating Conjunctions)

and	for	or	yet
but	nor	so	

Afterthoughts

(Conjunctive Adverbs)

accordingly	furthermore	likewise	then
also	hence	moreover	therefore
besides	however	nevertheless	thus
consequently	indeed	otherwise	
finally	in fact	so	

Connecting Adverbs

(Subordinating Conjunctions)

after	because	since*	when
although	before	so that	whenever
as	even though	than	where
as if	if	though	wherever
as long as	in order that	unless	whether
as soon as	rather than	until	while

*The expression *being that* is sometimes used to mean *since* or *because*. Normally, *being that* is not used in academic and professional writing.

Connecting Adjectives

(Relative Pronouns)

that	whom
which	whose
who	

Connecting Pronouns

how	which	whomever
that	whichever	whose
what	who	why
where	whoever	
whether	whom	

Although in the past grammarians did not deem it acceptable to start a sentence with a sentence connector, such as *and* or *but,* it is no longer considered "wrong" to do so. But it's up to you. Your choice will depend on the effect you want to make on your readers.

Afterthoughts. Sometimes an independent clause will follow another independent clause to which it is closely connected. But instead of using a sentence connector, you can use words that signal *afterthoughts.* Such words are listed in the sidebar on page 422. Here are some examples of pairs of independent clauses; the second clause in each pair is an afterthought. Notice that the two sentences contain semicolons and that a comma follows the afterthought word:

> The diseased elms were removed from Linwood; nevertheless, trees in the neighboring towns were stricken with Dutch elm disease.

> The trees in the neighboring towns were stricken with Dutch elm disease; indeed, it did no good to remove the elms from Linwood.

Dependent Clauses

A *dependent clause* contains a subject and verb and is introduced by a word that connects it to an independent clause. Dependent clauses contain ideas that are dependent on, or not as central as, the independent clauses to which they are attached. There are three kinds of dependent clauses: *adverbial, adjectival,* and *noun.* A sentence that contains a dependent clause is called a *complex sentence.*

Adverbial Clauses. Adverbial clauses contain ideas that are dependent, or not as central, as the independent clauses to which they are connected. Adverbial clauses help to change or modify the meaning of the main, independent clause. *Adverbial clauses work like adverbs because they answer the questions when, where, how, and why.* They tell you something is happening, has happened, or will happen. They begin with connecting adverbs such as those listed in the sidebar on page 422.

These are some examples of adverbial clauses:

> Even though the diseased elm trees were removed from Linwood

> If you want a reliable compact convertible

> Wherever there are children at risk

Notice that these clauses do not carry a complete message. When you read one of them, you look for the rest of the sentence. The rest of the sentence would be the independent clause.

Adverbial clauses can be written at the beginning, the middle, or the end of a sentence. For example, you could incorporate the first adverbial clause above as follows:

1. *Even though the diseased elm trees were removed from Linwood,* trees in the neighboring towns were stricken with Dutch elm disease.
2. The trees in the neighboring town were stricken with Dutch elm disease, *even though the diseased elm trees were removed from Linwood* and the neighboring trees were far away.
3. The elm trees in the neighboring towns were stricken by Dutch elm disease, *even though the diseased elm trees were removed from Linwood.*

Where you place the adverbial clause is determined by what you want to emphasize. You will usually start your sentence with the point you want to emphasize. Because sentence 1 starts with the fact that trees were removed, that is the emphasis of the whole sentence; sentence 2 emphasizes the trees in the neighboring town because those trees are mentioned at the beginning and the end of the sentence; and sentence 3 emphasizes that the trees were stricken with Dutch elm disease.

How you modify or change the meaning of your main, independent, clause will be determined by the connecting adverb that you use. If, for example, you used the word *because* instead of *even though* in sentence 1, the whole meaning of the sentence would change.

Because the diseased elm trees were removed from Linwood, trees in the neighboring towns were stricken with Dutch elm disease.

This version of the sentence states that the trees in the neighboring town were stricken with disease *because* the trees were removed from Linwood. Unless the removal process itself transferred the disease, this sentence doesn't make sense in this context.

Adjectival Clauses.   Adjectival clauses contain ideas that are dependent on the independent clauses to which they are attached. *Adjectival clauses function as adjectives because they modify the nouns in sentences.* Adjectival clauses begin with connecting adjectives such as those listed in the sidebar on page 422. These are some examples of adjectival clauses:

who inspected the trees

that would spread Dutch elm disease

Notice that these adjectival clauses are incomplete. When you read them, you look for the rest of the thought. The rest of the thought would be the independent clause. For clarity, place the adjectival clause as close as possible to what it explains. For example, notice how the adjectival clauses above are embedded in the following sentence:

> Mary, who inspected the trees, ordered the removal of the stricken trees that would spread Dutch elm disease.

If the adjectival phrase were placed much later, it would confuse readers:

> Mary ordered the removal of the stricken trees that would spread Dutch elm disease, who inspected the trees.

This sentence implies that Dutch elm disease, itself, had inspected the trees. That's absurd.

Remember that *who* is used to refer to persons, *that* is used to refer to persons or things, and *which* is used to refer only to things or events.

Noun Clauses. Noun clauses contain one of the connecting pronouns listed in the sidebar on page 422 and a verb. Noun clauses are dependent clauses because they cannot stand alone. A noun clause functions as a noun—a subject or an object that must be incorporated into an independent clause by a verb.

Here are some examples of noun clauses. Remember, the connecting pronoun transforms the whole clause into one noun:

Whoever owns an elm tree

That they couldn't save the trees

Read alone, these noun clauses are not meaningful. They must become either a subject or an object in an independent clause (a sentence):

Noun Clause as Subject:

Whoever owns an elm tree knows it may be stricken.

That they couldn't save the trees was a tragedy.

Noun Clause as Object:

They notified whoever owns an elm tree.

They knew that they couldn't save the trees.

Sentence Variety

If every sentence you wrote were short and started with the word *the,* your style would become choppy and boring for your readers:

> The storm started at 3:00. The rains were heavy. The forecasters were warning drivers. The drivers were swamped. The flash flooding swamped the drivers. The rescue squads were swamped too.

Compare this choppy report to its revised version:

> The storm, starting at 3:00, produced such heavy rains that despite the forecasters' warnings, not only drivers but rescue squads who were on the scene were swamped by flash flooding.

This sentence connects ideas and shows how they are related to each other. Notice some of the connecting devices:

Style Notes: Sentences

To analyze your sentence style, first circle the connectors (refer to the sidebar on page 422, which lists them). Then ask the following questions:

1. Do you tend to write short or long sentences?
2. Do you use sentence connectors? Which ones?
3. Where in your sentences (beginning or middle) do you tend to write sentence connectors?
4. Do you write sentences with afterthoughts? Which afterthought connectors do you use?
5. Do you use connecting adverbs? Which ones?
6. Where in your sentences (beginning or middle) do you tend to write connecting adverbs?
7. Do you use connecting adjectives? Which ones?
8. Where in your sentences (beginning or middle) do you tend to write connecting adjectives?
9. Do you use connecting pronouns? Which ones?
10. Where in your sentences (beginning or middle) do you tend to write connecting pronouns?

Challenge yourself to introduce more variety and meaning into your writing with sentence and clause connectors. Choose some connectors that you tend to avoid, and incorporate them into your next essay.

Verb Phrase: starting at 3:00

Prepositional Phrases: at 3:00, despite the forecasters' warnings, by flash flooding

Adjectival Clause: who were on the scene

The revised sentence is far more meaningful because it communicates how the author connects events. In your own writing, endeavor to use a variety of phrases and dependent clauses to connect and weave ideas into interesting sentences. Sentence connectors; connecting adverbs, adjectives, and pronouns; and participles and prepositions allow you to combine sentences to introduce meaning and variety into your style.

*D*eveloping Style ———————————————

1. *Together and Solo.* Identify which of the following groups of words is an adverbial clause, an adjectival clause, a noun clause, a sentence, or some combination of these. Start by circling prepositions and connectors. Add punctuation to complete sentences.

   a. Enduring the tedious conversation long enough, Cynthia finally fell asleep

   b. After the peace talks concluded

   c. Whoever finds it in his or her best interest

   d. Who you are often depends on who you know

   e. Because she refused to concede her position

   f. Approved for release, the prisoner spent the last night in prison distributing presents

2. *Together and Solo.* Here is an opportunity to practice writing dependent clauses. Choose words from the lists of nouns and verbs below. Feel free to add your own. Write serious clauses or humorous ones.

Nouns	**Verbs**
dust	wind (wound)
man	dive (dove)
courage	take (taken)
child	watch
bus	swirl
coin	go (gone)
coffee	reach

(continued)

Nouns	Verbs
freedom	forgive (forgiven)
watch	clear
wind	excuse

    a. Referring to the list of connecting adverbs on page 422, write five dependent clauses.

    b. Referring to the list of connecting adjectives on page 422, write five dependent clauses.

    c. Referring to the list of connecting pronouns on page 422, write five independent clauses.

3. *Together and Solo.* Combining the clauses you wrote in activity 2, write five interesting sentences. Experiment with sentence variety and meaning.

4. *Solo and Together.*

    a. To identify your style, review one of your own papers using the sidebar titled Style Notes: Sentences.

    b. Revise your paper so that you have a greater range of clauses and kinds and lengths of sentences.

    c. Discuss how your meaning changes with these revisions.

Parallel Construction (‖)

In order to show your reader that you consider certain ideas to be equally important, organize them into similar or *parallel* grammatical structures. If, for example, one of your ideas is expressed in a prepositional phrase, and all the other ideas you have to express are equally important, express all the ideas in prepositional phrases. Notice what happens in the following two sentences:

Marlene went to the dry cleaner, the drugstore, and the bakery.

Marlene went to the dry cleaner and to the drugstore, and then she went to the bakery.

In the first sentence, because all of Marlene's stops are expressed using an article-noun structure ("the _____"), the bakery is no more or less important than any other stop Marlene made. In the second sentence, the bakery is clearly a reward for having done her errands. All the other stops take a preposition-article-noun structure, but the bakery deserves a whole independent clause.

Using parallel structures provides you and your reader with a sense of order and *balance*. Notice how parallel structures are used in the following well-known expressions:

Parallel constructions	**Nonparallel constructions**
To be or not to be: that is the question.	To be or having lost your existence: to have that question.
I came; I saw; I conquered.	I came; there were things to see; victory was soon mine.
All's well that ends well.	If something ends well, all went fine.
A penny saved is a penny earned.	A penny saved is someone earning money.
A time to love, a time to hate; a time of war, and a time of peace.	A time to love, having been hated; to have time for war; you should want peace sometimes.

*D*eveloping Style

1. *Together and Solo.* Compare each nonparallel expression above to its original. To help you identify structures, circle words, punctuation, parts of speech, and phrase and clause structures that repeat. How are the meanings of the nonparallel expressions different? Which of each of the two expressions is more memorable? Why?

2. *Together and Solo.* Read the following expressions. What parallel structures are being used? To help you identify structures, circle words, punctuation, parts of speech, and phrase and clause structures that repeat.

    a. What did you do? Why did you do it? What will you do next?

    b. Having exhausted the medical supplies, having lost all the equipment, having tried all possible procedures, the doctor finally quit.

    c. Fireworks, barbecue, clear sky, ice cream, family, and friends— what more could we ask for on the Fourth of July?

    d. When chickens read and pigs fly, I'll organize my files.

3. *Together and Solo.* Listening to song lyrics, and noticing what you read, collect examples of parallel structures.

4. *Together and Solo.* Review your own papers for parallel structures. Mark problems with parallel structure with the symbol ||. Revise them for greater balance.

5. *Solo.* Challenge yourself to write some sentences that incorporate parallel structures. Review the examples offered on page 429 and in activity 2 as models. Then use the following structures to start:

   a. To _____ or to _____

   _____ .

   b. I_____ I _____I_____

   c. _____ ? _____ ? _____?

   d. Having_____ , having _____ , having , _____

   _____ , _____ .

PROBLEM SENTENCES

In academic and professional writing, most sentences must be complete and unified. Groups of words that are supposed to be sentences but don't meet these standards are called *fragments, run-ons,* or *comma splices.*

Fragments (frag)

Fragments are incomplete sentences. They usually come in the form of words, phrases, or dependent clauses punctuated with end marks—periods, question marks, or exclamation points—as if they were sentences. The following fragments are examples of phrases punctuated as sentences:

Prepositional phrases

In the garden.
During the operation?

Verb phrases

Spinning the wheel!
Dragged through the swamp.
Including these.

In some cases, transitional phrases signal fragments, as in these examples:

In some cases, dependent clauses.
For example, the money he stole.
Not to mention her lung capacity.
To be sure, ten dollars.

The following dependent clauses are examples of fragments. Their connecting words do not connect them to independent clauses.

Adverbial clauses

Because the experiment had not been properly designed?
Even though there were many arguments in favor of the defendant.

Adjectival clauses

Who had been inoculated against rubella.
Which was the first time the region had been explored!

Noun clauses

How you present yourself.
That the storm had passed over!

In some instances, single words can be correctly punctuated with end marks, as in the case of one-word answers to questions or a series of short questions. Strictly speaking, however, these words are not sentences:

Did they attempt to help the endangered seals? *No.*
Who was helping Carmen? *Mary? Kyomi? Jacob?*

A group of unpunctuated words can be long and still be a fragment. Even a long group of words can be missing an independent clause:

Whoever explored the region for the first time and was confronted with the spectacle of the snowcapped mountains after the arduous climb in dangerous terrain.

How would you complete the sentence?

Fragments may make your readers work too hard to understand you. Readers may give up because they are confused, or they may actually mis-read your intent. Fragments can also give your work a choppy, uncon-nected quality that may undermine your purpose. Revising fragments will help you to clarify what you want to say and to establish a better rela-tionship with your readers.

Identifying Fragments

The first step in revising fragments is to identify them. Use the following strategies to help you. Mark fragments with the word *frag.* If in the begin-ning you can't identify fragments in your own work, consult with others to help you to develop your skills.

Strategy 1.   *Check short sentences.* Do they start with prepositions, participles, or connectors? Do they start with transitional phrases such as *for example* or *not to mention?* If so, go to strategy 3 or 4.

Strategy 2.   *Read the paper aloud, front to back. Stop at every end mark*—period, question mark, or exclamation point. Exaggerate the stop. Notice if that breaks the connection between ideas. If so, go to strategy 4 or 5.

Strategy 3.   *Read the paper aloud, back to front.* To test your whole paper for fragments, read it starting with the last sentence and then read the sentence before it, and so on, until you have read the whole paper from back to front. *Circle* the first word of any series of words that does not complete a thought or make sense when read separately from what precedes and what follows it.

Strategy 4.   *Circle initial prepositions, participles, and transitional phrases* that start "sentences." Are these groups of words fragments? Consult with others to establish whether you tend to start fragments with certain prepositions, participles, or transitional phrases. If you do, regularly monitor the "sentences" that start with such words. Circle the words. Go to strategy 6.

Strategy 5.   *Circle initial dependent clause connectors.* Often, writers who write fragments tend to fall into a pattern of beginning fragments with dependent clause connectors such as *although* or *because* (connecting adverbs), *which* or *that* (connecting adjectives), or *whoever* or *that* (connecting pronouns). Notice whether you tend to write fragments that consist of dependent clauses starting with these words. If you do, read through your papers for fragments that start with these words. Circle the first word of these fragments.

Strategy 6.   *Review sentences by marking subjects and verbs.* If a series of words does not have both a subject and a verb, it cannot be an independent clause.

*D*eveloping Style

Together or Solo.   Read the following student paragraph. Using the strategies offered above, identify fragments.

```
     If only I could sleep. In the bedroom alone. I want to
hide from the world. In and out of the kitchen. In and out
of the bathroom. I'm wandering. Help! Agoraphobia. For exam-
ple, when I have to go to the store. I can't do it. I live
```

on deliveries and catalogs. Shop from the shopping channel.
Safe. Since I have a computer and a phone. My job is making
sales calls. But now I'm getting scared of making calls.
Help!

Revising Fragments

Once you have identified a fragment, you can revise it using one of the
following strategies.

Strategy 1.   *Delete the fragment.* Sometimes a fragment is a remnant
of an undeveloped thought or a typo. Delete any fragments that don't add
to the quality or readability of your writing.

Strategy 2.   *Give nouns verbs.* If your fragment is just a noun or
noun clause without a verb, give it a verb. This subject has no verb:

Fragment: The best dog in the show

Here a verb combines with the subject to form a sentence:

Sentence: The best dog in the show was trained by a ten-year-old
girl.

This noun clause has no verb:

Fragment: Whoever goes to the Fashion Institute of Technology.

This can be revised into a sentence by adding a verb:

Sentence: Whoever goes to the Fashion Institute of Technology *must
cope* with Manhattan's transportation system.

Or the noun clause can be added to a subject and a verb that needs an
object:

Sentence: The transportation system serves whoever goes to the
Fashion Institute of Technology.

Strategy 3.   *Give verbs and verbals subjects.* If your fragment is a
verb or verbal without a subject, revise it by giving it a subject:

> *Fragment:* Walked in the park.
>
> *Sentence:* Jeremy walked in the park.
>
> *Sentence:* Walked in the park, the dog was happy.
>
> *Fragment:* Including the garage fees.
>
> *Sentence:* Including the garage fees, the bill came to $300.

Strategy 4. *Connect phrases to sentences.* If your fragment is either a prepositional or verb phrase and the fragment is next to an independent clause, turn the end mark either preceding or following the phrase into a comma. Depending on which sentence it should be linked to, finish the sentence. In the following example, the strings of words starting with the participle *Accumulating* and the preposition *To* are fragments because they are only phrases. *The ice choked the region* is a sentence.

> *Fragments and Sentence:* Accumulating for thousands of years. The ice choked the region. The dinosaurs flourished. To the south.

Full sentences can be formed from this example by attaching the phrases as follows:

> *Sentences:* Accumulating for thousands of years, the ice choked the region. The dinosaurs flourished to the south.

Strategy 5. *Delete connectors or participles.* Sometimes you can create an independent clause (a sentence) just by deleting a connector or participle. In the following example, the strings of words starting with the participle *Accumulating* and the connecting adverb *While* are fragments:

> *Fragments and Sentence:* *Accumulating* for thousands of years. The ice choked the region. *While* the dinosaurs flourished to the south.

Full sentences can be formed by deleting the participle and connecting adverb. Note that the resulting prepositional phrase *for thousands of years* is added to the sentence *ice choked the region.*

> *Sentences:* For thousands of years, ice choked the region. Dinosaurs flourished to the south.

Strategy 6. *Connect fragments to sentences.* If your fragment is a dependent clause, and if it is either preceded or followed by a complete sentence, you can connect the fragment to one of the sentences. Depending on the sense you want to make, turn the period *preceding* or *following* the dependent clause into a comma. Here are three sentences. The clause starting with *Because* is a fragment; it is only an adverbial clause.

> The colleges sponsored a tennis tournament. *Because there were so many injuries.* They hired a sports doctor to coach the players.

If you attach the fragment to the preceding sentence, it will read as follows:

> The colleges sponsored a tennis tournament *because there were so many injuries.* They hired a sports doctor to coach the players.

The first sentence now states that the colleges sponsored a tennis tournament because there were so many injuries. That's silly. Tournaments are not sponsored because of injuries. This is what happens if you attach the fragment to the sentence that follows it:

> The colleges sponsored a tennis tournament. *Because there were so many injuries,* they hired a sports doctor to coach the players.

The second sentence now states that a sports doctor was hired because there were so many injuries. This makes sense. Whenever you attach a fragment to a complete sentence, make sure it appropriately expresses your meaning and purpose.

*D*eveloping Style

1. *Together and Solo.*

    a. Read the following advertisements and texts from product labels that use words, phrases, and dependent clauses as if they were sentences. Identify the fragments in each example. Circle prepositions, verbals, and connectors to focus your work. Turn the examples into complete sentences by deleting words, adding your own, or reorganizing. Use connecting adverbs, adjectives, or pronouns to add variety and meaning to your revisions. How do the meanings change? Would your revised versions satisfy the purpose of the advertisements? If so, with which audiences? If not, why not?

        1) How gender plays a role in the roles we play. The season premiere of *Our World* shows how gender affects how we see ourselves. How others see us. How it shapes our human identity. How do gender roles evolve? Are they a privilege? Or a prison?

2) Alaska. Where the bald eagles soar above your head. Where whales dive and otters splash right before your eyes. Alaska. If not now, when?

3) Sun-dried grapes. Because anything less is a compromise.

4) A Viking masterpiece. Wrought of tempered steel. 24K gold. Sterling silver. Hand-set crystal handles.

5) Well tolerated by most highly allergic individuals. No tablet binders, coatings, or colorings. Daily dose: one tablet with each meal.

6) Financial aid available. If you are eligible.

7) Wherever. Whoever. Whenever. Lion's Limousines.

b. Bring magazines to class and find advertisements that use words, phrases, or dependent clauses as if they were sentences. Revise the advertisements so that they are written in complete sentences.

2. *Together.*

a. Sometimes the best way to break a habit is to overdo it: eating too much chocolate or smoking too much at once can make you sick of chocolate or smoking. If you tend to write fragments by using dependent clauses as if they were sentences, this activity will help you to become aware of this tendency and to break the habit. In small groups, write a very long sentence fragment using a series of dependent clauses started by adverbial connectors. (Refer to the sidebar on page 422.) The goal is to write the longest sentence fragment without finishing it with an independent clause. An example of such a long fragment may sound like this:

> After the first frost encrusts the ground, when the ground starts to thaw, before the April rains fall, if you plan to grow leafy vegetables, as soon as you can, whenever it's a warm day...

Be sure to write dependent clauses and not just phrases. Recall that some words function as prepositions or connecting adverbs, depending on whether or not they are followed by a subject and verb.

b. Write these group fragments on the board and discuss whether they contain any independent clauses that finish the sentences. Write independent clauses that would turn the long fragments into sentences.

3. *Together or Solo.* Identify fragments in the following practice paragraphs:

a. People not having certain things taken care of. Concerns me to a great deal. Because I am a citizen of this city. If the people of the city have to deal with uncomfortable things. Like incinerators. That belch smoke and dirt. Every day makes me choke. Taxes paid.

   b. Photosynthesis is basic. To plant growth and development. Because there is no sun. That's why some plants don't green up. About fungi. Different processes.

   c. Women in the workplace. Because they don't have power. That's why they don't get promoted. Only men at the top. If you try to succeed. That's when they transfer you. Or they let a newcomer get ahead.

   d. The place I find significant. Where I enjoy spending my time is the Franklin Mall. I was totally confused. Because I didn't know the place. And it is huge. Walking in the mall. That's what I liked the best. Especially in the food area. Whatever you wanted. They had everything.

4. *Together or Solo.* Revise the paragraph filled with fragments on pages 433–434 and in activity 3. Strive to use as many of the strategies as you can. Use your imagination to add variety and interest to the resulting sentences.

5. *Solo and Together.* Identify fragments in your own papers and mark them *frag.* Revise them into complete sentences. Discuss how the meaning of your paper changes and clarifies with these revisions.

Run-ons

Technically, run-on sentences are two or more independent clauses that have been punctuated as if they were all one sentence. No connectors or punctuation marks are used to distinguish clause from clause. Some sentences, although they seem to run on and on—using a string of connectors—are *psychological* run-ons. The following sentence is a psychological and *not* a technical run-on:

> Because Harry was so determined to stuff and bake the turkey himself, Tania, who has always wanted him to follow his passion for cooking, promised to do all the shopping and cleanup to give Harry the support he needed during a busy season at his job, when otherwise he would have been too pressed to do all the usual shopping himself.

Because run-ons make it difficult to know where one sentence ends and another begins, they can confuse the reader. Read the following run-on sentence:

> John loves to run some other runners don't.

On first reading the sentence, you might read that John is running runners, the way a boss can run workers. By the time you read through the

PROBLEM SENTENCES AT A GLANCE

Fragments

A fragment is a nonsentence word group punctuated as if it were a sentence. Fragments can take these forms:

Noun	Transitional phrase
Verb	Adverbial clause
Prepositional phrase	Adjectival clause
Verb phrase	Noun clause

Identifying Fragments

If you tend to write fragments, notice if there are particular words with which you tend to start them. These ideas can help you identify fragments:

1. Check short sentences.
2. Read the paper aloud, front to back. Stop at end marks.
3. Read the paper aloud, back to front.
4. Circle initial prepositions, participles, and transitional phrases.
5. Circle initial dependent clause connectors.
6. Review sentences by marking subjects and verbs.

Revising Fragments

1. Delete the fragment.
2. Give nouns verbs.
3. Give verbs and verbals subjects.
4. Connect phrases to sentences.
5. Delete connectors or participles.
6. Connect fragments to sentences.

Identifying Run-ons and Comma Splices

1. Read the paper aloud. Do not stop for a breath unless there is an end mark.
2. Circle internal pronouns.
3. Mark subjects, verbs, and connectors.
4. Circle commas.
5. Distinguish technical from psychological run-ons.

Options for Revising Run-ons and Comma Splices

1. Add end marks.
2. Add sentence connectors.
3. Place semicolons between independent clauses.
4. Create afterthoughts.
5. Introduce a connecting adverb, adjective, or pronoun.

line, you realize that there are two separate thoughts. So you have to reread from the beginning of the line. Readers soon tire of having to reread and organize your words for themselves. Furthermore, run-on sentences make your writing seem cluttered or rushed. Readers will not want to spend any more time on your work than you do. But *just because a sentence is long doesn't mean that it is technically or even psychologically a run-on.* This long sentence is not a run-on:

> The research lab at the top of the hill is so hard to see from the bottom because it is behind the hill, which is thick with trees and shrubbery.

However, *even a short sentence can be a run-on,* as in this example:

> Run don't walk.

Punctuate the example so that it won't read as a run-on.

Comma Splices (CS)

A special form of run-on is the comma splice. Comma splices are two or more independent clauses that have been punctuated as one sentence with only commas between them. The word *splice* is used, as in the splicing together of tape or film. Here is an example of a comma splice:

> Maya Angelou has written several volumes of poetry, *Just Give Me a Cold Drink of Water 'Fore I Diiie* was the first and appeared in 1971.

In this example, the comma should be a period, because *Maya Angelou has written several volumes of poetry* is an independent clause and so is the clause that follows it.

One of the most common patterns of comma splices occurs in sentences that begin with pronouns, as in the following examples:

> Teenage pregnancy is a growing epidemic, *it* concerns me a lot. My parents worked hard to raise us, *they* never even complained.

These comma splices are to be distinguished from pronouns that follow a dependent clause, as in these correctly punctuated sentences:

> Because teenage pregnancy is a growing epidemic, *it* concerns me a lot. Although my parents worked hard to raise us, *they* never even complained.

Identifying Run-ons and Comma Splices

Consulting with others will help you to develop and sharpen your ability to identify run-ons and comma splices. Use the following strategies to help you.

Strategy 1. *Read the paper aloud. Do not stop for a breath unless there is an end mark*—period, question mark, or exclamation point. If you tend to write run-ons, have someone read your papers to you. Sometimes this will be enough to help you identify run-ons. Then go to strategy 3.

Strategy 2. *Circle internal pronouns.* A common way to create a run-on comma splice is to use a series of pronouns, as in the following example:

> He was not an unhappy child, *he* was content to care for his younger brothers, *he* cooked and mended their clothing, *he* created bedtime stories.

If you tend to link clauses that start with pronouns without using a sentence connector—*and, but, for, nor, or, so, yet*—between at least the last two of the clauses, circle the pronouns that are subjects in your paper. Write the symbol *CS* above commas that splice independent clauses together.

Strategy 3. *Mark the subjects, verbs, and connectors.* Determine which parts of sentences are dependent and independent clauses. Then, mark any sentences that run independent clauses together as if they were only one sentence. Mark them with the symbol *RO*.

Strategy 4. *Circle commas.* Read each segment that is marked off between commas or between a comma and an end mark. If the segment is an independent clause, if it is not connected to other sentences by a sentence connector, or if there are no dependent phrases or clauses attached to it, you have a comma splice. Analyze the example in strategy 2, using this system.

Strategy 5. *Distinguish technical from psychological run-ons.* Striving for variety and complexity in your sentence structure can help you to develop your mind and earn your readers' respect. Don't artificially shorten or break up psychological run-ons unless they are also technical run-ons, or confusing or boring to readers.

Developing Style

Together or Solo.   Using the strategies offered above, identify run-ons and comma splices in the following first draft by student Roy Smith. Distinguish psychological from technical run-ons.

> I am writing about my fiancée, she is the youngest in her family, she always had people there for her, doing things for her, like making decisions for her, solving all her problems, and that was because they would always think she wasn't able to make her own decisions or solve her own problems. Her parents were very loving and caring, she was always protected by them, in reality she was never alone.
>
> When my fiancée turned 15 years old, her mother passed away, she died of cancer, it was very painful for my fiancée. After that happened she moved in with her sister, and continued attending school. As the years passed by, she would talk to her family about getting her own apartment, a new car, finishing college, and getting her life going on her own, but she was surrounded by criticism, family members would always tell her, you can't manage on your own, it's too hard and you'll never make it, because you were never alone, there was always someone there for you, helping you out. Then they would tell her, it would be a waste of time for her to even try, because she would just end up back home. So that in turn made her stop and think about everything, it made her afraid of going out and getting what she really wanted in life, which was being an independent person, and having things of her own.

Revising Run-ons and Comma Splices

How you revise a run-on will depend, as it does for revising fragments, on your meaning and emphasis. Choose from the following four revising strategies.

Strategy 1.   *Add end marks.* Place a period, question mark, or exclamation point (depending on the purpose of the sentence) at the ends of your independent clauses. The following sentence is a run-on. Place a period where you believe one of the sentences ends.

> The Pilgrims and Puritans fled to New England to escape religious persecution some of them persecuted those who didn't share their beliefs.

Strategy 2.   *Add sentence connectors.* Place a sentence connector— *and, but, for, nor, or, so, yet*—between independent clauses. The run-on above can be revised as follows:

> The Pilgrims and Puritans of New England sought to escape religious persecution, *but* some of them persecuted those who didn't share their beliefs.

The comma has been added to separate the two long sentences, helping the reader distinguish the two ideas. The sentence connector *but* not only removes the run-on, but it also creates a much stronger statement. The word *but* provides a transition and meaningful link between the two sentences, showing an ironic contradiction in the behavior of some of the Pilgrims and Puritans. The word *but* shows that the writer objects to the behavior of the Pilgrims and Puritans who persecuted others.

Sentence connectors can be used with a series of parallel sentences, as well. One way to revise the comma splice from above is as follows:

> He was not an unhappy child. He was content to care for his younger brothers, he cooked and mended their clothing, *and* he created bedtime stories.

The sentence connector *and* is placed between the last two sentences. The preceding commas function like the word *and* when the connector is thus added.

Strategy 3.   *Place semicolons between independent clauses.* The word following the semicolon is not capitalized unless it is a proper noun. The run-on above can be revised as follows:

> The Pilgrims and Puritans of New England sought to escape religious persecution; some of them persecuted those who didn't share their beliefs.

The semicolon separates the two independent clauses while showing that the two ideas are closely related. This version does not imply the judgment made when the word *but* linked the two clauses.

Strategy 4.   *Create afterthoughts.* Create a transition between independent clauses by placing a semicolon after an independent clause, followed by an afterthought word and comma. (Refer to the sidebar with afterthought words on page 422.) The run-on above can be revised as follows:

> The Pilgrims and Puritans of New England sought to escape religious persecution; however, some of them persecuted those who didn't share their beliefs.

The semicolon divides the two sentences while showing that the ideas are linked. The word *however* emphasizes and clarifies the nature of the connection being made between the ideas. The comma following *however* causes the reader to pause briefly and thus notice the emphasis even more. Notice that this version also implies a judgment about the Pilgrims and Puritans.

Strategy 5.   *Introduce a connecting adverb, adjective, or pronoun to make one clause depend on the other.* If necessary, change the order of clauses. Reword portions of the sentences. In some cases, use commas to mark off clauses. Notice how the meaning changes when a connector is introduced and clauses are reordered:

Connecting adverb

Although the Pilgrims and Puritans fled to New England to escape religious persecution, some of them persecuted those who didn't share their beliefs.

Connecting adjective

Some of the Pilgrims and Puritans *who* fled to New England to escape religious persecution in turn persecuted those who didn't share their beliefs.

Connecting pronoun

Some of the Pilgrims and Puritans who fled to New England to escape religious persecution in turn persecuted those who didn't share their beliefs.

*D*eveloping Style

1. *Together and Solo.* Using the five strategies offered above, revise the following run-on comma splice in five different ways. Discuss how the meanings of these five versions change and vary.

   He was not an unhappy child, he was content to care for his younger brothers he cooked and mended their clothing, he created bedtime stories.

2. *Together and Solo.* Read and identify which of the following sentences are run-ons or comma splices. Mark them *RO* or *CS*. Revise run-ons and comma splices in at least three ways. How do the meanings change?

   a. While Mark didn't agree with the verdict, he respected the legal procedures that led to it.

   b. Julius Caesar crossed the Rubicon, he said there was no turning back.

   c. O'Keeffe painted skulls and other bones suspended in the sky most people find her work to be haunting.

   d. Music relaxes the mind, soul, and body tempo is the most important factor in its effect.

   e. I'm not going to let my coach down since she has been there to help, I'm going to try my best, because I want to show her that her help matters, and that's what I'm most concerned about now.

3. *Together or Solo.* Sometimes the best way to break a habit is to overdo and tire of it. This strategy helps you to become more aware of the nature and effects of the habit. In small groups, write a paragraph in which you create as many run-ons and comma splices as possible. Include some sentences that are correct. Then present your paragraphs to another group to identify and revise run-ons and comma splices. Compare your paragraphs and the variations in meaning that result from sentence problems.

4. *Together or Solo.* Revise the paragraph filled with run-ons and comma splices on page 422. Strive to use as many of the revising strategies as you can. Use your imagination to add variety and interest to your resulting sentences. How do the changes affect meaning and audience appeal?

5. *Together and Solo.* Identify run-ons and comma splices in your own and others' papers. Mark them with the appropriate symbols, *RO* or *CS*. In small groups or solo, revise these papers so that the sentences are effectively separated. Use a variety of strategies to break up run-ons. Discuss why you chose to revise as you did and how the revisions changed and clarified meaning.

Misplaced Modifiers (mod)

Modifiers are words and groups of words that modify or change the meaning of what you write. The simplest modifiers are adjectives, adverbs, and prepositional phrases. More complex modifiers are verb phrases and dependent clauses. When using a modifier, you should place the modifier as close as possible to what it is modifying, so that you will avoid confusing your reader. Also, if you misplace a modifier, you may find yourself unintentionally saying something humorous. For example, read the following sentence, which has a misplaced adjectival clause:

> The child was put to bed by his father who was crying and fretting with fatigue.

Of course, a father can be reduced to tears from fatigue. But the sentence above sounds humorous. The author most likely meant to say the child was crying and fretting from fatigue. Because the word *who* is closer to *father, who* sounds as if it were modifying *father* and not *the child*.

Be especially careful with verb phrases. The first subject that follows the verb phrase is what the verb phrase is modifying, as it does in the following sentence:

> Wrapping the broken vase in cloth, *Leslie* found the missing piece inside.

If the sentence had been written as follows, it would be illogical:

> Wrapping the broken vase in cloth, the missing piece appeared inside.

What this sentence implies, since *missing piece* is the first thing that follows the phrase *wrapping the broken vase,* is that the missing piece, itself, was wrapping the broken vase. That, of course, is absurd.

Similarly, the sentence would be confusing if the verb phrase followed the independent clause, *Leslie found the missing piece inside.*

> Leslie found the missing piece inside, wrapping the broken vase.

This implies that the missing piece, again, is wrapping the broken vase. Putting the verb phrase right next to Leslie would be more appropriate:

> Leslie, wrapping the broken vase, found the missing piece inside.

This sentence clearly states that Leslie, and not the missing piece, is wrapping the broken vase, because *wrapping* is right next to Leslie.

*D*eveloping Style

1. *Together and Solo.* Read the following sentences and identify modifying clauses and phrases. Discuss what the sentences imply. If a sentence is confusing or unintentionally humorous, revise it. In some cases, you can do this by moving the modifiers so that they are closer (or as close as possible) to what they modify.

   a. The swimming pool is very near our house, which is pleasant in hot weather.

   b. Running the risk of losing their jobs, the toys were being made on the factory premises by the workers for homeless children.

    c. Many people enjoy skiing having lived in Colorado.

    d. Proved to be effective, the town adopted the new water filtration system.

    e. The deer was injured by a car which jumped over the pasture fence.

    f. The coach lost the sixty pounds which improved his health tremendously.

    g. Same Day Laundry will not tear your clothes in machines, which we do carefully by hand.

2. *Together and Solo.* Sometimes the best way to break a habit is to overdo and tire of it. This strategy helps you to become more aware of the nature and effects of the habit. In small groups, create your own confusing or humorous sentences with misplaced modifiers. Include some sentences that are correct. Then present your list to another group to identify and revise misplaced modifiers. Compare your sentences and the variations in meaning that result from misplaced modifiers.

3. *Together and Solo.* Review your own papers for problems with misplaced modifiers. Mark these problems *mod* and revise for clarity.

AGREEMENT

Subjects and verbs must agree in number (both are singular, or both are plural). Pronouns must agree in number and person (first, second, or third) with the people, places, or things to which they refer. As you will see, problems with agreement can confuse readers and defeat your purpose. In this section, you will have an opportunity to review and refine your skills with subject-verb and pronoun agreement so that you can fulfill your purpose and engage your audience.

Subject-Verb Agreement (S-V)

Singular subjects take verbs with singular endings, and plural subjects take verbs with plural endings. Create subject-verb agreement with verbs in the present tense and subjects that don't end with -*s* in the singular, by adding an **-*s*** or **-*es*** to **either** the subject or the verb **but not both.** For example, notice where the -*s*'s are in the following sentences:

> The dog walk**s**.   (singular subject and verb)
>
> The dog**s** walk.   (plural subject and verb)

Notice that irregular verbs follow this pattern as well:

> The book ***is*** lost.   (singular subject and verb)
>
> The book**s** are lost.   (plural subject and verb)
>
> The horse ha**s** won.   (singular subject and verb)
>
> The horse**s** have won.   (plural subject and verb)
>
> The tower do***es*** not stand anymore.   (singular subject and verb)
>
> The tower**s** do not stand anymore.   (plural subject and verb)

The singular subject *dog* does *not* end with an added -*s*; therefore, the verb ends with an added -*s*. The plural subject *dogs* ends in an added -*s*; therefore, the verb does *not* end with an added -*s*. The same holds true for subjects and verbs that normally end with -*s* in their basic form, as for example the nouns *class* and *harness* or the verbs *pass* and *press*. The only difference is that -*es* is added to one or the other. Notice where the **-s'**s or **-es'**s are added in the following sentences to maintain subject-verb agreement:

The class pass**es**.   (singular subject and verb)

The class**es** pass.   (plural subject and verb)

The class walk**s**.   (singular subject and verb)

The dog pass**es**.   (singular subject and verb)

Some plural nouns are not formed by adding -*s* or -*es*. They include these irregular plurals:

Singular	Plural
child	children
curriculum	curricula
datum	data
deer	deer
foot	feet
goose	geese
she, he, it	they
louse	lice
moose	moose
mouse	mice
person	people
woman	women

Treat them as you would other plural words. Do not add the -*s* or -*es* to their verbs:

The children walk to school.

The five deer pass along the highway.

The people do not accept the new government.

Most plural subjects are created either by adding *-s* or *-es* to the singular form. Another way to form plural subjects is to join subjects with *and*. *An apple and a pear* is a plural subject and would take a plural verb (without an *-s* or *-es*) such as *make* in the sentence *An apple and a pear make a healthy lunch.*

Some subjects *seem* to be plural but are treated as singular, especially in academic and professional writing. These are *collective* nouns; pronouns formed with *any, every, no,* and *some;* and constructions using *each, either,* and *neither.* The rest of this section details how to identify and create subject-verb agreement with these singular subjects.

Collective Nouns.   Collective nouns refer to groups of things and are considered to be singular units. These nouns apply to more than one thing but take a singular verb (with an *-s* or *-es*). These are called *collective nouns.* The following nouns are examples of subjects that would take a singular verb:

class	family	school
college	flock	society
committee	government	team
community	group	tribe
company	herd	world
faculty	jury	

Here are examples of how to match such collective nouns with singular verbs in the present tense. *Don't be distracted by phrases with plural objects that precede the verb.*

The committee of doctors meets every week.

The team of players *is* going to win every game it plays.

The society makes its own rules.

Any, Every, No,* and *Some.   Some pronouns sound as if they should be treated as plural constructions but are treated as singular constructions in academic and professional writing. These pronouns are created by combining a word from the left column below with a word from the middle column.

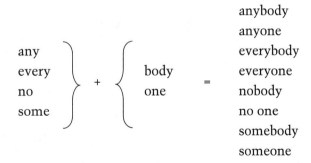

All these words, from *anybody* to *someone*, take a singular verb (with an added *-s* or *-es*). An easy way to remember that words such as *everybody* and *everyone* take a singular verb is to notice that *body* and *one* are singular. Here are examples of how to match singular verbs in the present tense with these constructions. *Don't be distracted by phrases or clauses with plural objects that precede the verb.*

Every**one** in the groups **is** working well with others.

Any**body** who knows those dances go**es** to that club.

Each, Either, and Neither.   *Each, either,* and *neither* are used with singular verbs (with an added *-s* or *-es*). Here are examples of how to match singular verbs in the present tense with these words. *Don't be distracted by phrases with plural objects that precede the verb.**

Either of the newspapers give**s** a forecast.

Each person writing the television scripts **is** a professional.

Neither Maria nor Sam do**es** well with aspirin.

To Be, To Have, and To Do.   Be especially aware of subject-verb agreement when you use forms of the verbs *to be, to have,* and *to do.*

---

*Note that although *and* between two or more subjects creates a plural subject, *or* or *nor* between two or more subjects does not. When *or* implies that only one or the other subject applies, then use a singular verb. For example, *An apple or pear is used in the cobbler* implies that only one fruit and not the other will be used.

VERBS AT A GLANCE

Present Tense of To Be *(Present Participle:* Being*)*

	Singular		Plural	
	Subject	*Verb*	*Subject*	*Verb*
1st person:	I	am**	We	are
2d person:	You	are	You	are
3d person:	He, she, it, or singular noun	is	They or plural noun	are

*Normally, *be* is not used as a singular or plural verb in academic and professional writing. However, *being* is often used as a present participle.

**Normally, *am* is only used with *I* as in *I am* in academic and professional writing.

Present Tense of To Have *(Present Participle:* Having

	Singular		Plural	
	Subject	*Verb*	*Subject*	*Verb*
1st person:	I	have	We	have
2d person:	You	have	You	have
3d person:	He, she, it, or singular noun	has	They or plural noun	have

Present Tense of To Do *(Present Participle:* Doing*)*

	Singular		Plural	
	Subject	*Verb*	*Subject*	*Verb*
1st person:	I	do	We	do
2d person:	You	do	You	do
3d person:	He, she, it, or singular noun	does	They or plural noun	do

These verbs are the most basic verbs in the English language and are used in all forms of writing by all communities. As Chapter 11 shows, language variations mark out different communities. Because forms of *to be,* *to have,* and *to do* are so widely used, you have to be especially flexible in

Verb Forms

Present Tense	Past Tense	Past Participle	Present Participle
cook	cooked	cooked	cooking
ring	rang	rung	ringing

Basic Tenses

Past Perfect (Earliest event; before other past events)	Perfect (Done up until now)	Past (Done)	Present (Now)	Future (To come)	Future Perfect (To be completed)
had cooked	has (have) cooked	cooked	cook	will cook	will have cooked
had rung	has (have) rung	rang	ring	will ring	will have rung

Progressive Tenses (continuous actions or conditions)

Past Perfect	Perfect	Past	Present	Future	Future Perfect
had been cooking	has (have) been cooking	was (were) cooking	is (are) cooking	will be cooking	will have been cooking
had been ringing	has (have) been ringing	was (were) ringing	is (are) ringing	will be ringing	will have been ringing

adjusting your use of them as you move from one cultural setting to another. Notice that the verbs for third person singular all end in *-s: is, has, does*. Refer to the sidebar on page 452 when you are revising your work for subject-verb agreement.

*D*eveloping Style

1. *Together and Solo.* Circle the subjects and verbs in the following sentences, and discuss whether the subjects and verbs agree in number, according to academic and professional standards:

   a. The committee need funds in order to study the fiscal crisis.

   b. Every person has to account for his or her own output.

   c. An apple and a pear keeps the doctor away.

   d. He want to apply to dental school within the next three years.

   e. The very idea that electricity can cause cancers seem ridiculous to some people.

   f. Neither of the teams want to lose.

2. *Together and Solo.*

   a. Using the list of collective nouns, write a variety of sentences in which the subjects are collective nouns and the verbs are in the present tense.

   b. Using the list of words formed with *any, every, no,* and *some,* write a variety of sentences in which the subjects come from the list and the verbs are in the present tense.

   c. Using the words *each, either,* or *neither* as subjects, write a variety of sentences in which the verbs agree in number with the subjects.

   d. Write a variety of sentences in which you use the present tense singular forms of *to be, to have,* or *to do.* For a challenge, use subjects recommended in activities 2a through 2c.

3. *Together and Solo.* Circle the subjects and verbs of sentences in one of your papers. Discuss whether the subjects and verbs agree. If they don't, mark them *S-V.* Revise any sentences in which the subjects and verbs don't agree.

Verb Tense Consistency (V-C)

Study the timelines offered in the sidebar on verb forms, which show you how different verb tenses are formed to indicate when something occurred. The first timeline shows the basic tenses. The second timeline shows how to form verb tenses that indicate activities or conditions in progress. A regular verb, *cook,* and an irregular verb, *ring,* are used as illustrations. Notice that all but the present and past tenses are formed by use of participles. The timeline for basic tenses uses the *past participle.* The timeline for actions in progress uses the *present participle.* (Refer to pages 416–420 for a discussion of how to form participles. The sidebar on pages 418–419 shows some irregular verbs.)

Provide your reader with a clear sense of when things happen. Unless you are very clear in your transitions, do not shift from one verb tense to another within or between sentences and paragraphs. Notice how confusing the following sentence is:

> I walk through the door and talked to the coach who will be standing by the equipment.

The sentence starts in the present tense with the verb *walk,* quickly shifts to the past tense with the verb *talked,* and then shifts to the future with *will be standing.* It would be much clearer if the verbs agreed in tense so that all were in the present tense or all were either in the past or future. Read the following examples, which are consistent in tense:

Present tense

> I *walk* through the door and *talk* to the coach who *is standing* by the equipment.

Past tense

> I *walked* through the door and *talked* to the coach who *was standing* by the equipment.

Future

> I *will walk* through the door and *will talk* to the coach who *will be standing* by the equipment.

*D*eveloping Style _____

1. *Together or Solo.* Read the following paragraphs of Ben Burton's essay, "The Gym." Notice that it is written in the present tense. Circle and revise all the verbs into the past tense. How does this change the tone and meaning of the essay? Which version do you prefer, and why?

The Gym

I raise my arm, grasp the handle, and pull open the door. When I or anyone else enters the gym, everyone temporarily stops doing what he or she's doing to see who it is.

The air is cold, stale, and stagnant. The smell of sweat slaps you in the face as you take your first breath. You hear the hum of several fans straining to circulate the thick air, and the clanging of weights. At times the gym sounds like a zoo full of animals, with everyone grunting, groaning, and some screaming to get in that last burning repetition.

I make my way to the counter and stumble over a piece of slightly torn blue carpet. I look at the tan walls and notice a new picture of some guy I don't know. I throw down my belt on the poorly made wood counter. Making a large thud, it attracts the attention of my friend Bob.

Bob, who manages the gym in the morning and afternoon sessions, is always up for a good conversation about lifting and is always eager to give advice. I sit down next to him on an old plastic crate, and without fail, he starts a conversation. This time it is about one of the most commonly talked-about subjects in the gym: steroids--drugs that are worshipped in the gym because of the incredible size and strength results they can help produce. He informs me of a new oral drug that has come out on the black market, but I disappoint him when I tell him I already heard of it. So, with the conversation ended, I decide to go lift.

2. *Solo.* Write a paragraph, entirely in the present tense, describing how you arrived at a given destination today. This paragraph will give your readers the feeling that they are moving through the day with you.

3. *Solo.* Write a paragraph, entirely in the past tense, describing the most memorable occasion you experienced last year.

4. *Together.* Discuss the paragraphs you wrote in activities 2 and 3. Focus on whether you were consistent in your use of verb tenses.

5. *Together and Solo.* Review your papers in process for consistency in verb tense. Circle all your verbs, and look for any shifts that could confuse your audience. Mark distracting shifts *V-C.* Revise your work for verb tense consistency.

Pronoun Agreement (pro)

A pronoun holds the place of a noun and refers to it. Sometimes it is not clear to whom or what a pronoun refers, especially in written English. The added challenge is to make sure that number, gender, and case agree as well. In this section, you have opportunities to explore and practice pronoun agreement for reference, number, case, and gender.

Pronouns and Reference

The *referent* of a pronoun is the noun that comes before the pronoun to which the pronoun refers. In the following sentence, *environmentalists* is the referent of the pronoun *they.*

> Environmentalists may ask us to do more work than we are used to, but they are our guides for preserving the planet.

Sometimes it is not clear what the referent of a pronoun is. For example, in the following sentence, *her* can apply to more than one person:

> Marilyn told Janet that her promotion was approved.

The pronoun *her* can refer to Marilyn, or Janet, or even another person. Sometimes the context will resolve the confusion. Often it will not. The example above could be clarified by revision. In this case, Janet was promoted:

> Hearing that Janet's promotion was approved, Marilyn called her to report the good news.

In this case, Marilyn was promoted:

> Relieved that the committee had approved her for promotion, Marilyn felt free to tell her friend Janet.

Pronouns, Number, and Case

Pronouns must agree in number with the person, place, or thing to which they refer. Pronouns must also be in the proper case—subjective, objective, possessive, or reflexive—depending on the role they play in the sentence. Refer to the sidebar on page 458 as you consider these issues.

If a construction is singular—a singular noun; a collective noun; forms of *any, every, no, some, either, neither,* and *each*—any pronoun that refers to that construction must be singular too. (Refer to pages 450–454 for a review of singular constructions.) Notice that the pronouns in the following sentences are all singular because they are referring to singular constructions. Notice, as well, that they are subjective, objective, possessive, or reflexive, depending on what role they play in the sentence.

Unless **John** excels on the entrance exam, **he** will not be able to enter the college of **his** choice.

The **faculty, itself,** decided to waive **its** salary increase so that no one would be fired.

Nobody wants to make up **his** or **her** mind on the issue.

Each woman chose **her** own specialty in the engineering class.

Neither of the doctors told us how **she** or **he** wanted to proceed with the treatment.

Someone on the men's swimming team had neglected to practice **his** backstroke.

The Four Cases of Pronouns

	Subjective		Objective		Possessive		Reflexive	
	Singular	*Plural*	*Singular*	*Plural*	*Singular*	*Plural*	*Singular*	*Plural*
1st	I	We	Me	Us	My/Mine	Our/Ours	Myself	Ourselves
2d	You	You	You	You	Your(s)	Your(s)	Yourself	Yourselves
3d	He	They	Him	Them	His	Their(s)	Himself*	Themselves*
	She	They	Her	Them	Her/Hers	Their(s)	Herself	Themselves
	It	They	It	Them	Its	Their(s)	Itself	Themselves
	One	Ones	One	Ones	One's**	Ones'	Oneself	—
	This	These	This	These***	—	—	—	—
	That	Those	That	Those***	—	—	—	—

*Normally, *hisself* and *theirselves* are not used in academic and professional writing.

**Notice that *one's* and *ones'* are the only possessive pronouns formed with apostrophes.

***Note that *this* and *that* are singular pronouns and *these* and *those* are plural. When used as adjectives, they must agree in number with nouns and verbs.

Pronouns that refer to plural nouns must be plural, as well:

> The *members* of the faculty decided to waive *their* salary increases so that no one would be fired.
>
> The *women* chose *their* own specialties in the engineering class.
>
> The *doctors* told us how *they* wanted to proceed with the treatment.

Pronouns and Consistency (P-C)

Provide your reader with a clear sense of whom or what you are talking about by being consistent with your use of pronouns. Do not shift back and forth from first person *(I)* to second person *(you)* or third person *(he, she, one,* or *it)*. Notice how confusing the following sentence is:

> If *one* considers the amount of time it takes to grow a tree, *you* feel a sense of responsibility toward the use of paper.

The sentence starts with the general pronoun *one* and then shifts to *you*. Your reader would expect *one* again, and so *you* is jarring (especially since *you* could be addressing the reader).

A more subtly confusing shift in pronouns occurs when you use the second person *(you)* when you are really talking about yourself. This is a habit that some people have when talking in person. The character Radar in the television program *M*A*S*H* had a tendency to use the word *you* in this way:

> You feel bad when your mother is having trouble on the farm and you're thousands of miles away and you can't do anything about it.

Radar, himself, was the one whose mother was having trouble. He, himself, was feeling frustrated.

In writing, be direct. Use *I* if you are speaking for yourself. For example, I could say, "You would hope that this example is clear" when actually it is more accurate to say, "I hope that this example is clear." Also, if you use *you* in your writing, be sure that you are addressing your reader directly. Do not use the second person *you* form when it would be more accurate to use the third person.

Pronouns and Sexism (P-Sx)

Language embodies gender differences. English retains remnants of old sexist beliefs. Starting with the end of the nineteenth century, we have

Style Notes: Nonsexist Language

Avoid sexism in your writing by adopting these strategies:

1. Refer to both sexes.
2. Order for balance.
3. Use plural forms instead.
4. Focus on ideas, activities, states of being, or things.

made strides in establishing equal rights for both sexes. But there is more to do. In writing, you can avoid sexism by paying close attention not only to what you write but also to how you use pronouns that refer to gender. Here are several strategies.

Strategy 1. *Refer to both sexes.* You may have noticed that in some examples in this book *he or she, his or her,* and *him or her* are used. In the past, only the masculine form of the pronoun was used, as in *Each person received his diploma.*

Strategy 2. *Order for balance.* You may also have noticed that this book does not comply with the customary order of always referring to the male gender first. Always putting the male gender first in such expressions is sexist. Create a balance by sometimes reversing the order. Use *she and he, her and his, her or him* as well. Of course, if everyone being referred to is female, use the feminine pronouns. Likewise, if everyone being referred to is male, use the masculine pronouns. If you find that your writing is overburdened with constructions such as *he or she,* use one of the following strategies.

Strategy 3. *Use plural forms, instead.* If you are referring to people in general, use the plural form. Instead of writing "A teacher is frequently asked for **his** or **her** ideas," write "Teachers are frequently asked for **their** ideas."

Strategy 4. *Switch from focus on persons to focus on ideas, activities, states of being, or things.* Instead of writing "A teacher is frequently asked for her or his ideas," write "A teacher's ideas are frequently sought." In the second version, the subject of the sentence is not *teacher* but *ideas*.

*D*eveloping Style

1. *Together and Solo.* Circle the pronouns in the sentences below and draw arrows to their referents. Discuss the following for each:
   - Do the pronouns agree in number, person, and case with their referents?
   - Are the pronouns consistent?
   - Do the pronouns agree in number?
   - Are the pronouns in the correct case?
   - Are the pronouns free of sexism?
   a. When Brenda was in New York visiting her sister, she took her to the theater quite often.
   b. When you take first-year English, they have to be prepared to learn how to write term papers.
   c. Everybody got their coats and left.
   d. Each of the men brought his proposal to the meeting.
   e. Because the Hungarians were so charming and hospitable, my friend and I enjoyed visiting it.

2. *Solo and Together.*
   a. Listen for examples of people using *you* when they mean to speak about people in general, or when they are indirectly speaking about themselves. Record as much as you can of what they say. Share these examples in class.
   b. Identify instances in your writing in which you use *you* not to address the reader but to speak in general or about yourself. Revise the papers to comply with standards of academic and professional writing.

3. *Together and Solo.* Revise the following sentences to remove any sexism. However, be careful not to remove appropriate gender distinctions. Make sure your pronouns agree in number, person, and case and that the referents are clear.
   a. When a doctor treats a patient, he must respect his right to refuse certain treatments.
   b. If a parent has to stay home with a sick child, she must have the opportunity to make up the time at work.

    c. A person who breastfeeds knows the satisfaction of giving his or her baby the best start in life.

    d. The average person knows more about what celebrities think than his locally elected officials.

    e. The president of the United States must be aware of his or her responsibilities as Commander in Chief.

4. *Together and Solo.* Following the instructions in activities 1 to 3, discuss your own work. Circle your pronouns. Mark problems with *pro, P-C,* or *P-Sx.* Revise your papers for pronoun agreement, reference, consistency, and nonsexist language. Discuss how your revisions affect meaning and audience appeal.

BLOOPER RULES OF GRAMMAR

Read the following "Blooper Rules of Grammar" that ask you to do what they don't do themselves. Revise the rules so that—although they will be less funny—they won't contradict themselves.

1. Each verb agree with its subject.
2. A pronoun agrees with their referent.
3. Don't never use no double negatives.
4. Everyone should use standard grammatical structures in their papers.
5. Using parallel structure, or not to use it, is your decision.
6. A fragment.
7. Comma splices are run-ons, run-ons are not always comma splices.
8. Having an important effect on meaning, you should always place the subject right after the verb phrase.
9. One must not shift your point of view.
10. When you write about a professional, do not be sexist in your treatment of him.
11. Run-on sentences ask your reader to absorb too much at once you should avoid using them besides they are hard to end.
12. The order of your words should your language community reflect.
13. Be consistent in how you used verb tenses within a sentence.

*C*hapter Review _____

Solo or Together respond to one or more of the following:

1. Which parts of this chapter did you most appreciate, and why?
2. If you were an instructor of writing, which five points would *you* stress from this chapter? Why?
3. Record questions that arose for you as you were working with this chapter, and discuss these in small groups or as a class.
4. How have you changed as a writer and reader as a result of working with this chapter?
5. Which parts of this chapter do you anticipate rereading?

Chapter 16

Punctuation and Style

This chapter offers opportunities to

—Develop perspective on **punctuation**

—Recognize **myths about punctuation**

—Learn the **purposes** of different punctuation marks

—Experiment with punctuation to alter **meaning**

—**Revise** your punctuation for **purpose** and **audience**

> No iron can pierce the heart with such force
> as a period put at just the right place.
>
> —*Isaak Babel, Short-story writer*

> Punctuation gives us the human voice, and all the
> meanings that lie between the words.
>
> —*Pico Iyer, Essayist*

How to Use This Chapter

You will find yourself focusing on different points of punctuation, depending on your needs and interests and on the guidance of your instructor. Don't expect yourself to learn punctuation *once and for all*, because you will learn and develop new insights into punctuation as long as you continue to read and write. Here are some possible ways to use this chapter:

1. Work through the chapter in the order in which it is written, choosing and doing the Developing Style activities as you go.
2. Refer to different parts of this chapter according to which punctuation element or mark you need to focus on.
3. Go straight to the Developing Style activities; if you get stuck, read what precedes them.
4. Display a copy of the punctuation chart in the sidebar on page 466, for easy reference during the writing process.
5. Adopt a particular punctuation mark and focus on it until you are satisfied that you understand its basic uses. Collect examples of it in your readings, use it consciously in your writing, and focus on it when you consult with others during the writing process. When you are revising, notice whether that punctuation mark could be added or deleted to enhance your meaning.
6. Create a lesson on a particular punctuation mark. (Refer to activity 3 on page 501.)

Punctuation, Purpose, and Audience

When you talk with someone in person, you communicate with more than just your words. You communicate with the tone, the loudness or softness, the pace, and the rhythm of your voice, and you communicate with your pronunciation, facial expressions, and body gestures. All these nonverbal cues give your listener a greater sense of what you're saying than your words alone could. In writing, punctuation serves the same purpose as your voice, expressions, and gestures. For example, in his article "In Praise of the Humble Comma," Pico Iyer remarks on the difference between these two expressions:

Jane (whom I adore)
Jane—whom I adore—

The parentheses in the first expression make the writer's adoration an afterthought, something that can be hidden. The dashes in the second expression highlight and emphasize the writer's feelings toward Jane. The meaning of an expression can change depending on the context, or situation in which it appears. If the expression "Jane (whom I adore)" appeared after the author had stated he adored Jane many times in what he was writing, putting "whom I adore" in parentheses (as an afterthought)

Style Notes: Punctuation at a Glance

Name	Mark	Origin	Meaning	Gesture	Use	Example
apostrophe	'	"step up"	contract / possess	flick away / beckon	contraction / possession	it's / John's
comma	,	"to cut"	introduce / / add	mark off	introduction / modifier / transition / comments / series	In the beginning, / John, the tallest one, / However, / Socialism, at least in theory, / a, b, c, and d
colon	:	—	point	to point	list / emphasis / summary	He saw the following: / He knew: this was it.
dash	—	"to rush"	emphasize	rush	interruption / list	Jane—whom I adore— / The numbers—1, 2, 3—
ellipsis	...	"fall short"	omit	cut	omission	The first...the last.
exclamation point	!	"call out"	emphasize	jab	emphasis	Help!
hyphen	-	"under one"	treat as one	connect	link / line ending	high-priced / end-ings
parentheses	()	"to put beside"	set aside	hide	insertions	Jane (whom I adore)
period	.	"cycle"	end	finish	sentence	Walk.
question mark	?	"to ask"	inquire	invite	questions	Why?
quotation marks	""	"exactly what"	highlight	highlight	direct quotes / irony / titles	"Why?" she asked. / It's "cool." / "Silent Night"
semicolon	;	—	half-stop	balance	sentences	Run; stop.
underlining (italics)		—	emphasize	draw attention	emphasis / mention / some titles	She knew. / I is the first word in I, Claudius. / Gone with the Wind

might make sense. If the writer had already emphasized "Jane—whom I adore" before and kept on emphasizing it, the reader would start wondering if the writer really meant it. So, although each punctuation element has its own personality, what it means also depends on where it appears. Raised eyebrows can mean many things, depending on the situation, from surprise to terror. When you are punctuating, be sensitive not only to the phrase, clause, or sentence you are punctuating but also to how the phrase, clause, or sentence fits into the larger piece.

Myths About Punctuation

Myths about punctuation may distract you from punctuation's main purpose: the making of meaning. Here are some of those myths:

> *Myth 1:* There is only one right way to punctuate a sentence.

> *Myth 2:* Punctuation always follows speech patterns.

> *Myth 3:* The best way to learn punctuation is by filling in blanks in a workbook.

> *Myth 4:* A sentence is a complete thought by itself.

As you work through this section, you will realize that these and other beliefs are only myths. You will be offered guidelines for using punctuation meaningfully, that is, to fulfill your purposes with your choice of audiences. You will be offered much more than the rules, for it is a myth that there is one best way to punctuate a sentence in any and every context. For each punctuation element, you will be offered a discussion of its strength, meaning, and the gesture it can make in a given situation. In addition, you will be offered some of the standard uses of that punctuation.

Strength. When language was chiseled into stone slabs in ancient Greece and Rome, the chiselers had to save space; therefore, they left no spaces between words and ran the words in two directions (see Figure 16.1). Otherwise, if the slabs were long enough, it would have been hard to find the way back to the beginning of the next line. The Greeks called this kind of writing *boustrophedon.* The word means "the way oxen move" and refers to how oxen would pull the plow in a field going *up* one row and turning at the end to go *down* the next. But, as you can see, it's hard to tell where words begin or end. The first punctuation element was the dot placed between words to separate them. Later, space itself was used to

```
THISIS
AWEHT
YTHEYW
ETOR
```

FIGURE 16.1   *Words Chiseled into Stone*

separate words, to emphasize their identity, or, in short, to punctuate words. For the purposes of our discussion, we will expand the definition of punctuation to include white space and other typographical elements that communicate any kind of separation, emphasis, or gesture.

Some punctuation elements do more than others. If you were to rank punctuation marks according to whether they were stronger or weaker, the comma would be "weaker" than the period, because the period marks off whole sentences, whereas the comma usually marks off only parts of sentences or lists.

Meaning.   In the discussion of punctuation elements below, you will be offered guidelines for how to use punctuation to communicate your tone and attitude toward your subject, purpose, and audience. Punctuation often determines your meaning and how it will be read by others.

Gesture.   Punctuation is a translation into written form of the body and voice gestures that accompany spoken language and lend it meaning. Therefore, the discussion of punctuation below will include comments on what gesture each punctuation element can make.

*D*eveloping Style

These activities are designed to help you recognize how much you know about punctuation and meaning and to interest you in learning more.

1. *Together.* List words you would use to describe your previous experiences with punctuation. Why would you use these words? Do your experiences with punctuation affect your perception of yourself as a writer? If so, how? If not, why not? What reactions do you have to focusing on punctuation now? What do you hope to learn, specifically, by working with this chapter?

2. *Together. A physics of punctuation.* The object of this activity is to rank punctuation marks according to their relative strengths. List all the punctuation elements you can think of, including capitalization

and different sizes of white space. You may want to start the list with the "weakest" punctuation element, either word spacing or capitalization, and end the list with the space suggested by the covers of a book. All other punctuations go in between. Rank the punctuations according to how much each element can do in terms of the following: emphasis, size of expressions the punctuation marks off, flexibility, and so on. For example, the semicolon can be ranked between the comma and the period. But where would you put the colon, and why? There is no absolute ranking. The important thing in this activity is to become aware of your current ideas about punctuation. As you discuss the rankings, you will notice what you know, which aspects of punctuation you focus on, and what questions you have about punctuating.

3. *Together.* Read the following groups of words. For each group, discuss how meaning changes with different punctuations.

   a. Woman, without her man, is a savage.
       Woman! Without her, man is a savage.
       Woman! Without her, man is a savage?
       Woman without! Her man is a savage.*

   b. He told her he was into shuffleboard, soap operas, and Lawrence Welk, before she managed to slip out the back door.

       He told her he was into shuffleboard, soap operas, and Lawrence Welk. Before, she managed to slip out the back door.

   c. Johnny's probably out there in the waiting room sitting in Dad's lap. Mary looks tired.

       Johnny's probably out there. In the waiting room, sitting in Dad's lap, Mary looks tired.

The Elements of Punctuation

Capitalization

The word *capitalize* comes from the Latin word *caput*, which means "head." To capitalize means that a word either

1. Heads a new segment of writing, or
2. Offers a gesture of respect.

Guidelines

1. **To head a new segment of writing, capitalize the following:**

    • **The first word of a sentence or title.**

---

*For this example, I am indebted to Gene Olson, *Sweet Agony II* (Portland, OR: Windyridge Press, 1983), page 75.

> ### *Capitals*
>
> 1. Head
>
>   - The first word of a sentence or title
>   - The first word of a quotation
>
> 2. Offer respect in
>
>   - Proper nouns
>   - Titles with names
>   - Titles of creative works

- **The first word of a quotation.** Capitalize the first word after an interruption only if it begins a new sentence.

    > "If you want a healthy garden," she said, gesturing to her compost heap, "you have to be willing to put up with some discomfort."

Note: Do not capitalize the first word after a colon unless it begins a sentence. If a sentence follows the colon, capitalization is optional.

2. **To offer a gesture of respect, capitalize the following:**

    - **Proper nouns,** including names of specific persons, places, religions, nationalities, languages, institutions, courses, historical periods, organizations, days of the week, months, holidays, movies, television series, documents, and brand names.
    - **Titles** when used as part of a specific name, as in "**Dr.** Martha Cottrell" or "Sammy Davis, **Jr.**"
    - **Major words in titles and subtitles** in books, articles, and creative works, unless the author specifically avoids doing so: Beethoven's Sixth Symphony is usually referred to as "The Pastoral Symphony."

The Comma (,)

The word *comma* comes from the Greek word *koptein,* which means "to cut." The comma marks off some word or words that *cut into* a phrase or clause in the same sense as you would *cut into* a waiting line. The comma marks off words that are used to introduce or modify other expressions. A comma

1. Marks off words, or
2. Adds words.

Without the comma, words, phrases, or clauses that have been introduced into a sentence could confuse a reader. For example, notice what happens without the comma in the following example:

If you fly Maryann will join you.

When you start reading this sentence—*If you fly Maryann*—it sounds like an airline advertisement, implying that *Maryann* is either the name of an airplane or a human being who can be flown like an airplane. You have to reread the sentence and regroup the words for yourself to realize that the clause *If you fly* is separate from the main point, which is *Maryann will join you*. If the comma is added in the logical place, before *Maryann*, the meaning of the sentence becomes clear on first reading.

A misplaced comma can be very expensive, as well. For example, it happened once that a congressional clerk was supposed to write, "All foreign fruit plants are free from duty." This meant that only fruit plants were to be admitted into the country without extra import cost. But in the process of writing, the clerk introduced a comma so that the sentence read: "All foreign fruit, plants are free from duty." The comma implied a list that included fruit and other plants because a comma sometimes functions as an abbreviation for *and*. The comma cut the important adjective, *fruit*, away from the word it modified, *plants*. This change cost the U.S. government over $2 million, because *all* fruit and *all* plants, not just fruit plants, were admitted without import cost.

Note: If a clause or a phrase cannot be cut out of a sentence without seriously altering the meaning, do not mark it off with commas. Read your sentence without the clause or phrase marked off with a comma or commas, and decide whether the essential thought has been altered.

Guidelines

1. **The comma marks off the following:**
    *   **Introductory word groups,** such as adverbial clauses or phrases (starting with connecting adverbs or prepositions).

        During the march on Washington, the protesters encountered supportive bystanders.

The Comma

1. Marks off

   - Introductory words
   - Certain adjectival clauses or phrases
   - Transitional expressions
   - Side comments or afterthoughts
   - Expressions that introduce direct quotations
   - Direct addresses

2. Adds

   - Dates, addresses, and titles
   - Items in a series
   - Independent clauses
   - Certain phrases or dependent clauses

Confusing Commas

1. Cut off verbs from subjects or objects
2. Begin or end a series
3. Precede parentheses
4. Accompany the word *and* joining two elements
5. Separate noun clauses from verbs

Because all new cars will have antilock brakes, driving in foul weather will be safer.

- **Certain adjectival clauses or phrases** that modify nouns or pronouns. If the clauses or phrases are essential to the meaning of the sentence, do *not* mark them off from the rest of the sentence:

Genetic engineering, which is a much disputed enterprise, is being researched in certain major universities.

In this sentence, the adjectival clause (starting with *which* and marked off by commas) is not essential to the meaning of the sentence. If you cut out the clause *which is a much disputed enterprise,* you would still have the essential message, which is

Genetic engineering is being researched in certain major universities. There are, however, adjectival clauses that *are essential* to the sentence. The following sentence does not make sense because commas mark off the essential adjectival clause starting with *who:*

People, who live in glass houses, shouldn't throw stones.

The commas mean that the clause could be cut out. But the sentence *People shouldn't throw stones* does not include the essential information that people *who live in glass houses* are jeopardizing themselves if they throw stones. The more reasonably punctuated sentence is this:

People who live in glass houses shouldn't throw stones.

There are phrases called *noun phrases* that reidentify a nearby noun. *If the noun phrase is not essential to identifying a specific person, place, or thing, mark it off with commas:*

Neil Postman, author of *Amusing Ourselves to Death*, argues that television is reducing our ability to reason.

If the noun phrase is *essential to identifying a specific person, place, or thing, don't use commas:*

The movie *Casablanca* has been colorized.

The poet Robert Frost wrote "The Road Not Taken."

If commas marked off the word *Casablanca*, then that word could be cut out of the sentence. The sentence would not retain its essential meaning, for it would read, "The movie *Casablanca* has been colorized." You would not know which movie was being referred to. Similarly, to write *poet Robert Frost* is the same as writing *General Patton.* You would not separate the word *General* from *Patton* or *poet* from *Robert Frost* by commas because the words *General* and *poet* provide essential information concerning the persons' roles.

- **Transitional expressions.** Afterthought words, such as *however, moreover,* and *nevertheless* (see page 422 for a complete list), and transitional phrases, such as *in fact* and *for example,* are sometimes marked off by commas.

  Moreover, the year-end report does not reflect contracts awarded in the fourth quarter.

- **Side comments or afterthoughts** that preface or interrupt the sentence.

  Yet, looking at the Ancient Egyptian wall paintings for the first time, one may find them bewildering.

  Socialism, at least in theory, is an attempt to improve conditions for all humans.

- **Expressions that introduce or modify direct quotations.**

  "Henry," he said, "I just remembered the answer to your question."

- **Direct addresses, questions, introductions, and expressions that serve as throat clearers.**

  Mr. President, I want to object to the new tax policy.

  Yes, they won the battle but lost the war.

  Well, it's about time.

2. **When the comma indicates something is being added, it is placed as follows:**

   - **Between elements in dates, addresses, and titles.**

     On July 17, 1984, the defendant entered the premises of my client, Cynthia Horton, M.D., at 1400 Washington Street, Bellville, Maine.

   - **Between items in a series.** This includes series of independent clauses, as in the first example:

     Caesar came, he saw, and he conquered.

     The butler purchased apples, caviar, and ham and cheese.

     In the second example, there are no commas between *ham* and *cheese* because they are often thought of as going together. A comma inserted between them would imply that one could be cut off from the other within the context of the sentence.

   - **Before connectors to independent clauses.**

     The vampire turned herself into a wolf, and her victim screamed.

   - **Before certain dependent clauses.** Whether you use a comma between the independent and dependent clause in a sentence depends on whether you want to emphasize the importance of the dependent clause. In the first example below, the dependent clause seems less strongly stated than in the second example, where the dependent clause is not cut off by the comma. Remember, the comma indicates that a portion of a sentence could be lifted out without significantly changing the meaning.

     Don't take drugs, if you want to be happy.

     If the dependent clause *if you want to be happy* were removed, the important point would still remain: *Don't take drugs*. The following sentence, however, implies that being happy depends strongly on not taking drugs:

Don't take drugs if you want to be happy.

Confusing Commas.   There are several uses of the comma that cut off parts of sentences in confusing ways. Whenever you are deciding whether to use a comma, notice which part or parts of a sentence the comma marks off. Sometimes, a comma may seem to mark off a part of a sentence for one reason when it is actually marking it off for another. In the examples below, you will be shown confusing uses of commas and commas that are used correctly although they appear to be incorrect:

1. **Do not cut off verbs from their subjects or objects.**

    Confusing:

    Caring for an infant, can be both the most frustrating and rewarding task a person can do.

    Jonathan crammed, all the cashews he could fit into the box.

    Clear:

    George, the cake decorator, created a huge basketball out of chocolate cake and orange icing.

    The comma after *decorator* is marking off the phrase *the cake decorator.* It is not cutting the subject, *George,* from the verb, *created.*

2. **Do not use a comma to begin or end a series** unless the comma ends a phrase or clause (in which case the comma is used not to mark off the series but to mark off the phrase or clause).

    Confusing:

    You should read a full range of materials including, newspapers, journals, magazines, and books, to make sure you have collected ideas from many different sources.

    Clear:

    For the new chicks, ducklings, and goslings, the incubator was the first parent they knew.

    The comma after *goslings* does not end the series *chicks, ducklings, and goslings;* it ends the whole phrase starting with *For.*

3. **Do not use a comma before parentheses.**

    Confusing:

    Whatever the effectiveness of vigorous exercise, (whether in individual or team sports), there is no substitute for a healthy diet in weight control.

4. **Do not use a comma when the word *and* joins two subjects, verbs, or phrases.**

   Confusing:

   The temple provided a place for worship, and served as a meeting place.

   Clear:

   The temple provided a place for worship and a shelter for passersby.

5. **Do not use a comma to separate noun clauses from their verbs.**

   Confusing:

   Whoever wants to succeed, must work.

   Clear:

   Whoever wants to succeed must work.

*D*eveloping Style

1. *Together and Solo.* Explain the differences in meaning in the sentences in activity 3 on page 469. In your explanation, refer to parts of the discussion of commas.

2. *Together or Solo.* Circle all the commas on half a page in a book you are reading. (You may choose a page from this book, if you like.) Why is each comma used? (In answering this question, refer to the explanations and examples of uses of the comma, above.) How does each comma help you better organize and understand what you are reading? Would you add or delete any commas? Why or why not?

3. *Together.* Punctuate the following sentences in two (or more) ways. Discuss how capitalization and commas change the meanings of the sentences. *To test whether a comma or commas should be included, experiment with cutting out parts of sentences they mark off.* If a sentence loses its essential meaning, then do not use the comma or commas. You may find that some punctuations create humorous sentences. In what situations would the different versions probably be used?

   a. come and watch the elephant eat debbie*
      come and watch the elephant eat debbie

   b. during the mexican american war 1846 1848 general santa anna lost every battle he fought

      during the mexican american war 1846 1848 general santa anna lost every battle he fought

---

*For this example, I am indebted to Pico Iyer, "In Praise of the Humble Comma," *Time,* June 13, 1983, p. 80.

c. the author of mind your own beeswax a self published novel made some serious points

the author of mind your own beeswax a self published novel made some serious points

d. i suspect you were right there
i suspect you were right there

e. camps that do not make safety the first priority should be shut down

camps that do not make safety the first priority should be shut down

f. when he swallows his eyes blink
when he swallows his eyes blink

g. therefore if we consider the effects of citrus on scurvy as in the example of early british sailors we will realize how some diseases have simple dietary solutions

therefore if we consider the effects of citrus on scurvy as in the example of early british sailors we will realize how some diseases have simple dietary solutions

h. the battleship formerly berthed in newport news virginia is now on active duty

the battleship formerly berthed in newport news virginia is now on active duty

i. she powdered her nose her appearance and her claims met the requirements for the modeling job

she powdered her nose her appearance and her claims met the requirements for the modeling job

j. god rest ye merry gentlemen
god rest ye merry gentlemen

4. *Together.* Write a long sentence in which you try to include every clear use of the comma cited in this section.

5. *Together and Solo.* Review your own papers, focusing on the comma. Where can commas be added or deleted to support your meaning and guide your reader? Revise your papers accordingly. How are the meanings modified or enhanced?

The Hyphen (-)

The word *hyphen* comes from the Greek word *huphen*, which means "together" or literally "under one." The gesture the hyphen makes is to connect. A hyphen is used for the following:

The Hyphen

1. Connects

   - Two or more adjectives used together before a noun
   - Paired words
   - Words broken across lines
   - Written fractions and compound numbers
   - Page numbers

2. Distinguishes two expressions

   - With prefixes such as *all-*, *ex-*, and *self-*
   - With confusing double and triple letters

---

1. To connect two words or parts of words, or

2. To distinguish two expressions.

The hyphen can give a powerful message, as the following example shows. According to Steven Greenhouse, in his March 28, 1990, article for *The New York Times,* during the 1990 revolutions in Eastern Europe, the Czechs and the Slovaks found themselves in an ethnic battle over a hyphen. The Slovaks wanted to rename Czechoslovakia "Federation of Czecho-Slovakia." The Czechs argued that including the hyphen is divisive because it implies that the Czechs and the Slovaks are separate and need to be put together.

Guidelines

1. **The hyphen connects two words or parts of words as follows:**

   - **With two or more words that function as an adjective before a noun.** Otherwise, the two words are separate.

She wrote a well-turned phrase.	Her phrase was well turned.
They sell a high-priced camera.	Their cameras were high priced.
Use a double-entry journal.	Write a double entry.

- **With paired words.** Many words in English were originally two or more words, but, since they were so often used together, after a while they became treated as one, such as the word *waterworks.* These words are called *compound words.* Your dictionary is your best guide to them. Here are some examples of related words. (Remember that connected adjectives are hyphenated only *before* the nouns they modify.)

Hyphenated	Compound	Separate
water-cooled (adj)	waterworks	water tower
high-riser (n)	highlight	high school
news-ready (adj)	newspaper	news release

In addition, you will discover other words that are hyphenated in current usage. These include some you may already know:

sister-in-law (n) no-show (n) good-for-nothing (n)

- **With words broken across lines.** If a word must be divided at the end of the line, there are several guidelines to follow.

Divide words between syllables. If you have a question as to where a syllable ends, consult your dictionary, which places dots between syllables. The same word root may be hyphenated in different ways for different forms of the word. For example, *indication* is hyphenated as in-di-ca-tion. But *indicative* is hyphenated as in-dic-a-tive. Sometimes, you may even want to check different dictionaries if you have a question. Here is an example of a hyphenated sentence:

We stored the lawn furniture, brought the garden hose indoors, and dragged the garden tools into the garage for safekeeping.

Never divide a one-syllable word at the end of a line.

Leave more than one letter at the end of a line and three or more letters at the beginning of the next line.

Divide a hyphenated word only at the hyphen.

- **With written fractions and compound numbers.**

one-fourth   thirty-nine

- **With page numbers.**

pages 43–77

2. **The hyphen distinguishes two expressions treated as one in these instances:**

   • **With prefixes such as *all-, ex-,* and *self-.***

   all-encompassing   ex-boss   self-fulfilling

   • **With confusing double or triple letters.**

   re-enter   cross-stitch   pre-engineered

*D*eveloping Style _____

1. *Together and Solo.* In small groups or solo, search through the dictionary and find thirty words that are hyphenated. Find thirty compound words—two or more words that function as one unhyphenated word.

2. *Together or Solo.* In small groups or solo, list thirty hyphenated adjectives. These may include ones you find in the dictionary and ones you create yourself. The ones you create may be serious or humorous.

3. *Together and Solo.* Choose a page from this chapter and mark words to indicate which ones could be hyphenated at the end of a line and where the hyphens could be placed. For example, the previous sentence could be marked as follows:

   > Choose a page from this chap-ter and mark words to in-di-cate which ones could be hy-phen-at-ed at the end of a line and where the hy-phens could be placed.

   Use the dictionary to confirm your hyphenations.

4. *Solo.* Keep an ongoing list of hyphenated and compound words from your readings.

_____

The Apostrophe (')

The word *apostrophe* comes from the Greek words *apo* and *strophe*, which together mean "step up." The name *apostrophe* describes how the punctuation looks. An apostrophe is used for the following reasons:

1. To replace letters or numbers.
2. To indicate possession.
3. To form some types of plurals.

The Apostrophe

1. Replaces letters or numbers
2. Indicates possession with the following:

   - Singular and irregular plural nouns with -'*s*
   - Plural nouns ending in -*s* with '
   - The last of conjoined nouns with a possessive
   - Pronouns such as *everyone* and *somebody* with -'*s*

3. Forms plurals of some letters and abbreviations

In the first case, think of the apostrophe as a hand flicking a letter away in order to pull the other letters together, as in the word *don't*. In the second, think of the apostrophe as a finger pointing to the owner.

Guidelines

1. **The apostrophe replaces letters or numbers as follows:**

   - **Where the letter or number has been removed, contract what's left into one word.**

they are	=	they're
do not	=	don't
she is	=	she's
something is	=	something's
something has	=	something's
let us	=	let's
1992	=	'92
it is	=	'tis, it's
because	=	'cause

A special case is the contraction of *will* and *not:*

will not	=	won't

Note that the word *ain't* is a contraction of *am not, is not, are not,* or *have not. Ain't* is not normally used in academic or professional writing, but this word is an example of the economy and elegance of spoken language: one word with many uses.

It's is always a verb contraction of *it* and *is* and never a possessive pronoun.

2. **The apostrophe is used to indicate possession as follows:**

   - **For singular and irregular plural nouns, add an apostrophe and an -*s*.**

     Singular: consumer   *Possessive:* consumer's
     Singular: hippopotamus   *Possessive:* hippopotamus's
     Irregular plural: children *Possessive:* children's

   - **For plural nouns ending in -*s*, add an apostrophe.**

     Plural: parents   *Possessive:* parents'

   - **For the last of conjoined nouns, add a possessive marker to the last noun only.**

     Conjoined nouns: Mary and William
     Possessive: Mary and William's
     Conjoined nouns: Teachers and parents
     Possessive: Teachers and parents'

   - **For pronouns such as *everyone* and *somebody* add an apostrophe and an -*s*.**

     Pronoun: everyone   *Possessive:* everyone's
     Pronoun: somebody   *Possessive:* somebody's

   Note: Except for *one's* and *ones'* possessive pronouns never take an apostrophe. **They already indicate possession by themselves.**

   hers, his, its, ours, theirs, yours

   Remember that the possessive pronoun *its* does not have an apostrophe so that you can distinguish it from the contracted verb *it's*.
   The only possessive pronouns that use an apostrophe are *one's* or *ones'*. If you want to say that the number *1* is used more than once, write *1s*. Both the contraction of *one is* and the possessive of *one* are written as *one's*. It is the only pronoun that functions this way.

3. **Use an apostrophe and -*s* to form plurals** of lowercase letters used as letters, capital letters that would otherwise be confusing, and abbreviations.

   Sydney wrote her *y*'s with elaborate curls.

   They embroidered the cloth with *S*'s, *A*'s, and *I*'s.

The audience was filled with M.D.'s and Ph.D.'s.

Do not use an apostrophe to pluralize numbers or words as words.

They grew up in the 1980s.
We don't want to hear any *ifs, ands,* or *buts* about it.

Developing Style

1. *Together and Solo.* Discuss how the meanings change in the following phrases and sentences. Imagine the situations in which the statements would be used. Which are confusing or illogical? How and why? Revise confusing or illogical phrases and sentences to make sense.

   a. I won't do it 'cause I don't want to.
   I will not do it because I do not want to.

   b. Everybodys' opinion is to be considered in the decision.
   Everybody's opinion is to be considered in the decision.

   c. Her parents' house is in disrepair.
   Her parent's house is in disrepair.

   d. Do'nt think twice: its' all right.
   Don't think twice: it's all right.
   Don't think twice: its alright.

   e. I've had it.
   I have had it.

2. *Together and Solo.* Choose papers you are currently writing and review them, focusing on the need for apostrophes. Add or delete apostrophes to clarify your meaning.

Quotation Marks (" ")(' ')

The word *quotation* comes from the Latin *quo,* which means "what." Literally, quotation marks mean "exactly what." The gesture or function of quotation marks is much like that of two spotlights highlighting *exactly what* is between them. Quotation marks are used as follows:

1. To indicate
2. To draw attention.

Quotation Marks

1. Indicate

   - Exact words
   - A quotation within a quotation
   - Titles
   - Meaning
   - Repetitions in lists

2. Draw attention to

   - Unusual use of a word
   - Slang or technical terms
   - Ironic tone

Guidelines

1. Quotation marks indicate the following:

   - **Exact words, whether they were spoken or written**. These are called *direct quotes.*

     Malcolm X once said, "Power in defense of freedom is greater than power in defense of tyranny and oppression."

     Words mentioned as words, traditionally placed between quotation marks, are now italicized. Refer to page 497 for a full discussion of how to punctuate words as words.

     Note: Indent and single-space long quotes of more than four typed lines. Check what style your academic discipline uses.

     The important matter is to find your own style, your own subjects, your own rhythm, so that every element in your nature can contribute to the work of making a writer of you. Study your own pages; among them you are to find some idea—preferably, this time, a fairly simple one—which offers you a good, obvious nucleus for a short story, an expanded anecdote...or a brief essay. You will have something to say on the subject which is more than a superficial comment. (Dorothea Brande, *Becoming a Writer* [Boston: Harcourt, 1934], p. 139.)

Indirect quotes, which refer to what someone says, are not placed within quotation marks. Indirect quotes are often, though not always, signaled by *that*.

> *Direct quote:*
>
> The engineer said, "The bridge is on the verge of collapse."
>
> *Indirect quote:*
>
> The engineer said that the bridge was on the verge of collapse.

- **A quotation within a quotation.** Use single quotation marks.

    "Stop saying 'you know' all the time," she said in exasperation.

- **Titles** of news and magazines articles, poems, stories, songs, chapters or sections of books, and episodes of television and radio series are placed within quotation marks.

    The article titled "The Taste of Fresh-Brewed" offered an analysis of thirty-three name-brand coffees.

- **Meaning.** There are times when you want to refer to meaning. Notice this sentence:

    Apostrophe means "step up."

    The expression is a shortened way of writing the following:

    Apostrophe means *exactly what* the expression "step up" means.

    Note: When writing dialogue, indent for the beginning of each change of speaker.

    > James Smith, deeply troubled, went to a psychiatrist.
    >
    > "My brother," he said, "thinks he's a chicken. He goes around pecking at things on the floor, squawks constantly, and flaps his arms."
    >
    > "Oh," the psychiatrist said. "How long has he been acting this way?"
    >
    > "About six months," James said.
    >
    > "Why didn't you come in sooner?" asked the psychiatrist.
    >
    > "To tell you the truth," James replied, "we needed the eggs."

- **Repetitions in lists.** The quotation marks indicate that exactly what is written above should be repeated.

For extended physical therapy	8/4/97	$ 50
" "	8/7/97	$100
" "	8/11/97	$ 50

2. **Quotation marks draw attention to the following:**

- **An unusual use of a familiar word.**

  The hyphen is one of the "weaker" punctuation marks.

- **Slang or technical terms.**

  Some of our sophomore classmates have a serious case of "beautyism."

  The contract was mostly "boilerplate."

- **Ironic tone.**

  Bart Simpson is not exactly an "overachiever."

  Note: Members of some academic and professional communities do not favor using quotation marks to draw attention to slang or puns, or to create an ironic tone.

Combine quotation marks with other punctuation elements as follows:

- **Within quotation marks.** Commas and periods are placed within quotation marks at the end of quoted material.

  "To begin," she said, "is half the work."

- **Outside quotation marks.** Colons and semicolons are placed outside quotation marks at the end of quoted material.

  Judge Wilson said, "The verdict stands"; nonetheless, the lawyers were already preparing another appeal.

Question marks and exclamation points are placed within quotation marks only when they are part of the quoted material. Compare the following two sentences:

Why did George say, "Go away"?
Why did George say, "Go away?"

The first sentence asks why George asserted "Go away." The question mark ends the whole sentence. The second sentence implies that George was asking whether or not to go away because the question mark ends

> **The Ellipsis**
>
> 1. Indicates omitted words
>
> **Parentheses**
>
> 1. Mark off side comments
> 2. Enclose letters or numbers

only the quote itself. If we were asking why George asked the question, the sentence would be written and punctuated as follows:

Why did George ask, "Go away"?

The Ellipsis (...)

The word *ellipsis* comes from the Greek word *elleipsis,* which means "to fall short." Use ellipsis points to indicate that you have deleted material from a quotation. Think of the ellipsis as dotted lines along which something was cut. Normally, ellipses are not used at the beginnings or ends of quotations. Put single spaces before, after, and in between. Note that the plural form of *ellipsis* is *ellipses.*

> Neil Postman writes, "Thinking does not play well on television, a fact that television directors discovered long ago.... It is, in a phrase, not a performing art."

*D*eveloping *Style* _____

1. *Solo.* Look through one of your textbooks from another course and find examples of quotations within the text. Notice how the author introduces quotes and which are indented and which single-spaced.

2. **a.** *Solo.* Choose a statement you recently read or heard that is meaningful to you in some way. Quote the statement *directly,* and write an essay about what it means to you. In your essay, refer to words and expressions in the statement.

   b. *Solo.* Write about your chosen statement, quoting the author *indirectly.* In this essay, do not refer to exact words and expressions used by the author.

   c.   *Together.* Read, discuss, and compare the differences between the essays in which you quote directly and the essays in which you quote indirectly. How do the meanings change? Which essays do you prefer, and why?

3. *Solo.* Choose a page of a book that interests you. Highlight several key phrases or sentences. (Refer to pages 110–116, 309–311, and 318–319 for discussions of key words and statements.) Write a short essay relating what the author says. Use long and short, direct and indirect quotes. Use ellipses to indicate portions that you have left out of direct quotes.

Parentheses [( )]

The word *parenthesis* (singular form of parenthese*s*) comes from the Greek words *para, en,* and *tithenai. Para* means "beside," *en* means "in," and *tithenai* means "to put." *Parenthesis* literally means "to put in beside." Parentheses

1. Mark off, or
2. Enclose.

A parenthetical remark adds extra material, afterthoughts, and tangents to the discussion. To put something between two parenthese*s* (note that this is the plural form of *parenthesis*) means that, if necessary, the added remark could be removed. Parentheses hide what is between them. That is why the example of "Jane (whom I adore)" could be so frustrating to a waiting Jane. Depending on the situation, parentheses can also serve the purpose of befriending or distancing a reader. Compare the attitudes that the following two examples can portray:

> We have to buy the more expensive gift for the boss (if you know what I mean).
>
> You look really terrific (for your age).

Guidelines

Parentheses are used in the following cases:

1. To mark off side comments.

> When you harvest herbs for drying, cut only the tops of the plants, about a third or quarter of its growth. (Parsley and chives can be cut further down.)

Art lies to us to tell us the (sometimes disquieting) truth.

2. **To mark off or enclose letters or numbers.**

The Graduate Management Admissions Test (GMAT) is required by most graduate schools of business.

The Fujiwara period of Japanese art (897–1185) was centered on the capital and dominated by the Fujiwara family.

If a whole sentence is included within parentheses, the end mark goes within the parentheses. If parentheses are included within a sentence, other punctuation marks that belong to the main sentence are put outside of the parentheses.

*D*eveloping Style

1. *Solo.* Collect at least five examples of the use of parentheses in books, newspapers, and magazines you are currently reading.

2. *Together.* Discuss the examples of uses of parentheses you collected. Revise several sentences to experiment with removing parentheses. Create additional sentences if necessary. What happens to the meanings of the sentences when formerly parenthetical expressions are incorporated into the regular text?

The Colon (:)

The word *colon* comes from the Greek word *kolon,* which refers to a unit of rhythm in poetry. The origin of the word does not clearly capture the meaning of the colon. Think of the colon as the tips of two fingers pointing either to indicate a list or to emphasize what follows. A colon is used in the following ways:

1. To direct attention, and/or

2. To introduce an explanation or summary.

Guidelines

1. **The colon directs attention to a list, a quotation, or the body of a business letter.**

There are three things you should never do at a cocktail party: put a lampshade on your head, drink from a bottle, or arrive early.

The Colon

1. Directs attention to lists, quotations, or the body of a business letter
2. Introduces an explanation or summary

Robert Foster states: "Venus is named for the goddess of love because it is visible only near sunrise and sunset."

Dear Ms. Winokur:
This is to acknowledge your payment.

2.   The colon introduces an explanation or summary as follows:

As I was falling asleep in Professor Dorman's class, I knew: this was going to be the end of me.

Hunting stories have a long history: they appear in different forms on the New England frontier of the eighteenth century.

Elizabeth Bishop wrote about fishermen, sandpipers, and seals: images of the sea.

Note: Do *not* capitalize the first word after a colon if it does not begin a new sentence. If a new sentence follows the colon, capitalization is optional.

When you go to Rome, visit the popular sites: the Tivoli Gardens, the Roman Colosseum, the Bernini Fountains, and the Sistine Chapel.

Confusing Colons.   If you place a colon after an incomplete sentence, as in the following example, you are separating a verb from its object. Just as placing a comma between a verb and its object is confusing, so too with the colon. When the colon is used to introduce a list, it must be preceded by a complete independent clause. Although this convention of punctuation is in transition, follow the traditional use. Notice this very sentence and the following examples:

Confusing:

To direct attention, you can: use a colon or a dash.

Clear:

To direct attention, you can use a colon or a dash.

Confusing:

The experts were: Hale, Leisenberg, and Foster.

Clear:

The experts were Hale, Leisenberg, and Foster.

Note: The colon following the word *Note* at the beginning of this sentence is correctly placed because "Note" is a complete sentence implying "You note this."

The Semicolon (;)

Think of the semicolon visually. It is half period and half comma. The semicolon balances sentences in these situations:

1. A period is too strong, or
2. A comma is insufficient.

Guidelines

1. **When a period is too strong a break** between independent clauses, and there are no sentence connectors (*and, but, for, nor, or, so, yet*), use a semicolon.

   The physician recommended that the terminal patient take that special vacation; there was nothing else the doctor could do.

   The carousel is still a favorite in amusement parks; people ride it more than the Ferris wheel.

2. **When a comma is insufficient** to mark off part of a sentence, use a semicolon as follows:

   - To make a transition into an afterthought, such as *nevertheless, furthermore, hence.*

     The job market was frozen; nevertheless, Mary was resourceful enough to get hired.

The Semicolon

1. Balances sentences when a period is too strong a break
2. Balances sentences when a comma is insufficient

   - Following an afterthought
   - In some series containing commas

The Dash

1. Emphasizes expressions
2. Frames a list or comment

- **To mark off a part of a sentence** when the items in the series contain commas.

  The mechanic had a whole shopping list of repairs to make: adjust the fan, air conditioner, alternator, and power steering belts; change the transmission, brake, and cooling system fluids; and tune up, align, rotate, balance, and repaint anything that he could find.

The Dash (—, --)

The word *dash*, used as a verb, means "to rush" or "move quickly." As an adjective, *dash* means "spirited" or "stylish." The dash, used as punctuation, gives writing these same qualities. Think of a dash as an arrow with two heads. Whereas parentheses hide what is written between them, the dash emphasizes or points arrows to what it marks off. Sometimes the dash is used when a list interrupts a sentence and a comma is too weak. In sum, a dash is used in these cases:

1. To emphasize expressions, or
2. To frame a list or comment.

Guidelines

1. **To emphasize.**

   Jane—whom I adore—is not only a successful business executive but a sensitive artist as well.

   Any increase or decrease in the proportion of people between the ages of sixteen and twenty-five in the total population affects the crime rate—which is what has happened over the past couple of decades.

2. **To frame lists or restatements.**

   The most famous baseball players—people such as Babe Ruth, Jackie Robinson, and Lou Gehrig—are immortalized in the Baseball Hall of Fame in Cooperstown, New York.

As the large "baby boom" generation—people born between 1946 and 1964—passed through its youthful years, crime rates rose sharply.

Because the dash is very strong, avoid overusing it. When you type a dash, use two hyphens. Do not leave spaces before or after the dash.

Developing Style

1. *Solo.* Collect examples of sentences that use the colon, the semicolon, or the dash, or some combination of them. Revise the punctuation in three of the sentences using commas or parentheses where possible. How do the meanings change?

2. *Together and Solo.* Write sentences using the following sequences of punctuation. You can write as much or as little as you want in the spaces between the punctuation marks. For sequences a, b, and c, experiment with using the same sentences and discuss how the meaning changes with the different punctuation marks.

   a. _____; _____.
   b. _____: _____.
   c. _____ — _____.
   d. _____: _____, _____; _____; _____.
   e. _____ — _____, _____, _____ — _____.

3. *Together and Solo.* Review your own papers, focusing on colons, semicolons, and dashes. Where can these punctuation marks be added or deleted to support your meaning and guide your reader? Revise your papers accordingly.

End Marks

The Period (.)

The word *period* comes from the Greek word *periodos,* which means "cycle" and implies an end. To use a period means that you have completed something. It means "stop, reflect." The period is used as follows:

1. **To end sentences that are not questions or exclamations.**

   Robert Frost's career as a poet did not really begin in earnest until he was nearly forty years old.

2. **To end short answers to questions.**

   Did the company reimburse me after I had called them six times? No.

End Marks

The period ends

1. Sentences
2. Short answers
3. Abbreviations

The question mark ends

1. Questions
2. Short questions in a series

The exclamation point emphasizes.

3. **In abbreviations.**

etc.	450 A.D.
e.g.	6:00 P.M.

The Question Mark (?)

The word *question* comes from the Latin word *quaestio,* which means "to ask." This mark is normally an invitation for a response. The question mark is used in the following cases:

1. **After a direct question.**

    Did the governor report the exact amount of fiscal deficit for the year?

    Note: Some questions, called rhetorical questions, are not genuine invitations for answers. Usually the situation will determine whether a question is rhetorical. A rhetorical question—implying that there is only one "right" answer—is meant to create a bond between the writer and the audience. (For a full discussion of rhetorical questions consult page 315).

    Is there any reason for this murder of innocent people?

    Are you ready to pay less taxes?

2. **In a series of short questions.**

    Will they research all the possible contributing factors to the development of cancer? Diet? Genetics? Environment? Lifestyle?

Notice that all the questions in the series begin with a capital letter, even though they are not complete sentences.

The Exclamation Point (!)

The word *exclamation* comes from the Latin word *exclamare*, which means "to call out." *Exclamation points emphasize words, phrases, or sentences.* Do not overuse exclamation points. Because the exclamation point *demands* attention, much like a jab in the arm, it can overwhelm and distance the reader. Notice the difference in your reactions to the following two versions of the same sentence:

> Help! These are the worst problems we've had in decades! There's a recession! Environmental destruction! Political tensions! What next?! No one seems to be catching on! We're committing suicide on this planet!

> Help! These are the worst problems we've had in decades: a recession, environmental destruction, political tensions. What next? No one seems to be catching on. We're committing suicide on this planet!

If you had to choose, who would you vote into a responsible government position, the one who wrote the first version or the one who wrote the second? Why?

*D*eveloping Style

1. *Solo.* Review the sections on fragments and run-ons in Chapter 15. Do some of the corresponding activities that address concerns you have with punctuating sentences in your own writing.

2. *Solo.* Collect examples of sentences for all the uses of end marks reviewed above. Use newspapers, magazines, or books as your resources. Change the end marks on three of these sentences. Do the meanings change? If so, how? If not, why not?

3. *Together and Solo.* Review your own papers, focusing on end marks, colons, and semicolons. Where can these punctuation marks be added or deleted to support your meaning and guide your reader? Revise your papers accordingly.

Underlining (Italics)

Written language has progressed from its earliest forms of marks on sand and stone to ink on paper. Today, typewriters and computers offer further ways of creating meaning and guiding the reader's attention with the

Underlining (Italics)

1. Emphasizes

    *   Words
    *   Titles
    *   Foreign words
    *   Words, letters, and numbers mentioned as themselves

written word. These typographical punctuations include italics (underlining), boldfacing, and shading. This discussion will focus on underlining (italics) because it is the most commonly used and available typographical punctuation. The more sophisticated typographical punctuations function, in part, as underlining (italics) does.

Italics are a slanted typeface on a printed page that some computer programs allow you to use in conjunction with a regular typeface on the same page. The working manuscript of this book was not printed with italics. Instead of italics, words were underlined. However, in its printed form, words that were underlined are now in italics.

Underlining is meant to emphasize and to draw attention to particular words.

Guidelines

Use underlining (italics) for emphasis in the following cases:

*   **Words.**

    The company will *not* abandon this project.
    Scientists insist that *yodoxin* is the cure.

*   **Titles** of books, plays, television series, newspapers, pamphlets, musical and artistic works, and long poems.

    In one semester, Lindsey studied *War and Peace, The Merchant of Venice, Forbes Magazine,* Beethoven's *Pastoral Symphony,* Chicago's *Dinner Party,* and Browning's *Sonnets from the Portuguese.*

*   **Foreign words** introduced into part of a sentence. Do not underline words that have been incorporated into English, such as *rendezvous* or *laissez-faire.*

    In ancient Hawaii, members of a family would hold a *ho'oponopono* until everyone in the gathering agreed to a peaceful solution to a problem.

- **Words, letters, and numbers mentioned as themselves.** To *use* a word as part of your discussion is different from *mentioning* it as itself. To understand the difference between using and mentioning a word, read the following sentence:

      Boston has six letters.

  This sentence is absurd because the city of Boston is likely to have more than six letters (in or out of envelopes) at any one time. The word *Boston* is being *used* in that sentence as if it were any other word. But the following sentence *does* make sense:

      Boston has six letters.

  What this sentence says is that the word *Boston* has six letters, because the word *Boston* is in italics. The italics emphasize the word to signal the reader that *Boston* is being mentioned as a word. In your own writing, underline words, letters, and numbers that you mention as themselves.

Developing Style

1. *Together and Solo.* The purpose of this activity is to give you practice in distinguishing whether a word, letter, or number is being *used* or being *mentioned* as itself. Read the following sentences. Which make sense and which don't? Which words should or should not be underlined? Revise them by underlining words, letters, and numbers that are mentioned as themselves.

   a. Chicago is a large city.

   b. Chicago is north of *Cleveland.*

   c. Othello had 3 daughters.

   d. 3 is a sacred number in many religions.

   e. How do you spell Cleveland?

   f. The G was barely visible on the slab.

   g. They say 1 is the loneliest number.

   h. Los Angeles means "the angels."

   i. Los Angeles means a lot to my Uncle Frank.

2. *Together.* The purpose of this activity is to give you practice using quotation marks, writing dialogues, and underlining to mention words. Review the use of quotation marks in direct quotations. Then brainstorm a list of overused words and expressions, such as *like, you know, yup, uh-huh, really,* and *good.* In pairs, or small groups, write dialogues that would last at least two minutes between a person who overuses a certain expression and another person, irritated by the repetition, who is trying to stop him or her from overusing the expression. Underline words when you are mentioning them:

"I wish you would stop saying <u>you know</u> all the time."

"Well, you know, it's a habit just like saying <u>like</u>—if you know what I mean."

Read the dialogues aloud. Although the dialogues may be serious, they are likely to be humorous.

Paragraphing (¶)

Usually, paragraphing marks off larger units of writing than end marks normally do. The word *paragraph* comes from the Greek words *para* and *graphos*, which together mean "writing to the side." Back during the days when language was carved into stone, one of the ways that new units of thought were marked off was by making marks by the sides of lines. Today, the white space that follows the last sentence of the previous paragraph, and the space indentation at the beginning of the line, mark off the beginning of a major shift in thought in a piece of writing. Paragraphing does one or both of two things for readers:

1. Frames, and therefore emphasizes, a major unit of thought, and
2. Gives readers a chance to reflect or readjust for a transition.

Because of these two functions of the paragraph, the end of a paragraph is a place to write those things that you want to have a lasting effect.

A paragraph can be as short as one word. For example, suppose there was a long paragraph describing a terrifying experience. It could be followed by a one-word paragraph:

Help!

The word *help*, framed by all that white space, cannot be missed. However, a sentence can be pages long, as often happens in legal documents. Forget any rigid rules you may have heard about how many sentences or how many paragraphs you should write in a given essay or other piece of

---

Paragraphing

1. Frames and emphasizes major units of thought
2. Gives readers a breather

writing. Forget, as well, any rigid rules about how long a sentence ought to be. Instead, challenge yourself to write shorter or longer sentences and paragraphs to develop your style, to fulfill your purposes, and to capture and engage your readers.

*D*eveloping Style

1. *Together or Solo.* Review the section on "The Body" on pages 179–194 in Chapter 7. Do the explorations that follow it.

2. *Together and Solo.* Review your own papers in progress for paragraphing. Notice if your paragraph breaks mark off sentences that belong together. Do your paragraph breaks give your readers time to reflect on what you've written, or do you rush readers from one idea to another without pauses? Revise your papers accordingly.

BLOOPER RULES OF PUNCTUATION

Read the following "Blooper Rules of Punctuation" that ask you to do what they don't do themselves. Revise the rules so that—although they will be less funny—they won't contradict themselves.

1. Don't, use a comma, where it isn't, necessary.
2. Its important to use apostrophe's with care.
3. The period. Is a mark of punctuation. Which is used only at the ends of sentences.
4. Do not separate a term of respect from the name of a person just because poet, W. S. Merwin didn't use punctuation.
5. Do not—under any circumstances—whether in business, academic, or personal writing—overuse the dash—it puts a strain on the reader.
6. Do not create overly-long-and-complex words with hyphenation.
7. NEVER capitalize a word all the way through unless it is a HEADING BECAUSE it is not acceptable in academic or professional writing.
8. Do not use "quotation marks" to draw "attention" to familiar expressions in "academic" writing.
9. Do not be someone, who overuses commas, and marks off phrases, that must be included, in the sentence, without commas.
10. Don't overuse exclamation points!!!!!

*D*eveloping Style

1. *Together and Solo.* Punctuate the following, using as great a variety of marks and elements as would make sense.

   ```
   because john was worried that people would not like him if
   his party was not successful as it was last time when he had
   it catered and he was able to afford it since he came into
   the inheritance which he blew on a weekend in las vegas he
   bought a pineapple ham cheesecake champagne salami horserad-
   ish and ritz crackers thinking he would make finger foods
   they all loved all of it went well although they thought he
   looked a bit bedraggled
   ```

2. *Together.* Divide your class into small groups. Each group is to find a long sentence or a group of sentences in a newspaper, magazine, or book, preferably with a variety of punctuation. Type the sentence (or sentences) without any punctuation or capitalization, and distribute

copies to another group or groups. Each group is to punctuate these sentences. Then compare your versions with the originals. How are your punctuations similar to or different from the originals? How do your sentences differ in meaning from the originals? Which versions would work best with which purposes and audiences? How would you change your own or the original versions?

3. *Together.* Divide the class into small groups. Each group is to adopt a particular punctuation that members want to learn more completely. Prepare a lesson for someone who will be entering college or for a grammar school child. Find or create examples to illustrate your lesson. Prepare activities to engage your audience. Use the ideas in this chapter, but vary them and create your own. Refer to other books to enrich your presentation. If you decide to use an idea directly from this chapter or any other work, be sure to follow the conventions of quoting.

*C*hapter Review

Solo or Together, respond to one or more of the following:

1. Which parts of this chapter did you most appreciate, and why?

2. Record five statements from this chapter that you want to remember.

3. Which Developing Style activities did you like best, and what did you learn from doing them?

4. What did you learn about yourself as a writer?

5. If you were an instructor of writing, which points from this chapter would *you* stress in teaching student writers? Why?

6. Record questions that arose for you as you were working with this chapter, and discuss these in small groups or as a class.

7. How do you plan to change as a writer as a result of working with this chapter?

8. Which parts of this chapter do you anticipate reviewing?

Index